IR

IR

THE NEW WORLD OF INTERNATIONAL RELATIONS

SEVENTH EDITION

Michael G. Roskin

Lycoming College

Nicholas O. Berry

Foreign Policy Forum

PEARSON
Prentice
Hall

Upper Saddle River, New Jersey 07458

Library of Congress Cataloging-in-Publication Data

Roskin, Michael G.
    IR: the new world of international relations/Michael G. Roskin, Nicholas O. Berry.—7th ed.
      p. cm.
    Includes bibliographical references and index.
    ISBN 0-13-613054-2
    1. International relations—Textbooks.   2. World politics—1945–1989—Textbooks.   3. World
politics—1989—Textbooks.   4. United States—Foreign relations—1945–1989—Textbooks.
5. United States—Foreign relations—1989—Textbooks.   I. Berry, Nicholas O.   II. Title.
    JZ1242.R67 2007
    327—dc22
                                                                    2006035706

Editorial Director: Charlyce Jones Owen
Executive Editor: Dickson Musslewhite
Associate Editor: Rob DeGeorge
Editorial Assistant: Jennifer Murphy
Senior Marketing Manager: Emily Cleary
Marketing Assistant: Jennifer Lang
**Director of Production and
  Manufacturing:** Barbara Kittle
Senior Managing Editor: Lisa Iarkowski
Production Liaison: Jean Lapidus
Production Assistant: Marlene Gassler
**Prepress and Manufacturing
  Manager:** Nick Sklitsis
**Prepress and Manufacturing Assistant
  Manager:** Mary Ann Gloriande

Director, Image Resource Center: Melinda Reo
Manager, Rights and Permissions: Zina Arabia
Manager, Visual Research: Beth Brenzel
**Manager, Cover Visual Research and
  Permissions:** Karen Sanatar
Image Permission Coordinator: Annette Linder
Cover Art Director: Jayne Conte
Cover Design: Bruce Kenselaar
Cover Photo: Michael G. Roskin
Interior Design: John Paul Mazzola
**Composition/Full-Service Project
  Management:** Kari Callaghan Mazzola
  and John Paul Mazzola
Printer/Binder: RR Donnelley & Sons Company
Cover Printer: Phoenix Color Corp.

This book was set in 10/12 Meridien.

Pearson Education LTD.
Pearson Education Singapore, Pte. Ltd
Pearson Education, Canada, Ltd
Pearson Education–Japan
Pearson Education Australia PTY, Limited

Pearson Education North Asia Ltd
Pearson Educación de Mexico, S.A. de C.V.
Pearson Education Malaysia, Pte. Ltd
Pearson Education, Upper Saddle River, NJ

10 9 8 7 6 5 4 3 2 1
ISBN 13: 978-0-13-613054-3
ISBN 10:   0-13-613054-2

Contents

CHAPTER 3   "WRONG, TERRIBLY WRONG": THE UNITED STATES AND VIETNAM   36

CHAPTER 4   CAN THE UNITED STATES LEAD THE WORLD?   53

CHAPTER 5   FROM RUSSIA TO THE SOVIET UNION   70

CHAPTER 6   FROM THE SOVIET UNION BACK TO RUSSIA   85

Part II   The Global South   103

Part III   The Eternal Threats   185

CHAPTER 15   THE CHALLENGE OF TERRORISM   228

Part IV   The Economic Blocs   243

CHAPTER 16   EUROPE DIVORCES AMERICA   24

CHAPTER 22 GIVING PEACE A CHANCE 342

FEATURE BOXES

Chapter 1

Chapter 2

Chapter 3

Chapter 4

Chapter 5

Chapter 6

Chapter 7

Chapter 8

Chapter 9

Chapter 10

Chapter 11

Chapter 12

Chapter 13

Chapter 14

Chapter 15

Chapter 16

Chapter 17

Chapter 18

Chapter 19

Chapter 20

Chapter 21

Chapter 22

PREFACE

What comes next? We do not have a clear picture of what the current global system is, much less of what the next one is likely to be. Some say that we have already left the "post–Cold War system" and entered a "post-post–Cold War system," unhelpful terms that explain little. Global systems—the distribution of power and motives of a given period—matter a great deal. They structure all countries' foreign and security policies. If we accurately comprehend the system that we are in—the "structure"—then we can make shrewd and effective policies. If we misunderstand the current structure—e.g., interpret the present system as a new Cold War bipolarity—then we can make terrible mistakes. Because we emphasize international systems and what they imply, we have been called "structural realists," a term we neither embrace nor reject.

This entails a review of IR history, and that is a problem. Few young people nowadays enter college with adequate background in twentieth-century history. Ask students questions about major events in the twentieth century and you are likely to face silence. It is all news to them. But they cannot be blamed; they don't know it because they have never been taught it. Accordingly, we take it as our task to do considerable backfilling in recent history, which we arrange largely by geographic area and use to illustrate one or more concepts of international relations. Many instructors have thanked us for this approach.

Some texts in international relations pay less attention to history, leaping instead into the future. These are the "world-order" texts that, we think, implicitly argue the following: "The twentieth century was a horrible century that showed the worst that humans can do to each other. But it was only an episode in the maturation of humankind and has little to teach us. The twenty-first century, a time of global cooperation, ecology, and equality, is upon us. We must concentrate on it and not on the unhappy past."

We find "world-order" approaches unjustified, or at least grossly premature. The world became more complex after the Cold War, which kept numerous problems suppressed or frozen. And the mechanisms to deal with these problems still depend on sovereign nations deciding if and when they want to participate. When people are determined to fight for what they believe is justly theirs, UN "peacekeeping" forces are useless. War—"contending by force," in Grotius's classic words—remains a part of international relations and cannot be wished away. Although we happily note in the concluding chapter that wars are becoming rarer, conflict is still the "stuff" of international politics. If world order does break out, we will be among the first to write a textbook about it.

We begin in Chapter 1 with system change and an overview of the international systems that have marked modern history. The present system still defies easy characterization. *Multipolar* does not capture the inequalities of the several "poles"; we consider *stratified, globalized, clash of civilizations*, and other models, most of them with major economic components. Chapter 1 also introduces the concepts of *power, state,* and *sovereignty,* which we believe are still fundamental to international relations.

System change has touched almost everything in international affairs, not just the obvious—the end of Cold War bipolarity between the superpowers. Unfortunately, the changes were hard to anticipate and sometimes led to increased violence. In the Persian Gulf, a tyrannical ruler strove to expand his realm because his previous superpower patron no longer could restrain him. Economic relations among the major industrial blocs—Europe, the Pacific Rim, America—have grown testier; fear of the Soviets no longer holds them together under a U.S. strategic umbrella. Proliferation of nuclear weapons, a minor issue during the Cold War, has become a major issue. The United Nations, previously little more than a talk shop, has developed as a crisis stabilizer. We discuss these and other consequences of system change in this book.

We believe that because system change is occurring before our very eyes, IR is more exciting and relevant than ever. In this new world there are new threats to guard against and new opportunities to take advantage of. As in earlier editions, we are trying to awaken young newcomers to the field to its fascinating and sometimes dramatic qualities, as well as acquaint them with its basic concepts and vocabulary. Toward this end, we include feature boxes titled "Concepts" and "Classic Thought," as well as "Economics," "Turning Point," "Diplomacy," and "Geography" feature boxes. We also include "Reflections" feature boxes, which recall the authors' personal experiences or ponder issues that affect students personally, to show that IR is not a distant abstraction.

■ Supplements

Companion Website™

www.prenhall.com/roskin   This Web site brings an on-line study guide to students. When students log on, they will find a wealth of study and research resources. Chapter outline and summary information, true/false tests, fill-in-the-blank tests, and multiple-choice tests, all with immediate feedback and chapter page numbers, give students ample opportunity to review the information. The site also includes links to sites pertaining to material covered in the text.

Instructor's Manual with Test Item File

For each chapter in the book, this supplement—available in print as well as downloadable format—contains a chapter summary, essay questions, and multiple-choice questions based on the material discussed in the text. (ISBN 978-0-13-613020-8)

Prentice Hall Test Generator

A computerized version of the test item file, this program allows full editing of the questions and the addition of instructor-generated test items. Other special features include random generation, scrambling question order, and test preview before printing. This program is available in Windows and Macintosh formats. (ISBN 978-0-13-613021-5)

Customized Readers

www.amongnations.com   Instructors can assemble their own readers based on the database of selections, **Among Nations: Readings in International Relations**.

Prentice Hall's sister company, Pearson Custom Publishing, has entered a partnership with the Council on Foreign Relations, bringing together expertise in on-line book-building technology with academic excellence. The Council formed a special editorial team—which includes *Foreign Affairs'* Managing Editor, Gideon Rose—to select the most influential articles on International Relations from *Foreign Affairs* and other prominent publications in the discipline. Along with suggested tables of content for specific courses and Prentice Hall texts, the Editorial Board has provided optional pedagogical apparatus.

Whether classic or current, theory or real-world applications, selections from **Among Nations** will bring important new perspectives to the classroom. This is the only on-line book-building resource of articles from *Foreign Affairs*. **Among Nations** provides access to all 1,500 articles published since the inception of *Foreign Affairs* magazine in 1922.

■ About the Cover Photo

The 1945 Hiroshima blast exposed two-year-old Sadako Sasaki to intense radiation. She developed leukemia and died ten years later. Japanese schoolchildren place colorful origami (the traditional Japanese art of folding paper to form flowers, animal figures, and other images) by her statue in the Hiroshima Peace Park in order to commemorate her and call for peace, which is, after all, the driving force in the field of international relations.

■ Acknowledgments

We owe a great deal of thanks to specialists who read and commented on our chapters and saved us from foolish misstatements. Ambassador Theresa A. Healy and Charles Ahlgren of the State Department made valuable suggestions for the chapter on diplomacy. Dr. Ed

Dew of Fairfield University perceptively reviewed our chapters on Africa and Latin America. Also, we thank the following reviewers for their helpful comments: Michael A. Colomaio of Alfred State College, Patrice McMahon of the University of Nebraska at Lincoln, Barbara Ann Rieffer of Bethany College, and Chris Van Aller of Winthrop University.

Responsibility, of course, lies with the authors, who are happy to receive your comments directly for incorporation into possible future editions.

Michael G. Roskin
roskin@lycoming.edu

Nicholas O. Berry
foreignpolicyforum@msn.com

IR

PART I

THE COLD WAR COME AND GONE

The Cold War dominated the latter half of the twentieth century and warped both of the main antagonists—the United States, and the Soviet Union. How they reached their present situations is thus worth study, both to show how the world got to where it is and to provide several concepts of international relations.

Chapter 1 looks at the big picture—the transformation of the *international system* in the twentieth century and what seems to be emerging in the twenty-first century.

Chapter 2 reviews America's encounters with the world and uses them to illustrate the slippery and changeable concept of *national interest*. Over various periods of U.S. foreign policy—the independence war, manifest destiny, imperialism, World Wars I and II, isolationism, and the Cold War—U.S. national interests and the strategies to carry them out have changed in response to new threats and opportunities. George F. Kennan's celebrated "containment" policy, for example, may be brilliant for one era but unworkable for the next (as Kennan himself lamented).

Chapter 3 shows how we got into and out of the Vietnam War, something most young people know little about. The gap here between *political generations* is great. Few high schools get around to Vietnam in their crowded history curricula. Vietnam was a searing U.S. national tragedy, altering our foreign policy, undermining the economy and our confidence in government, and spawning a counterculture generation. We learn that government can be "wrong, terribly wrong," in the words of Robert McNamara.

Chapter 4 brings us into the new world that U.S. foreign policy faces. Can we lead in this new, complex situation? Do we wish to practice *interventionism?* Have we turned *isolationist?* Should we be motivated by *ideals* or *self-interest?* Do we have the budget, armed forces, and congressional support with which to lead a world that often does not wish to follow us? Finally, do the institutions of our foreign policy tend to lead to policy errors and *bureaucratic politics?*

With Chapter 5 we turn to our Cold War antagonist, the Soviet Union, and how it came to be, how Russia turned into the tyrannical Soviet Union. Russia raises questions of *geopolitics:* Is geography destiny? What role does *ideology* play in foreign policy? Was the Cold War inevitable?

Chapter 6 explores why the Soviet Union collapsed. It considers how *misperception* of the outside world, *hegemony* over a costly empire, a failed *détente,* and increasingly critical *elites* driven by the *fear of falling behind* undermined regime *legitimacy.* Was Soviet foreign policy largely *internally* or *externally generated?* Finally, a word of warning: Russia under Putin has become authoritarian. Do not suppose our difficulties with Russia are over.

CHAPTER 1

STRANGE NEW WORLD

POWER AND SYSTEMS IN TRANSFORMATION

1. What is power?
2. How can some types of power be unusable?
3. What is an "international system"?
4. What systems has the world gone through over a century?
5. What kind of a system are we now heading into?
6. Will this new system be stable or unstable?
7. Are states and sovereignty still the foundations of IR?

International relations (IR) depend a lot on **power**, the ability of one country to get another to do (or sometimes not do) something. International laws and institutions are too weak to rely on them the way we rely on domestic laws and institutions. In **domestic politics** when we have a quarrel with someone, we "don't take the law into our own hands; we take him to court." In IR, it's sometimes the reverse. There is no court, and self-help may be the only kind available.

A **system** is the way power is distributed around the globe. An international system is a sort of "power map" for a certain time period. If you can correctly figure out what the current system is—who's got what kind of power—you know where you stand and how and when to use your power. For example, if many countries have roughly equal power, it is likely a "balance of power system" (explored presently). If one country has overwhelming power, enough to supervise the globe (unlikely), it might be a "unipolar system." The turbulent twentieth century witnessed four IR systems.

1. Pre-World War I: Dominance of the great European empires in the nineteenth century until 1914. In systems theory, this period exemplifies a balance-of-power system, but by 1910 it had decayed.
2. World War I through World War II: The empires destroy themselves from 1914 to 1945. With several major players refusing to respond to threats, the interwar period might be termed an "antibalance-of-power" system. It is inherently unstable and temporary.

3. Cold War: The collapse of the traditional European powers leaves the United States and USSR facing each other in a "bipolar" system. But the **superpowers** block and exhaust themselves from 1945 through the 1980s, and the bipolar system decays.

4. Post-Cold War: The collapse of the Soviet Union ends bipolarity, but ideas on the new system are unclear, ranging from "multipolar" (several power centers) to "zones of chaos" and from "globalization" to "clash of civilizations." We will consider several possibilities.

Do not reify these periods and systems. They are just attempts to get a handle on reality; they are not reality itself. **Reification** is a constant temptation in the social sciences. Students especially like to memorize neat tables in preparing for exams. Okay, memorize them, but take them with a grain of salt. Notice that in the foregoing breakdown one period overlaps with the next. The European empires, for example, did not turn off with a click in 1945; they phased out over three decades. To try to understand a confusing world, social scientists are forced to simplify a very complex reality into theories,

international relations   Interactions among countries. (See page 2.)

power   Ability of one country to get another to do its bidding. (See page 2.)

domestic politics   Interactions within countries. (See page 2.)

system   Interaction of many components so that changing one changes the others. (See page 2.)

superpower   Nation with far more power than others and the ability to wage many kinds of war nearly everywhere.

reification   Mistaking a theory for reality.

force   Application of military power.

Concepts

POWER

Power is widely misunderstood. It is not big countries beating up little countries. Power is one country's ability to get another country to do what it wants: A gets B to change its policy. There are many kinds of power: rational persuasion, economic, cultural, technological, and military. Typically, military power is used only as a last resort. Then it becomes **force**, a subset of power.

When Europe and the United States leaned on Iran to cease its uranium-enrichment program, Iran hinted it would cut oil shipments to the West. Iran was using its economic power to try to offset superior Western military power. When Ethiopia and Eritrea quarreled over their border, they mobilized their armies and got ready to use force. Powerful countries have great and several kinds of power at their disposal; they may have so much power that they rarely need to use force.

Sometimes, however, as the United States discovered in Vietnam, power is unusable. The crux of power, remember, is getting the other country to

change its policy—in the case of North Vietnam, to stop its forcible reunification with South Vietnam. Can American power really stop coca cultivation in the Andes, an area where government either cannot stop the activity or (in the case of Bolivia) supports it? If all your types of power—political, economic, and finally military—do not work in a particular situation, you turn out to be not nearly so powerful as you thought.

Power cannot be closely calculated. Even "powerful" countries do not always get their way. You can never be sure you will prevail. Your power may be unsuitable to the problem at hand, such as installing democracy in Iraq. Your attempt to persuade another country may lead to mounting resentments: "Who are you to tell us what to do?" (Washington often gets such replies from Beijing and Tehran.) Accordingly, power of whatever sort is best exercised with restraint. The question for our day is what kind of power we should emphasize.

models, time periods, and conceptual frameworks, all of them artificial. The systems approach is one such framework.

Why should we bother naming and analyzing international systems? Because if we misunderstand the system in which we operate, we can make terrible, expensive mistakes. For example, if we continue operating under the rules of the bipolar system of the Cold War—with its emphasis on military power—we will become frustrated and perplexed that our allies no longer follow our lead and that we seem to be creating new enemies. It will be like trying to play a game whose rules have changed. On the other hand, if we suppose we can stop massacres and promote democracy around the globe, we may collide with some nasty realities in "zones of chaos." Understanding the world system means you can go with the flow of events (and sometimes manipulate them) instead of working against them.

Concepts

SYSTEMS

A system is something composed of many components that interact and influence each other. Systems thinkers argue that if the logic of a system can be discovered, one can roughly predict its evolution or at least warn what could go wrong. The crux here is "interact." If something is truly a system, you cannot change just one part of it because all the other components also change. Systems thinking originated in biology. The human body is a system of heart, lungs, blood, and so on. Take away one component and the body dies. Alter one, and the others try to adjust to compensate. Systems can be stable and self-correcting or they can break down, either from internal or external causes.

After World War II, systems thinking spread to almost every discipline, including international relations. Thinkers—some focusing just on Europe, others on the entire globe—found that various systems have come and gone over the centuries, each operating with its own logic and producing variously stable and unstable results. Obviously, an unstable system does not last.

The strong point about systems thinking is that it trains us to see the world as a whole rather than just as a series of unrelated happenings and problems. It also encourages us to think about how a clever statesman may create and manipulate a system to get desired results. If he presses here, what will come out there? Will it be bad or good?

To some extent, international systems are artificial creations of varying degrees of handiwork. A

system that obtains the assent of the major powers and goes with the forces of history may last a long time. A system that harms one or more major players and goes against the forces of history will surely soon be overturned. Systems do not fall from heaven but are crafted by intelligent minds such as Metternich and Bismarck. This brings an element of human intelligence and creativity into international politics. It's not just science; it is also an art that brings with it hopeful thinking.

Does the world form a political "system"? It is surely composed of many parts, and they interact. The trouble is, few thinkers can totally agree on what the systems were, their time periods, and the logic of their operation. Looking at the four systems of the twentieth century, some would say there are only three, because the first and second should really be merged (the second was merely the decayed tail end of the first). Others would say, no, actually there are five, adding the period of the Axis dictatorships as a separate system.

Systems thinking is inexact, not yet a science. We have still not settled on what the present system is. In this chapter we consider several attempts to describe the current system and note that none of them is completely satisfactory. With each proposed system, ask two questions: (1) Does it exist, and (2) will it persist? That is, does the proposed system describe reality, and, if so, is it likely to remain stable and last for some time?

The European Balance-of-Power System

As we will consider in Chapter 7 on colonialism, in the nineteenth century Europe carved up the globe into empires and spheres of influence. Some say they did it for economic gain, but imperial costs usually outweighed profits. Prestige and fear of someone else getting the territory were big motivators. It was perhaps a foolish system and terribly unfair to the "natives," but it was a reasonably stable system and had several advantages for preserving peace. By denying their subjects self-rule, the imperial powers also denied them the possibility of going to war. Britain held down the latent violence between Hindus and Muslims in India. Upon India's independence in 1947, violence erupted as two lands emerged from the *Raj,* India and Pakistan, and they have fought three wars since. Their next war could be nuclear; both have the bomb. The imperial system, then, was not all bad.

balance of power Theory that states form alliances to offset threatening states.

Second, by carving up the globe in an agreed-upon fashion, the great empires mostly avoided wars among themselves. All powers understood that Britain had India, France had Indochina, the Netherlands had the East Indies, and so on. This has been called a **balance-of-power** system.

Some writers argue that during certain periods the power of the several major nations was similar, and they arranged this power, by means of alliances, to roughly balance. If country A felt threatened by country B, it would form an alliance with country C, hoping to deter B from aggression. Later, all of them might form an alliance to protect themselves from the growing power of country D. It did not always work, but it helped to hold down the number and ferocity of wars. For a balance-of-power system to function, theorists say, it took at least five major players who shared a common culture and viewpoint and a commitment not to wreck the system. Balance of power was like a poker game in which you decide you'd rather keep the game going than win all the money, so you refrain from bankrupting the other players. Graphically, it looks like this:

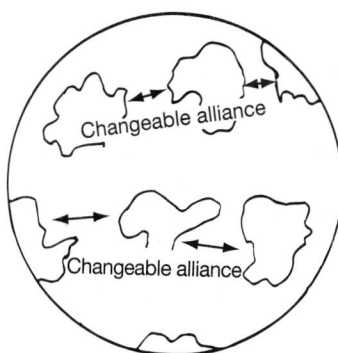

Historians detect two great ages of balance of power, from 1648 to 1789 and again from 1814 to 1914. The Thirty Years War, mostly fought in Germany, pitted Catholics against Protestants and was the bloodiest in history until World War II. By the time it was settled in 1648 with the Peace of Westphalia, Europe's monarchs had had enough of bashing each other and so constructed a balance-of-power system that endured until the French

Westphalian   System set up by 1648 Peace of Westphalia that made *sovereignty* the norm.

Metternichian   Conservative restoration of *balance of power* after Napoleon.

Bismarckian   Contrived and unstable *balance of power* from 1870 to 1914.

Revolution (1789) and Napoleonic wars (ending in 1814). The **Westphalian** system also established the concept of *sovereignty* (see discussion later in this chapter).

Napoleon overturned the old system with unrestrained ambition and a mass army that conquered most of Europe. When Napoleon played poker, he tried to bankrupt all the other players. (He also cheated.) Gone was the restraint that had characterized the old system. Once Napoleon was beaten, Europe's conservatives met under the guidance of Austrian Prince Metternich to construct a new balance-of-power system, sometimes called the **Metternichian** system. It worked moderately well for some decades, but only as long as monarchs restrained their ambitions and shared the values of legitimacy and stability. This slowly eroded with the effects of nationalism in the nineteenth century—especially with German unification in 1871—until it disappeared by World War I. There has not been a balance-of-power system since then. Some say there cannot be one again.

Many scholars reject the balance-of-power theory, pointing out that there were some nasty wars when power was supposed to be balanced, for example the Seven Years War (what Americans call the French and Indian War) of the 1750s or the Crimean War of the 1850s. Balance-of-power theorists counter by saying these were relatively small wars that did not wreck the overall system.

Turning Point

BISMARCK: SYSTEM CHANGER

If someone had told Prussian Chancellor Bismarck that the unified Germany he created in 1871 would lead to two world wars and the destruction of the nineteenth-century imperial system, he would have been aghast. Bismarck was a conservative, yet his handiwork brought radical, systemic change. Remember, in systems you cannot change just one thing, because everything else changes too. Bismarck supervised a giant change in the political geography of Europe—German unification—but this rippled outward, changing the global political system.

Before Bismarck, Germany had been a patchwork of small kingdoms and principalities. After unification, Germany had the location, industry, and population to dominate Europe. Bismarck thought unified Germany could live in balance and at peace with the other European powers. He was neither a militarist nor an expansionist. Instead, after unification, Bismarck concentrated on making sure an alliance of hostile powers did not form around his Second Reich. Trying to play the old balance-of-power game, Bismarck made several treaties with other European powers proclaiming friendship and mutual aid.

But the **Bismarckian** system was not as stable as the earlier Metternichian system (see above). Bismarck's unified Germany had changed the European—and to some extent global—political geography. German nationalism was now unleashed. A new Kaiser and his generals were nationalistic and imperialistic. They thought Bismarck was too cautious and fired him in 1890. Then they started empire building, arms races, and alliance with Austria. The French and Russians, alarmed at this, formed what Kennan called the "fateful alliance." Thus on the eve of World War I, Europe was arrayed into two hostile blocs, something Bismarck desperately tried to avoid. Without knowing or wanting it, Bismarck helped destroy Europe.

Some writers hold that not balance of power but **hierarchy of power** acts to preserve peace. When nations know their position on a ladder of power they are more likely to behave. The aftermath of a great, decisive war leaves a victor on top and a loser on the bottom, and this brings a few decades of peace. Critics say balance-of-power proponents have mistaken this hierarchy for a balance that never existed. All such hierarchies are temporary and eventually overturned as weaker states gain power and dominant states lose it.

hierarchy of power   Theory that peace is preserved when states know where they stand on a ladder of relative power.

Either way, the nineteenth-century system started decaying when two newcomers demanded their own empires. Germany and Japan upset the system with demands for, as Berlin put it, "a place in the sun." German unification (1871) and Japan's Meiji Restoration (1868) produced powerful, dissatisfied empires jealous of the existing arrangement. Tremors started around the turn of the century as Germany armed the Boers who were fighting the British, engaged Britain in a race to build battleships, and confronted France by boldly intervening in Morocco. At this same time in the Pacific, the Japanese took Taiwan from China, attacked and beat the Russians, and seized Korea.

If there had been a balance-of-power system during the nineteenth century, it was no longer operative by the start of the twentieth century. Balance of power requires at least five players who are able to make and remake alliances. Flexibility and lack of passion are the keys here. Instead, by 1914 Europe was divided into two hostile, rigid alliances. When one alliance member went to war—first Austria against Serbia—it dragged in its respective backers. By the time the war broke out, the balance-of-power system was no longer functioning.

■ The Unstable Interwar System

World War I was the initial act of Europe's self-destruction. Some fifteen million of Europe's finest young men died. Four empires—the German, Austro-Hungarian, Russian, and Turkish—collapsed. From the wreckage flowered the twin evils of communism and fascism. The "winners"—Britain and France—were so drained and bitter they were unable to enforce the provisions of the Versailles Treaty on the defeated nations. The international economy was seriously wounded and collapsed a decade later.

World War I led directly to World War II. The dissatisfied losers of the first war—Germany and Austria—joined with two dissatisfied winners—Italy and Japan (Japan participated in a minor way by seizing German possessions in China and the Pacific during World War I)—while another loser, Russia, tried to stay on the sidelines.

Another connecting link between the two wars was the failure of any balance-of-power system to function, this time by design. Balance-of-power thinking stood discredited after World War I. Some blamed the cynical manipulations of power balancers for the war. This is an unfair charge, as the system had already broken down before the war. Maybe balance of power is a defective system, but the start of World War I by itself does not prove that point. At any rate, the winning democracies—Britain, France, and the United States—chose not to play balance of power, and from their decision flowed the catastrophe of World War II.

interwar   Between World Wars I
and II, 1919–1939.

What do we call this strange and short-lived **interwar** system? It was not balance of power because the democracies refused to play. The dictators, sensing the vacuum, moved in to take what they could. We might, for want of a better term, call it an "antibalance-of-power system." Britain and France, weary from the previous war and putting too much faith in the League of Nations and human reason, finally met force with force only when it was too late; Germany nearly beat them both. Graphically, it looked like this:

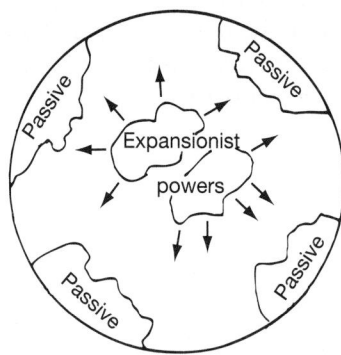

Stalin's Soviet Union also refused to play (see Chapter 5). Here it was a case of ideological hatred against the capitalist powers and the conviction they were doomed anyway.

Classic Thought

E. H. CARR AND REALISM

British professor E. H. Carr called the interwar period *The Twenty Years' Crisis, 1919–1939,* the title of his scathing and influential critique of the failure of the democracies to recognize world power realities. In so doing, Carr laid the groundwork for the Realist school that was picked up and amplified after World War II by Hans Morgenthau in the United States (see Chapters 2 and 19).

Carr divided thinkers on international relations into two schools, "utopian" and "realist." The utopians are optimists, children of the enlightenment and liberalism, and hold that reason and morality can structure nations' international behavior toward peace. Woodrow Wilson and his League of Nations are prime examples. Realists, on the other hand, are pessimists and stress power and

national interest. This does not necessarily mean perpetual war, for if statesmen are clever and willing to build and apply power, both economic and military, they can make aggressors back down. Implicit in this is a balance-of-power theory.

Between the two great wars Carr saw utopian fools unwilling to stand up to dictatorial beasts. The trouble with Realism is that you can't tell what is realistic until many years later, when you see how things turn out. Should you be constantly tough and ready to fight? What difficulties will that lead to? The application of a simplified version of Realism after World War II helped create and perpetuate the bipolar system of the Cold War, a dangerous system that led to a number of good-sized (but no nuclear) wars.

The United States also refused to play balance of power. Isolationism plus verbal protests to Japan over the rape of China were thought to keep us at a safe distance from the conflagration (see Chapter 17). We did not need much military might; we had two oceans. In 1941, both the Soviet Union and the United States learned they could not hide from hostile power.

bipolar The world divided into two power centers, as in the Cold War.

Europe destroyed itself again in World War II. Into the power vacuum moved Stalin's Red Army, intent on making East Europe a security zone for the Soviet Union. The Japanese empire disappeared, leaving another vacuum in Asia. The Communists, first in China and North Korea, then in North Vietnam, took over. The great European empires, weak at home and facing anticolonial nationalism, granted independence to virtually all their imperial holdings (see Chapter 7). The age of the classic empires was over, replaced by the dominance of two superpowers.

■ The Bipolar Cold War System

As we shall discuss in Chapters 2 and 5, the Cold War started within a couple of years of the end of World War II as Stalin's Soviet Union, intent on turning East Europe into a belt of Communist-ruled satellites, proved its unfitness as a partner for Roosevelt's grand design for postwar cooperation (see Chapters 2 and 21). Many feared that Stalin was also getting ready to move beyond East Europe. Probably by the spring of 1947 the Cold War was on, for that is when the United States openly stated its opposition to Soviet expansion and took steps to counter it.

The world lined up in one of two camps—or at least it looked that way—and that was how both the Soviets and Americans wanted it. Academic thinkers described this situation as **bipolar**. Bipolarity was a dangerous but in some ways comforting system. West and East blocs watched each other like hawks, constantly looking for opportunities to exploit in the other bloc and guarding against possible attack. It was a tense world, with fingers too close to nuclear triggers. Graphically, it looked like this:

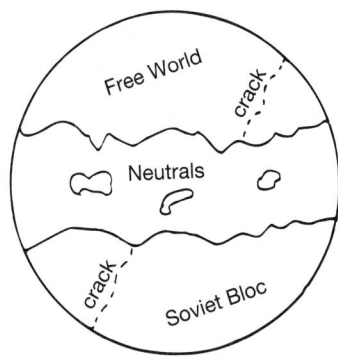

The bipolar system was seen as a "zero-sum game" in which whatever one player won, the other lost. If the Communist bloc stole a piece of the Free World, it won and the West lost. To prevent such reverses, war was always possible (Korea and Vietnam), even nuclear war (Cuba). Because both superpowers possessed nuclear weapons, though, they always kept their conflicts at arm's length, fighting them by proxy and not directly. Both understood that a direct conflict could quickly turn nuclear, ending both the system and their dominance. They hated each other, but they were not reckless. Better, each thought, to be prince of their half of the world than run the risk of mutual wipe-out. At no time did Americans tangle directly with Soviets. Still, everyone was jumpy, worried about possible gains and losses.

Some on both sides still hearken back to those days when life was simpler because you knew exactly who your friends and enemies were. The weaker allies of the superpowers, East and West Europe, mostly kept quiet and obeyed their leading power. NATO and the Warsaw Pact looked firm. Most members of each alliance had super-power military bases on their soil and accepted them as a form of protection. The comforting part about bipolarity was that you knew where you stood. For many today, life is too confusing.

If you look closely at the Cold War, however, you notice that it was never strictly bipolar. Some thinkers label it a "loose bipolar" system to account for the fact that between the two big "continents" were many "islands," neutral countries that deliberately avoided joining either camp. Both superpowers wooed these neutrals.

Was the bipolar world stable? It did not blow up in nuclear war and lasted nearly half a century, but it could not endure, for at least five reasons:

1. The bipolar system locked the superpowers into frantic *arms races* that grew increasingly expensive, especially for the weakening Soviet economy. More and more bought them less and less, for the armies and weapons thus produced did not succeed in protecting the superpowers or in extending their power; attempts to extend power collided with nationalism.

2. *Third World nationalism* arose, and both superpowers got burned fighting it. Playing their zero-sum game, the two superpowers tried to get or keep peripheral areas in their "camp." They pushed their efforts into the Third World until they got burned—the Americans in Vietnam and the Soviets in Afghanistan. Eventually both had to ask themselves, "What good is this war?"

3. At least one of the two camps *split*. One of the polar "continents" cracked apart and a large piece drifted away: the Sino-Soviet dispute (see Chapter 6). Dominance breeds resentment. The other "continent" developed some hairline fractures, as NATO grew shakier (see Chapter 16).

4. The economic growth of the *Pacific Rim* countries made both superpowers look like fools. While the military giants frittered away their resources in expensive weapons and dubious interventions, Japan and the Four Tigers turned their region into an economic giant (see Chapter 17).

5. The expensive arms race on top of an inherently defective economy led to the *Soviet collapse* in 1991. America, by outlasting its antagonist, in effect "won" the Cold War. The world that is emerging from the bipolar system, however, may not be completely to America's liking.

■ What Kind of New System?

The two momentous events of 1991 started discussions over how to name and describe the new system then being born, a task not yet accomplished. Notice that all of the possible systems suggested below have a question mark after them. Do not reify them.

multipolar   The world divided into many power centers.

unipolar   One power center.

Multipolar?

Many now see the world as **multipolar**—a system of several centers of power, some of them trading blocs, and all of them engaged in tough economic competition. No one nation or bloc dominates in this system. It would somewhat resemble the old balance of power system, but the blocs would be much bigger than nations, largely immobile, and competing by economics rather than warfare. Graphically, it would look like this:

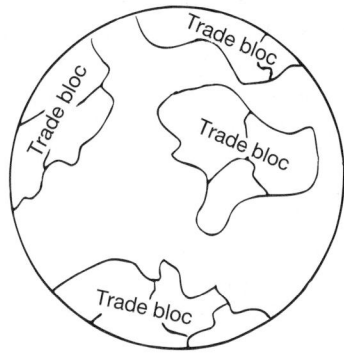

This model does not perfectly fit reality. The blocs—the European Union, the Pacific Rim, and others—cannot look after their own security; all need U.S. help. The West Europeans at first claimed they could settle things in ex-Yugoslavia by themselves, but within a few years they were demanding that the United States step in. South Korea, Taiwan, and Japan are powerful trade competitors with the United States, but all want free security from America. Without U.S. leadership in the world, little gets done. Would a multipolar system work if trade disputes became too great?

Unipolar?

Some thought the great events of 1991—the quick U.S. defeat of Iraq and Soviet collapse—produced a **unipolar** system. The United States would lead in constructing what President Bush senior called a "new world order" with the Gulf War as a model: The United States leads the UN and the middle-sized powers to stop an aggressor. In this model, only the United States now has the ability to project military power overseas, the political clout, and the vision to lead. Graphically, it would look like this:

The neo-conservatives of the younger Bush administration especially liked the unipolar view of the world and tried to implement it in Iraq. But a unipolar system is unlikely. America is clearly now the only military superpower, but economic factors and America's interest in the outside world may limit its leadership role. Are the American people and Congress willing to pay money and send troops to far corners of the globe? For how long? And are other lands willing to follow America in such enterprises? Or are they more likely to resent us? Notice how little we get our way in the world. Even a small power like Iraq did not bend to our will without war, and few allies supported us in that war.

Counterweight?

As the Bush 43 administration followed a unipolar model, many European lands, Russia, China, and other countries spoke of the need for a "counterweight" to U.S. power. They saw us as domineering and too eager for war. A counterweight model would look like a unipolar model stood on its head:

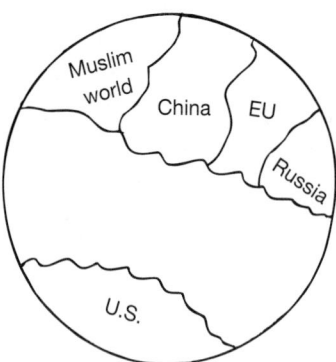

Here, instead of following the United States, many other countries agree among themselves to oppose and ignore us. They would provide no support for U.S.-led causes and would sharply criticize us on everything from unnecessary use of force to economic domination. We

would be labeled international bullies and politically isolated in
the world. Whatever we wanted, they would oppose. In the face
of massive U.S. military power, however, they would pose no security threat to us.

stratified   Power distributed in
layers.
globalization   The world turning
into one big capitalist market.

There are problems with this model too. The rest of the
world is disorganized and able to cooperate on little. Some op-
pose the United States on one question but support us on another. And when there is a serious problem, many beg for U.S. intervention; they understand that only we have the
power to curb dangerous aggressors and murderous civil wars. At times, especially in reaction to U.S. policy on Iraq, the world showed some tendency to form a counterweight,
but not a consistent one.

Stratified?

A **stratified** model combines the unipolar and multipolar models and may fit reality better. It sees roughly three layers. At the top are the rich, high-tech countries. The second layer
is that of middle-income industrializing lands. The third layer is a "zone of chaos" dominated by crime, warlords, and chronic instability. It is startling to realize that the world's
biggest single industry is now crime, much of it connected to the flow of drugs from the
poor countries to the rich countries. Graphically, it would look like this:

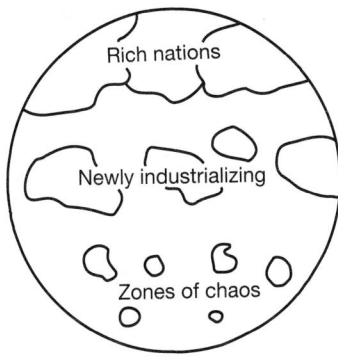

The top-layer countries can zap conventional targets with their advanced weapons,
but they cannot control the chaos of the bottom-layer countries, whose guerrillas and drug
cartels offer no good targets. Congo, Colombia, and Afghanistan are examples of chaos
that the top-layer countries would like to avoid but cannot. Many of the world's natural
resources—particularly oil—are in these chaos zones, so the first layer is inevitably drawn
into their difficulties. And the first layer's appetite for illicit drugs means the bottom layer
gets its tentacles into the top layer.

Globalized?

Even before the Cold War ended, **globalization** began to emerge (see Chapter 18). In an
ideal globalized system most countries become economic players in the world market, a
capitalist competition where goods, money, and ideas flow easily to wherever there are

customers. The motto of a globalized system: Make money, not war. The few countries that do not play, such as Cuba and North Korea, live in isolation and poverty. After some years, most countries want to play. Globalization can help promote worldwide economic growth. It might look like this:

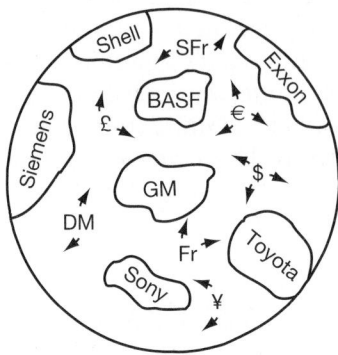

But there are many problems that limit and could end a globalized system. Most countries—including the United States—fear totally free trade. They see their industries closing under a wave of imports and respond with traditional protectionist measures to lock out foreign goods. Furthermore, is globalization a cause or a consequence of peace? Are the two intertwined? If so, what happens to one when the other is disrupted? Prosperity does not necessarily bring peace, as newly affluent countries demand respect, resources, and sometimes territory. As China got richer, it defined its borders more grandly, reaching far out into the South and East China Seas where there may be undersea oil. Globalization does not seem to work everywhere. East Asia has zoomed ahead, but Latin America has grown little, suggesting that sound policies and flexible cultures may be key factors. China turned itself into the "factory of the world" with which few countries can compete. How many low-cost producers can the world take? Some resent the American and capitalist culture of a globalized system: "McWorld." Globalization may have already peaked and be declining.

Resource Wars?

If a globalized system falls apart, it may do so over the scramble for natural resources, especially petroleum. As the Pacific Rim, particularly China, industrializes, it produces and drives far more motor vehicles. Its peoples want to live like Americans, who consume energy prodigiously. Where will this energy come from? Will the world stay open to the free flow of natural resources, or will nations seek exclusive deals with and control over the oil-producing areas? This is why questions of who owns the China Seas and who controls transportation corridors from the Persian Gulf and Central Asia loom larger and larger. We may already be engaged in resource wars, the 1991 and 2003 wars with Iraq (see Chapter 9).

Related to resource wars is *resource blackmail.* In an age of tight energy supplies, countries with oil and natural gas deflect outside pressures with credible threats to cut exports. Saudi Arabia, resentful of U.S. complaints, finds it impossible to increase oil production. Russia, unhappy with Ukraine turning westward, cut natural gas not only to Ukraine but to Europe. Everyone noticed. Iran, rolling in petroleum revenue, thumbs its nose at Western concern over its nuclear program. In the energy age, the weak have become powerful.

Clash of Civilizations?

Harvard political scientist Samuel P. Huntington in 1993 made intellectual waves with his theory that the post-Cold War world was dividing into eight "civilizations," each based mostly on religion: Western (with European and North American branches), Slavic/Orthodox, Islamic, Hindu, Sinic (Chinese-based), Japanese, Latin American, and African. Some of these civilizations get along passably well with others, but some seriously dislike and reject others. The biggest problem: Islamic civilization, which harbors major antipathy to Western and Slavic/Orthodox civilizations. (More on this at the start of Chapter 9.) Graphically, Huntington's "civilizational" theory would resemble the trade-bloc picture:

state   Country or nation, has *sovereignty.*

absolutism   Renaissance pattern of kings concentrating power in themselves.

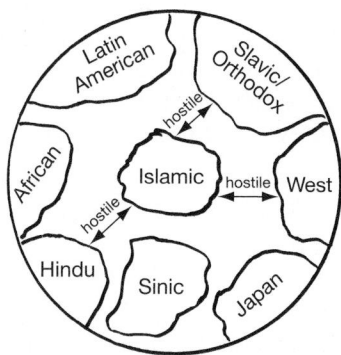

Indeed, some of these civilizations have formed trade blocs. The motive that guides their relations would not be trade, though, but deep-seated cultural dislikes and "kin-country" rallying. For example, Saudi Arabia and Iran, who detested Saddam's dictatorship in Iraq, opposed the U.S. invasion of Iraq in 2003. One should not invade a brother Muslim country. In Huntington's world, religion predicts international alignments better than commerce does. Few IR thinkers accept Huntington's theory; most think it contains some truth but is exaggerated.

Which, if any, of these models matches and explains international relations today? Would a combination provide a better fit? Can you come up with an accurate picture? Or will we just have to wait some years until the situation becomes clear?

■ Are States Here to Stay?

One may hope that the emerging international system will be an improvement, but its basic components are still sovereign **states**, and they tend to trip up plans for a peaceful, cooperative world. The concept of the modern state, nation-state, or the colloquial term "country" goes back about five centuries, when important changes rippled through West Europe. Thanks to gunpowder and cannons, monarchs controlled nobles and amassed centralized power, a movement called **absolutism**. Economies greatly expanded with new

strong state Modern nation-state able to enforce *sovereignty.*

inventions (such as printing) and the opening of trade to Asia and the Americas. The Roman Catholic Church lost temporal power as monarchs declared themselves supreme and secularized their kingdoms. To support their frequent wars, monarchs improved civil administration and tax collection. By the end of the horrible Thirty Years War in 1648, powerful modern states dominated West Europe.

Because they were so powerful—able to raise and fund large armies and navies—the modern **strong states** spread worldwide, for they easily conquered traditional lands. After they liberated themselves from colonial rule, the lands of Latin America, Asia, and Africa had also adopted the strong state form, although some were actually quite weak (see Chapters 7 and 10).

The American and French Revolutions in the late 1700s added a new twist to the strong state: mass enthusiasm and participation. Before, the affairs of state had been confined to a handful of kings and aristocrats; "subjects" (rather than citizens) kept silent and obeyed. With the spread of democratic ideas, citizens felt involved and patriotic. *Nationalism,* originating in the French Revolution and Napoleonic wars, also spread worldwide, assuming dominant, even lunatic, proportions in the twentieth century (see Chapter 8).

Concepts

THE STATE

States are generally defined as groups of humans having territory and government. This government, in turn, has the last word on law within its borders (*sovereignty,* which we consider presently). Only the state has a legitimate monopoly on coercion; that is, it can legally force citizens to do something. The mafia, of course, can force you to repay a debt, but it has no legal right to punish you. The Internal Revenue Service, on the other hand, can legally send you to prison for nonpayment of taxes.

Some use the term "nation-state," which adds the concept of nationality to state. Members of a nation-state have a sense of identity as a distinct people, often with their own language. Nation-states are fairly modern creations, probably not more than half a millennium old. International relations does not use "state" in the U.S. sense, such as the "great state of Kansas." In IR, in fact, the fifty American states are not states at all, because they lack sovereignty. They do not have the last word on law within their borders; the federal government in Washington does.

Most analyses of international relations take the nation-state as their starting point. State power overrides individual preferences. States can draft citizens and march them to war. Many states have a psychological hold on their citizens and inculcate and then command a sense of patriotism, not always for good ends. Along with this comes "we-they" thinking about foreign lands. "We" are peaceful folk simply trying to protect ourselves; "they" are plotting to harm us. U.S. and North Korean attitudes about each other are a current example. Each feels it is the aggrieved party.

Could the leading role of the state be eroding? States are not necessarily the first or last word in human organization. Throughout history, extended families, tribes, kingdoms, and empires have given way to more advanced forms of organization.

■ Is Sovereignty Slipping?

If the new international system is to be more peaceful and cooperative than the old, states will have to give up at least part
of their most basic attribute, their **sovereignty**. Part legal, part
power, and part psychological, sovereignty means having the

> **sovereignty**   Concept that each
> state rules on its territory.

last word in law, able to control your country's internal affairs and to keep other countries
from butting in. In a word, it means being boss on your own turf.

Sovereignty means countries can pretty much do as they wish. Pakistan in the past
has worked closely with the United States but ignored Washington's warnings not to produce nuclear devices. Islamabad decides what is in its national interest, not Washington.
Japan also depends on the United States for its security but resists purchasing more American goods. Tokyo decides what is good for the Japanese economy, not Washington. In
1990 Saudi Arabia asked for U.S. troops to defend its territory against Iraq. But these soldiers could not drink a beer until they crossed the border into Iraq; Saudi law prohibits all
alcoholic beverages (an incentive for U.S. troops to advance rapidly). Notice how sovereignty
in part offsets power, in these cases, U.S. power.

Sovereignty has always been partly fictional. Big, rich, and powerful countries routinely influence and even dominate small, poor, and weak countries. All countries are sovereign, but some are more sovereign than others. Lebanon, for example, lost its sovereignty
as it dissolved in civil war in 1975, its territory partitioned by politico-religious militias and
Syrian and Israeli occupiers. Israel's pullout from the south of Lebanon in 2000 scarcely
helped, as the territory was occupied by Hezbollah fighters, not by the Lebanese army.
Syria still controls much of Lebanon.

In our day sovereignty has been slipping as a sacred concept. The world community,
speaking through the UN, told Iraq that developing weapons of mass destruction was not
just Iraq's business but the world's business. The world felt ashamed that it did not inter-
fere in the massacre of 800,000 Rwandans in 1994. Can mass murder ever be a purely "internal matter"? Currently, the world condemns Sudan for genocide in Darfur; international

Concepts

SOVEREIGNTY

The root of the word *sovereignty* is *reign*, from the French for rule. The prefix is from the Old French for *over*, so a sovereign is someone who "rules over" a land (e.g., a king). Sovereignty is the abstract quality of ruling a country. The term gained currency in the sixteenth century when roy-alist scholars such as the Frenchman Jean Bodin, rationalizing the growth of the power of kings, decided that ultimately all power had to center in a monarch. By the 1648 Peace of Westphalia, Eu-ropean states were declaring themselves "sover-eign"—the last word in law—over their territories—and other states agreed to keep out of the internal affairs (such as religion) of other states. Although the age of royal absolutism passed, the notion of sovereignty remained, and now all states claim sovereignty.

Reflections

SOVEREIGNTY AND YOU

"Why, you can't do that to me; I'm an American!" say many young Americans who run into trouble with the local law while traveling overseas. But they can do that to you. They can do whatever they want to you; that is their right as a sovereign state. They can cane your behind until it bleeds for spray-painting cars (which Singapore did to one American youth). They can ignore (perhaps gleefully) a plea from the U.S. president for leniency. It's their law, and they can enforce it any way they like. What can the U.S. embassy or consulate do for you? Suggest an English-speaking lawyer. That's all. Remember, sovereignty means they are bosses on their own turf, so when you're overseas, you have to obey their laws. Your U.S. or other foreign passport gives you no special protection.

---

supranational   Power above the national level, as in the UN.

peacekeepers try to stop it. Nations can no longer hide their misdeeds behind the screen of sovereignty. Some say the *Westphalian* system is over.

Supranational entities have appeared. The European Union is now one giant economic market, and many important decisions are made in its Brussels headquarters, not in its members' capitals. EU members have surrendered some of their sovereignty to a higher body. Most have given up control of their own currency—a basic attribute of sovereignty—in favor of a new common currency, the euro. Now the EU is trying to build common foreign and defense policies. The trouble here is that if the EU goes all the way to European unification, it will not erase sovereignty but merely produce a bigger and stronger sovereign entity, one even harder to deal with. In place of many smaller states, we will face one big state. Further, the EU tends to economic protectionism, which could lead to trade wars, one of the themes of this book.

Key Terms

absolutism (p. 15)

balance of power (p. 5)

bipolar (p. 9)

Bismarckian (p. 6)

domestic politics (p. 3)

force (p. 3)

globalization (p. 13)

hierarchy of power (p. 7)

international relations (p. 3)

interwar (p. 8)

Metternichean (p. 6)

multipolar (p. 11)

power (p. 3)

reification (p. 3)

sovereignty (p. 17)

state (p. 15)

stratified (p. 13)

strong state (p. 16)

superpower (p. 3)

supranational (p. 18)

system (p. 3)

unipolar (p. 11)

Westphalian (p. 6)

Key Web Sites

Cold War International History Project (CWIHP)
http://cwihp.si.edu/default.htm

World Leaders of the World War I Era
http://www.lib.byu.edu/~rdh/wwi/bio/bios-home.html

International and Area Studies Links
http://www.clark.net/pub/lschank/web/country.html

To War or Not to War (Between the Two World Wars)
http://saul.snu.edu/syllabi/history/s97projects/towar/

Further Reference

Buzan, Barry, and Richard Little. *International Systems in World History: Remaking the Study of International Relations.* New York: Oxford University Press, 2000.

Clark, Ian, and Iver B. Neumann, eds. *Classical Theories of International Relations.* New York: St. Martin's, 1996.

Dougherty, James E., and Robert L. Pfaltzgraff, Jr. *Contending Theories of International Relations,* 5th ed. Boston, MA: Addison-Wesley Longman, 2000.

Ferguson, Niall. *The War of the World: Twentieth-Century Conflict and the Descent of the West.* New York: Penguin, 2006.

Klare, Michael T. *Resource Wars: The New Landscape of Global Conflict.* New York: Henry Holt, 2002.

Lundestad, Geir. *East, West, North, South: Major Developments in International Politics since 1945,* 5th ed. Thousand Oaks, CA: Sage, 2005.

Marks, Sally. *The Ebbing of European Ascendancy: An International History of the World, 1914–1945.* New York: Oxford University Press, 2002.

McWilliams, Wayne C., and Harry Piotrowski. *The World since 1945: A History of International Relations,* 6th ed. Boulder, CO: Lynne Rienner, 2005.

Opello, Walter C., Jr., and Stephen J. Rosow. *The Nation-State and Global Order: A Historical Introduction to Contemporary Politics.* Boulder, CO: Lynne Rienner, 2004.

Philpott, Daniel. *Revolutions in Sovereignty: How Ideas Shaped Modern International Relations.* Princeton, NJ: Princeton University Press, 2001.

Sheehan, Michael. *The Balance of Power: History and Theory.* New York: Routledge, 1996.

Sterling-Folker, Jennifer, ed. *Making Sense of International Relations Theory.* Boulder, CO: Lynne Rienner, 2005.

Wenger, Andreas, and Doron Zimmermann. *International Relations: From the Cold War to the Globalized World.* Boulder, CO: Lynne Rienner, 2003.

CHAPTER 2

AMERICA'S CHANGING NATIONAL INTERESTS

QUESTIONS TO CONSIDER

1. What is the national interest? Why is it often hard to define?
2. How could early U.S. foreign policy be described as "brilliant"?
3. What was the U.S. interest in "manifest destiny"?
4. Was Washington the original isolationist?
5. How did U.S. foreign policy pre–1898 differ from post–1898?
6. Why did the United States turn imperialist?
7. What is the difference between vital and secondary interests?
8. What does the owl of Minerva represent?
9. How did the Cold War flow naturally from World War II?
10. What was "containment"? Who invented it?

Americans had a national interest even before they became a nation. As the thirteen colonies evolved, they saw their interests differently from those of Britain. London wanted cheap raw materials, a closed market for British products, no undue expenses for defending the colonies, and colonial taxes to pay the defense and administrative costs of the colonies. The French and Indian War had cost a bundle and mostly served the interests of the colonists. Colonies should pay for themselves, figured London; they should not drain the royal treasury.

The American colonists wanted to sell their products to anyone, not just to Britain. They wanted to manufacture their own goods, not just buy British goods. They wanted the **Crown** to provide free security to let them expand westward. And they didn't want to pay taxes. (They still don't.) Years before 1776, American and British **national interests** had begun to diverge, leading straight to the Declaration of Independence.

Independence

Colonists had come to America to live free and get rich: "Life, Liberty, and the pursuit of Happiness." Any government that got in the way of these rights was a bad government—meaning Britain. The writers of the Declaration of Independence in 1776 also saw an opportunity: the likely assistance of France, which had an interest in weakening Britain, gaining an American ally, and opening America to French trade. The Americans sought sovereignty, in the words of the Declaration, to "have full power to levy war, conclude peace, contract alliances, establish commerce, and to do all other acts and things which independent states may of right do."

Crown   Powers of the British government. (See page 20.)

national interest   What is good for a country as a whole in international relations; often disputed. (See page 20.)

manifest destiny   Slogan calling for a U.S. continental republic.

The founding patriots began to pursue America's national interests rationally—not sentimentally, as is often depicted in novels and television series—by several interlocking strategies aimed at getting Britain to recognize the new "United States." They knew there would be a fight so they mobilized and equipped the colonial militias. They sought both military and diplomatic support from France, Spain, and whatever other European power might have a grudge against Britain. Franklin went to Paris to promise a U.S. alliance and trade and to try to foment a war in Europe that would tie down the British. The French, following their own national interests, saw a chance to weaken the British and provided major aid—weapons, troops, military advisors, and even a fleet. Paris was delighted to see the British weakened in the New World.

The sum of these strategies cost Britain too much, so Britain settled in 1782. To clinch the deal, Franklin secretly told London that the United States really sought no alliance with France, so it was easier to set the colonies free. The United States double-crossed France. In pursuing vital national interests, realism, not sentiment, rules. All in all, early American foreign policy was conducted brilliantly, bringing independence and recognition by the major European powers.

Manifest Destiny

After independence, U.S. national interests were redefined to suit the new, large, isolated nation. The weak Articles of Confederation had to be scrapped because they left us vulnerable to the European presence still in North America. The 1787 Constitution "provide[d] for the common defense" by a more centralized government that maintained an army and navy. We felt threatened by the Spaniards in Florida, the French in Louisiana, the British in Canada, the Russians in Alaska, and revolutionaries in Mexico. We gained most of these territories (except for Canada) with force and/or cash.

By the 1840s and 1850s Americans were convinced that they had a **manifest destiny** (predetermined by God) to claim and populate most of North America. National-interest thinking underlay each step. The United States, still small and vulnerable, did not like sharing the continent with major powers, especially European powers. With most of the continent populated by Americans, we would have little to fear. Land and unlimited immigration would make America a great power. And underneath was the old contingent necessity argument: If we did not take it, someone else would.

objective   Can be empirically verified.

subjective   Cannot be empirically verified, depends on feelings.

bluff   Not supporting a declared national interest with sufficient power.

The new technologies of the nineteenth century—the railroad and telegraph—made possible a continental republic. George Washington, even as the French Revolutionary wars raged, defined the U.S. national interest as staying out of European wars. In 1793 Washington declared neutrality, abrogating our 1778 alliance with France. With this, we got Britain to sign Jay's Treaty in 1794 and remove its forts in our West. Neutrality also prevented a divisive issue—for or against the French Revolution—from polarizing U.S. politics.

Concepts

NATIONAL INTEREST

Seemingly simple—what's good for the state as a whole in international affairs—national interest can be very tricky to apply. Intelligent people take opposite positions over what the national interest is at a given moment. The problem arises because the term is partly **objective** and partly **subjective**.

Geography plays a role. Close to home, national interest is objective and easy to define: Stay sovereign, that is, don't get conquered. This is considered a "vital" national interest. Sensing a threat, governments take security measures, such as increasing military preparedness and making defensive alliances. Security for the homeland is the irreducible minimum national interest. Historically, U.S. national interest was to get rid of outside powers on the North American continent; they were geopolitical threats.

Farther from home, national interests get subjective and sometimes "secondary." Should we worry about the other side of the world? If we trade a lot with it, say in petroleum, maybe we should. If a distant aggressor threatens to upset regional peace, maybe it is an interest, but we can't be sure. Some areas may not be a national interest. How can you tell? National-interest calculations are often based on estimates, analogies, and gut instinct, all of them fallible.

Who decides what the national interest is? Governing elites—the top or most influential people—do, but their judgment is often skewed by ideology, mistaken assumptions, the temper of the times, and individual, class, and regime interests. Is a leader pursuing the nation's interest or his own? To keep their power, many leaders whip up their people with nationalism under the banner of "national interest." Is North Korea's nuclear-bomb program really in its national interest, or is it the dangerously warped misperception of Kim Jong Il that the bomb gives his regime security?

What seems to be a national interest one year may turn out to be a mistake next year. Only hindsight tells you what your national interest had been in previous years, but then it's too late. In 1965, Washington defined South Vietnam as a vital U.S. national interest. Ten years later, few did. After 9/11, the Bush 43 administration defined "regime change" in Iraq as a vital U.S. national interest, and most Americans believed it. After the war, when no weapons of mass destruction were found but U.S. soldiers continued to be killed, some Americans began to wonder if ending the brutal Saddam regime had really been in our national interest. Slippery stuff, this national interest.

One important test: Do you have the *power* to back up what you have declared to be your national interest? If not, refrain from declaring it a national interest. Power and national interest are closely connected. Americans sometimes state grandiose national interests with insufficient power or intention of backing them up, a dangerous policy of **bluff**. America's national interest changes from one era to another. Our national interest during the Cold War was reasonably clear: Stop the spread of communism. What is it now? Snuff out terrorism worldwide? Is that a feasible U.S. goal?

Americans were pouring into the now French-held Louisiana territory, and France had wars enough in Europe. Jefferson's $15 million in cash in 1803 (without congressional authorization) pleased both us and Napoleon. It was hard to stay neutral and carry on commerce with Europe—we wanted to sell grain to the **Continent**—and this led to the War of 1812 with Britain, in which we tried to seize Canada. Several U.S. invasion attempts were repelled, Canadians note proudly. Some historians argue that we lost the War of 1812 but never admitted it. The British burned down the Capitol and White House and left; they still do not count it as a war.

Continent The European mainland.

Guerrilla warfare plus $5 million in cash persuaded Spain to cede Florida to us in 1819. With the independence of Latin America from Spain and Portugal, President Monroe issued his famous doctrine in 1823 that told Europe to keep out of our hemisphere and we would keep out of theirs (see Chapter 10). Threat of force against the British in Oregon (which included present-day Washington state) was mainly bluster, but it worked in 1846. American settlers in Texas started a war that we settled in 1848 by taking the West and giving Mexico a paltry $15 million. Cash alone, $7.2 million, bought Alaska from Russia in 1867.

Even Union diplomacy during the Civil War—the bloodiest conflict of the nineteenth century—was successful. Britain, whose interests in cotton almost pushed it to recognize the Confederacy, was dissuaded by Lincoln's freeing of the slaves. Britain had for decades worked against slavery worldwide, so Lincoln's move made British recognition of the South morally impossible. As the Civil War raged, France took advantage of U.S. weakness to set up a brief monarchy in Mexico. With the war over, we told them to scram, and they did.

Overall, U.S. foreign policy from independence through most of the nineteenth century was a spectacular success. Keeping the European powers distant, buying up their

Classic Thought

WASHINGTON'S FAREWELL ADDRESS

Some call Washington the first isolationist, for when he left office in 1797 he warned against "entangling alliances" with the European powers. Actually, it was a shrewd appreciation of U.S. national interests at the time. Why get locked into Europe's habitual and sometimes pointless bloodshed? We need neither allies nor enemies but should "cultivate peace and harmony with all."

The great rule of conduct for us in regard to foreign nations is, in extending our commercial relations to have with them as little political connection as possible. . . .
    Europe has a set of primary interests which to us have no or a very remote relation. Hence she must be engaged in frequent controversies, the causes of which are essentially foreign to our concerns. . . .
    Our detached and distant situation invites and enables us to pursue a different course. . . .
    Why forgo the advantages of so peculiar a situation? Why quit our own to stand upon foreign ground? Why, by interweaving our destiny with that of any part of Europe, entangle our peace and prosperity in the toils of European ambition, rivalship, interest, humor, or caprice?

Why indeed? Washington posed tough-minded questions that every generation of American leaders should ask anew.

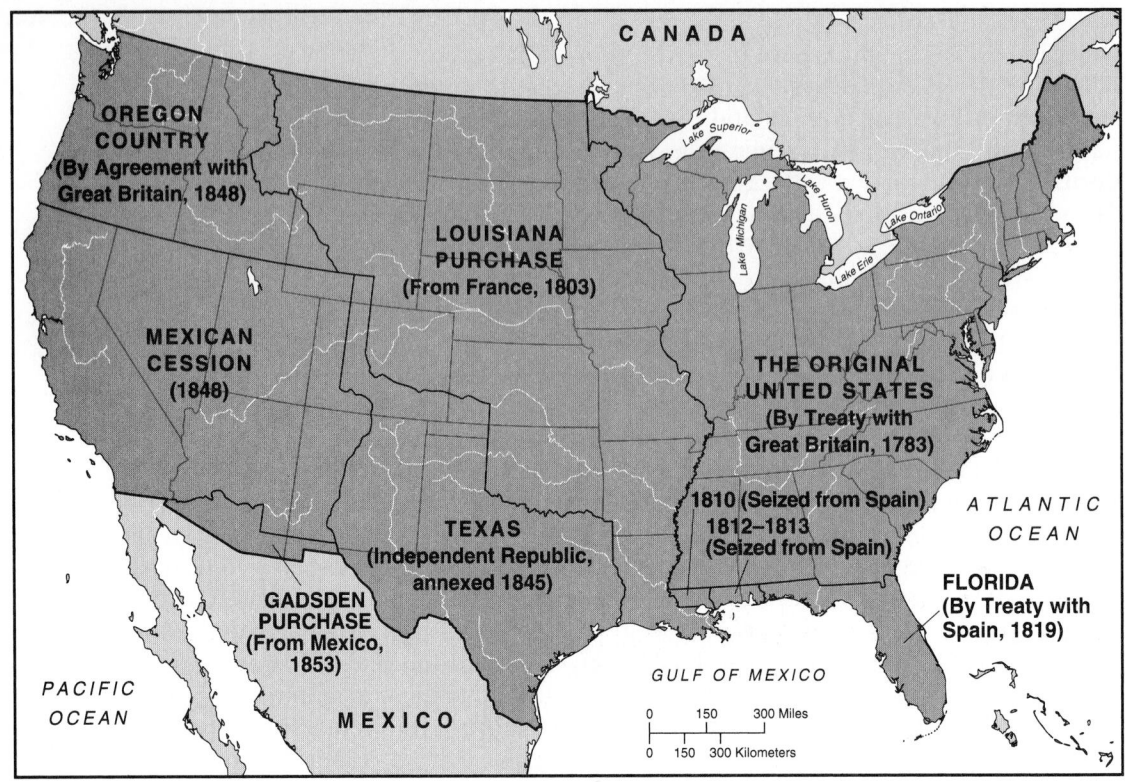

Expansion of U.S. Territory

strategy   Ends, ways, means.

imperialism   Spreading nation's power over other lands.

North American holdings cheap, and applying measured doses of force, the small, vulnerable United States grew into a continental republic, as planned. By the 1890s, however, the West had been won. Until then, policy goals had been clear, rational, limited, and feasible, for they focused on interests on this continent. The next era presented policy dilemmas and goals that were not nearly as clear and limited, for they focused on the other hemisphere. In the late 1890s, America started defining its national interests to include major activity overseas, and this brought a dispute that continues to the present over exactly what America's **strategy** in the world should be. How should we make our way in the world?

Imperialism

The causes for America's brief fling with **imperialism** are still controversial. Some see it as the continuation of a frontier spirit; once it reached the Pacific, it had to keep going westward. Imperial thinking in Washington—Mahan's seapower theory (see box on page 25) and the beginning of a large, modern fleet—started in the 1880s. In 1894, America faced a sharp economic depression, prompting some to see imperial expansion as a way to gain new markets for American goods.

The triggering event of the expansion—freeing Cuba from Spanish misrule—is only part of the story. Cuban patriots had revolted against Spain in the 1870s and were brutally crushed while the United States paid little attention. In the 1890s, when Cuba again revolted, we went to war over it. In a quarter of a century, Cuba had gone from noninterest to national interest. Besides, what did the Philippines have to do with Cuba?

The times had changed. In the 1870s America was still nursing its Civil War wounds and filling in the West. Americans ignored foreign affairs. By the 1890s things were different. The U.S. economy had shifted from agriculture to industry. A large, iron-hulled U.S. Navy had been built. Social Darwinism encouraged many Americans—including Teddy Roosevelt—to think of themselves as the "fittest" who were destined for world leadership over lesser (that is, colored) peoples. The European empires set an example for any country that aspired to be a "power." There was a race for colonies; we had to move fast if we wanted to grab what little was left, and the decaying Spanish empire was ripe for the taking. Germany was also interested in the Philippines and almost landed there. The circulation wars between the new high-speed presses of Hearst and Pulitzer fanned citizen interest in Cuba with lurid stories of Spanish brutality (especially against women). Editorialized Hearst proudly: "How do you like my little war?"

By the time of President McKinley, imperialists were defining the U.S. national interest as overseas expansion, a kind of new manifest destiny. The sinking of the battleship *Maine* in Havana harbor (probably from a faulty boiler) brought the cry, "Remember the Maine, to hell with Spain!" McKinley did not wish war but the country was inflamed, and the paralyzed Madrid government did not know how to get out of the mess without going to war and losing. This it did, quickly, in 1898.

All over America, volunteers signed up for what Teddy Roosevelt called "a splendid little war." The country had not had a war since the Civil War, and young men ached for adventure. Roosevelt went with his Rough Riders to Cuba but had earlier arranged with Admiral Dewey for the U.S. Pacific Fleet to wait at Hong Kong for a cable and then strike the pathetic Spanish fleet in Manila Bay.

With little fighting, the decrepit Spanish empire collapsed into American hands. Spain officially ceded the Philippines to the United States for $20 million. Again, force and cash.

Classic Thought

MAHAN'S SEAPOWER THEORY

In 1890, as the United States was busy expanding its fleet, U.S. Navy Captain Alfred Thayer Mahan published a book that told imperialists exactly what they wanted to hear. *The Influence of Sea Power upon History* argued that nations must expand or decline and that seapower is the key to expansion. To assure its overseas commerce, a nation needs a strong navy, which, in turn, needs colonies as "coaling stations" to service its ships. Mahan's model was the British fleet and empire. Among Mahan's followers was Theodore Roosevelt, who became assistant secretary of the Navy under President McKinley in 1897.

In one year, 1898, the United States took Cuba (ostensibly independent but a U.S. protectorate), Puerto Rico, and the Philippines, plus Guam, Hawaii, Wake Island, and American Samoa (in 1899). Suddenly, America was an empire.

Some Filipinos expected independence and fought the U.S. takeover. The Philippine Insurrection of 1899–1903 resembled the later Vietnam War: stubborn resistance, U.S. calls for more troops, ambushes, harsh reprisals, burning villages, and growing disgust and opposition on U.S. college campuses and in Congress. The insurrection provoked some belated rethinking: What are we doing on the other side of the globe shooting strange people who do not want us there? Is this really our national interest? Some "Anti-Imperialists"—including Mark Twain and Andrew Carnegie—bitterly denounced U.S. expansion overseas.

The United States expanded its interests to include China, where American traders and missionaries had long been active. In 1899–1900 Secretary of State Hay issued his famous "Open Door" notes that the China trade should be open to all and that China should not be broken up into European and Japanese spheres of influence. This began the U.S. policy of protecting China with words but with no troops or warships. The Japanese military concluded we were bluffing and ignored U.S. protests as they invaded China. We had disconnected national interest from power. It took Pearl Harbor to reconnect them. As for Hawaii, where American settlers had already taken over, we had better take it or Japan will. By 1900, the seeds of a U.S.-Japan war were planted.

The new U.S. Navy and merchant fleet had to be able to get quickly from the Atlantic to the Pacific. When Colombia dickered too long on a canal through its isthmus of Panama, Washington set up an independent Panama in 1903, held off Colombia with gunboats, and bought canal rights from Panama. Again, force and cash. With several Caribbean and Central American countries threatened with European intervention over debts, the United States intervened first, established customs receiverships to repay the loans, and thus kept the Europeans out (see Chapter 10). President Wilson sent U.S. forces into Veracruz and northern Mexico.

The abrupt shift from isolation to world power produced a backlash. The emerging academic discipline of international relations proffered legalistic and moralistic approaches to world problems. (One thinker in this area: political scientist Woodrow Wilson.) Politicians and scholars urged conflict resolution through binding arbitration. Peace movements sprang up. Americans were not accustomed to the cynicism that must accompany being a world power. Many still are not.

Expansion was easy, but it meant adding vulnerabilities and making enemies. Teddy Roosevelt regretted later that we had taken the Philippines, which now had to be defended from Japan. Some question if it was ever in our national interests to expand into East Asia, which led to war with Japan.

■ World War I

After war broke out in Europe in 1914, Germany tried to keep America out while Britain tried to get America in. German submarine warfare threatened U.S. shipping. Woodrow Wilson, with the legalistic-moralistic bent of the time, was president. He won reelection in 1916 with the slogan, "He kept us out of war." By early 1917, however, German submarine warfare pushed Wilson into the Great War. We had tried to stay neutral but could not.

Other forces were at work. An intercepted German telegram suggested to Mexico that it could recover lands lost to the United States in 1848. British propaganda blanketed the United States, emphasizing the barbarity of the "Huns." The ouster of the tsarist government in Russia in early 1917 now made the war look like a contest between democracy and autocracy. Wilson could sell the war as one "to make the world safe for democracy." Wilson also appreciated that the German conquest of Europe would threaten our national interest.

isolationism　U.S. avoidance of overseas involvement.

Realist　School of IR thought that emphasizes power politics.

U.S. troops arrived when the war was two-thirds over and tipped the balance against Germany. The war ended in late 1918. But the victors, particularly Britain and France, did not share Wilson's idealistic vision of a new League of Nations to keep the peace. They wanted revenge on Germany for their terrible losses. London and Paris accepted Wilson's League as part of the Versailles peace treaty but went on to strip Germany of territory and squeeze it for impossible reparations. The U.S. Senate refused to ratify the Versailles treaty and America, fed up with Wilson's idealism and the unreliable Europeans, slouched into **isolationism** (see Chapter 21).

Classic Thought

HANS MORGENTHAU ON NATIONAL INTEREST

A brilliant refugee scholar from Nazi Germany taught America about national interest. In so doing, Hans Morgenthau (1904–1980) founded the "**Realist**" school of international relations. Many Americans, immersed in legalism and moralism, disliked the concept of national interest, which smacked of the old and evil "power politics." To Morgenthau, national interest was the only thing that made sense in international relations. Once you understood a country's national interest, you could roughly predict its foreign policy moves. You could "look over the statesman's shoulder when he writes his dispatches; we read and anticipate his very thoughts."

Morgenthau thought national interest was largely objective and rational, because he defined it in terms of power. Intelligent statesmen could figure out what they must and should do to safeguard their nation's power, and outside observers could understand why they were doing it. Said Morgenthau: "International politics, like all politics, is a struggle for power." When facing the likes of Hitler

and Tojo, America needed power, not legalism or moralism, Morgenthau argued.

A nation's vital national interest is to secure its territory; this cannot be negotiated away. Other items may be "secondary interests" about which one may, depending on circumstances, negotiate and compromise. (For his rules of effective diplomacy, see Chapter 19.) Vietnam, like most of the Third World was not a U.S. interest; the conservative Morgenthau thought the war there was a stupid and useless crusade.

The trouble with Morgenthau's approach is that it made no provision for the irrational aspects of national interest, which sometimes dominate. It would be wonderful if all countries' national interests were rational; then they would be limited and predictable. Morgenthau's concept of a limited and rational national interest was actually a philosophical argument that countries should adopt such thinking, for then problems could be compromised by peaceful diplomacy. At bottom, the great realist was a great moralist.

■ Isolationism

Americans saw the World War as a failure. The tricky and unreliable Europeans hadn't learned a thing from the war. Even worse, they would not pay their war debts. Americans had fought and bled for nothing, was the feeling, and we must never do it again.

The United States in the interwar years had overseas interests but did not back them up; instead, we turned to law and rhetoric. Neither worked. The United States sponsored the 1921 Washington Naval Conference, which limited the number of battleships of the major seapowers. (Japan soon opted out.) The 1928 Kellogg-Briand Pact (named after the U.S. secretary of state and French foreign minister) outlawed war. Most states signed but did so in utter cynicism.

Atlantic Charter   1941 Roosevelt–Churchill agreement on peace aims and basis of UN.

This policy of words without deeds could not conceal the fact that the United States did not have the power to do much overseas. Between the two World Wars the army and navy shrank to almost nothing. The Philippines were lightly garrisoned and almost forgotten. The Great Depression focused Americans' attention on domestic economic recovery; the foreigners were simply trade competitors that had to be locked out of the U.S. market. In the Senate, the Nye Committee sought to blame U.S. involvement in the war on "merchants of death," U.S. bankers and munitions makers who had an economic interest in bringing us into the conflict. From these hearings grew the Neutrality Acts of 1935–1937, designed to keep us from ever being drawn into a similar war. Anyone who suggested we take a stand against aggression was howled down.

Interwar isolationism failed to recognize that the Axis powers—Germany, Italy, and Japan—threatened to create a closed, hostile world in which the United States was militarily besieged and economically isolated. U.S. national interests were massively threatened, but interwar isolationism blinded many Americans to this fact until Pearl Harbor. Then, almost too late, came understanding. The owl of Minerva flies at twilight.

■ World War II

For a growing number of Americans, the official outbreak of World War II in 1939 (it had been on in China since at least 1937) showed that isolationism was wrong. Franklin D. Roosevelt, who had served Wilson as assistant navy secretary, always admired Wilson and slowly restored a Wilsonian concept of national interest, one that extended our interests overseas. It showed up clearly in the **Atlantic Charter** (see box on page 29). FDR had learned the lessons of Wilson's failure—too idealistic—and moved only a fraction ahead of Congress and public opinion to bring the United States into the war and into a world leadership role.

Roosevelt's strategy was to aid Britain without alarming American isolationists, who thought that Britain in 1940 was defeated and that the war was none of our business. (Even the U.S. ambassador to Britain, the father of John F. Kennedy, thought so.) FDR circumvented the Neutrality Acts by allowing Britain to come and get U.S. goods under "Cash and Carry." The United States traded fifty old destroyers to Britain for a naval base in

Bermuda. With the fall of France in 1940 and Britain out of foreign exchange, **Lend Lease** simply gave war supplies to Britain and, after the 1941 German attack on Russia, to the Soviet Union. In getting these goods across the Atlantic, U.S. ships, including warships, became targets for German U-boats. We in turn depth-charged them in an undeclared war with Germany in the North Atlantic several months before Pearl Harbor. The Japanese attack on December 7, 1941, got both Churchill and Roosevelt off the hook. Churchill knew that Britain would now be on the winning side, and the U.S. isolationists fell silent. With U.S. leadership and supplies, the Allies won in 1945. This time the United States would play a constructive role in the world.

Lend Lease U.S. aid to Allies in World War II.

Wilsonian Idealistic projection of U.S. power to create a peaceful world.

Roosevelt avoided Wilson's mistakes. The United Nations Charter, separate from any peace treaty, was drawn up during the war while a common enemy cemented the alliance. U.S. military aid gave Washington great influence and induced many to accept the UN Charter. Declaring war on the Axis was the prerequisite for UN membership. Congress authorized the United Nations in 1943, this time with Republican consultation and support. In San Francisco in 1945, most of the world's nations signed the Charter. As if to underscore the U.S. role, the UN headquarters was to be in New York. (For how the UN worked, see Chapter 21.)

■ The Cold War

Roosevelt slowly and cleverly repudiated the interwar isolationism and revived the **Wilsonian** concept of a U.S. national interest that promoted peace and extended U.S. trade and influence overseas. The American people were ready for it, but Stalin refused to cooperate. Roosevelt thought he could charm Stalin into cooperation, but FDR died shortly before the war ended, and Stalin was suspicious of charm. America, to carry out the national interests FDR had defined during the war, now had to have a massive and permanent military establishment, some of it stationed overseas.

The Cold War began when the Soviets quickly began breaking the agreements made at the 1945 Yalta conference (see Chapter 5). They did not hold free, democratic elections in East Europe but installed Communist regimes subservient to Moscow, and they kept

Turning Point

THE ATLANTIC CHARTER

Meeting at sea off Newfoundland on August 14, 1941 (before America was officially in the war), President Roosevelt, who knew we would soon be in the war, and British Prime Minister Winston Churchill signed an idealistic statement of their war aims. They sought no territorial aggrandizement but wanted disarmament, self-determination for all nationalities, and freedom of trade and of the seas. The Atlantic Charter, the spiritual child of Wilson's Fourteen Points, formed the basis of the United Nations, NATO, and close U.S.-British cooperation.

Truman Doctrine   1947 presidential call to aid countries under Communist threat.

Marshall Plan   1947 call for massive U.S. aid to war-torn Europe.

containment   U.S. policy of blocking expansion of Soviet power; framed by Kennan in 1947.

McCarthyism   Senator Joseph McCarthy's early-1950s accusations of treason in high places.

many troops in East Europe. The United States had quickly demobilized after the war and left few troops in West Europe. As Churchill put it in 1946, the Soviets rang down an "Iron Curtain" to cut off East Europe. Local Communist parties plotted subversion in France and Italy, and Communist guerrillas almost won in Greece.

President Truman and his secretaries of state, George Marshall and Dean Acheson, soon grew alarmed that Moscow was closing off East Europe into brutal Soviet satellites and partitioning the peaceful, open world we had envisioned. Stalin started looking like Hitler, a dictator who had to be stopped. In the spring of 1947, Washington set forth interlocking policies of military, economic, and ideological opposition to the growth of Soviet power. The **Truman Doctrine**, **Marshall Plan**, and Kennan's "X" article—all of which came out within weeks of each other—defined U.S. national interest for decades.

At first **containment** was relatively cheap to carry out. We had the world's greatest industrial plant and the atomic bomb. U.S. airpower overcame the 1948–1949 Berlin Blockade. We formed NATO in 1949 (see Chapter 16). Things got more complex when the Soviets exploded their first atomic bomb in 1949; we no longer had a nuclear monopoly. China fell to the Communists that same year, and in 1950 the Korean conflict began. Truman sent troops to Asia and Europe without congressional or public approval. The president's powers here have never been settled (see Chapter 4).

Containment looked like an endless, unwinnable war with no clear goals. Americans like short, victorious wars with clear goals. Frustration and rage mounted within a U.S. public that was unused to global responsibilities and complexities: Why can't we fight and win? Is this Cold War going to last forever? Why don't we just drop our atom bomb on those Commies? Containment had its costs, and they played into the Republican electoral victories of the 1950s and into **McCarthyism**. The Democrats set up containment and then stood accused of not doing enough to carry it out. The United States became locked into a Cold War mentality.

Concepts

COLD WAR

The period of military and political tension between the United States and the Soviet Union that followed World War II was called the Cold War because it did not involve direct fighting between the two powers. Its dates are rather arbitrarily given as 1947–1989. Some say it started in 1946 and ended with the dissolution of the Soviet Union in late 1991. The two sides armed, sent troops into other countries, fought indirectly (as in Korea), and tried to keep their present allies and gain new ones from the enemy's camp. (See Chapters 1, 5, and 6 for more on the Cold War.) With the Cold War came the concept of "bipolarity," the world divided into two hostile camps.

Turning Point

A broke and weary Britain could no longer uphold its traditional interests in the Eastern Mediterranean and told Washington so in early 1947. Communist guerrillas in Greece controlled much of that impoverished country, and the Soviet Union strongly pressured Turkey for territories and control of the strategic Turkish Straits. President Truman felt we had to take up the burden and articulate a new policy and new U.S. national interests. It was a massive shift to **globalism**.

Truman told a joint session of Congress on March 12, 1947, that the United States must not only aid Greece and Turkey but more generally block Communist expansion. "[I]t must be the policy of the United States to support free peoples who are resisting attempted subjugation by armed minorities or by outside pressures," said Truman. "Great responsibilities have been placed upon us by the swift movement of events."

Truman thus made official the policy that had been brewing in Washington for many months. The United States would not return to isolationism but would actively oppose the Soviets worldwide. It was a new role for the United States, a much bigger and stronger one than Wilson or FDR had envisioned: permanent and global U.S. military and political activity.

A few weeks later, at the 1947 Harvard commencement, Secretary of State George C. Marshall proposed a massive program of U.S. aid to help war-torn Europe recover. Almost unnoticed at the time, this began foreign aid as a permanent part of U.S. foreign policy. The Marshall Plan, which swung into operation in 1948 and pumped some $12 billion into Europe, was a major part of the U.S. effort to contain Communist expansion. Washington even invited the Soviets and their satellites to participate, knowing that they would refuse, for the plan called for sharing economic data and joint economic planning. The Marshall Plan thus started West Europe on the road to economic integration (see Chapter 16).

At this same time, a quietly influential State Department official laid down the U.S. ideological line for the entire Cold War and coined the word "containment." George F. Kennan spoke Russian and had long studied Soviet behavior. Serving in the U.S. embassy in Moscow, he developed a strong dislike and mistrust of the Soviet Union and Stalin. During World War II, when the United States and the Soviet Union were allies, few in Washington would listen to Kennan's warnings that Stalin would be aggressive and expansionist after the war. With the start of the Cold War, Washington listened to Kennan.

Kennan turned a 1946 internal memo into an article for the influential *Foreign Affairs* quarterly. "The Sources of Soviet Conduct" appeared in the July 1947 issue and portrayed the Soviet Union as relentlessly expansionist both on ideological and geopolitical grounds. The Soviets feared and hated the West and sought to subvert democratic governments, wrote Kennan under the anonymous byline "X." (As a U.S. diplomat who dealt with Moscow, he didn't want his name used, but it soon leaked.)

U.S. strategy should be "a policy of firm containment, designed to confront the Russians with unalterable counter-force at every point where they show signs of encroaching upon the interests of a peaceful and stable world," Kennan urged. If held long enough, this would "promote tendencies which must eventually find their outlet in either the break-up or the gradual mellowing of Soviet power. For no mystical, messianic movement—and particularly not that of the Kremlin—can face frustration indefinitely without eventually adjusting itself in one way or another to the logic of that state of affairs." Kennan, who died at age 101 in 2005, could note with satisfaction that his policy finally worked. U.S. policy for the more than forty years of the Cold War was thus laid down in the spring of 1947.

Senator Joseph McCarthy in 1952, when his search for Communists in the U.S. government was at its height. (Ernie Sisto/The New York Times)

President Eisenhower did not repudiate containment but carried it out differently and in ways more acceptable to the public. His secretary of state, John Foster Dulles, preached the "rollback" of Communism but in practice was cautious. Eisenhower ended the Korean War with a threat to go nuclear and then let Dulles announce a policy of "massive retaliation" for future Soviet-bloc aggression. Ike's secretary of defense, Charles Wilson, called reliance on nuclear weapons "more bang for the buck" that allowed us to keep draft calls down. The American public at first liked projecting strength on the cheap. Critics, however, soon decried a policy that, according to Dulles himself, took us "three times to the brink of war"—and it would be a nuclear war.

The Democrats now portrayed Eisenhower's policies as passive and rigid. Now it was the Democrats' turn to use the Cold War to win elections: Just accuse the incumbent of not doing enough. *Sputnik* in 1957 gave Kennedy the idea of campaigning on an alleged "missile gap" that put the Soviets ahead in rocketry (it turned out to be untrue). Eisenhower had let the country fall asleep as the Soviet menace grew, Kennedy charged. (Decades later, Reagan copied this line from Kennedy.) JFK squeaked through to a narrow victory in 1960 with plans to increase defense spending, enlarge the armed forces, expand missile strength, and counter insurgencies with the Green Berets. Ike thought Kennedy was impetuous and mistaken. Ike was proud of having kept the United States secure at low cost with no more Koreas during his two terms.

globalism U.S. interests extending everywhere. (See page 31.)

Kennedy's can-do enthusiasm quickly met some harsh realities. The failure of the CIA-sponsored invasion of Castro's Cuba by anti-Communist exiles (see Chapter 10), planned under Eisenhower, painfully humiliated JFK in April 1961 and made him more determined to stop communism elsewhere. Kennedy's huge military buildup alarmed the Soviets; they saw it as a military threat. By 1962, the United States was ahead by a ratio of 7 to 1 in strategic missiles. Khrushchev, desperate to redress the imbalance, ordered some of his older, medium-range missiles placed in Cuba, closer to U.S. targets. This led to the Cuban missile crisis of October 1962. Khrushchev backed down, but it could have started World War III (see Chapters 4 and 6).

Some say the Cold War crested at that point and slowly began to subside. U.S.-Soviet relations became more flexible; several arms-control agreements were reached. The Sino-Soviet split removed the most threatening quality of the Communist movement—its unity—which U.S. policy had long tried to undermine. But the U.S. policy of containment was still deeply held as the national interest. Enshrined since 1947, it could not be modified or turned off. Kennedy himself did not question containment; instead, he brought it to its logical conclusion in Vietnam. It took the strain and frustration of Vietnam to make Americans see their national interest in a different light.

Concepts

MEAD'S FOUR SCHOOLS OF U.S. FOREIGN POLICY

In a much-noted 2001 book, Walter Russell Mead delineated four schools of thought or basic American approaches to foreign affairs that have variously combined and battled over the history of the Republic:

1. *Hamiltonian,* a commerce-oriented approach that seeks to make America secure and powerful by economic means, namely, promoting domestic prosperity and trade relations. Hamiltonians, found in the business and banking community, try to avoid war but will support it when pushed.

2. *Wilsonian,* an idealistic vision of peace through diplomatic agreements, international organizations, and international law. Wilsonians, often in the church and legal communities, are also very concerned with human rights and democracy and will go to war to vanquish brutal dictatorships.

3. *Jeffersonian,* a hands-off caution that too much foreign involvement can hurt domestic American institutions and throw away lives and money in unnecessary wars. We can't reform the world, criticize Jeffersonians, often academics and intellectuals, and we do best when we just set an example of democracy and prosperity.

4. *Jacksonian,* the view of the common man, is often ignorant and isolationist but prone to rage when America is attacked. Emotional and nonintellectual, Jacksonians are natural isolationists but once in a war demand total victory and aren't squeamish about civilian deaths. They dislike the Hamiltonian and Wilsonian approaches—too brainy and complicated—and prefer simple protection of Americans' jobs and a strong military.

U.S. foreign policy and its leaders are never just one of these schools, writes Mead, but shifting combinations of them. At times, they form alliances. The first three—Hamiltonian, Wilsonian, and Jeffersonian—are elite schools; the Jacksonian is a mass view and a permanent and powerful underlying element that foreigners cannot comprehend ("Those Americans are cowboys!") and U.S. politicians cannot ignore. Of Mead's categories, which seem to dominate American foreign policy now? Why?

Reflections

KENNAN ON HISTORY

George F. Kennan, a friend of my stepfather, Ambassador Felix Cole, kindly gave me some advice before I attended graduate school. He wrote:

All I can say is that I warmly support the thought that if political science is what you wish to pursue, you start by doing your M.A., and if possible, the doctorate in political history. I have misgivings about political science generally, as a subject, unless it is founded on serious historical study.

History reveals patterns of human behavior, what behavior shapes what events, and the likely consequences of those events. It is knowledge students of international relations cannot do without.

—N. O. B.

Key Terms

Atlantic Charter (p. 28)

bluff (p. 22)

containment (p. 30)

Continent (p. 23)

Crown (p. 21)

globalism (p. 32)

imperialism (p. 24)

isolationism (p. 27)

Lend Lease (p. 29)

manifest destiny (p. 21)

Marshall Plan (p. 30)

McCarthyism (p. 30)

national interest (p. 21)

objective (p. 22)

Realist (p. 27)

strategy (p. 24)

subjective (p. 22)

Truman Doctrine (p. 30)

Wilsonian (p. 29)

Key Web Sites

Marshall Plan from National Archives
http://www.nara.gov/exhall/featured-document/marshall/marshall.html

League of Nations
http://www.yale.edu/lawweb/avalon/leagcov.htm

The Versailles Treaty
http://ac.acusd.edu/History/text/versaillestreaty/vercontents.html

The Spanish-American War Centennial Web Site
http://204.182.127.43/war/

The Westward Expansion
http://www.msstate.edu/Archives/History/USA/19th_C./expand.html

The Atlantic Charter
http://www.msstate.edu/Archives/History/USA/WWII/charter.txt

The Truman Doctrine
gopher://gopher.law.cornell.edu/00/foreign/historical/truman.txt

Further Reference

Ambrosius, Lloyd E. *Wilsonianism: Woodrow Wilson and His Legacy in American Foreign Relations.* New York: Palgrave, 2002.

Beisner, Robert L. *Dean Acheson: A Life in the Cold War.* New York: Oxford University Press, 2006.

Boot, Max. *The Savage Wars of Peace: Small Wars and the Rise of American Power.* New York: Basic Books, 2002.

Gaddis, John Lewis. *Strategies of Containment: A Critical Appraisal of American National Security Policy during the Cold War,* rev. ed. New York: Oxford University Press, 2005.

Garthoff, Raymond L. *A Journey Through the Cold War: A Memoir of Containment and Coexistence.* Washington, D.C.: Brookings, 2001.

Graebner, Norman A. *America as a World Power: A Realist Appraisal from Wilson to Reagan.* Wilmington, DE: Scholarly Resources, 1984.

Hogan, Michael J., and Thomas G. Paterson, eds. *Explaining the History of American Foreign Relations,* 2nd ed. New York: Cambridge University Press, 2004.

Kagan, Robert. *Dangerous Nation: America's Place in the World from Its Earliest Days to the Dawn of the Twentieth Century.* New York: Knopf, 2006.

Kinzer, Stephen. *Overthrow: America's Century of Regime Change from Hawaii to Iraq.* New York: Times Books, 2006.

Magstadt, Thomas M. *An Empire If You Can Keep It: Power and Principle in American Foreign Policy.* Washington, D.C.: CQ Press, 2004.

Mead, Walter Russell. *Special Providence: American Foreign Policy and How It Changed the World.* New York: Knopf, 2001.

Schulzinger, Robert D. *U.S. Diplomacy since 1900,* 5th ed. New York: Oxford University Press, 2001.

Sloan, G. R. *Geopolitics in United States Strategic Policy, 1890–1987.* New York: St. Martin's, 1988.

Trubowitz, Peter. *Defining the National Interest: Conflict and Change in American Foreign Policy.* Chicago, IL: University of Chicago Press, 1998.

CHAPTER 3

"WRONG, TERRIBLY WRONG"

THE UNITED STATES AND VIETNAM

QUESTIONS TO CONSIDER

1. How did the Cold War influence us on Vietnam?
2. In what ways were we ignorant of Vietnam and the Vietnamese?
3. How long did France hold Vietnam?
4. How were the French ousted from Vietnam?
5. Why did the United States inherit the problem?
6. What is the crux of guerrilla warfare?
7. Did President Johnson lie about getting us into Vietnam?
8. Was a "decent interval" really necessary for us to get out?
9. How can you say a given war is "immoral"? Aren't they all?

Vietnam is intelligible only in the Cold War context. When the younger generation—born after the war ended in 1975—asks why we fought there, older Americans have difficulty explaining it. They form "political generations" (see box on page 37) with very different perspectives. Some of the older generation, raised in the Cold War, argue that the war made sense at the time: Continue containment; wherever communism is spreading, stop it. Eisenhower used the metaphor of "falling dominoes" to indicate what would happen if even one more country in Southeast Asia fell to the Communists. Any U.S. president who let communism expand was considered weak. The Cold War subverted U.S. national interest, which was presumed rather than examined.

Now, after the Cold War, the younger generation can dispassionately examine the U.S. national interest in the Vietnam War and find it wanting. The fall of South Vietnam to the Communist North in 1975 signified little or nothing. The very weak "dominoes" of Laos and Cambodia also fell, but nothing else. Far from being a rising tide, communism collapsed a decade and a half later in Europe, and Communist China and Vietnam turned from socialist to market-economic paths. We would have "won" in Vietnam if we had stayed out militarily and then signed up unified Vietnam to produce athletic shoes and clothing for the U.S. market, which it now does. But neither we nor the Vietnamese

Communists knew that at the time. In 1995, Robert McNamara, defense secretary to Kennedy and Johnson, went public with what had long been on his mind: "We were wrong, terribly wrong."

political generations The result of great events imprinting themselves on the young people who have lived through them.

■ The Colonized Colonialists

The Vietnamese originated as a South China tribe that kept pushing south. (Vietnam means South Viet.) Rice-farming lowlanders, they settled millennia ago in the Red River delta of what became known as Tonkin, roughly the northern third of present-day Vietnam. Historically, the Viets fought on two fronts, to the north against their colonial master, China, while expanding to the south, annihilating or pushing into the mountains the native peoples whom they still regard as *moi* (savages). The Viet war cry was *"Nam Tien!"* (March south). The Viets, for example, slowly penetrated and destroyed the powerful seafaring kingdom of Champa, causing the Cham people to disappear. By 1500 the Viets had taken the central third of Vietnam, called Annam ("pacified south"), and by 1800 they had occupied the southern third, later known as Cochinchina. Soon the French arrived with their own brand of colonialism. In the early nineteenth century, Viets invaded and occupied much of Cambodia until the French made them pull out.

It was ironic that the Vietnamese accused the French of colonialism, for the Vietnamese were fiercer colonialists than the French ever were. The Vietnamese were always a fighting, expansionist people. Even recently they continued their historical pattern, fighting China in the north while occupying Cambodia in the south. Americans are inclined to see Orientals as soft, meek, and passive—a huge mistake.

The French, like most colonial powers, stumbled into Vietnam with no clear plan or goal. In 1626 a brilliant French priest, Alexandre de Rhodes, arrived to try to convert the

Concepts

POLITICAL GENERATIONS

German sociologist Karl Mannheim argued that great events put their mark on an entire generation who carry the attitudes formed in their young adulthood all their lives. He called this **political generations**. World War I, for example, produced a war-weary "lost generation" throughout Europe. The Great Depression produced people who forever craved job security and welfare measures. Vietnam produced many Americans who are cautious about U.S. military intervention overseas.

One theory of war—not a completely valid one—uses the political generations approach. A generation that has experienced the horrors of war is reluctant to send its sons off to another war. This inclines the country to peace. The new generation, though, which has known only peace, picks up a romantic and heroic vision of war and tends toward an assertive foreign policy that may lead to war. We might call this a "forgetting" theory. The generation that forgets what war is like is more inclined to engage in it.

protectorate   Semicolony with some internal autonomy.

Vietminh   Communist Vietnamese anti-French liberation movement in the 1940s and 1950s, led by Ho Chi Minh.

monolithic   Composed of one single block with no splits or divisions.

Vietnamese. He devised an ingenious way to write the tonal language (sounds like a sing-song) with the Latin alphabet instead of its Chinese ideographs. This expanded literacy and Catholicism. Over the decades, French missionaries, traders, and military advisors (to warring Vietnamese factions) penetrated Vietnam piecemeal. When French citizens got in trouble, the mother country felt obliged to come to their rescue, a common pattern in imperial expansion. Between 1847 and 1883, French forces took over Vietnam, ruling Tonkin and Annam as **protectorates** and Cochinchina as an outright colony.

Of all the many peoples the French ruled in their imperial heyday, the Vietnamese were the feistiest and least willing to submit. Some never acquiesced to the French takeover and formed protests, underground parties, and revolts. The comfortable French *colons,* with their rubber plantations (Michelin) and *cercles sportifs,* were unaware that many natives hated them.

■ The First Indochina War

The Vietnamese Communists got their big break when the Japanese took over Vietnam in 1940, after France had fallen to Hitler. Since the Vichy regime in France was collaborating with the Germans, the French colonial regime in Vietnam did the same with the Japanese. In 1941, Ho sneaked back into Vietnam and founded the *Viet Nam Doc Lap Minh Hoi,* the Vietnamese Independence League, **Vietminh** for short. He chose the last of his many aliases to match the name of the Vietminh. The Vietminh gathered weapons, spied on the Japanese for the Americans, and plotted a postwar takeover.

Geography

VIETNAM AND CHINA

Dean Rusk, secretary of state under Kennedy and Johnson, depicted the North Vietnamese as a branch of Communist China, proxy soldiers for an aggressive, expansionist China that we had to stop. If he had read only a little Vietnamese history he would have learned that it is a series of Vietnamese revolts against Chinese imperialism. All of old Vietnam's heroes have been fighters against China. Geography has made Vietnam and China natural enemies, like trout and salmon.

It was, therefore, not surprising that in 1979, just four years after North Vietnam took the south, fighting broke out on the China-Vietnam border. (The Chinese started it and the Vietnamese won.) Other skirmishes flared. If U.S. decision makers had looked at Vietnamese geography and history—that it is China's enemy, not ally—American policies might have been quite different. We did not like communism in any form, but we failed to grasp that it was not **monolithic** but was instead divided against itself.

After the Japanese surrender in August 1945, Ho proclaimed Vietnam independent, even using phrases from the U.S. Declaration of Independence. Ho hoped to get U.S. support to block the return of the French. Roosevelt, in fact, had opposed letting the French back, but he died in April 1945. France, then under the provisional government of nationalistic General Charles de Gaulle, insisted on reclaiming its colonies. Paris held some unserious negotiations with Ho but insisted on keeping Vietnam subservient. Thus, two powerful, stubborn forces collided, and war was inevitable.

Dienbienphu French strongpoint taken by Vietminh in 1954.

In late 1946, the French and Vietminh forces clashed, and the first Indochina war was on. The Vietminh used guerrilla tactics and converted peasants to their cause. The French used more or less conventional tactics and tried to get the Vietminh to come out of the jungle for a "set-piece" battle where superior French firepower could destroy them. The Vietminh in 1951 did engage in a conventional battle and lost. Then they let the French walk into a trap of their own making: **Dienbienphu**.

Turning Point

HO CHI MINH

Born into a nationalist, educated family in Annam in 1890, Ho Chi Minh (not his birth name) led an incredible life. He went to an elite high school but got expelled for anti-French activities. Ho got a job on a ship and worked in various menial jobs in London, New York, and Paris. After World War I, the little, wispy Ho showed up at the Versailles peace conference in a rented black suit, representing Vietnamese aspirations for freedom from France. No leader spoke with Ho.

Ho found a better reception on the French left and became a founding member of the French Communist party (PCF) in 1920 for the simple reason that they, unlike the Socialists, favored ending colonialism. From the beginning, Ho was a Communist because communism promised liberation for colonies. Ho never cared much for its complex Marxist theories.

Ho became the PCF's expert on colonialism. The Communist International (Comintern) soon recognized Ho's talent and in 1924 sent him for training to Moscow, and then to China and Southeast Asia as a Comintern agent. Ho led a shadowy existence one step ahead of the police

as he organized an Indochinese Communist party. Like Lenin (whom Ho met in Moscow in 1922), Ho had a gift for languages; he spoke fluent French, Russian, English, Mandarin, two other Chinese dialects, and some German. Ho's small Communist party grew at the expense of other, more moderate Vietnamese nationalist parties. The Communists would simply turn over lists of members and leaders of the other parties to the French colonial police, who arrested them.

Ho even fought alongside Americans against the Japanese. One American OSS (precursor to the CIA) veteran recalled Ho as "an awfully sweet guy" who provided accurate intelligence. The OSS even gave some guns to Ho's fighters. From 1941 until his death in 1969, Ho led his people in nearly ceaseless warfare—against the Japanese, French, and Americans. Ho, who never married, made himself a quietly charismatic "Uncle Ho" to his people. No other Vietnamese leader had a fraction of his popular appeal. With the final Communist triumph in 1975, Saigon was renamed Ho Chi Minh City. (The locals still call it Saigon.)

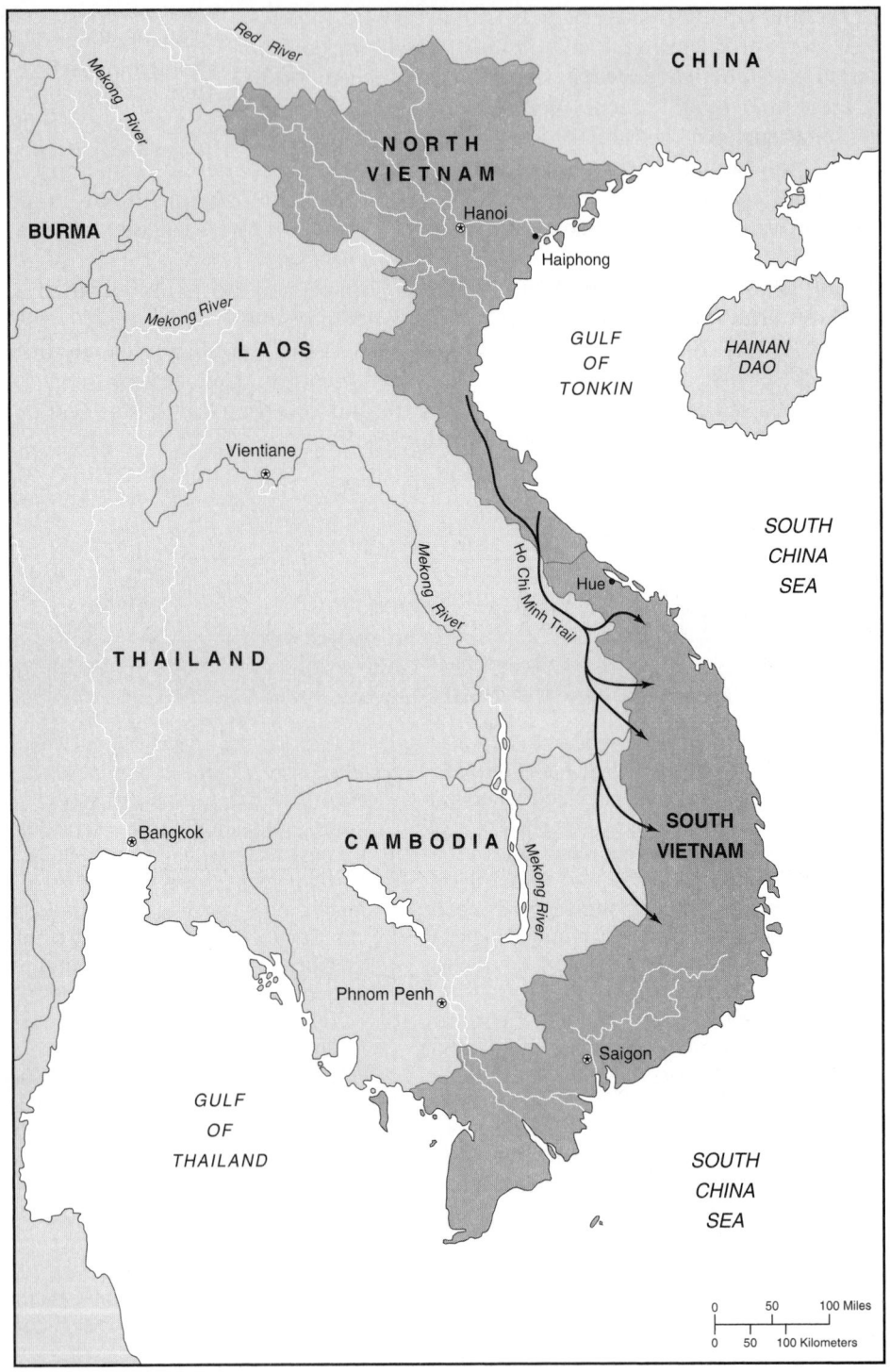

Vietnam and Vicinity

To interdict Vietminh supply lines from Communist China through the jungled mountains of northern Laos, the French in late 1953 airlifted 15,000 troops into a remote valley on the Laos border and dug in. The fortress of Dienbienphu was to serve as the base for patrols that would block the Vietminh. If the Vietminh attacked Dienbienphu, so much the better, the French supposed. But they failed to anticipate that the Vietminh would hand-wheel artillery through the mountains to surround and lacerate Dienbienphu. Over 50,000 Vietminh fought and tunneled closer, whittling down the isolated French. Paris called for U.S. help, but President Eisenhower cleverly passed the issue to key congresspersons, who rejected U.S. participation in Indochina; we had just gotten out of an unpopular war in Korea in 1953. Dienbienphu fell on May 7, 1954. It was, in the words of Bernard Fall, "hell in a very small place." That was it for French public opinion. A new premier, Pierre Mendès-France, promised to get France out of the war. The two sides met at Geneva, Switzerland, and by July 21, 1954, reached an agreement to end the war. It was a thinly disguised French defeat.

Geneva Accords 1954 agreement to end the first Vietnam war.

■ The United States and the Geneva Accords

The United States was never happy with the **Geneva Accords** that got France out of Indochina. They seemed to surrender to communism. President Eisenhower feared other lands of Southeast Asia would be next. The United States was present at Geneva but did not sign the accords and felt little bound by them.

As provided in the Geneva Accords, about a million refugees, mostly Vietnamese Catholics, fled from north to south Vietnam while perhaps a tenth as many Vietminh fighters went the other way. Some Vietminh buried their weapons and stayed behind in the south. The demarcation line across the narrow waist of Vietnam was never intended as permanent or to lead to the establishment of a separate country in the south, the Republic of Vietnam. (The north called itself the Democratic Republic of Vietnam.) That was the

Diplomacy

THE GENEVA ACCORDS

The 1954 Geneva Accords between the French and Vietminh included the following:

1. A cease fire
2. A "provisional demarcation line" across the middle of Vietnam
3. Regrouping of Vietminh forces and sympathizers to the north of this line and of the French and their sympathizers to the south of this line

4. Elections within two years in both halves of Vietnam on unification and under whom

If these provisions had been carried out, there would have been no South Vietnam. Instead there would have been elections in 1956, which Ho would easily have won—Eisenhower himself admitted that—leading to Vietnam's unification under a Communist regime, which is what happened anyway.

guerrilla warfare Small-unit, irregular struggle based on political revolution.

Americans' doing, seemingly in violation of the accords. Since we never signed them, argued Dulles, we were not bound by them, and neither was the anti-Communist government of South Vietnam that we set up. The demarcation line was the place to draw the line against Communist expansion.

The Americans thought they would do a lot better than the French. First, they saw the French as demoralized losers whose rigid doctrines were especially wrong for **guerrilla warfare**. Second, the French were colonialists who could not possibly win over a subject population. One young American congressman took a special interest in Vietnam. He had visited there in 1951 and predicted a French defeat because they were trying "to hang on to the remnants of empire" against rather than with the tide of Asian nationalism. Representative and later Senator John F. Kennedy (D., Massachusetts) urged us to ally ourselves with the forces of nationalism and use them to beat communism.

Washington thought it had the man for the job: Ngo Dinh Diem, who was both anti-French and anti-Communist, an authentic Vietnamese nationalist who would rally his people and keep the dominoes from falling. Unfortunately, Diem was a fanatic Catholic and looked down on Buddhists, a majority of South Vietnam's population. With U.S. blessing, financial aid, and military support, Diem was flown to Saigon in 1954 to found a new country called South Vietnam. At first things went pretty well.

Concepts

GUERRILLA WARFARE

Widely misunderstood, guerrilla warfare is not chiefly concerned with military tactics and equipment. The word first appeared in Spain—it is Spanish for "little war"—as Spanish partisans strove to expel Napoleon's legions. The word soon spread to connote small units of irregulars behind enemy lines who use hit-and-run tactics to confuse and wear down the enemy. As such, it is an ancient type of warfare, the strategy of the underdog against the superior forces of the occupier.

The crux of modern guerrilla warfare, though, is political. Some writers call it "revolutionary political warfare" or "people's war." It really depends on your ability to get the local people to support you against an unpopular government or foreign occupier. You work closely with the people, especially the peasants in the countryside, help them, organize them, redistribute land to them, provide literacy classes and political lectures, and levy taxes. You become, in other words, an underground government that slowly displaces the official government structure. In the words of Bernard Fall, an expert on Vietnam: "When a country is being subverted it is not being out-fought; it is being out-administered. Subversion is literally administration with a minus sign in front." The guerrilla fights a political war while the occupier fights a military war that just creates hatred among the local people.

The guerrilla is also trying to persuade the foreign occupiers to give up and go home. The war, expensive to the foreigners in money and blood, forces the public and politicians on the home front to ask what good this small, faraway country is to them. Pressure mounts for a pullout. Time may thus be on the side of the guerrilla. One axiom of guerrilla warfare: The guerrilla wins if he does not lose; the occupier loses if he does not win. A "last straw" military setback may persuade the occupier to quit: Dienbienphu for the French and Tet for the Americans.

Diem took a situation of near chaos and, by adroit use of military power, shaped it into what looked like a country. He ignored, of course, the call for Vietnam-wide elections in 1956. His police rooted out Vietminh "stay behinds."

Vietcong Informal name of Communist-led South Vietnamese National Liberation Front in the 1960s.

Diem made several mistakes. He ignored a program of reforms that the United States urged, including land reform to give tenant farmers a stake in the system. Paying high rents to greedy landlords drove some peasants to support the resurgent Vietminh, who now called themselves the National Liberation Front. The Diem regime dubbed them Viet Cong (Vietnamese Communist); they never called themselves that. Diem ignored a centuries-old tradition of village democracy by appointing as village headmen outsiders loyal to him personally. When the **Vietcong** came into the village at night to sentence and execute these headmen, the villagers did not especially mind. Diem's rigid personality was part of the problem. He trusted only his own family, and corruption was rife.

■ Kennedy's Commitment

In the late 1950s, Communist subversion grew in the South Vietnamese countryside, with assassinations of government officials, ambushes, and Vietcong tax collection among the peasants. Eisenhower had been able to put Vietnam on the back burner; Kennedy could not. Eisenhower sent only a 685-man U.S. military training mission to Saigon—the number set in the 1954 Geneva Accords—but made no specific U.S. commitments. By the time Kennedy was inaugurated in 1961, though, the Vietcong were gaining, and Kennedy decided to increase the U.S. presence. By the time JFK died in 1963, there were over 16,000 U.S. soldiers in Vietnam, and several had been killed in combat. Many observers feel that the point of no return came under Kennedy and that he bears primary responsibility for the U.S. commitment.

Kennedy's decision to up the ante in Vietnam was based on several factors. First, he was a vigorous young president who had campaigned on stopping the spread of communism

Concepts

WHAT IS A CIVIL WAR?

It sounds like a quibble now, but whether Vietnam was a civil war was one of the hot questions of the 1960s. The argument went like this: If Vietnam is a civil war fought within one country, it's really not much of our business. If it is an international war in which one country (North Vietnam) attacks another (South Vietnam), then it is right to help the victim. In 1964 North Vietnam did begin quietly sending troops into South Vietnam via the "Ho Chi Minh Trail" through Laos. In retrospect, the debate was laughable, for all "civil" wars have outside help and international ramifications. (By the way, what was the U.S. Civil War? Was it within one country or between two countries?)

in the Third World. Counterinsurgency was one of his pet projects, and he geared up the armed services to intervene in the developing lands. The Green Berets, for example, were his baby. Second, early in his first year he went through the humiliating defeat of the Bay of Pigs, the invasion of Cuba by CIA-trained anti-Castro forces. Third, that June JFK met with Soviet party chief Nikita Khrushchev in Vienna and exchanged blunt language about the spread of communism; Kennedy then felt he had to show Khrushchev that America had the will and ability to block Communist expansion. But fourth and probably most important, without U.S. help South Vietnam would soon fall, and that could hurt JFK's chances for reelection in 1964. During the entire Cold War, American presidents feared electoral punishment if another country went Communist on their watch.

Kennedy saw Vietnam as a proving ground for the new techniques of "counterinsurgency." If we could stop communism there, we could scare off the Communists from trying it elsewhere. Kennedy ordered counterinsurgency techniques applied to Vietnam. Green Beret "A teams" were sent into the hills to rally the natives. U.S. helicopters lifted troops quickly into battle and raked the enemy with machine guns. An ambitious program of "strategic hamlets" herded Vietnamese farmers into fortified villages that would keep out the Vietcong. During 1962, these measures seemed to turn the tide.

But by 1963, the war was being lost. The Green Berets could make few converts. The Vietcong learned how to shoot down helicopters. And the farmers hated being removed from their traditional villages to labor without pay on earthworks and moats for the strategic hamlets. Soon they started welcoming the Vietcong into the strategic hamlets. Diem, sensing doom, turned crazier than ever. His murder in a coup saddened Kennedy, who himself was gunned down three weeks later.

In the spring of 1963, JFK confided in his old friend Senator Mike Mansfield that he now agreed with Mansfield's argument to cut U.S. involvement in Vietnam. "But I can't do it until 1965—after I'm re-elected," JFK told Mansfield. Mansfield recalled in 1970, "There is no doubt that he had shifted definitely and unequivocally on Vietnam, but he never had the chance to put the plan into effect." Would Kennedy have done it?

We doubt it. First, Kennedy told few others about this plan, not even Vice President Lyndon Johnson. Second, right up to his death Kennedy kept emphasizing the U.S. commitment to Vietnam to stop the spread of communism. If he was thinking of pulling out, he would have begun minimizing the importance of Vietnam. Third and most important, by 1965 the situation in South Vietnam was terrible, both politically and militarily. A U.S. pullout would have led to an immediate Communist victory, something no president could stand for. Kennedy may have wished to pull out of Vietnam but circumstances, some of his own making, had locked him in.

■ LBJ: Victim or Villain?

Some writers have laid all responsibility for the war on Lyndon Baines Johnson. True, Johnson made the decisions to escalate until, by early 1968, more than half-a-million U.S. troops were in Vietnam. And he made the decisions in a tricky manner. But he was not precisely a free agent. First, the United States was already committed by JFK to stopping communism in Vietnam. Second, LBJ inherited all of Kennedy's advisors, and with only one exception (George Ball) they urged him to escalate. Third, he knew the Republicans would use it against him if Vietnam fell to communism. LBJ was trapped and tried to wiggle out by lying, promising he would not send U.S. troops to Vietnam even while he planned exactly that.

Johnson minimized the Vietnam issue during the 1964 election, allowing him to sweep all but six states. In secret, however, he had a staff develop plans to escalate the war. The plans called for a joint congressional resolution authorizing the president to do whatever needed to be done, including bombing raids on North Vietnam and U.S. troops sent into the south. When these plans came out in the "Pentagon Papers" in 1971, many Americans were furious that they had been deceived. The war had been planned in advance.

The first step of the plan fell neatly into place when North Vietnamese PT boats attacked (or allegedly attacked) two U.S. destroyers in August 1964. Neither U.S. ship was hit, and some critics charge that it was a trumped-up incident to secure passage of a joint congressional resolution. The destroyers were on a secret war mission, to back up South Vietnamese vessels that were raiding the North Vietnamese coast. LBJ never told Congress

Turning Point

THE TONKIN GULF RESOLUTION

With the passage of the 1964 Tonkin Gulf Resolution, as in the 1964 election campaign, LBJ did not so much lie as let gullible victims deceive themselves, the mark of a skilled con artist. First, LBJ did not tell Congress that the resolution had been drafted long before the incident at sea ever occurred. Second, he did not tell Congress that the destroyers had been engaged in warlike activity. Third, he indicated that he did not intend to use the resolution to go to war; it was just to make clear to the Communists that we stood firm.

This was the problem. Congress had gotten used to passing joint resolutions—which, when signed by the president, have force of law—during several Cold War crises. Strongly worded, they authorized the president to take whatever military steps were necessary. And every time, the Communists seemed to back down. The previous such resolutions were as follows:

- Formosa Straits (1955) to keep Communist China from taking Taiwan
- Middle East (1957) to block Soviet expansion in the Middle East
- Cuba (1962) to make the Soviets back down during the missile crisis

- Berlin (1962) to prevent a Soviet takeover of West Berlin

Congress passed the Tonkin Gulf Resolution thinking it would be like the previous resolutions—a show of resolve to make the Communists back down. The words in it, however, clearly authorized the president "to take all necessary measures to repel any armed attack against the forces of the United States and to prevent further aggression." Congress had signed a blank check, and LBJ filled in the amount and cashed it.

In 1967, when a State Department lawyer told Congress that Tonkin Gulf was "the functional equivalent of a declaration of war," Capitol Hill felt it had been tricked. But the resolution was precisely that. True, Congress misunderstood the context in which they passed the resolution; they did not know LBJ had specific plans to use it to go to war. Much of Congress's hostility to the White House during and after the Vietnam War traces back to congressional anger at having been deceived by LBJ's Tonkin Gulf Resolution, which was repealed in 1970.

Tonkin Gulf Resolution   1964
congressional permission for
president to go to war in
Vietnam.

about these patrols; instead, he portrayed the destroyers as peaceful victims of an unprovoked attack in international waters. Nothing gets American blood boiling quicker than that.

The White House sent to Capitol Hill the joint congressional resolution that had been prepared months earlier, and Congress speedily and nearly unanimously passed the **Tonkin Gulf Resolution**. Only two senators, Wayne Morse (D., Oregon) and Ernest Gruening (D., Alaska), voted no and predicted exactly what LBJ would do with the resolution: Take the country into a major war. No one believed them, and they were not reelected.

During 1965 the rest of LBJ's plan went into action. The military draft greatly increased, and most of the draftees went to "Nam." The "Rolling Thunder" air strikes against North Vietnam soon hit every worthwhile target. At first, public opinion overwhelmingly supported the president. Yes, nodded LBJ, who followed the polls closely, "but for a very underwhelming period of time." This was prophetic, for by early 1968 majority U.S. opinion opposed the war.

The public had been promised "light at the end of the tunnel" soon, but it never came. In 1965, the very year U.S. troops arrived in large numbers, so did large numbers of the North Vietnamese Army (NVA). From 1965 on, the war became more conventional and less guerrilla. Inflated "body counts" of enemy dead led people to wonder how enemy troop strength could keep growing. Real body counts of American dead—by the war's end 60,000—appeared every evening on television news. (An estimated 1.1 million Vietnamese perished.) Vietnam was the first TV war, and its vividness turned many people against the war. Students grew angry, rebellious, and finally alienated. The "flower children" and their drug culture appeared at this time. Some young men ran away to Canada to avoid the

Turning Point

TET

Tet, the Vietnamese lunar new year, was our Dienbienphu, the last straw that broke U.S. public support. In February 1968, the Communists, both Vietcong and NVA regulars, staged go-for-broke attacks throughout South Vietnam. The NVA took the northern city of Hue and executed thousands of civilians. A Vietcong suicide squad briefly invaded the U.S. embassy in Saigon.

Still, the U.S. and South Vietnamese forces held and inflicted heavy losses on the enemy. In numerical terms, we won Tet. In psychological terms, however, the Communists achieved their goal by puncturing LBJ's optimistic reports of progress in the war. Some conservatives claim Tet could have been a turning point in our favor, that if we had

stayed longer and fought harder, we could have won the war. But by then, few Americans wanted to.

Wide sectors of American society, including the business community, turned against the war. Senators Eugene McCarthy (D., Minnesota) and Robert Kennedy (D., New York) decided to challenge LBJ for the Democratic presidential nomination. The unknown McCarthy, supported by an army of enthusiastic young people ("stay clean for Gene") did surprisingly well in the New Hampshire primary. LBJ, the political pro who read the polls, knew he was finished and went on television to announce he would not run but would initiate peace discussions with Hanoi.

draft or to desert from the U.S. Army. Massive defense spending brought an inflation that lasted through the 1970s.

Matters came to a head with the **Tet** offensive. The American people would no longer stand for an open-ended commitment; the war had gone on long enough. Instead, they elected as president the man who promised to get us out with honor, Richard Nixon. Ironically, as vice president Nixon had favored U.S. military help for the French in 1954 when Johnson had opposed it.

Tet   Vietnamese new year; early 1968 North Vietnamese/Vietcong nationwide offensive.

Paris Accords   1973 agreement to end the second Vietnam war.

■ Extrication without Humiliation

President Nixon got us out of Vietnam at the same rate we had gone in. By late 1972 there were virtually no U.S. combat troops in Vietnam. Instead, there was "vietnamization," the turning over of weapons and responsibility to the Army of the Republic of Vietnam (ARVN, dubbed "Arvin" by GIs). But ARVN had never been much good. Officers were chosen on the basis of political, religious, or personal connections. Corruption was rampant. ARVN drafted young males capriciously—they once rounded up a Japanese-American who was with the CIA—but many deserted. Morale was terrible, and ARVN often shied away from engaging the enemy. Exasperated U.S. military advisors used to say of ARVN, "You can't transplant backbone."

U.S. forces had gone into Vietnam in the first place because ARVN could not handle things. What made us think they now could? President Nixon refrained from promising they could; he was merely giving them the chance. This was a major policy switch. The United States was no longer guaranteeing South Vietnam's security; now it was up to them. Could the United States have just "bugged out" quickly, in a few months? Nixon felt that abandoning an ally would have been dishonorable and would have ruined America's credibility with our allies.

The Nixon policy of "peace with honor" was actually a policy of extrication without humiliation. America should not look like it had been defeated. Nixon did not want a demoralized, beaten America, "a pitiful, helpless giant," in his words. The cost was high. About half of U.S. deaths in Vietnam occurred under Nixon for an essentially cosmetic rear-guard action.

Diplomacy

THE 1973 PARIS ACCORDS

The Americans got out of Vietnam much like the French did two decades earlier, with a fig leaf to hide their shame. The 1973 **Paris Accords** resembled the 1954 Geneva Accords: The white man got out so the Vietnamese could resume the struggle for mastery of their country. One major difference in the two accords: In 1973 there was no "regroupment." Instead, some 150,000 NVA troops were allowed to stay inside South Vietnam. Two years later, they took the whole country.

Public negotiations had already begun in Paris under LBJ, but they were leading nowhere. Secretly, Nixon's national security advisor Henry Kissinger met with North Vietnam's representative to slowly hammer out an agreement. (They were jointly awarded the 1973 Nobel Peace Prize.) When Hanoi balked, a massive "Christmas bombing" in late 1972 nudged them to sign. Saigon too needed heavy arm-twisting to go along with an agreement that left them to defend themselves with only material help from the United States.

On paper, Saigon had a good chance. ARVN actually had far more soldiers and equipment than the NVA. But they lacked morale, and when the NVA made a probing attack in the mountains in 1975, ARVN units panicked. Soldiers threw down their weapons and fled southward. An ARVN rifle, GIs used to joke, had "never been fired and only dropped once." The panic—for which there was no good reason—spread, and ARVN melted away. Billions of dollars of U.S. war material fell into enemy hands. This time the U.S. Congress refused to let President Ford get the United States involved again. Instead of fighting, South Vietnamese officials clamored to be evacuated to the United States.

They paid for their cowardice. Although there was no Cambodia-style bloodbath (some 1.7 million Cambodians were killed), many Saigon officials were executed and the remainder sent to prison farms for lengthy and brutal "reeducation." Over half-a-million South Vietnamese fled in overcrowded coastal fishing boats. Their greatest hope was to be admitted to the United States. Thai pirates raped, robbed, and murdered the "boat people" with impunity. Vietnamese who remained faced malnourished poverty as Communist bumblers wrecked the economy and turned Vietnam into one of the poorest countries in the world.

Finally, reformers in Hanoi—seeing how well the market economies of the region were doing—liberalized and welcomed foreign investment. The first to take advantage of it were the Japanese. The last were the Americans, although by the mid-1990s, they too were in on the deal. In 1995 Hanoi and Washington opened full diplomatic relations. Vietnam (like China) became partly capitalist and tied to the world market. Hanoi's Communist rulers disliked this but could not argue with 7 percent annual growth. Aside from unifying their country on their terms, the Vietnamese Communists fought for an ideology doomed to failure.

Diplomacy

KISSINGER'S "DECENT INTERVAL"

Before he became President Nixon's national security advisor, Harvard professor Henry Kissinger confided privately that the best the United States could hope for in getting out of Vietnam was a "decent interval" of two to three years between our withdrawal and a Communist takeover, so it would not look like a direct U.S. defeat. This is what Kissinger got: two years between the Paris Accords and the fall of Saigon. There is no evidence that Hanoi agreed to any such interval; it just worked out that way.

Morality and Feasibility

Americans are given to moralizing about foreign policy; it is part of our religious heritage. Are we doing good or evil? we constantly ask ourselves. Most other countries hold such discussions to a minimum. Vietnam unleashed a torrent of moral analyses. The White House constantly assured the public that our actions were moral; many clergymen and professors argued they were immoral. Our analysis follows.

just war   Doctrine of medieval Catholic philosophers that war under certain conditions can be moral.

First, the American policy of trying to block the spread of communism was moral. Politically, economically, and morally, Communist countries were blights, some worse than others. Most have now ousted their Communist regimes, a clear indication that the system failed. The strongest anti-Communists were citizens of Communist countries. You didn't know how bad it was until you lived under it. There's the rub. How could we communicate to people who had not yet tasted Communist rule just how bad it was? And, as in Vietnam, how could we reach them when the local Communists had managed to capture the *nationalist* movement?

Classic Thought

WAR AND PEACE

"THEY MAKE A DESERT AND CALL IT PEACE"

Roman historian Tacitus showed some guilt over what Rome had done during its conquest and subjugation of England. The Roman Empire did eventually bring peace, but it was a cynical kind of peace, a peace of the graveyard. Critics of the Vietnam War often recalled Tacitus's bitter remark—"They make a desert and call it peace"—and suggested that it was what we were doing in Vietnam.

"WE HAD TO DESTROY THE VILLAGE IN ORDER TO SAVE IT"

The statement "We had to destroy the village in order to save it," made by an American officer (a sort of unwitting Tacitus) explaining why a certain Vietnamese village had to be leveled, was widely reported because it seemed to encapsule what we were doing in Vietnam. After we finished "saving" Vietnam, what would be left?

AQUINAS ON "JUST WAR"

St. Thomas Aquinas in the thirteenth century deplored war but admitted that a war could be just provided that the following criteria were met:

1. It aimed at defending and reestablishing peace.
2. The cause itself was just.
3. Noncombatants were not harmed.
4. The means used were proportional to the ends.

St. Thomas's "proportionality" doctrine is his most important. It means you do not nuke a country over fishing rights. Some thinkers felt the U.S. war in Vietnam passed on points 1 and 2 but failed on points 3 and 4.

feasibility   Able to do without
excessive force or cost.

It was nationalism that gave communism its strength. The Vietminh beat the French because they had the force of Vietnamese nationalism on their side; the French were foreign colonizers. The Americans unwittingly stepped into the French role; we looked like new colonialists. The Vietcong did not know or care about Marx or Lenin; they were fighting to get the foreigners out of their country. How would you feel if your country was occupied by an army of eight-foot aliens with green complexions, who did not speak your language or eat your food but could sure mess with your women? Would you believe them if they told you they were here to liberate you? This is how the Vietnamese saw us.

Under such circumstances, how do you save people who do not want to be saved? Making matters worse was the ineptitude of the Saigon regime; it was incapable of rallying its people. And the more the United States "helped" Saigon—with money, food, experts, and so on—the weaker it became. In place of political and moral support from the South Vietnamese, we relied on firepower, which was counterproductive. People who have seen their homes, farms, and children destroyed by artillery, napalm, or Zippo lighters hate the foreigners who have done these things. The more we fought, the worse it got. We were destroying the country in order to save it. Eventually, our moral goal was subverted by immoral means.

The Vietnam Veterans Memorial in Washington was the focus of the nation's pent-up emotions over the war. Here a veteran tearfully remembers his fallen buddies. (Michael G. Roskin)

Morality and **feasibility** are closely linked in international affairs. If a goal, however moral, is infeasible, trying to attain it by brute strength leads to immorality. We must ask not only what our goals are, but whether they can be achieved without doing more harm than good. As we ceaselessly used to point out to the Communists, the end does not justify the means.

Are there any lessons to be learned from the Vietnam experience? We suggest the following:

1. Use care in picking the government you wish to help; make sure it is incorrupt and popular.
2. Do not help too much. People have to fight for their own freedom. If we do the fighting for them, they become dependent, demoralized, and resentful. The more money you give them, the more corrupt they become.

3. Issue no visas to local citizens. Make it clear to them that the United States is not an escape hatch. If they lose, they will have to live under a dictatorship.

4. Make sure local nationalism is on your side, that the enemy has not captured it. If you look like colonialists, you have no chance.

5. Armed forces cannot win hearts and minds. An army does one thing: destroy. Therefore, use your army sparingly, quickly, and away from population centers.

6. Survey the geography to make sure it does not give your enemy advantages such as secure base areas, sanctuaries, or supply routes.

7. Remember that Americans do not like long wars and quickly lose patience.

8. Obtain the informed consent of Congress to make sure they are fully behind you. Do not attempt to sneak by with a "functional equivalent of a declaration of war."

9. Immediately increase taxes to soak up defense spending and block inflation.

Key Terms

Dienbienphu (p. 39)

feasibility (p. 50)

Geneva Accords (p. 41)

guerrilla warfare (p. 42)

just war (p. 49)

monolithic (p. 38)

Paris Accords (p. 47)

political generations (p. 37)

protectorate (p. 38)

Tet (p. 47)

Tonkin Gulf Resolution (p. 46)

Vietcong (p. 43)

Vietminh (p. 38)

Key Web Sites

U.S.-Vietnam Relations: A Chronology
http://acs.oakton.edu/~wittman/chronol.html

Vietnam Information
http://www.batin.com.vn/vninfo/vninfo.htm

Vietnam: Yesterday and Today
http://acs.oakton.edu/~wittman/

Further Reference

Ellsberg, Daniel. *Secrets: A Memoir of Vietnam and the Pentagon Papers.* New York: Viking, 2002.

Fall, Bernard B. *The Two Viet-Nams: A Political and Military Analysis,* 2nd rev. ed. New York: Praeger, 1967.

———. *Last Reflections on a War.* Garden City, NY: Doubleday, 1967.

FitzGerald, Frances. *Fire in the Lake: The Vietnamese and the Americans in Vietnam.* New York: Random House, 1972.

Halberstam, David. *The Best and the Brightest.* New York: Random House, 1972.

Isaacs, Arnold R. *Vietnam Shadows: The War, Its Ghosts, and Its Legacy.* Baltimore, MD: Johns Hopkins University Press, 1997.

Karnow, Stanley. *Vietnam: A History,* rev. ed. New York: Penguin Books, 1991.

Lamb, David. *Vietnam, Now: A Reporter Returns.* New York: PublicAffairs, 2002.

Logevall, Fredrik. *Choosing War: The Lost Chance for Peace and the Escalation of War in Vietnam.* Berkeley, CA: University of California Press, 1999.

Maraniss, David. *They Marched into Sunlight: War and Peace, Vietnam and America, October 1967.* New York: Simon & Schuster, 2003.

Neu, Charles E. *America's Lost War: Vietnam, 1945–1975.* Wheeling, IL: Harlan Davidson, 2005.

SarDesai, D. R. *Vietnam: Past and Present,* 4th ed. Boulder, CO: Westview, 2005.

Schulzinger, Robert D. *A Time for Peace: The Legacy of the Vietnam War.* New York: Oxford University Press, 2006.

Sheehan, Neil, Hedrick Smith, E. W. Kenworthy, and Fox Butterfield. *The Pentagon Papers.* New York: New York Times, 1971.

CHAPTER 4

CAN THE UNITED STATES LEAD THE WORLD?

QUESTIONS TO CONSIDER

1. Has the United States practiced interventionism? When?
2. Is the opposite of interventionism isolationism?
3. Is U.S. foreign policy cyclical? Caused by what?
4. How were the doctrines of postwar presidents similar?
5. What is the elite-mass split on U.S. foreign policy?
6. Should U.S. foreign policy be based on ideals or self-interest?
7. How important are bureaucracies in forming foreign policies?
8. Is the United States well-structured for foreign policy?
9. How does unilateralism turn into isolationism?
10. Can the interventionist policies of Bush 43 be sustained?

Suddenly, on September 11, 2001, the United States got a new foreign policy, one that plunged us deeply into the Middle East. An enraged America sent troops to overthrow two regimes, Afghanistan's and Iraq's. Before 9/11 the Bush 43 administration had denounced "nation-building" and keeping U.S. forces abroad. Peacekeeping and humanitarian missions were out. From the end of the Cold War until 9/11, **foreign policy** played a minor role in the media, Congress, and presidential elections. In his 2002 State of the Union address, however, President Bush put us into a struggle with an "axis of evil"—Iraq, Iran, and North Korea. From near-isolationism, muscular U.S. interventionism became the Bush policy.

Few nations followed us in this struggle. 9/11 and the Taliban in Afghanistan disgusted nearly all, so most countries approved of the quick U.S. ouster of the obnoxious Afghan regime in late 2001. Some even helped us. As Bush's plans for war against Iraq emerged during 2002—the "axis of evil" speech was its kickoff—world support turned to opposition. Bush's case against Iraq—that it had weapons of mass destruction and sponsored terrorism—seemed unproved and exaggerated. America moved against Iraq with few allies. Only Britain contributed combat forces.

foreign policy   The way a country deals with the outside world. (See page 53.)

interventionism   U.S. willingness to use military force overseas.

The two Clinton administrations, 1993–2001, focused on domestic politics and had little to say about foreign policy. Its first national security advisor, Anthony Lake, spoke of "enlargement of democracy" to replace containment of communism, but there was little follow-through. Its second secretary of state, Madeleine Albright, preached a major U.S. role in preserving peace, but Congress and the American people were skeptical. The simple fact was that Americans of all political persuasions could not agree on what America's role in the world should be. In the absence of a threat, America tends to revert to its traditional impulse: isolationism. Bush 43 was basically an isolationist. He disparaged Clinton's overseas efforts and indicated we would not get or stay involved in the Balkans, Middle East, or Africa. Instead, we would build a missile shield. The Middle East, however, forced U.S. involvement. With 9/11 we witnessed the latest of many shifts between noninterventionism and interventionism in U.S. foreign policy.

From Interventionism to Caution

From roughly Pearl Harbor in 1941 to Vietnam in the late 1960s, the United States practiced an interventionist foreign policy. At its high point in the 1960s, U.S. commitments nearly covered the globe to encircle what was then called the "Sino-Soviet bloc." Everything was our business, and we sent troops to dozens of countries. Mostly we were successful, or at any rate we seemed to be successful. U.S. foreign aid and troops staved off Soviet expansion into West Europe. U.S. forces pushed back a Communist attack in Korea. CIA-sponsored coups ousted undesirable governments in Iran and Guatemala. We acted like the world's policeman.

Vietnam, however, was one intervention too many. U.S. foreign policy shifted in a noninterventionist direction during Vietnam and was slow and reluctant to return to the sweeping **interventionism** of pre-Vietnam years. Under President Reagan, U.S. interventionism

Concepts

INTERVENTIONISM

The great French foreign minister Talleyrand (see Chapter 19), when questioned about a policy of noninterventionism, replied: "Ah, yes, noninterventionism. A philosophical and metaphysical term meaning approximately the same as interventionism." The cynical Talleyrand indicated that not interfering in the affairs of another country can have as great an impact as interfering.

Intervention means projecting your power into another country to make, maintain, or unmake foreign governments. As used in this chapter applied to U.S. foreign policy, interventionism is a policy of using U.S. armed power overseas. When the United States sends its troops to other lands, it is pursuing an interventionist foreign policy. CIA sponsorship of a coup or insurrection is interventionism too, but of a less public variety. When, on the other hand, Washington is unwilling to send troops or spooks (CIA operatives), it is pursuing a noninterventionist policy. There can be in-between positions; the willingness to use some forces overseas in certain circumstances might be called a moderate interventionist policy.

enjoyed an upsurge. Soviet power is aggressive and expansionist and must be stopped, decreed the White House. Defense spending increased sharply. U.S. troops were dispatched to Beirut (a catastrophe) and Grenada (a mini-victory). President Bush 41 sent troops into Panama and the Persian Gulf with mixed public support. America looked interventionist again. Then Soviet power collapsed; there was no more enemy. Many Americans wondered what we were doing overseas: The Cold War is over and we won, so let's go home. Even members of Congress who had been hawks during the Cold War turned **noninterventionist**. Strange coalitions of protesters—unionists, environmentalists, leftists, Christians, anarchists—tried to disrupt international meetings and prevent U.S. trade normalization with China. They claimed America's involvement with the outside world was wrong and harmful.

noninterventionism The unwillingness to use military force overseas.

U.S. foreign policy seems to swing like a pendulum from interventionism to noninterventionism about once a generation. Americans reacted to World War I by slouching into "isolationism" and swearing that we would never get involved in helping the ungrateful Europeans again. With the rise of German and Japanese militarism, however, isolation was impossible, as Pearl Harbor demonstrated. The generation that fought in World War II became imbued with a globalism that was more or less the opposite of the interwar isolationism. Now everything overseas mattered. We intervened more and more until we eventually got burned in Vietnam. Coming out of Vietnam, we swore never to get involved in anything like that again. A similar mood appeared after the 2003 Iraq War.

■ Are Americans Basically Isolationists?

The Cold War retained domestic support because the Soviets and their allies were perceived as a threat to the United States. With that over, the American public and Congress moved back to less involvement. Political scientist Gabriel Almond observed in 1950 that "an overtly interventionist and 'responsible' United States hides a covertly isolationist longing." By the 1990s, this longing was no longer covert; leading figures of both parties opposed interventionist policies. Domestic concerns dominated politics. Allies were increasingly seen as uncooperative and unfair trade competitors.

Classic Thought

SPYKMAN ON INTERVENTION

Nicholas Spykman, educated in the Dutch institute for colonial administration, brought with him to Yale a geopolitical perspective on world affairs. Spykman (pronounced SPEAKman) posed the classic question of U.S. foreign and defense policy in 1942: "Shall we protect our interests by defense on this side of the water or by active participation in the lands across the oceans?" In other words, to intervene or not to intervene? The answer for Spykman, writing only days after Pearl Harbor, was clear: Intervene before it is too late. The answer for our day is not so clear.

behavioralism   Studying humans by empirical evidence, often quantified.

Pollsters found few isolationist views in the American public. Rather consistently, Americans say they support U.S. involvement in the world, even if that means sending troops. The questions are mostly asked in the abstract, though, with no mention of how many lives and dollars Americans are willing to expend. As the body bags and costs to taxpayers start coming home, attitudes reverse. Public opinion is volatile; it can support a cause one year and abandon it the next. It often seems contradictory. Americans were pleased with the first President Bush's foreign policy successes, even as they criticized him for spending too much time on foreign policy instead of on domestic U.S. problems. The success of the quick 1991 Gulf War shot his popularity up to record levels, but within a year opinion turned negative over a brief economic recession. The strong support for the Iraq War in spring 2003 by 2005 turned negative as casualties and costs mounted.

The U.S. public is frequently divided and hesitant. Before U.S. peacekeeping forces were sent to Haiti in 1994, opinion was split about whether to intervene or stay out. Americans were not eager to rush into that complex situation and were relieved when we took over quickly and easily. Political scientist John Mueller found similar patterns of declining public support for the Korean, Vietnam, and Iraq wars. After three years of U.S. casualties with no clear end, public opinion was negative on all three wars. Public opinion after 9/11 was angry and strongly interventionist but soon wished to bring American troops back from Iraq.

Concepts

A CYCLICAL THEORY OF U.S. FOREIGN POLICY

A **behaviorally** inclined political scientist, Frank L. Klingberg, accurately predicted in a 1952 article that the U.S. interventionism then current would end in the late 1960s. A social scientist who can predict anything deserves respect. Klingberg quantified such indicators as naval expenditures, annexations, armed expeditions, diplomatic pressures, and mention of foreign matters in presidential speeches and party platforms to discover alternating moods of "introversion" (mostly staying home) and "extroversion" (expanding U.S. power and influence outside its borders). (See table at bottom of righthand column.)

On average, introvert periods lasted twenty-one years, extrovert twenty-seven. If you add twenty-seven to 1940, when the United States entered an extrovert phase, you get 1967, which turns out to be the very time the United States tired of overseas involvement in general and Vietnam in particular.

Klingberg, of course, did not know when he wrote that Vietnam would become a major U.S. war or political issue. He merely suggested that based on past performance we could expect extroversion to end in the late 1960s. We can even take it a step farther. Adding twenty-one years (average length of introvert phase) to 1967, we get 1988. Did we indeed return to extroversion? Or was the whole cycle thrown off by the Cold War so that the introvert phase did not start until 1989? What phase are we in now?

Introversion	Extroversion
1776–1798	1798–1824
1824–1844	1884–1871
1871–1891	1891–1919
1919–1940	1940–

There is also an **elite** versus **mass** split on foreign affairs. Better-educated, attentive Americans in leadership positions think that world events are important, and almost all support a U.S. world leadership role. The mass public, on the other hand, generally thinks that things overseas have little impact here; fewer support an active U.S. role in the world. With little enthusiasm or understanding, they show "apathetic internationalism." A 1997 Pew Research Center survey found that 63 percent favored expansion of NATO, but only 10 percent could name even one of the three nations that were about to join—

elite The top or most influential people.

mass The rest of us.

idealism Basing foreign policy on moral, ethical, legal, or world-order principles.

self-interest Basing foreign policy on national interest.

Poland, the Czech Republic, and Hungary. (You knew all three, didn't you?) Elites usually support foreign aid and use of troops overseas more than the mass public. Only elite opinion sustains U.S. foreign policy; the masses rarely care.

The Continuity Principle

Presidential candidates of one party usually denounce the foreign policies of incumbents of the other party. Once in office, however, the new president generally follows these policies and sometimes takes them farther. Candidate Bush 43 criticized Clinton's policy of

Reflections

IDEALS OR SELF-INTEREST?

Young people often wonder what they should base their foreign-policy views on, **idealism** or **self-interest**. Many learn from school and church a moralistic tradition that leads to idealism, aiming for the good of the world. Some are then exposed in college to the notion that foreign policy should be based on the "national interest"—looking out for the good of one's country (see Chapter 2 for the U.S. search for its national interest).

Which approach is right? Either can be fraught with peril. An idealistic policy of sending "peacekeeping" forces to feed the starving in Somalia can lead to armed clashes and an ignoble retreat. The good intentions of this policy are no substitute for a hard-edged analysis of Somali politics. But a national-interest approach can be so narrow that it misses dangers that are brewing. Thinking only of self-interest, we might ignore a regime of Muslim fanatics that is distant and none of our concern. That is the way we treated Afghanistan from

1989 to 2001. But Afghanistan became a nest of terrorists, who bombed U.S. ships and embassies and finally destroyed the World Trade Center. We should have paid more attention to Afghanistan earlier.

Idealism and self-interest are not always at odds. Sometimes the smartest thing to do is to help others, who in turn become trading partners and customers. U.S. Marshall Plan aid for Europe after World War II paid off many times over in prosperity on both sides of the Atlantic. Beware of analyses that are too idealistic or self-interested. Are the policies feasible? What are their long-term consequences likely to be? Beware also of policies that are idealistic but difficult to follow up in practice. Americans are always wary of getting "bogged down" in distant conflicts. A policy needs a certain amount of idealism, but to be accepted must also be presented as promising a payoff. We must construct policies that merge idealism and self-interest.

keeping U.S. troops in Kosovo. After six months in office, President Bush called them "essential." There is more continuity than change from one administration to the next. Candidate Bush criticized Clinton's use of troops overseas and "nation-building," but after Bush became president he did much more of both than Clinton ever envisioned.

The continuity principle shows up in the policies commonly associated with one president that were often initiated by his predecessor. The Eisenhower doctrine of massive nuclear retaliation was implicit in Truman's actions; Eisenhower just made it explicit. Nixon's withdrawal of U.S. forces from Vietnam actually began under Johnson. Reagan's massive defense buildup actually began under Carter. Clinton's defense cutbacks actually began under Bush 41. Many things happen earlier than is commonly thought.

To be sure, there are sometimes shifts from one administration to another. Kennedy found Eisenhower's defense budget and strategy entirely unsatisfactory—he won election in 1960 in part by denouncing Ike's caution—and he redid the Defense Department with major new funding. Kennedy shifted U.S. attention to the developing areas of Asia, Africa, and Latin America. Vietnam was but one example of JFK's strong interventionism. Reagan, also an interventionist, took a leaf from Kennedy's book in his similar defense buildup in the 1980s.

Diplomacy

PRESIDENTS AND THEIR "DOCTRINES"

During the Cold War, most U.S. presidents articulated policies that journalists quickly dubbed their "doctrines." The policies were seldom that simple, and calling them "doctrines" tends to make them sound more clear-cut than they were. Nonetheless, they are convenient handles to help us remember who stood for what. Notice that all these doctrines are just variations on the first, the Truman Doctrine, sometimes called the "containment" policy, from George Kennan's 1947 article (see Chapter 2). The overall goal of U.S. foreign policy did not change much: Stop communism. Only the intensity and costs changed.

President	Years	Doctrine
Truman	1945–1953	Contain the expansion of communism, presumably everywhere.
Eisenhower	1953–1961	Use nukes and spooks to prevent Communist or other radical takeovers.
Kennedy	1961–1963	Respond flexibly to communist expansion, especially to guerrilla warfare.
Johnson	1963–1969	Follow through on Kennedy Doctrine by committing U.S. combat troops in Vietnam.
Nixon	1969–1974	Supply weapons but not troops to countries fighting off communism.
Ford	1974–1977	Continue Nixon Doctrine.
Carter	1977–1981	Make clear to Soviets that Persian Gulf is a vital U.S. interest.
Reagan	1981–1989	Sponsor anticommunist guerrillas who are trying to overthrow pro-Soviet regimes.

Why is there considerable continuity? Most obviously, the Cold War posed the same basic challenge to all presidents from Truman through Reagan; the Soviet threat could not be ignored. Next, campaign rhetoric is one thing, reality quite another. It is easy for a challenger to denounce an incumbent for not doing enough, ignoring problem areas, or failing to develop new technology. Once in the White House, though, the new president discovers that things are not so simple. A candidate speaks to a domestic audience; a president suddenly discovers that the entire world is listening. Would Bush 43 really pull U.S. peacekeepers out of Kosovo? It would look like betrayal of a commitment and end any U.S. leadership role in Europe. So Bush kept them in Kosovo. Campaign sound bites win votes, but Congress and allies refuse to cooperate.

deficit A federal budget that spends more than it takes in.

entitlements Required federal expenditures, such as Social Security and Medicare, to large classes of U.S. citizens.

constraint A limit on decision-making.

dove Favors peace, a noninterventionist.

Pentagon Defense Department main building.

Joint Chiefs of Staff Committee of top generals and admirals.

Another factor is the U.S. federal budget **deficit**, which in 2006 was about $250 billion, a constraint on further spending. Even Republicans balked at major new outlays to rebuild Iraq. **Entitlements** dominate the budget, and politicians fear voter anger at cutting Social Security or Medicare or raising taxes. In short, presidents face numerous **constraints**; they are not free to do everything they originally thought they could.

Resuming military conscription, for example, would require a major crisis and act of Congress. Americans have never liked the draft; young men during Vietnam especially disliked it. Nixon defused student anger in 1973 by ending the draft and going to the all-volunteer army (AVA), the case ever since. The AVA is highly trained and effective but relatively small. From a high of 3.5 million active-duty military personnel in 1968 (the Vietnam peak), total U.S. troop strength for all services fell to 1.4 million in the 1990s and stayed there. As Iraq dragged on, it became difficult to recruit enough qualified people to maintain that level. Many recruits now come from depressed rural areas where young people are patriotic and need jobs.

The U.S. military is overstretched. Much of the Army's and Marine Corps's active-duty combat forces are overseas, most in Iraq. Some soldiers got three and even four tours there. Few are available for new missions. Service abroad is hard on marriages and families. Spirited U.S. forces quickly crushed the Iraqi regime but soon had to keep order in a hostile Iraq after the war. Many said their job was done and wanted to return home. The Army's top general, Eric Shinseki, warned of pursuing a "twelve-division strategy with a ten-division army."

Some critics speak of the "military mind" and assume that officers are eager for overseas intervention. This is far from the case; often the biggest **doves** in an administration are the **Pentagon** chiefs. It is their people, after all, who get killed. The top U.S. generals often give presidents cautious advice about deploying overseas. They know they are overstretched and how rapidly public and congressional opinion can change when casualties mount. The president may be commander-in-chief, but when the **Joint Chiefs of Staff** talk, the president listens. The biggest constraint on presidential decision making, however, is Congress.

■ A Contrary Congress

The precise role of Congress in foreign affairs has never been defined. Rather, it has changed over the years, mostly declining. A nagging ambiguity came with the Constitution, which says Congress declares war but also says the president is commander-in-chief. Which power overrides? Must the president wait until Congress passes a declaration of war before using troops overseas? The problem had come up before, but with Vietnam it surfaced with a vengeance.

War Powers Act **1973**
congressional time limit on
president's use of troops in
hostilities.

As we discussed in Chapter 3, that war was never formally declared. Instead, President Johnson used a joint resolution of Congress that empowered him to stop Communist aggression. The senators and congresspersons did not fully understand that passing (nearly unanimously) the 1964 Tonkin Gulf Resolution gave the president a blank check. Even after it was repealed, Nixon argued that the president's power as commander-in-chief allowed him to conduct the war and even expand it into Cambodia. Rage grew in Congress because they were essentially helpless spectators to a president's war-making whims. To try to remedy this imbalance, in 1973 Congress passed (over President Nixon's veto) the **War Powers Act**, giving the president only ninety days to use troops overseas without congressional approval.

No president, Republican or Democrat, has liked the War Powers Act. They claim it usurps their prerogative as commander-in-chief, and they have easily circumvented it. The president simply doesn't report to Congress that he has sent troops into "hostilities or situations where hostilities are imminent." In 1982, when President Reagan sent U.S. Marines into Beirut, he carefully noted that they were "peacekeeping" forces and thus not involved in hostilities. Congress backed down and voted to allow him eighteen months to use the Marines for peacekeeping, even though the situation was dangerous. Congress, in effect, repealed its own War Powers Act. Then a suicide truck bomber killed 241 sleeping Marines in their barracks, and the president ordered all troops withdrawn. At no time, however, did he admit they were in hostilities.

Several times in recent decades U.S. forces have clearly been put into hostilities, but the White House never reported it as such, so the War Powers clock never started ticking. And there is nothing in the act that forces a president to report hostilities. The White House's reply will always be, "Hostilities? What hostilities?" The War Powers Act was defective, unenforceable, and probably unconstitutional (under the 1983 *Chadha* decision outlawing legislative vetoes).

In 1990, after Iraq invaded Kuwait, President Bush 41 quickly sent U.S. forces to defend Saudi Arabia. He did not ask Congress for authority to do this and said the troops' mission was "wholly defensive." In January, as the troop buildup peaked, Bush asked Congress for a joint resolution authorizing the use of force to fulfill UN resolutions, which the United States had sponsored. Congress debated it and said yes on January 12, 1991. Five days later, Desert Shield turned into Desert Storm as the air campaign began. On day 39 of the war (February 24), the ground campaign began. Bush concealed his aims, but it is now clear that he aimed for war from the beginning. Congress went along after the plans were made and the troops deployed.

After 9/11 President Bush 43 claimed broad war powers and in a highly emotional atmosphere got congressional support (but not a declaration of war) to invade both

Afghanistan and Iraq. He also asserted inherent presidential powers during an emergency to detain suspects worldwide and eavesdrop on phone calls. Some critics feared the president's claim to nearly unlimited war powers warps the constitution. Congress, far from checking the president, generally follows him and votes the war funds he requests.

alarmism   Exaggerating dangers to promote a policy.

The Founding Fathers did not have this in mind. They gave the power to declare war only to Congress. Gradually, though, this power became irrelevant. A president can take diplomatic and military steps that lead the country into hostilities. Then, after the first shots

Concepts

CONGRESS AND FOREIGN POLICY

Congress, although it generally follows the president's lead in foreign policy, can play a meddlesome or mischievous role. It does not consistently follow principle, president, public opinion, or pressure group. At times it seems to delight in tripping up presidential policy, especially when the president is of another party. A Republican-dominated Congress, for example, blocked President Clinton's measures in several areas:

- The Senate (only the Senate, with a two-thirds majority, approves treaty ratification) rejected treaties to ban nuclear tests and land mines, treaties that most of the world wanted.

- Congress passed laws to punish foreign firms that do business in Cuba, Iraq, or Iran. Other countries, including America's own allies, ignore the U.S. laws.

- Most of the world signed a treaty limiting the emissions of "greenhouse gases" in an effort to prevent global warming. Clinton went along with a diluted version, but the U.S. Senate rejected it.

- The administration geared up for trade talks to bring new Latin American partners into our free-trade area, but Congress, fearful of loss of American jobs, shot the talks down before they started.

- With much congressional opposition, the United States finally took a lead in Bosnia and Kosovo ("Clinton's war"),

but Congress wanted the few thousand Americans there brought home soon.

- The Senate Foreign Relations Committee chairman blocked everything he opposed, leaving some ambassadorships unfilled. An extremely able diplomat, Richard Holbrooke, had to wait fourteen months before Senate confirmation as ambassador to the UN.

- Congress cut the State Department's budget and foreign aid, shrinking the U.S. presence overseas. Many consulates closed.

- Congress delayed for years U.S. dues owed to the U.N., the World Bank, and the World Health Organization.

Some critics claim actions like these amount to "creeping isolationism." To get congressional support presidents often use either a crisis or massive pressure. Then the Congress rallies around a president and speaks of "bipartisan foreign policy." Such was the case after 9/11. Presidents often sound alarm bells and call a situation a desperate emergency. **Alarmism** can be dangerous and go too far without critical thinking. Kennan complained that his "containment" policy (see page 30) was exaggerated and misapplied. A president may also enlist powerful interest groups. In 2000 Congress voted to normalize trade with China despite public, especially labor, opposition. Pressure in favor of it from big business was unusually heavy.

National Security Council The
president's foreign-policy
coordinating body.

have been fired, he asks Congress to support the effort. Congress
automatically goes along, because "our boys" are already being
shot at. In much of foreign policy, Congress is bypassed: secret
funds for Nicaraguan contras, secret arms sales to Iran, secret
understandings with Kuwait and Saudi Arabia. Such end runs
have built a storehouse of congressional resentment that comes out from time to time in
the form of hostile committee hearings, accusations of executive wrongdoing, budget cuts,
and the blocking of administration policies and appointments (see box on page 61). Congress has a built-in inefficiency—designed that way by the Constitution's authors—that
can delay and block U.S. foreign policy. It also trips up a U.S. leadership role.

■ Is the Structure Defective?

As Alexis de Tocqueville observed in the 1830s, a democratic republic such as the United
States will always have trouble conducting a coherent foreign policy. Democracies have to
pay attention to public opinion; tyrannies don't. The need to win elections produces crowd-
pleasing but oversimplified slogans and unrealistic policies. U.S. administrations appoint top
officials from business, the law, and academia for a few years. Many are talented amateurs,
in office only a few years. No secretary of state, for example, has been a career Foreign
Service Officer.

The very structure of the U.S. foreign affairs community is also a problem. Big and
sprawling, it often seems controlled by no one. More than a dozen federal departments
and agencies focus on foreign affairs. (For the complexity of even a small U.S. embassy,
see Chapter 19.) Attempting to coordinate these branches fell to the **National Security
Council** (NSC), but that brought new problems (see box on page 63). Secretaries of state,
nominally the nation's overseers of foreign affairs, battle over turf with secretaries of defense and national security advisors, usually losing.

The Iran/contra foul-up of the 1980s illustrated what could go wrong. Oliver North, a
Marine lieutenant colonel on the NSC staff, in connection with nongovernmental fundrais-
ers and "consultants," directed a harebrained scheme to sell U.S. weapons to Iran and use
the profits to support the Nicaraguan contras in defiance of the will of Congress and U.S.
laws. Who was responsible? It was hard to say. And that is one of the problems of U.S. foreign policy: Exactly who gives the orders for what? If left divided, the various departments
and agencies work at cross-purposes without coordination or communication. If centralized under the NSC or the Defense Department, other agencies feel overridden and misused by enthusiastic amateurs whose chief qualification is their friendship with or access
to the president. Recent presidents have conducted foreign policy with a handful of close
associates; they simply bypass the conventional structures.

Can the structure be fixed? Some have suggested requiring the national security advisor to be confirmed by and answerable to Congress, just as the secretaries of state and
defense are. This would help control secret schemes, but it would give Congress more
scrutiny of the White House than most presidents would wish. Presidents like their national security advisors to be responsible only to them; this gives them flexibility and secrecy. Another proposal is to designate the secretary of state as the top and responsible
person in foreign affairs. But the secretary cannot be assured of cooperation from the

other branches; the Pentagon, CIA, NSC, and the new Homeland Security can ignore or fail to inform him.

After 9/11, a new structural problem became clear. The CIA, FBI, Immigration and Customs Enforcement (ICE), and state and local police barely communicated with each other. By law and by corporate culture, the CIA gathers information but does not share it with other agencies. It prepares reports only for the president and a few other top officials. The CIA had no interest or way to share with other agencies signs that al Qaeda was preparing a major strike. The CIA has massive foreign-area expertise but no law-enforcement powers. The FBI, on the other hand, has great law-enforcement powers but no foreign-area expertise. It would be nice if the CIA and FBI talked to each other and even better if they communicated with local police and immigration officials, the front line in the war on terror. There is not yet a single computer system that links all relevant agencies. The new Department of Homeland Security, established in haste in 2002, was supposed to integrate and coordinate our efforts, but the FBI and CIA are not under its supervision.

The United States is not well structured to conduct a concerted, rational foreign policy. And, for deep-seated reasons, it is not likely to become so. Americans and their Congress fear a secretive, centralized system. A superagency in charge of U.S. foreign policy goes against the American grain. The uncoordinated, sprawling nature of the

Diplomacy

NATIONAL SECURITY COUNCIL

As the United States geared up for the Cold War, Congress streamlined and partially centralized foreign and defense policymaking with the National Security Act of 1947. The act set up the Central Intelligence Agency and provided for a National Security Council composed of the president, vice president, and secretaries of state and defense.

Various presidents have used the NSC differently, some a little and some a lot. Over the decades though, its centralized power has grown, and it has developed a large staff to assist the president. By the time of the Nixon administration, the NSC staff—which was not mentioned in the 1947 law—had become more important than the NSC itself or the regular departments.

The head of this staff is called the national security advisor, a presidential appointee not accountable to Congress. The president picks these advisors and their helpers mostly from academia and the military. The most famous (and probably most effective) was Harvard professor Henry Kissinger, who soon eclipsed Secretary of State William Rogers. Bush 43 relied more on National Security Advisor Condoleeza Rice than on Secretary of State Colin Powell. After 9/11, Vice President Dick Cheney and Secretary of Defense Donald Rumsfeld took the policy lead; Powell did public relations. Then, amidst mounting criticism of our Iraq policy, Bush assigned Rice to coordinate it, angering Rumsfeld. In general, the national security advisor has the president's ear more than anyone else in foreign policy.

The NSC staff has a number of things going for it that enhance its power. First, it is close to the president, not across town. It is an information clearinghouse, receiving all State, Defense, and CIA cables and reports. It is small and thus moves faster and leaks less; the president can trust it. Many in Congress and the conventional departments are vexed that the NSC, which started as a simple policy-coordinating device, has turned into an unaccountable superagency.

U.S. foreign policy community is likely to continue, and presidents who think they are in charge of policy may find that the structure is in charge of them.

■ Do Bureaucracies Make Foreign Policy?

One of the fads in political science, popular in the 1970s, was to analyze decisions in terms of the **bureaucracies** who carry them out and often influence them. We may have an image of decision makers sitting in a quiet room, rationally discussing a problem and coming up with a logical solution. But what if the material they have been fed is skewed or incomplete? What if the civil servants are telling their bosses what they want to hear? Will the decision then be a rational one? And can we be certain the civil servants will execute the decision the way the decision maker wants it?

bureaucracies   Career civil servants organized into various departments and bureaus.

Cuban Missile Crisis   1962 showdown over Soviet rockets in Cuba.

Bureaucracies have lives and interests of their own, but do they really make policy? Vietnam has been analyzed in terms of bureaucratic politics. When presidents issued orders to stop the Communists in Vietnam, they didn't want to hear any back talk about how difficult it was or that it was a lost cause. They wanted a "can-do" response from enthusiastic military and civilian officers. Accordingly, reports came back from the field that U.S. aid, advisors, and programs were working. The bureaucrats were telling the presidents what they wanted to hear. Overly optimistic reporting, in this view, deepened U.S. commitments in Vietnam.

Concepts

BUREAUCRATIC POLITICS

In a widely read 1969 article, Harvard political scientist Graham Allison claimed the 1962 **Cuban Missile Crisis** unrolled the way it did because of "bureaucratic politics." The term caught on and gave birth to a new subfield. Later evidence suggested the study omitted key factors.

Specifically, Allison found that the crucial factor was the timing of evidence presented to the president and his advisors that the Soviets were placing missiles in Cuba. This depended on when the U2 spyplane flew. The flight was delayed a week because the Air Force and CIA squabbled over who was to pilot it. If it had flown earlier, it would have given the National Security Council time to consider other, less confrontational options. But if it had flown later, it would likely have led to one of the warlike options the military was urging

on President Kennedy. So, the timing of information gathering depended on bureaucratic politics, and that is what made all the difference.

However, tapes of Kennedy's words at the time, edited by Harvard historian Ernest May, show that at no time did JFK consider a military strike of any sort. He had recently read Barbara Tuchman's *Guns of August* and learned how World War I began as a series of misunderstood moves that escalated to total war. Kennedy was not going to let things spin out of control. Accordingly, the options that Allison thought were on the NSC table—air strikes, amphibious landings, parachute drops—were never on the table. Kennedy, from the beginning, decided he would not use them. Bureaucratic politics had little or nothing to do with his decision.

This view was widely accepted until the 1971 publication of the "Pentagon Papers," a secret Defense Department history of decision making on Vietnam. The papers showed that, in general, the reports from well-informed officials were accurate and pessimistic; no one promised a short or easy war. The public relations material cranked out for the press, to be sure, was foolishly optimistic; the insider reports were coldly sober. Some of the toughest and most realistic warnings came from the CIA. There is no evidence from the Vietnam experience that bureaucrats deceived presidents.

unilateralism Foreign policies without allied help or consultation.

Once the decisions had been made, however, the various bureaucracies did their utmost for the war effort. They are disciplined services and obey orders. There were, of course, the usual bureaucratic foul-ups and rivalries, but all worked in pursuit of goals laid down by the White House. By the same token, U.S. Ambassador April Glaspie was not a free agent when she told Saddam Hussein in July 1990 that the United States would not get involved in Iraq's quarrel with Kuwait. She was following a U.S. policy to stay friendly with Baghdad. Neither she nor the State Department bureaucracy were fully to blame for this blind and foolish policy. Bureaucratic politics does take place, but it usually does so after the stage has been set and directions given by the White House.

Some blamed "the bureaucrats" for letting 9/11 happen. The several agencies totally failed to follow up on warnings or to cross-communicate, but they were created and given their missions by Congress. The problem was that no one—not the president, Congress, or the agencies themselves—could understand that we were in a new era with new threats. Agencies designed for the Cold War were clumsy in dealing with decentralized terrorism. Once set up, agencies tend to rumble on unchanged: "But we've always done it that way here." Agencies do not recreate or reform themselves; that is up to the president and Congress. By most accounts, President Bush 43 alone was in charge of U.S. policy on Iraq.

■ The Unilateralist Temptation

Related to isolationism in U.S. history is **unilateralism**, doing things ourselves and not in concert with other countries. As we saw in Chapter 2, Washington warned against "entangling alliances," and until World War II we entered into no formal alliances, not even in World War I. We did not join the League of Nations. Sponsoring the UN and North Atlantic Treaty were major breakthroughs, for at last we were formally "entangled" in the world. Not all Americans like that. Some say it infringes on U.S. sovereignty. Should the UN or NATO tell us when and where to go to war? Should they be able to stop us from going to war when we deem it necessary? Should American soldiers serve under foreign generals? Should Congress pass laws and ratify treaties to please foreigners or to serve our own interests?

This is the unilateralist temptation that the administration of Bush 43 slipped into, with help from the neo-cons (see box on page 66). It works like this: If we must do something in the world, we try to persuade NATO allies and UN members to support us, but we do not depend on them. They are timid, divided, and wrong, unable to take clear stands against evil. We must do it ourselves. Bush's unilateralism resonated with American tradition and found much public support. For example, when 178 nations signed a 2001

neo-conservative Use of conservative methods for liberal goals.

global climate treaty, the Kyoto Protocol, that sought to curb greenhouse gases, Bush called it "fatally flawed" and ignored it. Overall, the United States signs few treaties; the neo-cons say they restrict us.

Unfortunately, U.S. unilateralism turns much of the rest of the world against us, isolating us. We figure: Only we have the trained, mobile, and high-tech armed forces that can move rapidly in a coordinated way to overthrow evil regimes in places like Afghanistan or Iraq. Waiting for allies takes too long and brings communication and coordination problems. In purely military terms this is quite true, but it ignores the political problems that flow from unilateral actions. It creates the "counterweight" system we discussed in Chapter 1: The rest of the world criticizes America and refuses to follow its lead.

Many Americans respond, "So what? Who needs them?" We do. We need them as markets and as investors. Without huge amounts of foreign investment and savings pouring into the U.S. economy, we would be in severe economic decline. We need their cooperation

Diplomacy

THE RISE OF THE NEO-CONSERVATIVES

The Vietnam War spawned student radicalism in the 1960s, but soon a reaction to it set in. By 1970 several important thinkers, mostly academics and Democrats, repudiated the pacifism and relativism that had made a home in the Democratic party. They soon took the name "**neo-conservatives**" because many were liberals who rediscovered conservative values and approaches. One founder of the movement, Irving Kristol, famously defined a neo-conservative as "a liberal who's been mugged by reality." Vietnam may have been a mistake, but Soviet power was still a threat, they argued. We had to keep up our military strength and not be afraid to use it. Some worked for Sen. Henry ("Scoop") Jackson, a hawkish Democrat from Washington state. Many published scathing arguments in learned journals of opinion. More and more of them abandoned the Democrats and worked in Republican administrations and think tanks.

In contrast to old-line Republican conservatives, who are inclined to caution and isolationism, neo-cons preach muscular intervention abroad. America can and must both eliminate security threats and build a better world. We should not be shy about

promoting American values in the world, and we should not be timid in taking a leadership role. The world is dangerous, and bad governments should be changed. Some neo-cons served in the Reagan administration and liked his reference to the Soviet Union as an "evil empire." Getting tough with Moscow and increasing U.S. defense spending triggered the fall of the Soviet empire, they claim.

Neo-cons came into their own in the Bush 43 administration. Bush is more of a traditional conservative, but he was influenced by neo-cons. The neo-con *Weekly Standard* magazine became required reading in Washington. Several neo-cons were named to high positions in Defense and State, most prominently political scientist Paul Wolfowitz as Rumsfeld's deputy secretary. According to some accounts, Wolfowitz, who had been obsessed with Iraq for years, immediately after 9/11 emphasized to Bush that Iraq was building weapons of mass destruction and sponsoring terrorism. A neo-con speechwriter, David Frum, is responsible for Bush's "axis of evil" speech. It is still not clear how much influence the neo-cons had on Bush; he may have quickly come to his own conclusions after 9/11 with no help from them.

to fight terrorism, drugs, and crime. We cannot police the entire globe by ourselves; we are already stretched thin. We need their political support and their peacekeeping forces even if they do not contribute to a shooting war. Unilateralism is a cousin of isolationism, and that, as you recall from our discussion of the interwar period, leads to global chaos and aggression that can be stopped only with a major war. The biggest U.S. foreign policy problem now is our tendency to go it alone.

To Lead or Not to Lead?

From our discussions in this chapter, it might seem that a policy of U.S. leadership in the post–Cold War world is infeasible. There are too many obstacles and constraints. Budget deficits, isolationist attitudes, an unsteady Congress, a too-small military, an incoherent structure, and a unilateralist strategy could keep the United States from a leadership role. And that would be a pity. As we will explore in subsequent chapters, the world is chaotic, but the right application of the right kind of power—sometimes economic, sometimes diplomatic, sometimes military, but always in a coalition of partners—at the right time and place, can head off many world problems before they become threats to peace and stability. If we stand back from the world scene, some of these problems will grow until they require drastic measures. Then we will wish we had taken more interest earlier on.

In the words of Theodore Roosevelt, the presidency really is a "bully pulpit." When the president speaks, just about everybody listens. A U.S. president who understands the opportunities now available and who can explain them to the American people and to the world can really put America in a leadership position. The American people also harbor other tendencies that a president could appeal to, such as a feeling of pride that the United States is just and powerful and can lead other nations. Americans enjoy playing a positive role in the world. If we do not lead, no one will.

Key Terms

alarmism (p. 61)

behavioralism (p. 56)

bureaucracies (p. 64)

constraint (p. 59)

Cuban Missile Crisis (p. 64)

deficit (p. 59)

dove (p. 59)

elite (p. 57)

entitlements (p. 59)

foreign policy (p. 54)

idealism (p. 57)

interventionism (p. 54)

Joint Chiefs of Staff (p. 59)

mass (p. 57)

National Security Council (p. 62)

neoconservative (p. 66)

noninterventionism (p. 55)

Pentagon (p. 59)

self-interest (p. 57)

unilateralism (p. 65)

War Powers Act (p. 60)

Key Web Sites

Cuban Missile Crisis, 1962
http://www.seas.gwu.edu/nsarchive/nsa/cuba_mis_cri/cuba_mis_cri.html

War Powers Resolution, 1973
http://www.msstate.edu/Archives/History/USA/20th_C./warpowers.973

National Security Council
http://www.whitehouse.gov/WH/EOP/NSC/html/nschome.html

U.S. Senate Committee on Foreign Relations
http://www.senate.gov/~foreign/

U.S. State Department
http://usinfo.state.gov/

Foreign Affairs magazine
http://www.foreignaffairs.org

Foreign Policy Association
http://www.fpa.org/

Further Reference

Cameron, Fraser. *U.S. Foreign Policy after the Cold War: Global Hegemon or Reluctant Sheriff?*, 2nd ed. New York: Routledge, 2005

Fisher, Louis. *Congressional Abdication on War and Spending*. College Station, TX: Texas A&M Press, 2000.

Fukuyama, Francis. *America at the Crossroads: Democracy, Power and the Neoconservative Legacy*. New Haven, CT: Yale University Press, 2006.

Haass, Richard N. *The Opportunity: America's Moment to Alter History's Course*. Boulder, CO: PublicAffairs, 2005.

Hoffmann, Stanley, with Frédéric Bozo. *Gulliver Unbound: America's Imperial Temptation and the War in Iraq*. Lanham, MD: Rowman & Littlefield, 2004.

Holsti, Ole R. *Public Opinion and American Foreign Policy*. Ann Arbor, MI: University of Michigan Press, 1996.

Jervis, Robert. *American Foreign Policy in a New Era*. New York: Routledge, 2005.

Johnson, Chalmers. *The Sorrows of Empire: Militarism, Secrecy, and the End of the Republic*. New York: Metropolitan, 2005.

Lieven, Anatol, and John Hulsman. *Ethical Realism: A Vision for America's Role in the World*. New York: Pantheon, 2006.

Mandelbaum, Michael. *The Case for Goliath: How America Acts as the World's Government in the 21st Century*. Boulder, CO: PublicAffairs, 2005.

Moens, Alexander. *The Foreign Policy of George W. Bush: Values, Strategy, and Loyalty*. Williston, VT: Ashgate, 2004.

Nye, Joseph S., Jr. *Soft Power: The Means to Success in World Politics.* Boulder, CO: PublicAffairs, 2005.

Prestowitz, Clyde. *Rogue Nation: American Unilateralism and the Failure of Good Intentions.* New York: Basic Books, 2004.

Rothkopf, David. *Running the World: The Inside Story of the National Security Council and the Architects of American Power.* Boulder, CO: PublicAffairs, 2005.

Woodward, Bob. *State of Denial: Bush at War, Part III.* New York: Simon & Schuster, 2006.

CHAPTER 5

FROM RUSSIA TO THE SOVIET UNION

1. What has been the impact of geography on Russia?
2. Who has invaded Russia? Approximately when?
3. Can a country practice an ideological foreign policy?
4. What was Stalin's argument for forced industrialization?
5. Was Stalin paranoid? What evidence is there?
6. What was the Hitler-Stalin Nonaggression Pact?
7. When and how did the Soviet Union enter World War II?
8. What were the main provisions of Yalta?
9. What was the Cold War about and when did it begin?

Consider the impact of geography on U.S. and Russian history. The new United States quickly became master of its continent, taking whatever land it wished by force and/or cash. Few threats came from overseas; the United States entered all its wars by choice. For most of its history, the United States had a small army and navy because it needed little armed power. Large oceans on either side kept would-be adversaries distant.

Russia had no such protection; the original Russia was landlocked and flat as a pancake. Diplomat and historian George Kennan, in his famous 1947 article, suggested that much Soviet foreign policy behavior was forged from "centuries of obscure battles between nomadic forces over the stretches of a vast unfortified plain. Here caution, circumspection, flexibility, and deception are the valuable qualities."

With no natural barriers, Russia was open to easy invasion from both the east and the west. The first Russian state was erased by the **Mongol** hordes in 1240, and much of the population was enslaved. ("Horde" is one of the few Mongol words to make it into English; *ordu* meant a gigantic army on the prowl for conquests.) Americans never faced a horde. Russians still remember the thirteenth century and are racist about the East and its millions of clever, aggressive people.

Ivan III, the Duke of Moscovy, in the fifteenth century pushed back the **Tatars** and built a new Russian state. His grandson, Ivan IV, known as "the Terrible," continued expanding Russia by brutal means in the sixteenth century. To Russians, his "terribleness" is good; it means strong and strict in crushing both foreign invaders and those who would weaken the Russian state from inside. Russians still like such rulers.

There are some remarkable constants to Russian/Soviet **geopolitics**. One has been the struggle for secure, year-round access to the high seas, especially a "warm-water" port that does not ice over in winter. In the early eighteenth century, Peter the Great strove to overcome the landlocked and backward status of the Russia he inherited. He pushed back the Turks to gain access to the Black Sea and the Swedes to gain his "window to the west" on the Baltic, where he built St. Petersburg, a magnificent new capital. Peter was also the first tsar to tour West Europe. Impressed by its advanced industries, he ordered them copied in Russia. Peter thus set the pattern of importation of Western technology and forced modernization from the top down, a pattern that persisted for centuries. Peter was the great expansionist and modernizer of Russia and is highly honored today.

The Baltic, however, freezes in winter, and its exit to the Atlantic is flanked by Denmark and Norway (both now NATO members), making access insecure in time of war or tension. Access to the North Russian ports of Archangel and Murmansk is around Norway's North Cape. On the Pacific, the port of Vladivostok ("master of the East") freezes, and ships leaving it can reach the open sea only under U.S.-Japanese surveillance.

The great prize for Moscow has long been Istanbul and the Turkish Straits. For centuries, tsars longed to liberate the original center of Orthodox Christianity and secure the Straits for the unhindered traffic of Russian warships and merchantmen from the Black Sea. In ten wars over two centuries, Russia pushed back the Ottoman Empire. If Russia had won in World War I, the prize would have been hers, for Turkey fought alongside Germany. Exactly like the tsars, Stalin tried to gain the Straits at the close of World War II, for that would have turned the Black Sea into a Russian lake. For Russia, geopolitics is a constant.

Mongols   Thirteenth-century conquerors of Eurasia. (See page 70.)

Tatars   Descendants of the Mongols (not *Tartars*).

geopolitics   The impact of geography on international politics.

Reflections

PETER WATCHES A MASS HANGING

In a Leningrad (now St. Petersburg) art museum many years ago I heard a guide explain a large painting of Peter the Great on horseback watching the hanging of hundreds of his soldiers. They hadn't been paid in years and had mutinied; therefore they had to hang. When some of the foreign tourists protested that this seemed a little harsh, the guide said no, the discipline was absolutely necessary to keep Russia strong. Looking devotedly at Peter in the painting she sighed, "He was wonderful." Today, few Russians object to Putin's strong-hand rule.

—M. G. R.

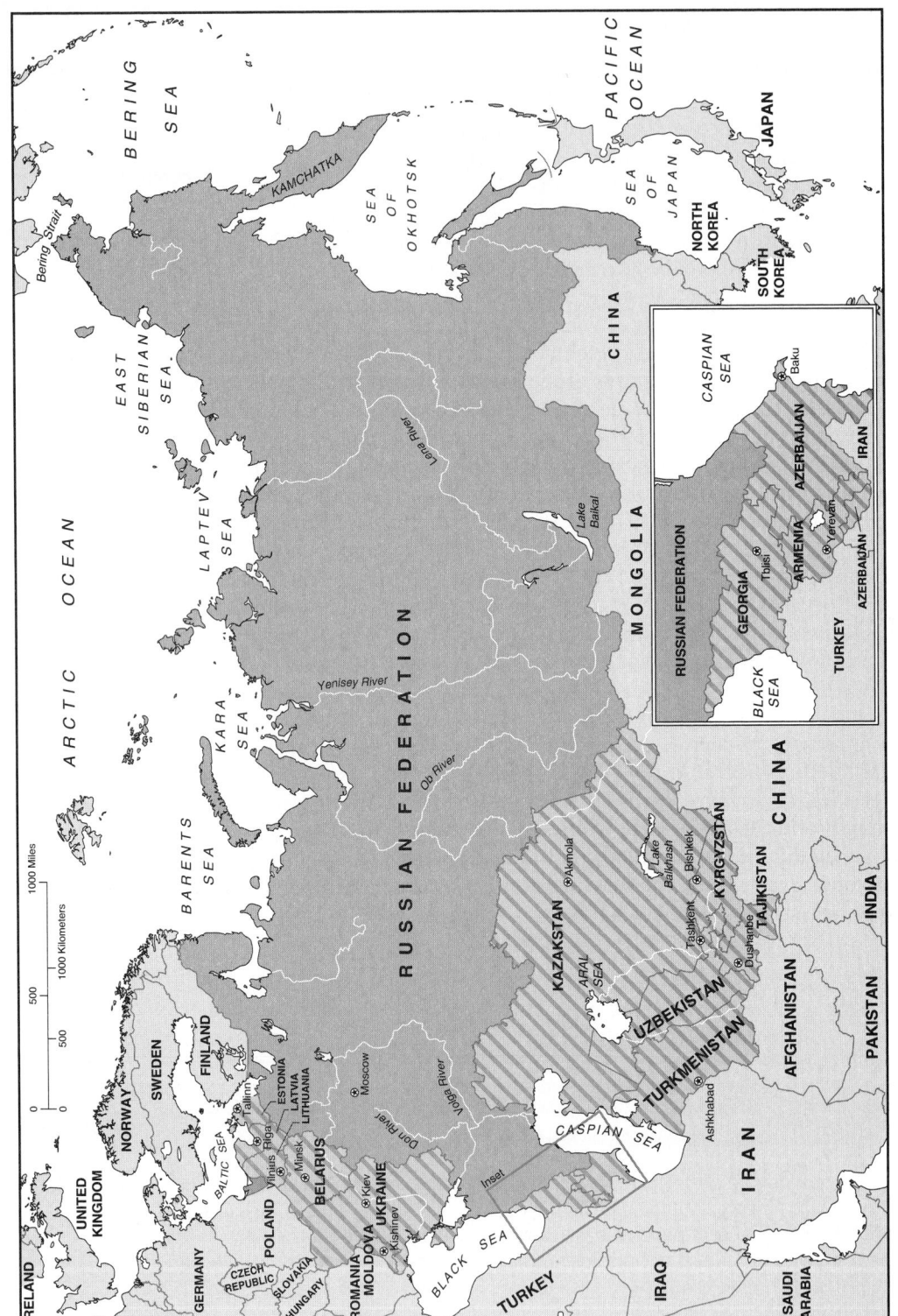

Russia

■ Invasion from the West

The Mongol conquest pulled Russian civilization backward while the rest of Europe expanded intellectually, economically, and militarily. Looking east, various European powers saw Russia as ripe for invasion and plunder. The Teutonic knights pushed eastward along the Baltic, conquering Slavic peoples until stopped by the Russians under Alexander Nevsky in 1242. From 1707 to 1709, a powerful Swedish army under Charles XII battled through Russia until it gave up, exhausted. In 1812 Napoleon actually occupied Moscow. In World War I, German forces penetrated deep into Russia.

Lebensraum German for "living space"; theory that countries must expand to gain room for their population.

In 1941, Hitler assembled the largest army in history—it included not only Germans but Italians, Hungarians, Romanians, and even Spaniards—and sent it to conquer and enslave Russia. The bulk of Hitler's forces were sent against Russia, and the biggest battles of the war occurred in the east. The Soviet Union lost twenty-six million people to the Nazis. The United States in World War II lost fewer than half a million.

Geography

GEOPOLITICS

The study of the effects of geography on international politics sprang up in the nineteenth century, partly to justify imperialist expansion. To think geopolitically, you first need to be looking at a map or possibly a globe. Then you must ask such questions as the following:

- How far is this area from my homeland?
- If this area were in hostile hands, could it be a threat?
- What are the natural barriers to invasion, such as seas or mountains?
- What is the value of this area in terms of natural resources, industry, trade, protection from invasion, or a base for extending influence?
- How costly would it be to extend my influence into this area?
- Could I do it indirectly by means of diplomacy and commerce, or will it take troops?

- If I do move into this area, what new problems will I incur?
- Will the people there welcome me or hate me?

Expansionist leaders ignore these questions and misuse geopolitics to launch wars, often harming themselves. The Nazis embraced a nutty **Lebensraum** geopolitics. Countries tend to define their geopolitical interests too broadly, leading to interventionist foreign policies. When England strove to prevent the domination of the Netherlands or the eastern Mediterranean by a hostile power, it was playing geopolitics. When the United States issued the Monroe Doctrine or took the Philippines, it was playing geopolitics. Moscow still holds traditional geopolitical views and tries to control bordering countries.

■ War and Bolshevism

War has had a far more profound impact on Russia than on the United States. Defeat produced at least two systemic upheavals in Russia. The Mongol conquest led to the founding of the centralized and militarized Russian state under Ivan. World War I led to the collapse of tsarism and the founding of the Bolshevik state under Lenin. War has produced only incremental changes in America, for example, enhanced presidential power. The United States has never gone through national annihilation or, with the exception of our Civil War, national tragedy. The Russians have.

socialism   State ownership of economy to end class differences.

Marxism   Militant, revolutionary form of *socialism.*

mobilization   Getting an army ready for immediate war.

Without war, in fact, there would have been no Soviet Union. The tsarist regime early in the twentieth century had numerous problems but none big enough to bring it down. It was an antiquated political system that attempted to concentrate all power in the hands of the "autocrat," the tsar. Russian intellectuals grew fed up with this system that seemed intent on preserving the past. Many of them turned to **socialism** and **Marxism**, but only a few belonged to the small, underground Russian Social Democratic Labor party.

Russia was changing, though, and in time might have evolved into a constitutional monarchy with popular input. The economy was growing, and new industries were creating both a working class and a middle class. Russia's humiliating defeat in the

Diplomacy

WORLD WAR I: THE SLAVIC CONNECTION

The causes of World War I are many, but one was the resentment of Slavic peoples of Eastern Europe at being part of the Austro-Hungarian Empire. Serbs, Croats, Slovenes, Czechs, Slovaks, and Poles in this multinational empire started to stir in the nineteenth century as they picked up the twin impulses of nationalism and *Pan-Slavism,* the feeling that all the Slavic peoples are related and under the benevolent protection of the largest Slavic nation, Russia. Pan-Slavism was especially important in the Balkans as Serbs, Montenegrins, and Bulgars struggled to free themselves from the Muslim Turks; they turned naturally to their "big brother," the Eastern Christian Russians. Even today, Serbs turn almost instinctively to Russia for help.

Further, Russia's imperial ambitions in the Balkans rivaled those of the Austrians; both pressed southward against the weakening Ottoman Empire. In 1908 Austria annexed Bosnia, which the neighboring independent kingdom of Serbia also claimed. (Notice the similarity to the recent Serbian claim to Bosnia.) In 1914 Bosnian-Serb nationalists assassinated Austrian Archduke Franz-Ferdinand, and Vienna, in revenge, demanded a virtual takeover of Serbia. Belgrade refused, and Austria attacked.

Serbia turned to Russia for help, and the tsar ordered the **mobilization** of the huge Russian army. In the meantime, Germany gave Austria blank-check support to punish the Serbs. The German kaiser, alarmed at the Russian mobilization, also mobilized, and the little war turned into World War I, the seminal catastrophe of the twentieth century. Without the Slavic connection, the war would have been a minor Balkan conflict between Austria and Serbia.

Russo-Japanese War of 1904–1905 triggered the abortive 1905 revolution. The tsar promised a democratically elected parliament, the *Duma* (the name of Russia's parliament today). He let it do little, but it planted the notion of democracy. Without war, evolution rather than revolution would have been Russia's probable path.

ideology	Belief system that society can be improved by following certain doctrines; usually ends in *-ism*.

World War I doomed that. The Russian army was large but backward. Incompetent generals—the same ones who had lost to the Japanese a decade earlier—flung their divisions against the numerically smaller German forces, who ground the Russians to a quick halt. Within a year the eastern front (like the western front in France) was stalemated. By 1916 the Russian army started coming apart; troops mutinied and returned home. Peasants seized their masters' lands. Early the following year, with the economy and army near collapse, a group of moderates seized power and forced Tsar Nicholas II to abdicate.

The Provisional Government, as it was called, knew Russia could not fight Germany much longer but felt duty-bound to stay in the war so as not to betray its Western allies. (America entered World War I only in April 1917 and shipped much material support to North Russia.) But Russia was unable to stay in the war. Spurred by radical agitators, the army further disintegrated. The government—by July it was under moderate Alexander Kerensky—was attacked domestically from both left and right. The left won. In November the Bolsheviks, who had been building their strength on the *soviets* (councils) that dominated the cities, seized power, shot the tsar and his family, and began negotiations with Germany to take Russia out of the war. If Kerensky had taken Russia out of the war earlier, he may have been able to prevent the Bolshevik takeover. Either way, Russia would have left the war.

In getting Russia out of the war, the Bolshevik leaders made at least two mistaken assumptions. First, Lenin had developed an **ideology** according to which revolution might

Turning Point

THE NORTH RUSSIAN INTERVENTION

Few Americans are aware of it, but Russians and Americans have fought each other, at the end of World War I. The western allies were horrified at the Bolsheviks taking Russia out of the war, for that meant the Germans could transfer a million troops from east to west. The Bolsheviks were considered traitors and German agents. Much war material, most of it American, had been sent to the North Russian ports of Archangel and Murmansk, where, it was feared, it would be captured by the advancing Germans. The British and Americans sent small contingents there in 1918. Some thought the West could help the White Russian forces fighting in the civil war, but they could not.

The operation was confused and accomplished nothing. But by the time the war ended in November, the North Russian ports were frozen shut. The Americans had to stay until mid-1919 and they fought minor skirmishes with the newly formed (by Leon Trotsky) Red Army. Americans and Soviets shed each other's blood, albeit not very much of it.

The problem, studied closely by diplomat and historian George Kennan, was that all the British and Americans could think about was winning the war, whereas all the Bolsheviks could think about was consolidating their revolution. Neither side could accept the other's motives as legitimate. Some say the Cold War started in 1918 in North Russia.

Brest-Litovsk   1918 treaty
dictated by Germany to get Russia
out of World War I.

Comintern   Short for Communist
International; the world's
Communist parties under
Moscow's control.

begin in Russia but would soon sweep over the industrialized world. There was indeed much socialist unrest throughout Europe, and Bolsheviks encouraged it. The capitalist war would end with a proletarian revolution, so there need be no formal treaty ending the war, they fantasized.

Lenin's second mistake lay in thinking the Germans would be so delighted to get Russia out of the war they would be lenient in their peace demands. They were not. The Germans demanded large areas of western Russia and an independent Ukraine. Lenin balked. For the first time he was tasting the responsibility of power. Before, he had been a revolutionary trying to overthrow state power. Now, ironically, he was trying to preserve the power of the Russian state. Ideology collided with reality. With Russia weak and disintegrating, in March 1918 Lenin glumly accepted the German *Diktat*. Only Germany's collapse in November (the fresh American troops tipped the balance on the western front) made the **Brest-Litovsk** treaty a dead letter and saved Russian lands from German takeover.

■ Spreading the Revolution

The revolution did not spread, even though War Minister Trotsky sent the new Red Army westward into Poland. There the forces of newly reestablished Poland (it had been divided among Germany, Austria, and Russia for a century and a half) under Pilsudski pushed the Reds back and took more territory for Poland, lands inhabited mostly by Belarussians and Ukrainians that Stalin eventually got back.

By the end of 1920, Lenin realized that the revolution was not going to spread worldwide, and attempts to do so only encouraged the hostile capitalist powers to intervene in Russia. The Reds had not yet won their desperate civil war against the Whites and needed no more enemies. So Lenin dropped efforts to export revolution and concentrated on protecting the Soviet Union and consolidating Communist—as the Bolsheviks now called themselves—power. After 1920, the Soviet Union was cautious about using force to expand.

Instead of military power, Lenin turned to sympathetic socialists all over the world, where socialist parties were splitting into moderate democratic socialists and committed revolutionary socialists who looked to Moscow for guidance. In the years 1920 and 1921, new Communist parties broke off from most socialist parties. The Communists accused the socialists of being unrevolutionary, timid, and soft on capitalism. Communist and socialist parties in Europe became natural enemies; where one was strong, the other was weak.

Lenin instituted a disciplined, centralized international organization, the **Comintern**, and demanded that member parties obey Moscow to the letter and place the good of the Soviet Union—"the world's first socialist country"—above that of their own country. Communists believed that helping the Soviet Union was aiding the cause of socialism and thus followed the most absurd twists and turns of Soviet foreign policy. For believers, communism became a secular religion, with its center in Moscow.

■ Stalin's Policy Mistakes

When Lenin died in 1924 he left no designated heir. One of his last messages, however, urged the Communist party to reject Stalin as "too rude." By then, however, Stalin had gained control of the party structure, using his position as the party's general secretary to handpick supporters for leading party positions. This enabled him to beat and exile Trotsky. By 1927, Stalin was in firm control of both domestic and foreign policy. In 1928 Stalin instituted the first **Five-Year Plan** of forced industrialization and the collectivization of agriculture. Brutally, the Soviet Union became a major industrial power.

Five-Year Plans   Stalin's forced industrialization in the 1930s.

pragmatism   If it works, use it.

Stalin's aim was not just economic growth for its own sake but an industrial basis to enable the Soviet Union to withstand foreign onslaught. In an oft-quoted 1931 speech to managers, Stalin stressed why they needed to maintain the rapid tempo of industrial growth:

> To slow down the tempo means to lag behind. And those who lag behind are beaten. The history of Old Russia shows . . . that because of her backwardness she was constantly being defeated . . . beaten because of backwardness—military, cultural, political, industrial, and agricultural backwardness. . . . We are behind the leading countries by fifty to one hundred years. We must make up this distance in ten years. Either we do it or we go under.

Concepts

IDEOLOGY AND FOREIGN POLICY

An ideology is a belief system or theory that aims to improve society. Usually ideologies end in "ism," as in liberalism, conservatism, socialism, communism, or Islamic fundamentalism. The opposite of ideology is **pragmatism**, but it is often in the service of an ideology. Even Americans have ideological motives, a combination of free market, democracy, and Christianity. Sometimes, of course, ideology is not seriously believed but serves as a mask for pragmatic self-interest.

Can a foreign policy be ideological? Yes, provided it does not cost too much. When it does, ideology goes on the back burner or out the window. A revolutionary regime can start intensely ideological, determined to spread its doctrine, but when it encounters resistance and threats to its very existence, it usually tones down its ideology. Sometimes it becomes completely pragmatic and forgets its ideology. Notice how first Lenin and then Stalin made pragmatic compromises.

Was Soviet foreign policy ideological? It certainly started that way, but very quickly Marxism-Leninism became entwined with Soviet national interest. Russia was the first Communist country, so its interests were the same as communism's. That was the line Lenin and Stalin used on gullible Communists around the world. What's good for Russia is good for communism, they argued. This was ideology in the service of national interest.

Notice also Stalin's ideological flip-flops: First ignore the Nazis (early 1930s), then work against the Nazis (mid-1930s), and later make a deal with the Nazis (1939). With every zigzag Stalin offered ideological excuses that faithful Communists accepted. Stalin was simply practicing cynical power politics designed chiefly to keep Stalin powerful. Take strongly ideological foreign policies with a grain of salt. They are usually either temporary fanaticism or disguised pragmatic self-interest.

paranoid Unreasonably
suspicious of others.

Spanish Civil War   1936–1939
conflict in which Nazis and
Communists aided opposite sides.

Many hold that Stalin was **paranoid**. He started fearing that Trotsky, expelled from the Soviet Union in 1929, still had supporters inside the Communist party and Red Army, which he had founded. Chronically insecure, in 1934 Stalin instituted the Great Purge, which killed perhaps a million party comrades—including all generals and most colonels—on suspicion of being suspicious. At this same time, Stalin had millions of ordinary Soviets—farmers who resisted collectivization, workers late to work, ethnic minorities—arrested and sent to Siberia, where most died in slave-labor projects. All together, over fifteen million Soviets died under Stalin's orders. This is not the working of a normal mind. (Iraq's Saddam Hussein modeled himself on Stalin.)

In foreign policy, Stalin, who had no experience with other countries, made dreadful mistakes. In the late 1920s he ordered the Chinese Communist party to affiliate with the Nationalists; he argued that China was not ready for a proletarian revolution. Chiang Kai-shek massacred the Communists, who started having success only when, under Mao Zedong, they ignored Stalin. The roots of the Sino-Soviet conflict go back to Stalin's bad advice.

In Europe, too, Stalin misunderstood the situation. Here he told Communist parties to keep their distance from "bourgeois" parties and not cooperate with them, not even with socialists. When the Depression hit Germany, the Nazi vote grew rapidly. Only one combination could have stopped Hitler, a joint Social Democrat-Communist front, which Stalin rejected. He ordered the German Communists to call the Social Democrats "social fascists," as bad as Hitler. After Hitler took power in 1933, Communists and Social Democrats alike paid for Stalin's blunder with their lives.

Turning Point

THE SPANISH CIVIL WAR

In the 1930s the weak Spanish Republic split in two. General Franco's conservative Nationalists rebelled against the leftist Popular Front government in 1936. The bitter Civil War that ended with Franco's victory in 1939 was a curtain raiser and proving ground for World War II. Mussolini and Hitler immediately came to Franco's aid and tried out their aerial bombardment techniques. Stalin had the Comintern recruit the International Brigades and sold the Republic tanks and artillery. Some thirty-two hundred Americans fought for the Republic in the Lincoln Brigade; half of them perished.

The Communists, under Stalin's orders, played a very moderate role during the **Spanish Civil War**. They actually crushed Trotskyites and Anarchists who wanted a proletarian revolution. Stalin's idea here was to convince the British and French—who stayed neutral while fascists murdered a sister democracy—that the Soviets could be reliable partners in opposing fascism. Too late, London and Paris realized that Hitler and Mussolini were just sharpening their knives in Spain and that the other democracies would be next.

Realizing his mistake much too late, Stalin then ordered the Comintern to work for "popular fronts" with any and all antifascist parties. Communists now tried to explain that they were really just democrats who were trying to put an end to fascism. Popular Front governments were briefly in power in France and Spain. Stalin's idea in the second half of the 1930s was to get Britain and France as allies against a rearming Germany that was rabidly anti-Communist.

nonaggression pact Treaty to not attack each other.

Winter War Stalin's invasion of Finland, 1939–1940.

London and Paris were too war-weary and anti-Communist to accept Stalin's offer. Who could trust Stalin? After they failed to respond to his overtures for an anti-Hitler coalition, Stalin pulled the most amazing and cynical reversal of modern history: He made a deal with Hitler. All over the world, Communists were stunned (many quit the party) at the 1939 Hitler-Stalin **nonaggression pact**. Stalin likely reasoned that if the British and French refused to work together with him to block Hitler, his only recourse was to protect the Soviet Union by a treaty that would leave Britain and France to face Germany alone.

Part of the blame here must be placed on the rigidity and stupidity of the London and Paris governments of that time. Standing together with Moscow against Hitler, the three could have prevented World War II. Instead, at Munich in 1938, Britain and France handed Czechoslovakia to Hitler. In Stalin's paranoid vision, the British and French were trying to get the German war machine aimed eastward, at the Soviet Union. Stalin simply turned the tables on them with the nonaggression pact. A week after the pact was signed, Hitler invaded Poland in September 1939, the official start of World War II. Stalin quickly occupied the eastern third of Poland—that was a secret part of the agreement—thus getting back the territory Poland had taken in 1921.

Diplomacy

THE WINTER WAR

In late 1939, Stalin was both impressed with the rapid German conquest of Poland and worried that the Finnish border was too close to Leningrad (formerly and now again St. Petersburg), his second-largest city. Finland, where the Whites had beaten the Reds two decades before, was friendly with Germany. Stalin offered Helsinki some territory further north in exchange for land near Leningrad. The Finns, fearing a trick to breach their defenses, refused, and Stalin attacked. Not only would he get the territory, he figured, but he'd show Hitler that the Soviet Union could do in Finland what the Germans had just done in Poland.

It was a blunder. The Red Army had been decimated by Stalin's purges and suffered enormous casualties at the hands of the hardy and tenacious Finns. Finally, in March 1940, the Finns had to settle, but the **Winter War** showed how weak the Soviet Union was and thus encouraged Hitler to invade in 1941.

■ The Great Patriotic War

The Hitler-Stalin Pact of 1939–1941 was strange and unstable. The blood-enemy Nazis and Communists stopped cursing each other. The Soviet Union shipped much grain and petroleum to Germany. French Communists disparaged their own country's war effort. Stalin thought Britain and France, both of which had declared war when Hitler invaded Poland,

Stalin in his office at the Kremlin, 1938. (Central State Archives of Cinematographic and Photo Documents/The New York Times/NYT Photos)

would be about an even match for Germany. The two sides would exhaust themselves and leave the Soviet Union as the strongest power in Europe. But that did not happen. In May and June 1940, the "phony war" ended as German tank columns slashed through the north of France. Members of the French government fled to England, and aged Marshal Pétain signed a humiliating peace with the German occupiers. Britain stood alone, and some thought it would crumble.

Stalin had made another blunder. Instead of an exhausted Germany, the Soviet Union now faced a triumphant Germany. Still, Stalin thought Hitler would leave him alone. The Soviets even made fairly stiff territorial demands when they took over the Baltic states of Lithuania, Latvia, and Estonia as well as a part of Romania called Moldavia. This angered Hitler and attracted his attention eastward again, to his old first hate, the Slavic people in general and Communists in particular. In late 1940 he gave orders for a huge military buildup for the invasion of the Soviet Union the following year.

One puzzle is why Stalin let the Soviet Union be taken by surprise in the Nazi attack of June 1941. Stalin had received over a hundred intelligence reports about the attack—some from his own spies—but he refused to believe them. Intelligence is worthless if you don't believe it. The British also informed Stalin of the impending invasion they had gleaned from breaking German codes, but paranoid Stalin smelled a British trick to pull him into the war.

Stalin's orders were firm: We are friendly with the Germans; therefore there will be no invasion. Stalin had built his policy on the Hitler-Stalin Pact and could not admit error, for that might give enemies a chance to bring him down. Paranoids always have to be right. When the invasion hit, Stalin had a nervous breakdown; he disappeared into his Kremlin apartment for two weeks. When he emerged, however, he rallied the Soviet people successfully. Moscow's line for years was that the Soviets knew all along what Hitler was up to and used the time to prepare. Why then were they caught so unprepared?

Barbarossa ("Red Beard," the name of a German king who perished on a crusade) nearly succeeded. Over half a million Soviet soldiers were captured during the first month. Russia is geographically tough to conquer, though. As an invader penetrates eastward, his supply lines become long and the front expands as Russia becomes broader. Mud in spring and snow in winter slow movement. The Russian winter is fierce, and the German troops had no winter clothing. Hitler was confident they would soon be in winter quarters. In November German troops neared Moscow, but there they stalled. Winter came early, and reinforcements from Siberia held the line. By early 1943, with the Nazi defeat at Stalingrad, perceptive Germans knew they could not win.

From then on, the Soviet army pushed the Germans painfully across East Europe back to Berlin. When the war in Europe ended in May 1945, the Soviets had won not by superior weapons, leadership, or tactics—the German army was far better in these areas—but by letting the foe exhaust himself in the attack and then pushing him back by means of greater manpower. It was a costly and traditional way to wage war, but it saved Russia.

> **Yalta** Early 1945 agreement by Stalin, Churchill, and Roosevelt on who got what in Germany and East Europe.

Yalta

In early 1945, the Big Three wartime leaders—Roosevelt, Churchill, and Stalin—met in the Soviet Crimean resort of Yalta to decide the fate of East and Central Europe. Some Republicans accused Roosevelt and the Democrats of giving East Europe to the Soviets at **Yalta**. The word "Yalta" became synonymous with "treason." Yalta was sloppy diplomacy but not treason. The Soviet army had already conquered most of the territories in question and was not about to give any back. It was not yet clear how far east the Allies would get; they could have taken more of Germany and Czechoslovakia.

The two sides at Yalta also had different definitions of the "democracy" that was to come to East Europe. The West meant liberal democracy, with parties competing in free and fair elections. The Soviets meant "people's democracy," the ouster of capitalists and conservatives, with power going to the "party of workers" (i.e., the Communists). The misunderstandings over Yalta were part of the causes of the Cold War.

Diplomacy

THE YALTA AGREEMENT

1. Poland would get new borders, losing territory in the east to the Soviet Union and gaining it in the west from Germany. In effect, Poland was picked up and moved over 100 miles westward.

2. The countries of East Europe would be democratic and friendly with the Soviet Union.

3. Germany would be divided into three (later four, when France was added) zones for temporary military occupation. Berlin would be likewise divided.

4. Germany would be disarmed and would pay heavy reparations for the damage it had caused, especially to the Soviet Union.

■ The Cold War

The **Cold War** was the period of political and military tension between the United States and the Soviet Union that followed World War II. Some writers say the Soviet refusal to depart from northern Iran after the war triggered the hostility in 1946. Others say the Truman Doctrine of 1947 (see page 30) was the beginning. Still others say the 1948 Berlin blockade and airlift signaled the start. The main underlying element to the Cold War, however, was the Soviet takeover and communization of the nations of East Europe from 1945 to 1948. Every time Stalin installed another Communist government in East Europe, the West became angrier at Stalin for repudiating the Yalta agreement—which called for free and democratic governments in Europe—and more fearful that he was ready to move into West Europe.

Cold War   Period of armed tension between Soviet Union and West, roughly 1947 to 1989.

The Cold War probably crested with the 1962 Cuban missile crisis, but some feel it ended with Nixon's and Kissinger's efforts at détente in the early 1970s. A few think it then revived with the Soviet invasion of Afghanistan in 1979, becoming Cold War II. But most now think the Cold War lasted until the Berlin Wall fell in late 1989.

The Cold War shows the paradox of the insecure empire. By the end of World War II, Stalin had achieved what the tsars had only dreamed about. Russia was the most powerful European nation and was protected by a security belt across East Europe. But within two to three years this very fact had so alarmed the Western nations, now led by the United States, that they rearmed and opposed the Soviet Union in every corner of the globe. Stalin had called into life a hostile coalition of virtually all the other industrialized countries in the world. Stalin, who used to warn his subjects of "capitalist encirclement," created precisely that. The more secure the Soviets tried to become, the greater insecurities they faced. The insecure tsarist empire had become the insecure Soviet empire.

Classic Thought

KISSINGER ON ABSOLUTE SECURITY

"Absolute security for one power means absolute insecurity for all the others," wrote Harvard political scientist Henry Kissinger, who later served Nixon as national security advisor and secretary of state. Kissinger had concluded that a revolutionary country—such as France after 1789—has good reason to feel insecure and fearful that other states will try to snuff out its revolution before it becomes a threat to them. Therefore, the revolutionary state can feel secure only by crushing all neighbors. This explains Napoleon and his compulsion to conquer all of Europe.

Kissinger thought it also explained the Soviet drive to expand its power. The Soviet Union, a revolutionary country in a world of conservative powers who hated it, could become secure only by destroying all potential rivals. The insecurity of revolutionary states thus naturally fuels expansionist tendencies. But by attempting to obtain perfect security, an impossibility, the insecure nation makes all other nations highly nervous, and they seek to counteract the menace by building their own power. It was a profound insight, and one that explains Soviet behavior and the Cold War in general.

Key Terms

Brest-Litovsk (p. 76)

Cold War (p. 82)

Comintern (p. 76)

Five-Year Plans (p. 77)

geopolitics (p. 71)

ideology (p. 75)

Lebensraum (p. 73)

Marxism (p. 74)

mobilization (p. 74)

Mongols (p. 71)

nonaggression pact (p. 79)

paranoid (p. 78)

pragmatism (p. 77)

socialism (p. 74)

Spanish Civil War (p. 78)

Tatars (p. 71)

Winter War (p. 79)

Yalta (p. 81)

Key Web Sites

A Chronology of Russian History by Bucknell University
http://www.bucknell.edu/departments/russian/chrono.html

History of Russia by the Russian National Tourist Office
http://www.interknowledge.com/russia/rushis01.htm

The Marxism/Leninism Project
http://www.idbsu.edu/surveyrc/Staff/jaynes/marxism/marxism.htm

Further Reference

Dallas, Gregor. *1945: The War That Never Ended.* New Haven, CT: Yale University Press, 2006.

Gaddis, John Lewis. *We Now Know: Rethinking Cold-War History.* New York: Oxford University Press, 1997.

Kennan, George F. *Russia and the West under Lenin and Stalin.* Boston, MA: Little, Brown, 1961.

Lieven, Dominic. *Empire: The Russian Empire and Its Rivals.* New Haven, CT: Yale University Press, 2002.

Merridale, Catherine. *Ivan's War: The Red Army, 1941–1945.* New York: Metropolitan, 2006.

Murphy, David E. *What Stalin Knew: The Enigma of Barbarossa.* New Haven, CT: Yale University Press, 2005.

Pipes, Richard. *Russia under the Bolshevik Regime.* New York: Knopf, 1994.

Powaski, Ronald E. *The Cold War: The United States and the Soviet Union, 1917–1991.* New York: Oxford University Press, 1997.

Read, Anthony, and David Fisher. *The Deadly Embrace: Hitler, Stalin and the Nazi-Soviet Pact, 1939–1941.* New York: Norton, 1988.

Sempa, Francis P. *Geopolitics: From the Cold War to the 21st Century.* Somerset, NJ: Transaction, 2002.

Trenin, Dmitri. *The End of Eurasia: Russia on the Border between Geopolitics and Globalization.* Washington, D.C.: Carnegie Endowment, 2002.

Ulam, Adam B. *Stalin: The Man and His Era.* New York: Viking, 1973.

———. *Expansion and Coexistence: Soviet Foreign Policy, 1917–1973,* 2nd ed. New York: Praeger, 1974.

CHAPTER 6

FROM THE SOVIET UNION BACK TO RUSSIA

QUESTIONS TO CONSIDER

1. How did we perceive the Soviet Union? Were our perceptions accurate?
2. How did Khrushchev start the Sino-Soviet split?
3. What was Soviet hegemony over East Europe?
4. What is the difference between *détente* and *entente?*
5. How was Afghanistan for the Soviets like Vietnam for us?
6. How did productivity trip up Soviet economic growth?
7. Was it possible to reform the Soviet system?
8. What is the theory of imperial overstretch?
9. How is Russia a continuing problem?

During the Cold War, many American analysts and politicians portrayed a powerful Soviet Union expanding relentlessly. Fear and **worst-casing** led us to overestimate Soviet power. We now see that the Soviet giant had feet of clay and was declining at an accelerating rate. Its army devoured one quarter of the economy. Its empire drained it in subsidies. Its technology fell farther behind every decade. Chronic shortages were producing massive discontent. Hatred fumed among the Soviet nationalities.

U.S. politicians, academics, and journalists did a poor job in alerting us to the extent of Soviet decay. When Soviet power collapsed between 1989 and 1991, analysts could see that they had overestimated Soviet strength for decades. We now see that the Soviet Union headed into difficulties both at home and abroad after the death of Stalin in 1953. The problem is a permanent one in human psychology: how to perceive clearly. (More on *misperception* theory in Chapter 12.)

■ Khrushchev and the Loss of China

After Stalin died, Kremlin chiefs competed for power. By 1955, Nikita Khrushchev, party general secretary, followed Stalin's path by naming his supporters to key positions and stacking the deck to beat his rivals. He still faced opposition within the party, namely thousands of mini-Stalins, stodgy bureaucrats who fought economic innovation and retarded growth. How to get rid of them? At the 1956 party congress, where Khrushchev thought he was speaking behind closed doors, he delivered a stinging, hours-long denunciation of the "crimes of Stalin" that included everything from blunders in the war to murdering party comrades. In this way, Khrushchev thought he could shake loose Stalin's influence and more firmly establish his own power. Khrushchev intended the speech to have a purely domestic impact.

worst-casing Tendency to see enemy as stronger than he is. (See page 85.)

But nothing is purely domestic anymore—a point sometimes lost on American politicians—and soon the speech leaked out with disastrous international consequences. All over the world, Communists who had been worshipping Stalin suddenly learned that the terrible things long said in the West about Stalin were true. Everywhere, Communist parties split; many members quit in disgust. In Hungary, radically reformist Communists took over until Soviet tanks intervened. The same thing nearly happened in Poland.

In China, Mao Zedong had not been consulted about Khrushchev's speech and opposed it. Even though Mao did not slavishly follow Stalin, Mao still used Stalin as a symbol and

Concepts

HEGEMONY

Hegemony, from the Greek "to lead," means holding sway over other lands. Powerful countries are said to have hegemony over weak neighbors when they can to some degree control their foreign and domestic policies. During the Cold War, the Soviet Union was clearly the hegemonic power in East Europe. Some argue that the United States exercises hegemony over Central America.

Countries are driven to practice hegemony— and few countries admit to practicing it, for it connotes a kind of imperialism—by the fear of being made vulnerable. Moscow calculated that it needed East Europe as a defensive shield. Washington strongly dislikes hostile powers establishing footholds in the Western hemisphere. Both felt they had to extend their control and influence because if they did not, someone else would take what were deemed vital areas. This is the "contingent necessity" argument, and it is almost always a winner: "If we don't take it, someone else will." This is the kind of geopolitical argument that is accepted uncritically and sometimes foolishly in times of tension.

The trouble with hegemony is that the underdog countries detest it. Most Central Europeans, for example, hated Soviet hegemony and were unreliable allies. Some West Europeans resented U.S. hegemony; Paris still feels this way. Hegemony wins few long-term friends.

he disliked the impulsive and reckless Khrushchev for damaging the world Communist movement. Mao repudiated Khrushchev's leadership and took China on ultraradical paths in both foreign and domestic policy. Mao called for world revolution just as Khrushchev was warning against the dangers of nuclear war. In 1960, the Soviet Union yanked all its foreign aid and experts from China. The two called each other "revisionist," a Communist swear word. China revived old border claims going back to tsarist days, and in 1969 the two sides skirmished on their Manchurian border.

hegemony   Leading or dominating other countries.

Balkans   Easternmost Mediterranean peninsula.

legitimacy   Citizens feeling that government's rule is rightful.

Central Europe   That part of Europe between Germany and Russia.

This split helped drive China toward the United States. As the Americans withdrew from Vietnam in the early 1970s, Beijing started perceiving the Soviet Union as its biggest threat. Feelers went out, leading to President Nixon's 1972 visit to China, a process that culminated in full diplomatic relations in 1979. The relationship was a plus for both sides. The Soviets had to keep about one-quarter of their army on the long Sino-Soviet border. China did not have to fear the two superpowers ganging up on her, but the Soviets had to worry about a U.S.–China combination aimed against them. The loss of China shattered the Soviet bloc and contributed to the decline of communism as a global force. Nixon must be given credit for this clever balance-of-power diplomacy.

■ Restive East Europe

Through the long Cold War, East Europe seemed to be trapped permanently under Soviet **hegemony**. Stalin, Khrushchev, Brezhnev, and even initially Gorbachev swore they would never give up the broad belt from the Baltic through the **Balkans** that served as Russia's defensive shield. In 1989, the Soviets gave up East Europe.

East Europe caused difficulties for Moscow from the beginning. Stalin's takeover of the region brought an American response, the origin of the Cold War. This meant massive military expenditures and blocked improvement of relations with the West. Stalin initially robbed the East European lands, but his successors found they had to calm them by sweetheart deals on Soviet raw materials, especially oil. Maintaining the East Europeans—who had higher living standards than Russians—thus was an expensive subsidy from the Kremlin.

One Communist country, Yugoslavia, slipped out of the Soviet camp in 1948 because of Stalin's clumsy handling of Tito, who refused to be his puppet. Albania departed in 1961 to pursue an ultraradical Mao-type policy. As for the others, there was no end of difficulties. Most East Europeans disliked the Soviets, and most accorded their local Communist regimes little **legitimacy**. In **Central Europe** there were anti-Communist movements and uprisings, most of which were brutally put down. This, of course, solved nothing; it just made Central Europeans hate the Soviets more and prolonged the Cold War with the West. Eventually, Mikhail Gorbachev was able to perceive that the costs of retaining this empire were too high.

East Europe

Khrushchev and the Cuban Missiles

The Cold War peaked in October 1962 when U.S. spy planes showed the Soviets building missile bases in Cuba. The world was never closer to nuclear war. The crisis originated in 1957 when the Soviet Union stunned the world with the first earth-orbiting satellite, *Sputnik* ("fellow traveler"). America panicked, for it seemed to prove that the Soviets were ahead of us in missile strength. Young Senator John F. Kennedy used the phrase "missile gap" to describe our peril and help him win the presidency (narrowly) in 1960. Like President Reagan two decades later, Kennedy embarked on a major defense buildup that stressed more and better missiles. Actually, the United States had always been ahead in missile strength, but it took Washington a while to realize this. In the meantime, the Department of Defense cranked up a big missile program.

The Kremlin viewed this with alarm. The Americans were now surging even further ahead in missiles. Soviet military rockets were few, short-range, and inaccurate, and Soviet generals knew it. The missile gap favored the Americans. How to fix the imbalance? Khrushchev came up with a quick and cheap fix to the range problem: Put some missiles in Cuba. Besides, Castro had asked for protection from the United States.

Word leaked out from Cuba that something was up, and a U2 camera plane on October 14 confirmed the worst: The Soviets were constructing missile bases and were nearly finished. The president's top advisors huddled nonstop. (For more on U.S. decision making at this time, see pages 33 and 64.) Kennedy chose a naval blockade because it stopped short of shooting at Russians and gave them a way out. Decades later, it was learned that

Geography

CRUSHING REBELLIONS IN CENTRAL EUROPE

At one time or another, every country of Central Europe rebelled against communism and Soviet control. Note that they did not start until 1953; Stalin's death fostered the hope that things might soon get better. At no time could the Kremlin regard Central Europe, Russia's supposed defensive shield, as permanently pacified. Note also that there were no rebellions in the Balkans. Any ideas about what might explain this difference?

- Czechoslovakia, 1953: Antiregime rioting broke out in Pilsen and started spreading; crushed by Soviet forces.
- East Germany, 1953: East Berlin workers, fed up with conditions, protested and then rioted, and unrest started spreading throughout East Germany; crushed by Soviet tanks.
- Hungary, 1956: The most famous and bloodiest uprising. Intellectuals' criticism of the regime led to a Budapest demonstration that police fired on. Mobs murdered secret policemen, and the liberal Communist Imre Nagy (rhymes with "lodge") took power. The Soviets pretended to pull out, then invaded and battled through Budapest's streets. Nagy was promised safe conduct but was arrested and shot.
- Poland, 1956: At this same time, Poles rioted against a regime of rigid Stalinists. Soviet tanks almost rolled, but at the last minute Warsaw brought in a new Communist leader, Gomulka, who had been imprisoned under Stalin.
- Czechoslovakia, 1968: The "Prague Spring" blossomed when the old Stalinist chief was bumped by reformist Alexander Dubcek, who began dismantling socialism amid popular joy. Soviet tanks rolled in August to oust Dubcek—but not kill him—and put in the conservative Husak.
- Poland, 1970 and 1980–1981: A series of worker strikes, starting at the Gdansk shipyards, toppled one corrupt Party chief after another and led to the formation of Solidarity, a giant union that enrolled nearly a third of all Poles and eventually brought down the Communist regime.

WHO WAS WHEN: SOVIET LEADERS AND THEIR ACCOMPLISHMENTS		
Party Chief	**Ruled**	**Main Accomplishments**
Vladimir I. Lenin	1917–1924	Led Revolution; took Russia out of World War l; beat Whites in Civil War.
Josef Stalin	1927–1953	Forced industrialization; made pact with Hitler; beat Germany in World War II; took East Europe; made China ally.
Nikita Khrushchev	1955–1964	Crushed Hungarian uprising; gained influence in Egypt; made Cuba an ally; boosted missile strength; alienated Mao's China.
Leonid Brezhnev	1964–1982	Gained Soviet clients in Angola, Ethiopia, South Yemen, and Syria; achieved brief détente and then military parity with U.S.; invaded Afghanistan.
Yuri Andropov	1982–1984	None–tenure too brief.
Konstantin Chernenko	1984–1985	None–tenure too brief.
Mikhail Gorbachev	1985–1991	Pulled out of Afghanistan; INF treaty with Reagan; attempted to reform system but only collapsed it.

détente   Relaxation of tensions between hostile countries.

the Soviets already had three dozen nuclear warheads in Cuba; if we had invaded they would have used them. We would have retaliated, and a nuclear World War III would have started.

As the Soviet ships with oblong crates on their decks steamed toward Cuba, the world held its breath. The ships stopped and then turned back, and the Kremlin offered a deal: no Soviet missiles in Cuba if Washington promised not to invade. It was a good face-saving solution, but it hurt Khrushchev in Kremlin politics, and two years later the Politburo voted him out of office for both foreign and domestic "harebrained schemes." He really was rather impulsive.

■ Brezhnev and Détente

Vowing to work for "a generation of peace," President Nixon in the early 1970s took steps to relax tensions with the Soviet Union. The time seemed right for it. The American people and Congress were sick of the Vietnam War; they wanted to end the draft and to reduce military spending. Nixon promised to deliver on both. Domestic pressures set the scene for Nixon's **détente**.

Nixon visited Moscow, signed a treaty limiting missiles (SALT I), and encouraged trade with the Soviet Union. It looked like the Cold War was giving way to a new era of businesslike negotiations. Then things began to go wrong. Starting in 1973, the Nixon presidency was paralyzed by the Watergate scandal, which led to Nixon's resignation in 1974.

Powerful congressional voices on the left and right attacked détente. The Soviets did not play by what the Americans thought
were the ground rules of détente. They built up their missile
strength and increased their troops in East Europe. They picked
up new clients in the Third World. They persecuted Jews at home. Many Americans, especially in the right wing of the Republican party, believed the United States was being
deceived. Détente failed because Moscow was not ready for it.

> **republic**   Main Soviet/Russian civil division, like U.S. state.

Afghanistan: A Soviet Vietnam

In 1989, after nearly a decade of fighting, the last Soviet troops withdrew from
Afghanistan. Afghanistan was a catastrophe for the Soviets, much as Vietnam had been
for America. Both nations learned the hard way that intervention in the Third World is
difficult and dangerous.

On an extremely elite basis, a handful of elderly Brezhnev cronies in 1979 ordered the
Soviet military into a bad situation. Several reasons have been suggested. First, a Communist regime—that had taken over in a coup in 1978—was threatened with overthrow
and needed help. Second, if the Afghan *mujahedin* (Muslim holy warriors) won, they would
spread their creed into the restive Soviet Muslim **republics**. Third, Soviet control of

Diplomacy

DÉTENTE

French for "relaxation of tensions," in traditional diplomatic usage détente meant that two countries moved a step away from armed hostility. That
was all. It did not mean the hostile powers established a new, peaceful relationship. As used
by Nixon and Kissinger in the early 1970s, however, the term suggested a new era of peace between the United States and the Soviet Union.
Overused and oversold, détente became a dirty
word by the 1976 presidential campaign, implying giving in to the Russians, and was never used
after that.

Two Stanford professors—historian Gordon
Craig and political scientist Alexander George—
emphasized that the move from hostility to trust
takes many steps, all of them reversible. In classic
diplomacy, the first step away from armed tension
was *détente.* If the process went further, the two
countries achieved a *rapprochement,* French for

approaching each other, getting together again
to establish reasonable relations. If that worked,
they might go on to reach an *entente,* a mutual
understanding of who had what turf. And if that
succeeded, one side could conceivably offer the
other a goodwill token, called in classic diplomacy *appeasement,* a term that became a swear
word after Chamberlain tried to appease Hitler in
1938. Eventually, if the two countries saw a mutual advantage, they could even form an *alliance,*
a pact to help defend each other.

The seventeenth- and eighteenth-century prac-
titioners of diplomacy understood that these stages
could not be rushed or skipped over. The process
might stall at any stage or even go back to hostility. Craig and George indicate that Nixon and
Kissinger should have observed the caution of traditional diplomacy and not have pretended that a
détente was a rapprochement or entente.

Afghanistan would put them near the strategic Strait of Hormuz, through which passes much of the world's oil.

The costs for the Soviets were high. They kept some 120,000 troops in Afghanistan; about 15,000 Soviets died. Like the United States in Vietnam, there was no end in sight for the Soviets in Afghanistan. The Soviet public was told little about the war, only that it was their "internationalist duty" to defend the Soviet motherland against Afghan bandits backed by the United States. Many disbelieved this official line. Returning Soviet servicemen told of a dirty war and serious morale and drug problems among the troops; dozens defected.

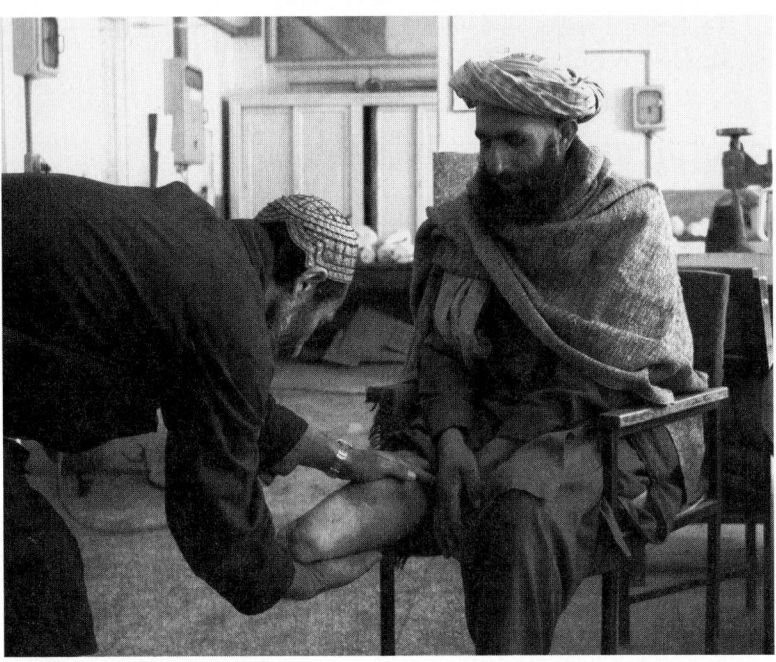

Countless Afghans lost limbs by stepping on land mines dating back from the Soviet Union's war in Afghanistan, from 1979 to 1989. (Ozier Muhammad/The New York Times)

The Afghan war cost the Soviet Union friends and influence, especially in the Muslim world. Moscow's détente with the United States crashed. President Jimmy Carter declared he "learned more about the Soviets in one week" than in all previous years. He began a U.S. arms buildup, canceled grain sales to the Soviet Union, and pulled the American team out of the 1980 Moscow Olympics. The harsher international climate increased burdens on the Soviet Union and contributed to the system's collapse a few years later. The year of the Soviet pullout, 1989, is the year the Kremlin also lost East Europe. With the opening of the Berlin Wall in November 1989, the Cold War was effectively over. The cause: Soviet weakness.

■ Why the Soviet Collapse?

Marx theorized that capitalism has to produce a series of depressions and an angry working class. Eventually, there will be a depression so big and a working class so angry that they will seize power and usher in a new system, socialism. Capitalism was doomed; socialism—meaning here state ownership of the means of production—was sure to come. About the only people who believe this now are found on a few U.S. college campuses. Marx was right that the economic system underpins everything else, but it turns out that socialism is the defective system, not capitalism.

There are at least two ways you can get economic growth. The first is by dumping more **inputs** into the system: labor, capital, raw materials, and energy. You mobilize every resource to increase production. The second way is to become more efficient, using labor, capital, and so on to produce more outputs with the same or fewer inputs. Economists argue that only the second way yields long-term, sustainable economic growth. The Soviets boosted production but not **productivity**, the efficiency with which things are produced. On the first path, you eventually run out of inputs. With the second path, you make gradual gains in productivity, largely technological, that you can keep up forever—as long as you get new ideas—and gradually make your economy more efficient. As a gas company ad says, "The future belongs to the efficient."

inputs The ingredients of economic growth: labor, capital, raw materials, energy.

productivity How efficiently goods are produced—that is, using fewer *inputs.*

The Soviet economy had high production but low productivity. It turned out lots of poor-quality goods inefficiently because it was technologically backward. In a centrally directed economy, there are few plans, money, people, or incentives to innovate and become more efficient. Some Soviet economists knew this, and under the brief Khrushchev "thaw" in the early 1960s they suggested market-type reforms to invigorate the Soviet economy. None were implemented and with Khrushchev's ouster in 1964 would-be reformers laid low.

From the 1930s through the 1960s, the Soviet system showed impressive growth, but it was due to more and more inputs, not to greater efficiency. By the early 1970s, many of the inputs had reached their limit, but productivity was still low. Soviet economic growth

Concepts

ELITES

Political scientists call the top or most influential people in a political system its "elites," the people with real political clout. Exactly who is an elite is hard to say, but they are a small fraction of 1 percent of the population. Although few elites are poor, they are not necessarily the richest people.

Typically, a country has several elites: a governmental elite of top officeholders, an industrial elite, a military elite, and so on. Countries may have specialized elites: a party elite in the Soviet Union or a Muslim theocratic elite in Iran. Much of political life consists of struggles, often out of public sight, among and within elites to control the country's direction. Typically, the masses then follow.

Most thinkers agree that foreign policy is inherently an elite game. Often only a handful of people formulate a country's foreign policies. In the United States, it is the National Security Council with occasional consultation with top members of Congress. In the Soviet Union, it was the Politburo, the dozen or so people at the top of the Communist party structure.

Diplomats use a nation's capital as shorthand for the country's foreign-policy elite. They say "Paris" or "Moscow" instead of France or Russia. This is more accurate than saying "the Russians," as 99.999 percent of Russians have no say in foreign policy. Try to avoid "they" in reference to citizens of other countries, as it suggests "they" are united in hostility toward us. Americans often discover that people in hostile countries are quite friendly to Americans. Governments and peoples are not necessarily one and the same.

glasnost   Policy of media openness under Gorbachev.

perestroika   Gorbachev's wish to restructure the Soviet economy.

backwardness   Lacking modern qualities.

slowed, in some years to near zero. At least two groups of Soviet elites grew restless at this decline: economists who understood how backward the Soviet system was and some members of the Soviet military who understood that war is increasingly high-tech and that the Soviet Union was falling behind the Americans. These two elites wanted reform, and both welcomed Mikhail Gorbachev to power in 1985.

■ Gorbachev and Collapse

Mikhail Gorbachev never intended or even imagined the collapse of the Soviet system; he just wanted to reform it. He could not understand that reforming Communist systems is like trying to vaccinate a balloon. Gorbachev inherited a declining Soviet economy. Many thinking Russians knew that reforms were necessary to break the grip of the corrupt bureaucracies. Gorbachev did institute **glasnost** and **perestroika**, but these just made things worse. Under glasnost, citizens and the press began to complain loudly and bitterly. Especially dangerous—and totally unforeseen by Gorbachev—was that the many nationalities that made up the Soviet Union began to voice their suppressed feelings. Perestroika promised much but delivered little; by 1989 food shortages were getting serious. Constantly battling conservative forces (as had Khrushchev), Gorbachev hesitated for years and never adopted a serious economic reform plan.

The declining Soviet economy pushed Gorbachev to genuine détente; he desperately needed Western aid and trade. He first met with President Reagan in Geneva in 1985. The two hit it off and built a climate of mutual trust. In late 1987, in the White House, they signed the important treaty on intermediate-range nuclear forces (INF) that got rid of a whole class of atomic weapons (see Chapter 14). The one bright spot on Gorbachev's horizon was his relationship with the United States.

Concepts

THE FEAR OF FALLING BEHIND

Backwardness and how to overcome it is the great theme of Russian history. (Remember the Stalin quote in the previous chapter?) We see in the anxiety of the Soviet (now Russian) reformers one of the great motivating factors for state behavior of the new international system: the fear of falling behind technologically. If you do fall behind, you will be hurt economically and militarily.

Your living standards and global competitiveness will decline, and others will know that you are vulnerable in a showdown with a more high-tech power. The 1991 and 2003 Gulf Wars showed what happens when military technology levels get way out of balance. Accordingly, countries go to great lengths to catch up with high-tech leaders.

Soviet hegemony over East Europe limited this relationship. Besides, Gorbachev did not like the old-line Brezhnevite leaders who still ran East Europe. In 1988, Gorbachev began telling the East Europeans it was time to develop their own glasnost and perestroika. But the East European regimes lacked legitimacy, and as soon as they began to give an inch, their citizens took a mile. In partly free 1989 Polish elections the Communist regime was trounced, and, after a telephone call from Gorbachev, the Polish Communists stood aside for an anti-Communist Catholic prime minister. In the summer of 1989 a more liberal Hungarian Communist government opened the border with Austria, letting thousands of East Germans slip out to West Germany. Then Czechoslovakia did the same. Rioting broke out in East Germany. The regime gave the order to fire on the rioters; instead, liberal Communists took over and opened the Berlin Wall in November, marking the end of the Cold War.

Gorbachev never had a sound vision of the future; he thought he could "fix up" communism. By now a second or third elite generation, much better educated and exposed to new critical ideas, knew the system had to reform. The party split between conservatives and liberals, with the liberals gaining political influence. Gorbachev at first sided with the liberals to initiate decentralizing reforms.

But halfway economic reforms undermine the system. The new market sector kept bumping into the state sector, creating monumental economic breakdowns and inflation. Gorbachev alternated between reforming and stalling almost annually. By 1990, Russians were fed up with Gorbachev's zigs and zags; even as he was celebrated in the Western media, his popularity at home slumped toward zero.

Meanwhile, some of the more liberal party members quit and won elections as non-Communists. In 1991, Boris Yeltsin won the presidency of Russia, by far the largest republic of the Soviet Union, in the first free election in the thousand years of Russia's history. This gave Yeltsin a legitimacy that Gorbachev lacked, for Gorbachev had never been popularly elected to anything. During the attempted coup of August 1991—carried out by Gorbachev's handpicked cabinet—Yeltsin stood firm, citizens rallied to him, the military split, and the coup plotters lost their nerve.

Concepts

LEGITIMACY

An important term in political science, legitimacy means a feeling among citizens that the regime's rule is rightful and should be obeyed. It has the same root as "legal" but is psychological, a connection between governed and government. Where legitimacy is high, as in Sweden, the government can pass a law and it will be obeyed with little need of coercive enforcement. Where legitimacy is low, as in East Europe under the Communists, citizens obey only grudgingly and the regime needs many police to enforce laws. The speed with which East European regimes collapsed showed how little legitimacy they had.

At the end of 1991, Gorbachev was out and the Soviet Union ceased to exist, replaced by fifteen independent republics, twelve of them associated in a loose and undefined "Commonwealth of Independent States." The red banner over the Kremlin turrets came down, replaced by the old Russian flag of white, blue, and red stripes. In less than three-quarters of a century, the Soviet Union had been born under Lenin, grown to brutal Stalinist maturity, slowly declined under Brezhnev, and died during an attempt at rejuvenation by Gorbachev.

◼ Foreign Policy: Generated Internally or Externally?

Do national leaders make foreign policies on the basis of internal politics, needs, and demands, or do they make policies as reactions to threats and opportunities perceived from abroad? In other words, is foreign policy mostly generated internally or externally? The Soviet Union is a good case study.

One school of analysis saw Soviet foreign policy as the product of domestic pressures, such as jockeying for political power among the elite or the need for top leaders to show their people some kind of progress. If they could not deliver rapid improvements in living standards, at least they could give Soviet citizens the feeling of belonging to a mighty and growing empire. Some analysts saw Soviet foreign policy as driven by ideology. Marx and Lenin foresaw the collapse of capitalism, and the Kremlin felt it must help this process along. Such approaches defined Soviet foreign policy as mostly internally generated.

Geography

THE SOVIET SUCCESSOR STATES

Where there used to be one Soviet Union, there are now fifteen independent states, many of them, to be sure, still dominated by Moscow. These states can be grouped by geography into three groups of three, plus a large Central Asian group of five (the five "stans," meaning "place of"), plus one Romanian-speaking republic.

Slavic Republics	Russian Federation, Ukraine (no "the"), Belarus (ex-Belorussia)
Baltic Republics	*Lithuania, *Latvia, *Estonia
Caucasian Republics	Georgia, Armenia, †Azerbaijan
Central Asian Republics	†Turkmenistan, †Kazakstan, †Kyrgyzstan, †Uzbekistan, †Tajikistan
Romanian-Speaking Republic	Moldova (ex-Moldavia)

*Those states not in the Commonwealth of Independent States.
†Predominantly Muslim countries.

Another school of analysis emphasized that the Soviet Union lived in a hostile world and was constantly reacting to events and opportunities. If the Soviet Union felt threatened, it tried to overcome its weakness in order to equal its foes. If one of its clients was under attack, it came to the rescue. In this view, the Kremlin's foreign policies were largely externally generated.

imperial overstretch Theory that powerful nations tend to overexpand and weaken.

In any given situation, of course, there will be both internal and external factors. Why, for example, did the Soviets invade Afghanistan? An ideological commitment to communism (an internal factor)? Or the threat posed by a hostile Afghanistan on the Soviet border (an external factor)? The two are difficult to untangle. And what caused Mikhail Gorbachev to reduce tensions with the United States? Was it Reagan's military buildup and firm positions on arms control (external factors)? Or was it the economic weakness and growing discontent inside the Soviet Union (internal factors)? Three theories of the demise of the Soviet Union illustrate the internal-external question:

1. **Imperial Overstretch**: Yale historian Paul Kennedy argued in his controversial 1987 bestseller *The Rise and Decline of the Great Powers* that major powers tend to expand until they overexpand. Imperial expenses and slower economic growth then drain them into decline. The Habsburg and British empires are good examples, but "overstretch" fits the Soviet experience too. Spending perhaps 25 percent of GDP on defense and subsidizing satellite and client states was too much for the Soviet economy. Related to this theory is the view that the upturn in U.S. defense expenditures under Reagan forced the Kremlin to realize that their economy could stand no more. This explains why Gorbachev became flexible on arms control, Afghanistan, East Europe, and domestic economic reforms. This type of analysis fits into the "externally generated" mode of thought.

Diplomacy

GEORGE F. KENNAN ON RUSSIA AND THE WEST

Diplomat-turned-historian George F. Kennan (see Chapter 2) taught America about Russia. But he also changed his mind about Russia. The deeply conservative Kennan authored the 1947 "containment" doctrine in his famous "X" article, which laid down a tough anti-Communist line that he later regretted.

In his early writings Kennan called the Communists "snake-like" in their hostility to the West. Once out of the foreign service, Kennan reflected on the Cold War and disliked it. In his magisterial *Russia and the West under Lenin and Stalin* (1962), he began to see the rivalry more evenhandedly and even to assign some of the blame to America for ignorance and inconsistency. One of his longstanding themes is that the United States tends to conduct a "legalistic-moralistic" foreign policy instead of a realistic one. Hans Morgenthau (page 27) argued along the same "realist" lines.

Kennan also deplored what he thought was the excessive militarization of U.S. policy; he had in mind greater emphasis on diplomatic and economic forms of containment. How long would containment take? In his 1947 "X" article, Kennan suggested that in ten to fifteen years we would see some cracks in the Soviet edifice. He was right. In 1956, Khrushchev's de-Stalinization speech started splitting the Communist world. In 1960, China departed from the Soviet camp. In Kennan's vision, patience is more important than weapons.

2. Defective System: Another approach, focusing on the "internally generated" side, argues that the Soviet economic and political system was inherently defective. Communism does not work very well; over time it runs down. At first the command economy rapidly builds a heavy-industry base, but then the central planning mechanism hinders a more advanced and complex economy. People now need incentives; without them, workers refrain from exerting themselves and the system declines more. With political life monopolized by the Party—which treats its members well—the regime ignores mass discontent until it boils over. No Communist system has so far reformed itself; those that try collapse.

3. Bungled Reform: A third approach starts with what happens when Soviet elites admit the validity of point 2, that the economy really is running down. They know about and want the living standards of West Europe. They urge reforms, but the halfway reforms just make things worse. The conservative party structure stalls and sabotages reforms. The reformers seek a "middle way" between communism and capitalism, but there is no middle way. Conflicts among the Soviet nationalities come out with unexpected viciousness. Under these circumstances, almost any reform efforts will appear "bungled." In trying to fix the system, they broke it.

Restoring Russian Power

There are two problems with Russia, the material problem and the psychological problem. The material problem is that capitalism in Russia did not work the way it was supposed to (see box on page 99). Many Russians, especially in rural areas, are worse off than ever. Health standards and medical care, never very good, plummeted. Russians have few children but a high death rate. The average Russian male lives to only 60. Russia's population, now down to 142 million, declines by some half-million a year.

weak state One unable to govern effectively; corrupt and crime-ridden.

KGB Soviet intelligence and security police.

Russia became a **weak state**, one in which lawlessness and corruption flourish. Most "banks" are simply money-laundering operations. All *biznesmeny* pay bribes to officials and protection to the *mafiya*. Members of parliament, journalists, bankers, businessmen, and ordinary citizens are routinely gunned down by *keelers,* who are never caught, suggesting the police are in on the deal. Said one Russian: "The only lawyer around here is a Kalashnikov."

The psychological problem is that Russians have also lost their national pride. Not long ago they had a mighty empire, one that could stand up to the Americans. First they lost East Europe, then they lost the historic Russia constructed by the tsars that stretched unbroken from Poland to the Pacific. Now it is fragmented into countries that had no names until Stalin invented them. One Russian cartoon showed Peter the Great spanking Yeltsin for giving away the Russian empire. Putin called the Soviet breakup "the greatest geopolitical catastrophe of the twentieth century" and is doing all he can to reverse it.

It is not surprising, then, that many Russians have turned, as they have historically, to strong-handed leadership. Observers for some years expected a turn to authoritarianism and saw it coming in either Yeltsin, extreme nationalists, or an ex-general. Instead it came with a veteran **KGB** officer, Vladimir Putin, who came out of nowhere to be first appointed prime minister, then acting president, and then in 2000 elected president. Some suspect that Putin, who was also head of the new Russian intelligence service, the FSB, has files on who has stolen what and uses them to obtain compliance. Putin's takeover amounts to a quiet KGB coup. Most of his top officials are former KGB.

privatization   The selling of state-owned assets to private interests.

kleptocracy   Rule by thieves.

Putin is an authoritarian but not a Stalin. He swore to crush the rebellious Chechens. He cracked down on critical journalists and brought the energy industry and main news media back under state control. Putin now faces essentially no media criticism or serious political rivals. Freedom House, which monitors democracy around the world, downgraded Russia from "partly free" to "not free." Putin broke the ultrarich "oligarchs" and got much of their properties back under state control. He increased the role of the Russian presidency—already strong under Yeltsin—and got an obedient majority in the Duma. He reined in Russia's eighty-nine disobedient republics by carving Russia into seven big districts, each with his handpicked supergovernor (five of them ex-KGB) in charge. Putin's initial popularity faded with the lack of democracy, corruption, and endless war in Chechnya, but his control of the government and media and lack of a credible alternative got him reelected in 2004, an election that was not completely free or fair. Russia is not a democracy.

What does this mean for Russia's foreign policy? Already under Yeltsin, there was a nationalistic hardening, one that Putin expanded. Foreign aid workers and nongovernmental organizations have been barred from Russia. Putin does not like them monitoring Russian affairs, especially the brutal war in Chechnya. Many Russians, including top leaders, view America as domineering and arrogant. They think we plotted to bring down the Soviet Union and then Russia (by bad economic advice). They sided with Serbia and deplored the U.S. war in Kosovo. The Kremlin sees the eastward expansion of NATO as a threat and U.S. plans to build an antimissile shield as a breach of the 1972 treaty that would make

Economics

WHOSE FAULT?

Under Yeltsin in the 1990s, the Russian economy declined greatly, perhaps by half, to less than $4,000 per capita GDP (see page 169). (By 2005, thanks to the high price of oil, it had rebounded to $11,100.) Russia **privatized** most of its state-owned industries by selling them ultracheap to a handful of insiders who became billionaires. These "oligarchs" sold off assets and stashed the profits in foreign banks rather than reinvest them in Russia.

Who's to blame for Russia's economic collapse? Some observers—both Russians and Americans—charge that American economists gave bad economic advice. The economists retort that their advice was sound—it worked in Poland—but was not implemented by Moscow. Critics say the advice failed to take into account Russia's lack of legal, political, and cultural support for capitalism to work right. The result was monumental rip-offs and **kleptocracy**. The advisors say they warned against precisely that but were ignored. Either way, Russian economic reform was badly bungled, and Russia took years to recover.

CIS Commonwealth of
Independent States; grouping of
most ex-Soviet republics.

America invulnerable. But there is nothing they can do about either issue, so they say little.

Putin phoned his sympathy to President Bush immediately after 9/11 and supported the U.S. overthrow of the Taliban in Afghanistan, even accepting U.S. use of bases in Central Asia. He exchanged visits with Bush, who thought Putin was America's permanent friend. Like most Europeans, however, Putin opposed the 2003 war with Iraq. Putin did not pursue policies directly hostile to the America; he knows Russia is too weak. The Russian army has shrunk to under 1 million and is badly fed and trained. Putin's goal is that of any KGB officer: restore Russian power. To do this, he patiently plays whatever cards he has:

1. Restore Russian pride by nationalistic moves and symbols, showing Russians and the world that they are still major players and must be respected. Putin travels and receives foreign leaders a lot to emphasize Moscow's importance. Visiting is a cheap way to boost prestige and importance.

2. Keep Russia together. No region will depart the Russian Federation. Any that try, like Chechnya, will be dealt with forcefully. Putin recentralized power in the Kremlin through his seven supergovernors.

3. Recover the "near abroad" of former Soviet republics, using the **CIS** as a cover. Belarus has all but remerged into the Russian Federation. The landlocked Central Asian republics have little choice but to stay close to Moscow. The Caucasus is militarily dependent on Russia. The Baltic states will not willingly return to Russia; trying to force them back would lead to conflict with the West. Ukraine prefers to face west, but Moscow fights that tendency.

4. Regain influence in neighboring lands, chiefly by oil and natural-gas deals. Where pipelines run, political influence follows. In late 2005, Russia briefly cut gas to Ukraine and out to Europe, a warning to an energy-dependent Europe. Moscow will not be able to recover its East European satellites, all of them now in NATO, but it can induce caution and respect in them.

5. Russia's future is with Europe, so Russia will seek a strategic and economic partnership with the European Union but will not join it. It wants a counterweight to U.S. "hegemony." In opposing the 2003 Iraq War, Putin played the "us Europeans" card. Russia, jealous of its sovereignty, has no interest in joining the European Union.

6. Get along with the United States but nothing more. Like most Russians, Putin feels Russia got little from the United States except bad advice. Russia's markets and investors are mostly in Europe, not America. The Bush administration pays little attention to Russia, something that does not bother Putin.

Russia's foreign policy shows much continuity with the Soviet Union's, because geography determines a good part of national interest. If Russia pursues its interests by economic means and without threats or force, we should not worry. That would be normal IR. But Russia's power to disrupt—through arms sales, export of dangerous military technology (nuclear, bacteriological, and chemical), and cutting natural gas shipments—is still dangerous.

We were naive in assuming that Russia would quickly become democratic, capitalistic, and pro-American. Eventually it may, but not for some years. Russia, since the collapse of the ruble in 1998, has enjoyed good economic growth of over 6 percent a year. Production is up, inflation down, and the ruble stable in relation to other currencies. The jump in world oil prices gave Russia a revenue windfall. Russian labor costs are half those of Poland or Mexico, one-twentieth those of Germany. Russia has fabulous natural resources and resourceful people. In time, Russia could become prosperous, democratic, and friendly, but do not expect it soon.

Key Terms

backwardness (p. 94)

Balkans (p. 87)

Central Europe (p. 87)

CIS (p. 100)

détente (p. 90)

glasnost (p. 94)

hegemony (p. 87)

imperial overstretch (p. 97)

inputs (p. 93)

KGB (p. 98)

kleptocracy (p. 99)

legitimacy (p. 87)

perestroika (p. 94)

privatization (p. 99)

productivity (p. 93)

republic (p. 91)

weak state (p. 98)

worst-casing (p. 86)

Key Web Sites

Radio Free Europe/Radio Liberty
http://www.rferl.org

Russia Today
http://www.russiatoday.com/

Russian Embassy in Washington, D.C.
http://www.russianembassy.org/

REESWeb Russian and East European Studies Web
http://www.pitt.edu/~cjp/

List of Russian WWW sites
http://weblist.ru/

Russian and East European Network
http://reenic.utexas.edu/reenic.html

Further Reference

Andrew, Christopher, and Vasili Mitrokhin. *The World Was Going Our Way: The KGB and the Battle for the Third World.* New York: Basic Books, 2006.

Brzezinski, Zbigniew. *The Grand Failure: The Birth and Death of Communism in the Twentieth Century.* New York: Scribner's, 1989.

Bugajski, Janusz. *Cold Peace: Russia's New Imperialism.* Westport, CT: Praeger, 2004.

Donaldson, Robert H., and Joseph L. Nogee. *The Foreign Policy of Russia: Changing Systems, Enduring Interests,* 2nd ed. Armonk, NY: M. E. Sharpe, 2002.

Fowkes, Ben. *The Disintegration of the Soviet Union: A Study in the Rise and Triumph of Nationalism.* New York: St. Martin's Press, 1997.

Fursenko, Aleksandr, and Timothy Naftali. *Khrushchev's Cold War: The Inside Story of an American Adversary.* New York: Norton, 2006.

Lane, David. *The Rise and Fall of State Socialism: Industrial Society and the Socialist State.* Malden, MA: Blackwell, 1996.

Malcolm, Neil, Alex Pravda, Roy Allison, and Margot Light. *Internal Factors in Russian Foreign Policy.* New York: Oxford University Press, 1996.

Malia, Martin. *The Soviet Tragedy: A History of Socialism in Russia, 1917–1991.* New York: The Free Press, 1994.

Munton, Don, and David A. Welch. *The Cuban Missile Crisis: A Concise History.* New York: Oxford University Press, 2007.

Petro, Nicolai, and Alvin Z. Rubinstein. *Russian Foreign Policy: From Empire to Nation-State.* New York: Longman, 1997.

Shleifer, Andrei, and Daniel Treisman. *Without a Map: Political Tactics and Economic Reform in Russia.* Cambridge, MA: MIT Press, 2000.

Trofimenko, Henry. *Russian National Interests and the Current Crisis in Russia.* Brookfield, VT: Ashgate, 1999.

Wegren, Stephen K., ed. *Russia's Policy Challenges: Security, Stability, and Development.* Armonk, NY: M. E. Sharpe, 2003.

Zimmerman, William. *The Russian People and Foreign Policy: Russian Elite and Mass Perspectives, 1993–2000.* Princeton, NJ: Princeton University Press, 2002.

PART II

THE GLOBAL SOUTH

What to call the five-sixths of humankind that lives in the poorer countries of Asia, Africa, and Latin America? Some still call it the Third World, because it is neither the rich, industrialized First World nor the communist Second World, most of which has collapsed. Some call it the "developing areas," "newly industrializing countries" (NICs), or "emerging markets." We like the "Global South," because it is mostly closer to the equator than the more industrialized and largely stable Global North. It is highly varied, with some countries making good progress out of poverty and toward democracy while others are stuck in backwardness and warfare. It is in the Global South that we find the "zones of chaos" mentioned in Chapter 1.

In Chapter 7 we use the dramatic transformation of South Africa to illustrate the demise of the colonial mentality and the end of five hundred years of global imperialism. When the superpowers ended the Cold War they stopped propping up minority regimes, and these regimes then sought accommodation rather than fighting the masses alone. The greatest accommodation occurred in South Africa, where Nelson Mandela and his African National Congress took over power without a bloody showdown. South Africa is now a crucial test of multiracial democracy and economic development.

Chapter 8 traces the development of Arab and Israeli nationalism. Much of modern Middle Eastern history flows from the struggle of these two peoples for the same land. Most Palestinians and Israelis now realize that after five nasty wars and two Palestinian *intifadas*, the only way to live together is to live apart in separate homelands. After many tries, peace still eludes, and militants on both sides sabotage the peace process.

Chapter 9 shows that mixing oil with religion in the Persian Gulf can produce a clash of arms and, some say, a clash of civilizations. The wars revealed splits in Islam, splits in the Arab world, and the power of the region to draw the United States into two wars with Iraq and likely a long stay. We discuss the 2003 war and its aftermath at some length.

Chapter 10 turns us to Latin America, which we try to ignore but cannot. A U.S. war with leftist guerrillas and drug lords threatens. Spanish colonialism bequeathed Latin America statism, poverty, and economic dependency. The United States has repeatedly intervened in Central America and the Caribbean, each time fostering instability. Guatemala and

Cuba have been especially difficult and dangerous. Recent Mexican elections show that Latin America can modernize and democratize.

Finally, Chapter 11 explains why some states are rich and others are poor. Literacy, technology, and attitudes about progress are key factors. So is the population explosion in the Third World. A high birthrate retards growth and fuels a great migration to the First World, raising questions of integration, jobs, official languages, and the power of market capitalism to feed the world.

CHAPTER 7

SOUTH AFRICA AND THE END OF COLONIALISM

QUESTIONS TO CONSIDER

1. Why do good intentions often fail in Africa?
2. How big were the colonial empires?
3. How did South Africa under apartheid show a colonial mentality?
4. What was the impact of the British hold over and departure from India?
5. What external factors forced South Africa to change?
6. What is the fallacy of halfway reform as practiced by the white regime in South Africa?
7. What is the impact of a charismatic leader, such as Kenya's Kenyatta and South Africa's Mandela?
8. What has happened to most African lands after their independence?

The world does not know what to do with Africa. Some say the situation in much of the continent is so hopeless that we should just keep out. Africa has few success stories. Much of it is wracked by economic decline, civil war, mass murder, and an explosion of AIDS. (One of the worst: South Africa, where one-fifth of adults are infected). Overall in Sub-Saharan Africa, per capita GDP declined from $700 in 1981 to $450 in 2002. (Of that GDP, 45 percent is concentrated in South Africa, the region's only industrialized economy.) Well-intentioned help often goes wrong. The United States attempted to bring food and order to **anarchic** Somalia but abandoned it when eighteen U.S. soldiers were killed in street fighting in 1993. Taking the wrong lesson from that, in 1994 we sent no soldiers to prevent tribal massacres in Rwanda. Instead, we set up refugee camps in neighboring Congo, which made the massacres spill over into the Congo and get worse (see box on page 113). In Sierra Leone, the United Nations tried to restore peace but its peacekeepers were disarmed and held by rebels, who stole diamonds and chopped off arms. A few U.S. troops could have stopped the death and chaos of a collapsing Liberian regime, but we did not send them. The major powers see much danger and little payoff in African peace operations, so they rarely intervene.

anarchic   Lacking government or order. (See page 105.)

failed state   Collapse of sovereignty, essentially no national government.

pan-Africanism   Movement to unite all Africa.

colonialism   The gaining and exploitation of overseas territories, chiefly by Europeans.

One of the biggest problems in dealing with Africa is that several of its countries are **failed states** that only pretend to have governments. They cannot feed their people or keep order. Prime example: Somalia. Lawlessness rules. Rebel groups—often teenagers with Kalashnikovs—loot and murder. As Gertrude Stein said of Oakland, CA, "There's no there there."

Some of these countries—set up for the convenience of European imperialists—should not exist. Under normal circumstances, many would have merged into larger units or have broken up into more natural tribal units. But the Organization of African Unity (renamed the African Union in 2002) decided to keep the colonial borders because there was no good way to redraw them, and if states combined many officials would lose their jobs. Thanks to the imperialists, adjacent countries have different official languages (English, French, Portuguese). What the colonialists set up, Africans have accepted, although some still dream of **pan-Africanism** that would erase these pernicious imperialist borders.

Nature has not been kind to Africa. Much of the soil is poor. In some times and places there is too much rain, in others too little. Insects and disease thrive, people do not. For these reasons and for most of history, Africa has been thinly populated by hardy subsistence farmers scattered in small villages. Family and survival were all that mattered, not organization or economic growth. Africa rarely developed the European type of "strong state" or nationalism (exceptions: Ethiopia and the Zulus). Almost defenseless, traditional Africa was first deranged by the Arab slave trade on the east coast and the Portuguese on the west before European colonialists, often with African troops, easily took over.

Many of Africa's problems trace back to Europeans, first to **colonialism** and then to the Cold War. The Portuguese in the fifteenth century worked their way down Africa's coast but left the kingdoms and cultures of the interior untouched. In the nineteenth century, the Europeans erased much traditional culture by carving up Africa into unnatural colonies that they attempted to educate, Christianize, and exploit. The Europeans gave their colonies artificial borders, overcentralized administration, and no legitimacy before casting them free to become pawns in the Cold War. A few Western-trained elites—imitation Europeans—took over, interested only in self-enrichment. Africa has been misused for centuries.

The Cold War did, however, force us to pay some attention to Africa. Support by outside powers—the United States, Soviet Union, Britain, and France—brought with it some stability. With the Cold War over and that support withdrawn, chaos has grown. Now, few care much about Africa. One U.S. government specialist on Africa, aware that his expertise was no longer in demand, sadly joked: "Africa is a dagger—aimed at the heart of Antarctica."

South Africa is an interesting case study because it preserved a colonialist mentality longest, one sustained by Cold War rivalries. Then, with the Cold War over, its two main antagonists—the whites-only government and the African liberation movement—lost their outside backers and had to start talking with each other. The end of the Cold War system set in motion new forces. At almost the same time that the Soviet Union let East Europe break free, Pretoria freed Nelson Mandela from a life sentence in prison. Just as the Soviet Union collapsed, the white South African regime sat down for talks on a new constitution with its former black enemies. International systems have a big impact on domestic politics.

■ The Colonial Mentality

South Africa was frozen into a peculiar pattern that continued a colonialist social and economic structure—the last remnant of the days when the European empires blanketed the globe and a few whites ruled many natives. Although South Africa had long ago cut its ties to Holland and Britain, it was still psychologically colonialist, taking us back to a time when empires covered most of the world. It is quite startling to make a list of non-European countries that were never colonies, for the list is awfully short: Thailand, Turkey, Ethiopia, Afghanistan, and Japan. China and Iran were reduced to semicolonial status.

Over a two-century span, the European powers were forced back to Europe. The first loss was Britain's thirteen colonies in North America. Next, in the early nineteenth century, came Spain's and Portugal's ouster from Latin America. Germany and Turkey lost their

Concepts

COLONIALISM

Colonialism is first a legal condition wherein a land lacks sovereignty; ultimate lawmaking authority resides in a distant capital. London controlled the laws governing India, Paris those of Indochina, and Brussels those of the Congo. Second, the "natives" were kept politically powerless, as the imperial power deemed them too backward and ignorant.

Colonialism often involved economic exploitation by the imperial country. The colonies supplied cheap agricultural and mineral raw materials, which the imperial country manufactured into industrial products that it sold back to the colonies. Marxists argue that colonies were captive markets that were kept poor to enrich imperialists. Actually, most colonies cost imperial governments more to administer and defend than they earned. Individual firms, to be sure, often made lush profits.

Racially, colonies were governed on the basis of skin color and according to the principle that "the lowest of the Europeans is higher than the highest of the natives." A French policeman directing traffic in Hanoi was superior to a Vietnamese doctor. A Dutch clerk in Jakarta was the social better of an Indonesian professor. Racism was woven into the fabric of colonialism, contributing much to the psychological rage felt by the leaders of independence movements: "You can't treat me like dirt in my own country!" These social and psychological factors are still alive in South Africa.

Was colonialism morally wrong? Unquestionably. But it was also inevitable, the logical outcome of the encounter between a restless, dynamic West and a traditional Global South that looked like easy pickings. (Only one traditional land held off the Europeans: Japan. Any ideas why?) The imperial powers had no right to conquer and govern others, but they did have guns. If only Europe had stayed home! (Of course, then there would be no United States.) "Colonial" has a nice sound to Americans, connoting Pilgrims, shoppes, and gracious living. It has a bitter ring for most other peoples. Colonialism left a chip on the shoulders of the Global South and helps explain why much of it has been anti-West.

Southern Africa

decolonization   The granting of
independence to colonies.

empires in World War I, but most of those territories were taken over by the victorious British and French under mandates of the League of Nations. Real **decolonization** did not come until after World War II, first as a trickle and then as a flood: India and Pakistan in 1947, Israel (formerly Palestine) in 1948, Indonesia (Dutch East Indies) in 1949, Ghana (Gold Coast) in 1957, then, in 1960, seventeen countries, mostly British and French colonies in Africa. By the mid-1960s, all the old colonial empires had been liquidated except for Portugal's African holdings. In 1975, Lisbon too gave way. After Rhodesia became Zimbabwe in 1980, South Africa stood alone as the last bastion of white power in Africa.

South Africa started as a colony when the Dutch East India Company set up a "refreshment station" at the Cape of Good Hope in 1652. Dutch farmers, or *Boers,* slowly pushed their way inland, taking whatever land they wanted and subjugating the natives. During the Napoleonic wars, Britain took the Cape and later Natal province. Many Boers hated English rule and trekked to the interior to set up two small republics, the Transvaal and Orange Free State. British imperialists—including Cecil Rhodes, founder of the Rhodes scholarships—picked a fight with the Boers in 1899 in order to seize their gold- and diamond-rich lands. The Boer War was no easy fight, and the British finally resorted to putting Boer families into "concentration camps" where typhoid killed some 26,000. The Boers capitulated in 1902, but their descendants, now called Afrikaners, won control of the political system and viewed themselves as the victims of British imperialism.

> **apartheid** South Africa's system of strict racial segregation from 1948 to the early 1990s.

In 1948, the Afrikaners, who constitute 60 percent of the white population, won elections with their National party and passed laws that built a thorough and complex system of racial segregation they called **apartheid** (literally, apartness). Blacks were kept separate and down. There was no such thing as a mixed neighborhood, church, school, or sports team. Blacks needed permits to get jobs in urban areas, and the jobs had to be those whites did not want. Blacks were given a limited and inferior education. In the name of "influx control," blacks had to show a passbook on demand and could be "endorsed out" of an urban or white farming area to a desolate black homeland. Eventually, it was envisioned that ten black homelands—scattered parcels of land forming 13 percent of South Africa's territory—would become independent. Blacks would be citizens of Bophuthatswana, Transkei, Ciskei, or other homelands and only temporary workers in white South Africa. This would deprive them of all citizenship rights in South Africa and make them easier to control. Blacks had not the slightest voice in their future, and protest was illegal.

To us as outsiders, it is inconceivable that human beings would long stand for such treatment. To Afrikaners, who were used to living in a racially, socially, and psychologically colonial situation, it seemed normal that the black majority would acquiesce to the fate assigned it by the white government. Because blacks are still backward and tribal, argued many whites, they are happiest with their own people in their homelands.

Reflections

GOLD COAST INTO GHANA

Decades ago at UCLA I knew three students from the Gold Coast, a British colony for 113 years on the bulge of West Africa. In 1957 it became Ghana, and they became Ghanians. They were intensely proud. "Under the British," one of them told me, "we could have no feeling of patriotism for our country, because it wasn't our country. Now it's ours." The students predicted an unleashing of Ghana's energy and rapid progress now that the British overlords were gone.

Ghana's progress foundered, however. Its U.S.-educated president, Kwame Nkrumah, turned himself into a pro-Soviet dictator. "The Redeemer," as he called himself, concentrated on show projects, including statues of himself, rather than on economic growth. In 1966 the army overthrew Nkrumah in the first of several military coups. Democracy never had much of a chance; the economy stagnated and living standards deteriorated, the experience of many African countries since independence. I wonder what has become of my friends and what they think now.

—M. G. R.

◼ The Wind of Change

Black South Africans tried peaceful protest for half a century. The African National Congress was founded in 1912 to petition the government for equal rights. They were ignored and silenced. In 1960, after police killed sixty-nine peaceful protesters at Sharpeville, the ANC decided that they could deliver their message only by violence against select targets; the bomb would be an attention-getter. In 1960 the ANC was banned by the government

Turning Point

INDIA SPLITS IN TWO

Before the British, India was a patchwork of princely states. Hindus predominated, but there were many Muslims, and the two religious communities disliked each other. The British East India Company arrived in the seventeenth century and slowly took over the subcontinent. London had no plan to conquer India; it just happened, as commanders such as Robert Clive felt driven to expand to secure their original outposts. Untamed adjacent areas were always a security threat, so it was necessary to conquer them. By the time of the American Revolution, British governors-general ruled India.

British rule was not all bad. They brought in relatively few soldiers and civil servants and trained Indians to fill the lower ranks of both the army and bureaucracy. By keeping sovereignty in London, British rule temporarily dampened conflict between Hindus and Muslims. The British introduced railroads, hospitals, the telegraph, and modern education. Without the English language, Indians would have trouble communicating nationwide, for there was no single Indian language. (Hindi is a language of northern India; southerners disliked it.) By giving Indians the tools to communicate, colonialism invented Indian nationalism. In modernizing India, the British sowed the seeds of their own departure, for the more educated and aware Indians became, the less they could stand the arrogant British.

The Indian National Congress (INC) was founded in 1885 by a group of British-educated Indians to press for democracy and eventual independence. The present Congress party (now in opposition) is thus over a century old, a factor conferring

institutional stability. Unfortunately, in 1906 the Muslim League was founded to press for separate treatment and territories for India's many Muslims. The movement for self-rule thus split.

Mohandas K. Gandhi, an Indian lawyer who had sharpened his skills in South Africa for twenty years, introduced "nonviolent resistance" into the nationalist movement in 1918 (his inspiration: American writer Henry Thoreau). Through the 1920s and 1930s, Gandhi built a following throughout India by mounting simple, direct protests the masses could understand. He walked from village to village, wore homespun cloth (some of it spun himself), led a boycott on salt taxes, and went on hunger strikes.

In World War II, the British feared Japan would take India (some Indians sided with the Japanese), so they promised independence after the war. In 1947 Britain delivered, but the Muslim League refused to be part of an India with a Hindu majority. With sovereignty now up for grabs, murderous rioting broke out. Under the guidance of Lord Mountbatten, Pakistan was split off from India as a predominantly Muslim country. Some twelve million people fled their home territories—Muslims going to Pakistan and Hindus to India—in the largest population transfer in history. Gandhi was horrified at the communal violence and was himself assassinated by a Hindu fanatic who thought Gandhi was soft on Muslims. The British had long warned of Hindu-Muslim violence. "Without us," they said, "you people will kill each other." This was the bottom-line argument of colonialism, one heard in South Africa until recently.

but went underground. The ANC's president, black lawyer Nelson Mandela, was apprehended and sentenced to life in the harsh prison of Robben Island off Cape Town. This enhanced his genuine **charisma**, and black South Africans worshiped him.

charisma Personal drawing power of some politicians.

There was no shortage of warnings about an explosion in South Africa. Prime Minister Harold Macmillan told South Africa's whites-only parliament in 1960 that "the wind of change" was blowing over Africa as dozens of former colonies got their independence. In response, the Union of South Africa became the fully independent Republic of South Africa (RSA). (It returned to the Commonwealth in 1994.) Unlike a colony, South Africa's Europeans have no mother country to turn to.

Through the 1960s the National party relentlessly built its apartheid system. Opposition leaders were silenced by prison or death squads and opponents were "banned"—barred from normal social contact, political activity, or even being quoted. Apartheid started breaking down in the mid-1970s, however, and even some militant Afrikaners began to lose their nerve.

The international picture changed. Portuguese rule in Angola and Mozambique ended. Heretofore, these colonies, along with Rhodesia, provided a protective belt of white rule against the newly independent states of black Africa. Suddenly, in 1975, South Africa shared borders with black Marxist regimes armed and advised by the Soviet bloc. Trade sanctions did little good—they just gave South African industry protection and incentives to grow—but in 1985, international bankers started doubting South Africa's creditworthiness and refused it new loans. Virtually all countries depend on such loans (actually

Turning Point

THE AGONY OF ALGERIA

A colony with many European settlers is much harder to decolonize than one with few, for the settlers fight for their lands and privileged position. Such was the case with Algeria. The French arrived in 1830 to crush piracy but soon turned it into a colony where a million European *colons* dominated the Muslim majority. Algeria was even declared part of France. Algerians served in the French army but could not become French citizens.

Algerian nationalists, inspired in part by Egypt's Nasser, began their fight for independence in 1956 with bank robberies and bombings. The European power structure fought back ferociously, with killings and bombings of its own. Murder became nearly random.

The French army, having just lost Indochina, was determined to win. They used torture freely. When French leaders talked about ending the war, the French army began a military coup in 1958. At the last minute, retired General Charles de Gaulle was called to head a new government. The settlers and army thought he would keep Algeria French, but he led France out of Algeria with a series of referendums. With Algerian independence in 1962, a million bitter colons gave up their farms and businesses and resettled in France.

Algeria's horrors did not end. Its military regime with a socialist slant botched the economy. Unemployment soared, and millions went to France (many illegally). Islamic fundamentalists harvested mass anger and were about to oust the regime in elections in 1992. Instead, the regime repressed the Islamists, who lashed back with murder, sometimes of whole villages. The death toll since 1992: over 75,000.

"rollovers" of old loans), and their cutoff jolted South Africa's business community into thinking of how to end their isolation. Some argue that what really got the attention of sports-mad South African whites was the international boycott of their teams.

In 1976 bloody violence broke out in Soweto (standing for South-West Townships), the sprawling black housing area near Johannesburg. Rejecting a new law requiring black pupils to learn Afrikaans (the Dutch-based speech of Afrikaners), students protested, and the police gunned down some seven hundred of them. Thousands of young blacks dedicated themselves to revolution; some fled to neighboring countries to enroll in the ANC's fighting arm, *Umkhonto we Sizwe*, Spear of the Nation, founded by Nelson Mandela. The Soweto violence was a major radicalizing event in the lives of young blacks.

Reform instead of Revolution

By the time Pieter Willem Botha took over as prime minister in 1978, anyone with half a brain knew something had to give. Pretoria announced "apartheid is dead" and eased up on the hateful system. The reforms, however, were weak and did little for most blacks, who were still confined to their townships and could not own property. Said Botha, "One man, one vote is out. That is to say, never." Frustration and discontent mounted. To talk about reforms and then not deliver only heightens revolutionary feelings.

In 1989 came a more decisive reformist, F. W. de Klerk. In early 1990 he released Nelson Mandela from prison along with dozens of other ANC figures. Parliament repealed the apartheid laws, and the white regime and black opposition began a dialogue, culminating in an interim constitution in 1994 under which South Africa held its first one-person-one-vote elections. The new parliament, in which the ANC was the largest party, then elected Mandela president; both the parliament and cabinet were multiracial and included all but the extremists on both sides. It was an amazing breakthrough, a sort of domestic decolonization.

Turning Point

ANGOLA AND MOZAMBIQUE

Until the 1970s South Africa had a protective belt of white-ruled colonies to its north. Angola and Mozambique were Portuguese colonies, defined as part of Portugal by the stubborn Lisbon dictatorship. In the 1960s, with arms from Communist countries, guerrillas began a fight that gradually drained tiny, poor Portugal. In 1974 the Portuguese army, fed up with unwinnable warfare, toppled the dictatorship. Portugal gave the colonies their freedom in 1975, but fighting did not stop. Rebel armies, based on dissident tribes and funded by the United States, Soviet Union, Zaire, and South Africa, ravaged both new countries.

The new revolutionary regimes eagerly embraced the Communist way, with catastrophic results. The white settlers fled, leaving the countries' infrastructure unstaffed, and the economies spiraled downward. By the 1990s both had abandoned Marxist paths and turned to pluralism, free markets, and capitalism with mixed but better results. The revolutionary leaders finally wised up to the fact that Marxism sounds good when you're fighting in the bush but is no way to economic prosperity. Revolution in Southern Africa, as elsewhere, ran its natural course from impassioned extremism to sober pragmatism.

■ God Save Africa

Nkosi Sikelel' iAfrika (God Save Africa), the stirring anthem of the ANC, became South Africa's national anthem in 1994 and could serve as the prayer for the entire continent. All the world's poorest countries are in Africa; only a few have shown spurts of economic growth. There are few democracies in

divide and rule   Roman and British ruling method of setting subjects against each other.

Turning Point

CONGO: STILL THE HEART OF DARKNESS

The Congo, once called Zaire, shows the very worst of what has happened to Africa. The Congo, two-thirds the size of West Europe and the personal property of King Leopold of Belgium from 1885 to 1908, was run as a tidy and profitable prison camp. To get a chilling feel of Belgian colonialism, read Joseph Conrad's *Heart of Darkness,* set in the Congo.

As most of Africa got its freedom, Congolese rioted and Brussels hastily gave the Congo independence in 1960. The pro-Soviet Patrice Lumumba won elections, but several forces (including the CIA) plotted to kill him. He was assassinated in 1961. The Belgians had trained and prepared no one to lead—there were three Congolese high-school graduates in all the giant territory—and Belgium was delighted as tribal warfare broke out and the Congo fell apart. The Belgians' game was to break off mineral-rich Katanga province in the south as a puppet state of their mining company and keep on milking it for profits. UN Secretary General Dag Hammarskjold died in a 1961 plane crash while trying to restore order in the Congo. UN intervention (and some covert U.S. operations) put the Congo back together under the dictatorship of Colonel Joseph Mobutu.

The United States backed Mobutu as an anti-Communist force for stability. He hyped nationalism by renaming the country Zaire and himself Mobutu Sese Seko. He was also one of the world's biggest crooks, who took much of Zaire's wealth while his people grew poorer. A per capita GDP of $90 puts Congo at the very bottom of the poorest countries. Mobutu stayed in power three decades by cutting his officials and supporters in on the corruption—

the way it works in much of Africa, where to be a government official means to collect bribes. With the Cold War over, the United States lost interest and stopped supporting Mobutu.

Then tribal violence spilled over from neighboring tiny Rwanda, also a former Belgian colony. Belgium had played classic **divide and rule** by setting up one tribe, the Tutsis, to be aristocratic masters and another tribe, the Hutus, to be underlings. As was often the case in Africa, colonialists invented tribes and tribal hatreds. When the Belgians left Rwanda in 1962, Hutu-Tutsi fighting and massacres flared every few years. One factor: population growth in an overcrowded land. The average Rwandan woman bore eight children.

The latest chapter of horror began in 1994 as Hutu *genocidaires* massacred between 500,000 and 800,000. Many Tutsis fled into Zaire and joined a rebel army led by Laurent Kabila that easily ousted Mobutu in 1997. No one, not even his own soldiers, helped the supercrook. But Kabila (assassinated by a bodyguard in 2001), who renamed the country the Democratic Republic of Congo, was worse than Mobutu; in addition to the standard corruption, civil war continues, abetted by outside armies. Rwandan and Ugandan forces fought each other over diamonds. Revenge killings by Rwandan Tutsis of Hutu refugees in eastern Congo took approximately 2 million lives, most from starvation and disease. The combined Rwanda-Congo death toll is estimated at 3 million, the world's worst since World War II. And the world paid little attention. Only France sent some peacekeeping forces. The Congo is a failed state, due in large part to colonialism and outside intervention.

tribalism   Identifying with tribe
rather than country.

Africa, and Africa's presidents almost never lose reelection. South Africa could be different and serve as a beacon for the rest of Africa. It has the only major industrial plant on the continent and a modern, high-tech infrastructure. With the fall of trade barriers and boycotts—the "divestment" campaigns that rattled some U.S. campuses in the 1980s—the South African economy is now open to major foreign investment. The potential market for the southern part of Africa is big—with more than 110 million people—and South African products now flow freely into most African countries. South Africa could thus serve as the industrial spark plug for the southern part of the continent. South Africa's president since 1999, the intelligent Thabo Mbeki, who studied economics in Britain, understands the importance of markets. He also showed impatience with opposition and denied facts such as AIDS.

But South Africa is dangerously fragmented. The worst break is not between blacks and whites but among blacks, specifically between the largest tribe, the Zulus, concentrated in KwaZulu/Natal province, and all the other Africans. As in the rest of Africa, **tribalism** still governs much of politics. South Africa's unemployment problem is staggering, the case in much of the Global South. Half of South Africa's black citizens are unemployed or underemployed. Jobs must be created, and fast. The only hope for this is rapid foreign investment. But foreign investors seek stability and rule of law. Corruption, endemic in the Global South, grew in South Africa as new black officials did financial favors for themselves and friends. Black citizens grew angry when the promised jobs, housing, and health care did

Turning Point

BAD WAY IN ZIMBABWE

Zimbabwe shows what can go wrong in South Africa, just to its south; that is, it could turn into a corrupt, impoverished dictatorship. Rhodesia, a British colony, declared its independence in 1965 under a white minority government that imitated the South African apartheid structure. Soon guerrilla fighting broke out, and an international embargo tried to isolate the Rhodesian economy. In 1980, the exhausted white government finally handed over power to Robert Mugabe, who revived the ancient name of Zimbabwe.

President Mugabe, bright and well-educated, won election in 1980 and ever since, along with his party, the Zimbabwe African National Union (ZANU), which is based on the majority Shona tribe and uses violent election tactics. As is standard in Africa, politics is tribal. Mugabe's forces killed thousands of the minority Ndebele tribe and then amalgamated their party into ZANU-Popular Front in 1987, trying to make a one-party state.

ZANU-PF mismanagement brought severe economic decline. Since 2000, the opposition Movement for Democratic Change (MDC) wins over a third of the seats, mostly in urban and Ndebele areas. The MDC suffers intimidation and murder, and outside observers call elections unfair. Mugabe's ZANU-PF, with a lock on rural and Shona districts, wins majorities.

Most of the good farmland was owned by a tiny white minority. Mugabe denounced them and ordered their lands taken but gave them only to army and ZANU-PF supporters. The economy tumbled into inflation, 70 percent unemployment, and hunger. Many of the remaining whites departed, taking their skills with them. Could dictatorship and decline be the future of South Africa?

not quickly materialize. The crime rate shot up. Whites hunkered behind spiked fences; many quietly emigrated. A Truth and Reconciliation commission uncovered some of the horrors of the recent past, but that did little to calm families who had lost loved ones to police torture.

Will Thabo Mbeki have the moral authority to keep South Africa together? Charismatic founders, such as Nelson Mandela and Kenya's Jomo Kenyatta, are examples of how power in Africa (and Latin America) tends to be personal, not institutional. Their successors have less personal power and a harder time governing. Mbeki attempted to bolster his power by demanding that South Africa's whites give up some of their economic privileges and make way for blacks in business and government. He introduced a forceful affirmative-action program that persuaded some whites to leave. The nasty part of South Africa's transition from colonialism to freedom could still be ahead. South Africa, while it avoided a revolution, could fall into the pattern of many African countries of violence, corruption, and decline.

Key Terms

anarchic (p. 106)

apartheid (p. 109)

charisma (p. 111)

colonialism (p. 106)

decolonization (p. 108)

divide and rule (p. 113)

failed state (p. 106)

pan-Africanism (p. 106)

tribalism (p. 114)

Key Web Sites

African Studies (UPenn)

http://www.sas.upenn.edu/African_Studies/AS.html

African News

http://www.africanews.org/

British Broadcasting Corporation

http://news.bbc.co.uk/

Financial Mail

http://www.fm.co.za/

Daily Mail & Guardian

http://www.mg.co.za/

Daily Nation (Kenya)

http://www.nationaudio.com/News/Daily/Nation/Today/index.html

Africa Online

http://www.africaonline.com

Further Reference

Adelman, Howard, and Astri Suhrke, eds. *The Path of a Genocide: The Rwanda Crisis from Uganda to Zaire.* Rutgers, NJ: Transaction, 1999.

Ansprenger, Franz. *The Dissolution of the Colonial Empires.* New York: Routledge, 1989.

Cocker, Mark. *Rivers of Blood, Rivers of Gold: Europe's Conquest of Indigenous Peoples.* New York: Grove, 2001.

Howe, Stephen. *Empire: A Very Short Introduction.* New York: Oxford University Press, 2002.

Husband, Mark. *The Skull Beneath the Skin: Africa after the Cold War.* Boulder, CO: Westview, 2001.

Jones, Bruce D. *Peacemaking in Rwanda: The Dynamics of Failure.* Boulder, CO: Lynne Rienner, 2001.

Love, Janice. *Southern Africa in World Politics: Local Aspirations and Global Entanglements.* Boulder, CO: Westview, 2005.

Lyman, Princeton N. *Partner to History: The U.S. Role in South Africa's Transition to Democracy.* Herndon, VA: U.S. Institute of Peace, 2002.

Mandela, Nelson. *Long Walk to Freedom.* Boston, MA: Little, Brown, 1994.

Meredith, Martin. *The Fate of Africa: From the Hopes of Freedom to the Heart of Despair; A History of Fifty Years of Independence.* New York: PublicAffairs, 2005.

Wrong, Michela. *I Didn't Do It for You: How the World Betrayed a Small African Nation.* New York: HarperCollins, 2005.

CHAPTER 8

ETERNAL WARFARE IN THE HOLY LAND

QUESTIONS TO CONSIDER

1. What is nationalism and where did it come from?
2. How did Israelis and Arabs become nationalistic?
3. How and why did the British help set up the Arab-Israel dispute?
4. How many wars has Israel fought? When were they? What was their underlying cause?
5. What strategy did Kissinger use to end the 1973 war? Is there a message in this for current peace attempts?
6. Is the conflict a clash of religions or just about land?
7. What role can the United States can play in the peace process?
8. Can there eventually be Arab-Israeli peace? How?

How did two peoples become attached to the same piece of land? History and religion helped create two communities in each of which a *national consciousness* grew that was fixated on the same territory of **Palestine**. Thus two strong *nationalisms* evolved at odds with each other and still block peace efforts. Can they be overcome?

■ The Making of Jewish Nationalism

Jewish peoplehood is rooted in the Holy Land and Scripture. The ancient Hebrews were conquered by Assyria, Persia, Alexander the Great, and Rome. They became a dispersed people but preserved a sense of their nationhood through the Old Testament.

Scattered through the Roman Empire and beyond, over the centuries millions of Jews converted—sometimes by force—and assimilated into local life. Mixing went the other way too, and in Israel today one can meet Jews who look like Germans, Spaniards, Russians, Turks, Arabs, Indians, you name it. The connection between people and land is not racial but psychological. Jewish life in Europe ranged from tolerable to horrible. Jewish

Palestine Ancient Holy Land, part of Fertile Crescent bordering the Mediterranean, Egypt, and Lebanon. (See page 117.)

Zionism Jewish nationalism focused on gaining and keeping Israel as a Jewish state.

nationalism A people's sense of identity and unity, often exaggerated and focused against foreigners.

life in Arab lands was generally better, as Islam historically has tolerated Christian and Jewish minorities. Nationalism in the nineteenth century awakened Jews much as it did colonial peoples. Every people, nationalism taught, was supposed to have their own country. Jews in the late nineteenth century began devising their own nationalism, **Zionism**.

A key event in Zionism was the Dreyfus Affair of the 1890s, in which a Jewish French officer was convicted on fake evidence of spying for Germany. France, a society badly split since the Revolution, split again as reactionaries reviled Jews and liberals defended them. An assimilated Jewish journalist at Dreyfus's trial, Theodor Herzl, was horrified by the anger and violence that appeared in France and concluded that Jews could be safe only with their own country. In 1896 he published *Der Judenstaat* (The Jewish State) and became the principal advocate and organizer of modern political (as opposed to religious) Zionism. In 1897 he organized the first Zionist Congress and predicted that within fifty years his dream of a Jewish state would be a reality. He was off by only one year, for Israel was proclaimed a state in 1948.

Concepts

NATIONALISM

Nationalism is the sometimes angry belief in the independence of one's people. It often includes resentment or hatred of alien rulers or threatening foreigners: "No foreigners will push us around!" It is the strongest and most emotional of the world's ideologies. Most of the world's peoples—including Americans—are nationalistic, some a little and some a lot.

The modern concept of *nationality* came with the absolutist monarchs in the sixteenth century who tried to replace local consciousness (e.g., Burgundian) with national consciousness (e.g., French). **Nationalism**, however, didn't get going until the French Revolution, which, because it was based on "the people," gave the French an exalted view of themselves as Europe's leaders and liberators. (To get a feel for the emotional power of nationalism, listen to the French national anthem, "La Marseillaise.")

Wherever Napoleon's arrogant legions conquered, they awoke nationalism among other Europeans. Nationalism teaches that it is deeply wrong to be governed by foreigners. French occupation gave life to Spanish, German, and Russian nationalism. (To see how a francophile Russian learns to hate the French and become a Russian nationalist, read Tolstoy's epic *War and Peace*.) During the nineteenth century, one people after another discovered their national identity and demanded their own nation.

The European empires inadvertently spread nationalism. By administering different peoples as one unit and educating them in a common language and culture, the colonialists taught the "natives" to think of themselves as one people and to resent being governed by foreigners. During the twentieth century, nationalism covered the globe. The more recently a country has been a colony, the more nationalistic it tends to be, for its grudges against foreigners are still vivid. It is especially dangerous when nationalism becomes entwined with religion, as in India, Pakistan, ex-Yugoslavia, Chechnya, and the Middle East.

Aiding recruitment for Herzl's new movement were conditions in Russia, which at that time included eastern Poland, the area of heaviest Jewish population. The tsarist government encouraged *pogroms* (anti-Jewish riots) to deflect mass discontent onto Jews. Many Jews emigrated to West Europe and America, but a few, imbued with Zionism, settled in Palestine.

In 1900 Palestine was a sleepy part of the **Ottoman** Turkish empire, its small population mostly Arab. The Zionists saw Palestine as an unpopulated wasteland, and Zionist immigrants believed Herzl's dictum, "The land without a people shall have a people without a land." They barely noticed the local Arabs. The young Zionists were secular (some were even atheists), socialist, and pioneering. Jewish nationalism was their religion, and working the soil was their worship.

The Zionists were few in number but well organized. A Jewish National Fund raised money abroad, and a Land Development Company bought land and trained young Jewish settlers who set up *kibbutzim* (communal farms) and *moshavim* (cooperative farms). The pioneers drained swamps and irrigated deserts. Hebrew was revived as a spoken language, no longer just for prayer. In 1903 Tel Aviv ("Hill of Spring") was founded as a modern Jewish city, just north of the Arab port of Jaffa.

Ottoman   Turkish empire in Balkans and Middle East from fourteenth century to World War I.

Islam   Faith founded by Muhammad in seventh-century Arabia.

Muslim   Adherents of *Islam*, also adjective.

caliphate   Muslim empire.

■ The Making of Arab Nationalism

Arab nationalism is also rooted in religion, in the **Islam** that exploded out of Arabia in the seventh century. Muhammad believed he was the last prophet of Allah (Arabic for God). His recitation of God's words formed the *Koran,* or holy book. Arabic thus became the liturgical language of **Muslims** (meaning those who surrendered to the will of God). As Islam spread, so did the Arab language and culture. Arabic and Hebrew are related languages.

Arab invaders spread the new faith like wildfire, and in a few decades Islam blanketed the present Middle East, Persia, Central Asia, Western India, North Africa, and Spain. They also founded **caliphates**, which culturally were far ahead of Europe, which was then stuck in the Dark Ages. Thanks to Arabic translations, the ancient Greek classics survived and spread into Christian Europe. Medicine, the arts, and commerce flourished under Arab empires.

Concepts

ZIONISM

Europe turned nationalistic in the nineteenth century, and with this came anti-Semitism. Feeling threatened, some of Europe's Jews revived their old dream and coined the term Zionism in the 1880s to describe the new sense of Jewish nationalism that sought to return Jews to Palestine. Zion is the Jerusalem hill from which David and Solomon ruled. Not all Jews were or are Zionists or want to settle in Israel.

These caliphates crumbled over time. The Christian crusades and a brutal Mongol invasion in the thirteenth century weakened Arab civilization. No longer able to expand, it atrophied. Portugal opened the sea route around Africa to the Orient, bypassing Arab traders. Muslim mysticism turned Islam from a tolerant and eclectic faith to a narrow and reactionary one. By the time the Ottoman Turks, themselves Muslims, expanded through the Middle East in the sixteenth century, there was little Arab resistance. The Arab lands fell into the "sleep of centuries" as backwater provinces of the Ottoman Empire.

In the nineteenth century, however, Europe's nationalism also rippled into the decaying Ottoman Empire. Arab officers in the Ottoman army resented not being treated as equals with Turkish officers. Some formed conspiratorial cells aiming for Arab independence. An "Arab awakening" began with a literary revival in Lebanon in the mid-nineteenth century, much of it led by Arab Christians. Half-forgotten classics spoke of the glory of Arab culture and history.

Diplomacy

PROMISES, PROMISES

Desperate in World War I, Britain made promises to win allies and paid no attention to how the promises overlapped and contradicted each other, leading to angry conflict later.

1. *The McMahon-Hussein Letters:* The British boss of Egypt, Sir Henry McMahon, exchanged ten letters with Sherif Hussein in 1915–1916 to encourage the Arabs to revolt against the Turks. McMahon agreed with Hussein that there should be an Arab land, but he left the borders vague. Hussein wanted the entire Arabian peninsula and Fertile Crescent (including Palestine). McMahon hedged, but the Arabs thought they had a deal.

2. *The Sykes-Picot Agreement:* At the same time, Britain, France, and Russia secretly agreed to carve up the Ottoman Empire after the war. The Arabs could have the Arabian peninsula, but Britain and France would divide the Fertile Crescent into spheres of influence, the British in Palestine and Mesopotamia and the French in Syria and Lebanon. The Bolsheviks published the agreement to show how dastardly the imperialists were. Sykes-Picot

was clearly at odds with the McMahon-Hussein understanding.

3. *The Balfour Declaration:* In the fall of 1917 the British cabinet, to win worldwide Jewish support for the war effort, issued a declaration named after the foreign secretary:

His Majesty's Government view with favour the establishment in Palestine of a national home for the Jewish people, and will use their best endeavours to facilitate the achievement of this object, it being clearly understood that nothing shall be done which may prejudice the civil and religious rights of existing non-Jewish communities in Palestine.

Notice that the declaration promised no Jewish state, just a "national home," and that it looked out for Arab rights as well. Nonetheless, it seems to be at odds with the preceding two agreements. How many people can you promise the same land to?

The first Arab Congress met in Paris in 1913 to seek Arab self-rule within the Ottoman Empire. Istanbul refused. On the eve of World War I, Arab nationalists saw that they needed a powerful ally to free them from the Turks. Like the Zionists, the Arab nationalists lined up British power for their own nationalist ends. Britain in World War I launched both Zionist and Arab nationalist movements into a contest for land.

mandate   League of Nations grant of semicolonial power to Britain and France over former German and Turkish possessions.

■ World War I and the Mandate

Turkey allied with Germany in World War I. Istanbul knew that Britain, France, and Russia coveted pieces of the Ottoman Empire. A British officer, T. E. Lawrence, organized the Arab revolt of 1916 to oust the Turks from the Fertile Crescent and expand the British empire. But the Arabs in this revolt, led by Hussein, the Sherif of Mecca and Medina, thought they were fighting for Arab self-rule. Britain meanwhile encouraged the Zionist movement as a means of mobilizing Jewish opinion in the United States and Russia to support the war effort.

Britain soon torpedoed Arab aspirations. Britain and France divided the Fertile Crescent and ignored Arab protests. In 1922, the new League of Nations, which Britain and France dominated, gave them **mandates** over the region. The British did, for a while, honor the Balfour commitment to let Jews have a national home in Palestine, and from 1919 to 1931 an average of ten thousand Jews entered annually, not a major influx. Angered at British betrayal and fearful that Jewish immigration would take over the country, Palestinian Arabs rioted against Jews in 1920 and 1921, leaving over one hundred dead. This began the violent confrontation between the two communities.

In the 1930s, anti-Semitic regimes in Germany and Poland accelerated Jewish immigration to Palestine. Jewish organizations bought more land, and this led to more Arab rioting. In 1936 civil war between Arabs and Jews broke out. A Jewish self-defense force, the *Haganah,* was organized; it later became the core of the Israeli army. Kibbutzniks tilled the soil by day and fought off Arab attacks by night.

Diplomacy

BRITAIN INVENTS JORDAN

The original League mandate on Palestine included present-day Jordan as well. In 1921 the British split off Transjordan ("the land beyond the Jordan") and gave it to one of Hussein's sons as a reward for his help in expelling the Turks. The British advised Transjordan's king, subsidized him, and equipped and trained his army, the Arab Legion. In 1948, as the British pulled out of Palestine, the kingdom was renamed Jordan. Some Israelis argue that Jordan's origins as part of Palestine mean that Palestinians already have a state—on the other side of the Jordan River. No Palestinians buy this argument.

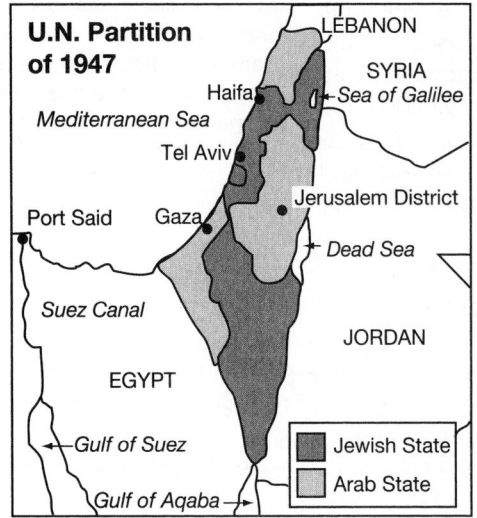

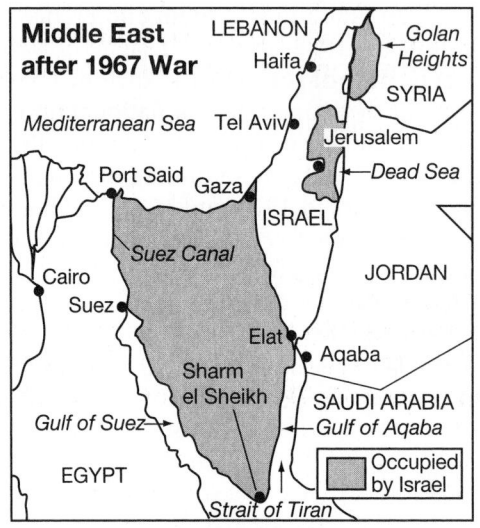

Shifting Middle East Maps

By 1938 there were 413,000 Jews in Palestine, still a minority because the Arab population had grown too. By 1939, Britain knew that war was coming and that Germany desired the region's strategic position and petroleum. Hitler indeed sent two armies toward the area, one through Russia into the Caucasus and another across North Africa into Egypt. German agents encouraged the Arabs (and Iranians—see Chapter 9) to revolt against the British. Britain was scared and tried to calm the Arabs.

In 1939 Britain issued a **white paper** that severely re-stricted Jewish immigration; only 75,000 more would be al-lowed over the next four years. The Arabs were calmed, but the Zionists felt betrayed. Britain closed the immigration door precisely when Europe's Jews needed a refuge. Still, the Jews of Palestine had to support the British. Said Zionist leader David Ben Gurion: "We will fight the White Paper as if there were no war and fight the war as if there were no White Paper."

white paper Major diplomatic policy statement.

Holocaust Nazi genocide of Jews.

partition The formal division of a disputed territory.

The war turned Zionism from a romantic dream to a tough demand for a Jewish state. As Jews desperately sought to leave Europe, there was practically no place that would take them. They were the "boat people" of the 1930s and 1940s. The British barred them from Palestine. Some Zionists, including two who later became prime ministers of Israel (Men-achem Begin and Yitzhak Shamir), in rage and frustration turned to terrorism against the British mandate: "The Nazis kill us, and the British won't let us live."

The discovery of the Nazi death camps in 1945 clinched the Zionist argument, an argument made since Herzl: Jews would never be safe until they had their own coun-try. The Nazis had exterminated some six million Jews while the world paid little atten-tion. The survivors demanded to be let into Palestine, and Zionists demanded a Jewish state. Jewish terrorists in Palestine murdered British soldiers. To fight for a Jewish state was the highest morality; anyone who got in their way was immoral. Israelis developed a mind-set to never again trust their fate to others—no one gave a damn during the **Holocaust**—and to this day Israelis dislike outsiders proposing "peace plans" that threat-en their security.

▌ The 1948 War

Britain's position in Palestine became untenable after World War II. Broke and exhausted, Britain in 1947 threw the problem to the new United Nations. A UN commission recom-mended **partition** of Palestine into a checkerboard of Arab and Jewish areas with a neu-tral Jerusalem (see maps on page 122). The UN General Assembly voted for the plan 33 to 13 with 10 abstaining. Both the United States and the Soviet Union and most of their al-lies voted for the plan, but all of the Middle East states voted against. Moscow saw it as a way to get Britain out of the Middle East and enhance their own role. Both Washington and Moscow immediately recognized the new state of Israel.

The Jews, at this point about a third of Palestine's population, accepted partition, but the Arab states and the Palestinian Arabs rejected it. Arabs, contesting Israel's right to exist, saw no reason to compromise. On May 14, 1948, as the British mandate ended, Ben Gu-rion proclaimed the state of Israel, and five Arab armies—Egypt, Syria, Iraq, Jordan, and Lebanon—moved in to grab a piece of Palestine.

The Arabs got a shock. The Haganah fielded an army of 40,000, half of them World War II veterans, and scrounged up war-surplus weapons or made their own. Their best weapon was high morale born of desperation. If they lost, the entire Jewish population would be "pushed into the sea." Israeli military doctrine is based on *ayn brayra,* no alternative.

With the exception of Jordan's British-officered Arab Legion, the Arab armies fought poorly. No Arab country wanted a separate Arab country of Palestine. Israel beat all but the

**Sinai Campaign   1956 war in
which Israel took Sinai.**

Jordanians, who occupied and held what is today called the West Bank plus East Jerusalem with the Old City and most holy sites. Israel held West Jerusalem.

Under UN auspices (see Chapter 21) in 1949, Egypt, Syria, Jordan, and Lebanon agreed to truces with Israel but not to peace. Israel now held 80 percent of the Palestine mandate. Some 700,000 Palestinian Arabs fled Israel; their property was declared "abandoned" and seized. The permanent core of the Arab-Israel conflict has been and still is the Palestinians.

The 1956 War

The 1956 war, also known as the Suez Crisis and **Sinai Campaign**, again illustrates the role of outside powers in starting and ending Arab-Israeli wars. Britain and France attacked Egypt, and the United States and USSR pressured them to clear out.

Egyptian President Gamal Abdul Nasser was a new breed of Arab leader. The Egyptian army, humiliated at its defeat by the Israelis, blamed the corrupt monarchy, and under Colonel Nasser's leadership carried out a coup against King Farouk in 1952. Nasser saw himself not simply as an Egyptian nationalist but as the leader of a pan-Arab movement. He supported the Algerian nationalists against the French and opposed the U.S.- and British-backed Baghdad Pact that sought to keep Soviet influence out of the Middle East.

Events unrolled quickly as each side enraged the other. It began with Palestinian refugees. In the Gaza Strip, under Egyptian control since 1948, some Palestinians became *fedayeen*, "self-sacrificers," who made raids into Israel. They were armed and trained by Egypt as part of Nasser's policy of using conflict with Israel to arouse and unify all Arabs under his leadership. Israel retaliated with major raids on Egyptian posts in the Gaza Strip. Enraged, Nasser sought arms. The United States and Britain refused, but the Soviet Union was happy to sell enormous quantities. With Soviet weapons, Nasser built up his forces in the Sinai facing Israel, and Israel grew nervous.

Disappointed that Nasser was turning to the Soviets, the United States and Britain withdrew their offer to help fund construction of Egypt's dream, the Aswan Dam on the Nile. Angered by this withdrawal, Nasser nationalized the British- and French-owned Suez Canal on July 26, 1956. It was a vestige of colonialism, he argued, and now Egypt needed its revenues to build the Aswan Dam. Enraged by Nasser's canal takeover, Britain and France quietly colluded with Israel to take the canal back. Israel would strike first, and they would come in to "protect" the canal.

On October 29, 1956, Israeli forces streaked through the Sinai toward the Suez Canal. London and Paris issued ultimatums to both sides to withdraw ten miles from the canal, and invaded and seized the canal zone on November 5. The 1956 war ended with Israel in possession of the Sinai and Britain and France in possession of the canal. Nasser was beaten but not defeated. Eisenhower was angry that London and Paris moved on Egypt against U.S. advice. This last gasp of British and French imperialism would only push Arab nationalists closer to the Soviets, Ike reasoned. The United States supported a UN resolution to oust the invading forces and used economic pressure to get the British and French to withdraw from Suez, which they did in December.

Israel took more persuading. Ike threatened economic sanctions and promised to get Egypt to open the **Tiran Strait** to Israeli shipping. With a UN Emergency Force (UNEF) to patrol the Sinai, Israel pulled out in March 1957. In 1956, as in subsequent wars, the victors had not won, and the war settled nothing.

Tiran Strait   Narrow entrance from Red Sea to Gulf of Aqaba.

Six Day War   1967 war in which Israel took Sinai, West Bank, and Golan Heights.

preempt   To strike first on the eve of war.

▌ The Six Day War

One result of the 1956 war was that Egypt and Syria became Soviet clients. Fedayeen again raided, and Israel retaliated. In 1963, Israel began a project to divert water from the Jordan River (a creek in U.S. terms), angering Syria and Jordan. Regional tensions mounted. By spring 1967, events took hold of Nasser and pushed him toward war. He may have been bluffing; the Israelis called it. Nasser declared he was ready for war with Israel, and Israelis took the threat literally. This was in part the clash of two cultures: Arabs are given to exaggerated rhetoric, Israelis to straight, blunt talk.

Much of the blame for the **Six Day War** must rest on Syrian and Soviet lies. Syria held the Golan Heights overlooking Israel's lush Upper Galilee and shelled Israeli farmers; in response Israeli jets hit Syrian gun positions and shot down six Syrian MIGs. Damascus lied, saying that Israel was massing troops in the Galilee to attack Syria. What, Damascus demanded, was Nasser, the great hero of the Arabs, going to do? Syria was goading Nasser into a strong response.

Israel denied any such intent and invited the Soviet ambassador to take a look; in this small valley troops are easily visible. The ambassador declined but repeated that Israel was preparing to invade Syria. Nasser had to show he would aid Syria. He ordered the UN forces out of the Sinai, where they had served as truce observers since 1957. Then he closed Tiran to Israeli shipping and ordered a troop buildup in the Sinai. On May 30, 1967, he signed a defense pact with King Hussein of Jordan; he already had such an agreement with Syria. The cautious Hussein had previously stayed clear of involvement with Nasser and had not threatened Israel.

Israel was thus surrounded by hate-filled Arabs screaming "war." Israel's narrow neck between Jordan and the sea was less than ten miles wide in places. Israel's attitude grew out of its geopolitical situation: Either we **preempt** or we're doomed. Israel quietly began mobilizing reservists. On June 4 Jerusalem learned that the United States would not force open the Tiran Strait as pledged in 1957. America was bogged down in Vietnam. Israel felt endangered and abandoned and on June 5 preempted.

The results were breathtaking and horrifying. Using tactics from U.S. military training courses, Israeli jets first destroyed Egyptian warplanes on the ground and then Egyptian armor. Israel streaked across the Sinai and reached the Suez Canal June 8.

Jordan began shelling Israel and gave the Israelis the excuse they had been looking for since 1948 to take the Old City of Jerusalem, which they did with three battalions. Jerusalem was declared reunified and forever the capital of Israel, a superemotional symbol. Israel also took the entire West Bank.

The Golan Heights were the hardest for Israel: uphill against Syrian bunkers from June 8 to 10. The Israelis swore they would never relinquish the strategic Golan and incorporated it

logistics   The supplying of an
army.

into Israel in 1981. The Israelis in 1967 knew time was short. The superpowers saw the danger of the war expanding. Moscow threatened to intervene as its clients' armies collapsed, and Washington told Jerusalem to wrap it up fast. The Six Day War was short because of the superpowers.

The three Arab countries lost 14,000 soldiers, Israel only 700. It looked like a brilliant, astonishing victory, a model of training, daring, morale, and competence. But again the war settled nothing. Israel had not taken an Arab capital city or the heartlands of its three foes; the superpowers saw to that. There was no pressing need for the Arabs to "sue for peace," as in classic diplomacy. Instead, they announced in a Khartoum meeting that September: "no negotiation, no recognition, no peace." The United Nations passed the evenhanded Resolution 242, the basis of peace plans ever since, that asked Israel to withdraw and the Arabs to accept Israel's existence on peaceful terms. Both sides ignored 242, each claiming it could not trust the other side. The stage was set for the 1973 war.

Israel, in the flush of victory, also acquired a major problem. The recently seized West Bank and Gaza Strip contained 1.3 million Palestinians—now numbering over 3 million—most of them refugees from the 1948–1949 war or their descendants. Israel would now have to govern the people it wanted to get rid of in 1948.

■ The 1973 War

Egyptian President Anwar Sadat, who took over upon Nasser's death in 1970, believed that Israel's occupation of the Sinai, Golan Heights, and West Bank, had to be challenged, partly to cure the defeatist psychology of Arabs and the victorious psychology of Israelis and partly to make the superpowers take an active interest.

Diplomacy

LOGISTICS AND PEACE

The 1973 war showed that modern warfare consumes munitions at a prodigious rate. War becomes highly dependent on **logistics**. Said Israel's defense minister in 1973: "We are firing shells this afternoon that we did not have in the country this morning." They got them by a U.S. airlift across the Atlantic with aerial refueling. U.S. airlift capacity allows it to project power like no other country.

U.S. Secretary of State Henry Kissinger was no specialist on the Middle East, but he had written books on the balance of power. When Israel was losing, the United States had to resupply it. But Kissinger knew that another Israeli victory would not lead to peace. It would be a repeat of 1956 and 1967. So Kissinger discreetly held up resupplying

Israel, which soon did not have the munitions to move further. Neither side won or lost in 1973; they psychologically balanced.

In "shuttle diplomacy," Kissinger jetted repeatedly between Cairo, Jerusalem, and Damascus, securing truces that held. In both the Sinai and Golan, he mapped out strips of no-man's land flanked by strips thinly patrolled by each side, backed up by strongly held zones. The idea was to separate their main forces. The belligerents signed. The agreement formed the basis of a peace treaty between Egypt and Israel. Based on the idea that power should balance, Kissinger produced a brilliant piece of diplomacy.

On October 6, 1973, Egyptians and Syrians struck a surprised Israel. Over two thousand Soviet-made Syrian tanks penetrated the lightly held Golan Heights. Israel repelled them in the biggest tank battle in history. Meanwhile, Egyptian forces crossed the Suez Canal and broke through Israel's lightly held Bar Lev Line and into the Sinai. In a bold gamble, Israeli General Ariel Sharon crossed his forces to the west side of the canal and cut off the Egyptians on the east.

October War 1973 Arab-Israeli war, also called Yom Kippur or Ramadan War.

PLO Palestine Liberation Organization, mainstream resistance party that formerly ran *PA*.

At this point, the United States and USSR, after desperately resupplying their clients, tried to enforce another UN cease-fire. Moscow threatened to send troops to aid the Egyptians. President Nixon then put U.S. forces on worldwide alert to deter Soviet intervention. U.S. delay in resupplying Israel stopped Israel's further advances. As before, outside powers decided things.

The war, known as the **October War**, jolted the world. Arab oil exporters embargoed oil shipments to countries deemed pro-Israel (the United States and the Netherlands) and then quadrupled the price of petroleum. This kicked up world inflation for years. Militarily, the world's armies took careful note, for the war demonstrated that small, guided missiles could knock out jets and tanks. The Arabs had shown that Israel was not invincible. Heavy Israeli losses (2,500 dead to 8,000 Syrians and 8,000 Egyptians) made Israel worry about a long war.

The psychological change enabled Anwar Sadat to amaze the world. In 1977 he accepted Israel's invitation and flew to Jerusalem for face-to-face talks with Israeli Prime Minister Menachem Begin. Sadat spoke to the Israelis not as a loser but as an equal. This led to the Camp David talks at the president's Maryland retreat in 1978. President Carter mediated and cajoled Begin and Sadat into the first Arab-Israeli peace treaty, completed in 1979. Each side emerged with something. Sadat got the Sinai back and more U.S. aid to head off food riots by Egypt's poor. Begin got an opportunity to split Israel's Arab enemies—Egypt was expelled from the Arab bloc—and increased U.S. financial support.

■ The Rise of Palestinian Nationalism

The 1978 Camp David agreement left the most crucial problem vague, and it led to another war. Israel pledged to accept "Palestinian autonomy," but nothing came of it. Land seizures for new Israeli settlements in East Jerusalem and the West Bank increased; now some 400,000 Israelis live there. Palestinian nationalism grew, mostly under the **PLO**, headed by Yasser Arafat. Palestinians had been treated badly by the British, the Israelis, and other Arab countries, who used them for their own purposes. Everywhere they were homeless and foreigners. No Arab country wanted them in large numbers. In a colossal irony, the Palestinians became like Jews, a dispersed and sometimes suspect people with no national home. And like Zionists, Palestinians concluded they needed their own country.

Israel's takeover of the West Bank and Gaza Strip in 1967 ended any illusions about Egypt or Jordan "protecting" the Palestinians. This also allowed Palestinians to work in Israel and view for the first time their ancestral land, but as noncitizens. Israelis treated them with disdain, and there was little contact between the two communities. The hatred got worse.

ARAB-ISRAELI WARS		
Year	Name	Result
1948–1949	Israeli Independence	Israel founded on most of Palestine.
1956	Sinai Campaign	Israel beats Egypt, takes Sinai.
1967	Six Day War	Israel takes Sinai from Egypt, West Bank from Jordan, Golan Heights from Syria.
1973	October War	Israel repels Egypt and Syria.
1982	Lebanon Incursion	Israel invades southern Lebanon.
2006	Hezbollah War	Israel in Lebanon again.

intifada   Arabic for uprising; includes suicide bombings.

Hezbollah   ("Party of God") Iranian-sponsored Lebanese Shi'a militia.

A number of factors led to two bloody **intifadas**. The fate of Palestinians has dangled unresolved for decades. They still have no country of their own. Israeli settlements, roads, and security fences in the West Bank continued to grow, taking more Palestinian land and hacking the territory into small pieces. The Palestinian birth rate is one of the world's highest. In a century, the number of Palestinians has grown from half a million to five million, many of them in other countries. Coupled with a ruined economy, this produces armies of unemployed, angry youth. Muslim extremism has grown across the Middle East, inspiring some youths to become terrorists and suicide bombers. Every act of Palestinian terrorism produces brutal Israeli reprisals—demolition of homes, "targeted assassinations," and tough occupation restrictions—which inflame more Palestinians.

The 1982 War

In 1975, Lebanon fell apart in a civil war between Christians and Muslims, and this allowed the PLO to set up a state within a state, "Fatahland," in southern Lebanon. A dozen Lebanese religio-political militias battled, some of them backed by Syria, which took over eastern Lebanon, an area it had long claimed. Israel invaded Lebanon in June 1982 to knock out Palestinian bases and help put Christians back in power, but the Israeli army bogged down fighting Muslim militias. U.S. "peacekeeping" forces arrived but soon began supporting the Christians. Misguidedly, we took sides in a civil war. A **Hezbollah** truck bomb killed 241 sleeping U.S. Marines, and we withdrew. Israel pulled back but kept a roughly nine-mile-wide "security zone" in southern Lebanon. Hezbollah fighters bombed and ambushed the Israelis weekly until they withdrew entirely in 2000. In 2006, Hezbollah kidnapped two Israeli soldiers, and Israel responded with another invasion that did massive civilian damage. Some count it as the sixth Arab-Israeli war. Hezbollah boasts that it is the only Arab force to ever beat the Israelis.

■ Is There Hope?

War is easy; peace is hard. Peace negotiations, opposed by **rejectionists** on both sides, can quickly collapse. In a climate of tension and frustration, extremists fuel a downward spiral. Four Arab-Israeli wars (1956, 1967, 1982, and 2006) were triggered by terrorist attacks on Israel. Palestinian militants say only violence works, because Israel seizes their land and ignores their rights. And Israeli militants say they are entitled to retaliation because the Arabs want to kill them. Down and down the spiral goes.

rejectionist Those who reject compromise peace.

Cooler heads on both sides know that they must strike a deal, but both are constrained by fears of what could go wrong and by their own militants. Israel cannot govern millions of angry Palestinians on the West Bank without becoming an authoritarian police state. Israelis fear, however, that a Palestinian state would be a terrorist training camp that had the goal of recovering all of historic Palestine. Many Palestinians still wish to destroy Israel.

Israeli settlements in the West Bank are major obstacles. Settlers were lured by a mixture of religion and affordable housing. Rightist Israelis claim these areas are theirs by biblical right, that they have been paid for in blood, and that turning them over to Israel's sworn enemies would be suicidal. Liberal and leftist Israelis say that giving up these settlements for a lasting peace would be worthwhile.

Israeli troops amass near the border with southern Lebanon in 2006 to fight Hezbollah. (Rina Castelnuovo/The New York Times)

Fatah   Yasser Arafat's armed party that dominated *PLO*.

Palestinian Authority   Quasi-government of Palestine.

Hamas   (Arabic for "zeal") Armed Palestinian Islamist party, founded in 1987.

Muslim Brotherhood   Original modern Islamist movement, founded in Egypt in 1928.

Moderate Palestinians know they must come up with a Palestinian state soon without conceding too much or extremists will spark a new war, and Israel will be tempted to "transfer"—a euphemism for expel—thousands of Palestinians out of the West Bank and take over most of it. Rejectionists on both sides are happy to block the peace process. The 2000 intifada exploded when a rightwing Israeli ex-general (and later prime minister), Ariel Sharon, defiantly visited Jerusalem's top Muslim holy site. Thousands died, mostly Palestinian youths, many of whom volunteered for suicide bombings. Among both Palestinians and Israelis, many cheer the *failure* of peace talks, arguing they give away too much to the other side.

In 2006 Israel completed construction of a long fence to keep Palestinian suicide bombers from reaching Israel. In 2005, Sharon ordered some 8,500 Israeli settlers out of the Gaza Strip; many resisted. These moves marked an Israeli unilateral solution. Jerusalem in effect says, "Look, Arabs won't negotiate and can't stop violence, so we'll do what we must to make Israel secure." But the wall did not stop Hamas and Hezbollah rockets and infiltrators. In 2006, after Hezbollah kidnapped two Israeli soldiers, Israel retaliated with air strikes deep into Lebanon, and Hezbollah fired some of its 12,000

Concepts

CAN EXTREMISTS TURN PRAGMATIC?

Militant Palestinian organizations tend to evolve, slowly and grudgingly, from passion to practicality. The PLO, founded in Egypt in 1964, began with fiery radio rants calling for the destruction of Israel—one reason Israel preempted in 1967. Meanwhile Yasser Arafat developed his **Fatah** into a guerrilla force and with it took over the PLO in 1969. The PLO became a Palestinian government in exile successively in Jordan, Lebanon, and Tunisia, always hunted by the Israelis.

In 1988 King Hussein dropped Jordanian claims to the West Bank, indicating it should become a Palestinian state. The 1991 Gulf War (see next chapter) left the PLO broke and isolated, and it moderated, turning from raids to diplomacy. Arafat—not always backed by more militant Palestinians—accepted the existence of Israel and began off-and-on negotiations with it. Norwegian mediation brought the Oslo Accord in 1993, which, among other points, created the **Palestinian Authority** (PA).

The PA now controls the Gaza Strip and parts of the West Bank but is not yet a state. Arafat was PA president until his death in 2005.

Arafat longed to overthrow Israel, but he could not and so was forced to become more pragmatic. **Hamas**, related to the much-older **Muslim Brotherhood**, swore to destroy Israel and carried out suicide bombings. Hamas became bigger than the corrupt and ineffective PLO by delivering charity, schooling, and health care. Hamas won the 2006 PA parliamentary elections and took over the PA government. After Israel pulled out of the Gaza Strip, militants there shot rockets into Israel and kidnapped an Israeli soldier. The Hamas government seemed to have ruined any chances for peace. The big question: Can extremists get realistic? Will fierce Israeli reprisals and economic hardship force Hamas, which is dedicated to the destruction of Israel, to abandon its goal and negotiate?

Iranian-supplied rockets into Israel. The major powers achieved a cease-fire before the conflict escalated into full-scale war.

Peace in the Middle East at times seems impossible. Rabin and Arafat in 1993 pledged on the White House lawn to work for peace, but in 1995 an Israeli fanatic gunned down Rabin at a peace rally. Egypt and Israel signed a peace treaty in 1979, Jordan and Israel in 1994, but it led only to "cold peace" with little contact, commerce, or good feeling. Both treaties happened because at a certain point the two sides had more to gain than to lose by ending the state of war. Both treaties were sponsored by the United States, which delivers major foreign aid to all three countries. Israel gets some $3 billion in U.S. aid annually, Egypt some $2 billion. If the United States cut its gifts of grain to Egypt, food riots would break out. U.S. and EU aid supports the PA. Aid gives leverage.

Israel-Palestinian talks have at times made progress, but three questions block a deal. Israel must give up many—perhaps most—of its settlements in the West Bank to make a territorially coherent Palestinian state. Many Israelis refuse. Palestinians want the right of return, to go back to the homes and farms they fled in 1948. Israelis see they would soon be swamped and reject the demand. Palestinians also insist on sovereignty over East Jerusalem. Israelis swear that Jerusalem is eternally theirs. The issue is emotional and symbolic, but symbolic concessions can sometimes work around problems. What exactly is "sovereignty" and what exactly is "Jerusalem"? There is some wiggle room here that could lead to a compromise. Peace between Palestinians and Israelis could produce an economic boom in the region. If they cannot compromise, there will soon be another, major war.

Lessons of the Arab-Israeli Conflict

1. Nothing gives an eternal claim to land. The belief that history or the Bible or God gave territories to certain people leads to war without end.

2. People have long memories, especially of injustice. The Israelis remember the Holocaust, and the Palestinians remember their lost homeland. For peace, memories must fade.

3. Outside powers start conflicts. British, U.S., and Soviet arms, money, and policy set up Middle East wars.

4. Terror begets terror. All sides have practiced terrorism, which guarantees terrorist responses and blocks peace.

5. One war leads to another. A clear causal line connects World War II to 1948, to 1956, to 1967, to 1973, to 1982, and to 2006.

6. Do not lie or bluff about war. Your adversary may take it literally.

7. You cannot ignore inconvenient people. Neither Israelis nor Palestinians will disappear.

8. A few extremists can upset the peace process. If hardliners guide events, there will be no peace.

9. A committed outside mediator is essential for the peace process. If the United States does not do it, no one will.

10. We are entitled to despair but better not. Giving up and letting Arabs and Israelis murder each other is immoral and could produce a bigger war, one that could hurt us.

Key Terms

caliphate (p. 119)

Fatah (p. 130)

Hamas (p. 130)

Hezbollah (p. 128)

Holocaust (p. 123)

intifada (p. 128)

Islam (p. 119)

logistics (p. 126)

mandate (p. 121)

Muslim (p. 119)

Muslim Brotherhood (p. 130)

nationalism (p. 118)

October War (p. 127)

Ottoman (p. 119)

Palestine (p. 118)

Palestinian Authority (p. 130)

partition (p. 123)

PLO (p. 127)

preempt (p. 125)

rejectionist (p. 129)

Sinai Campaign (p. 124)

Six Day War (p. 125)

Tiran Strait (p. 125)

white paper (p. 123)

Zionism (p. 118)

Key Web Sites

HyperQur'aan Project
http://www.uoknor.edu/cybermuslim/cy_quraan.html

Arab Net
http://www.arab.net/

Jerusalem Post
http://www.jpost.com/

Israeli Foreign Ministry
http://www.israel-mfa.gov.il/

Lebanese Embassy
http://www.erols.com/lebanon/

Further Reference

Bickerton, Ian J., and Carla L. Klausner. *A Concise History of the Arab–Israeli Conflict,* 5th ed. Upper Saddle River, NJ: Prentice Hall, 2006.

Cordesman, Anthony H. *The Israeli-Palestinian War: Escalating to Nowhere.* Westport, CT: Praeger, 2005.

Creveld, Martin van. *Defending Israel: A Strategic Plan for Peace and Security.* New York: St. Martin's, 2005.

Kimmerling, Baruch, and Joel S. Migdal. *The Palestinian People: A History.* Cambridge, MA: Harvard University Press, 2003.

Meital, Yoram. *Peace in Tatters: Israel, Palestine, and the Middle East.* Boulder, CO: L. Rienner, 2005.

Morris, Benny. *Making Israel.* New York: I. B. Tauris, 2004.

Oren, Michael J. *Six Days of War: June 1967 and the Making of the Modern Middle East.* New York: Oxford University Press, 2002.

Rabinovich, Itamar. *Waging Peace: Israel and the Arabs at the End of the Century.* New York: Farrar, Straus and Giroux, 1999.

Ross, Dennis. *The Missing Peace: The Inside Story of the Fight for Middle East Peace.* New York: Farrar, Straus and Giroux, 2004.

Rubenberg, Cheryl A. *The Palestinians: In Search of a Just Peace.* Boulder, CO: Lynne Rienner, 2003.

Thomas, Baylis. *How Israel Was Won: A Concise History of the Arab-Israeli Conflict.* Lanham, MD: Lexington Books, 1999.

Wasserstein, Bernard. *Israelis and Palestinians: Why Do They Fight? Can They Stop?,* 2nd ed. New Haven, CT: Yale University Press, 2005.

CHAPTER 9

OIL AND TURMOIL

THE PERSIAN GULF

QUESTIONS TO CONSIDER

1. Why is the Persian Gulf region so important?
2. What are the strategic waterways of the region?
3. What is Huntington's civilizational theory?
4. What are the differences between Iran and the Arab countries?
5. Why did Iran erupt in Islamic revolution?
6. What were the first, second, and third Gulf Wars about?
7. Why did Saddam use chemical weapons in the first but not the second or third Gulf War?
8. How did U.S. diplomacy blunder in Iran and Iraq?
9. Would you be willing to fight to keep Gulf oil flowing?

The U.S.-led war against Iraq in 2003 was quick and brilliant, but occupation of Iraq was long and messy with no easy way to get out. Most Americans agreed that Saddam Hussein was a bloody and aggressive dictator who deserved to be ousted, but few knew much about Iraq or the complexities that would follow a war. Soon many turned critical. Washington had neglected a very basic point: In the Middle East, nothing is simple.

Most Americans would like to keep out of the Middle East, but its oil, politics, and even religions draw us in. Islam is not just a religion; it is a distinct civilization that does not easily bend or compromise with the modern world. Islam has always divided the world into the *dar es-salaam* (house of peace, meaning the Islamic world) and the *dar al-harb* (house of war, the non-Muslim world). Muslim fundamentalists still see the world this way: us versus them.

In the Gulf, religion fuses with nationalism to become a political tool with which to push out foreigners, first the British, now the Americans. If this were Tierra del Fuego it might not matter, but the Gulf region contains the world's greatest oil reserves, a strategic prize. Two-thirds of the globe's proven petroleum reserves are in the countries that border the Persian Gulf. Another large reserve is around the **Caspian** Sea. Neither of these are stable areas.

■ Irascible Iran

Iran is Muslim but not Arab. It is heir to the much older civilization of Persia and speaks the Indo-European tongue of Persian. Arabs conquered Persia in A.D. 642 and converted Persians from Zoroastrianism to Islam, but in 1501 Iran adopted the **Shi'a** offshoot in contrast to the **Sunni** Islam of most Muslims.

In the nineteenth century, **Persia**, then in decline, became the prey of outside powers. The Russians in the north, who were rounding out their empire in the **Caucasus** and **Central Asia**, gained economic concessions and territory from the corrupt Qajar **shahs**. The British, pushing up from India, did the same. In 1907, the two powers divided Persia in a treaty that assigned each **spheres of influence** in which they dominated and controlled trade. Persia, like China, was reduced to semicolonial status; Persians hated it and vented their anger from time to time on foreign diplomats. Iranians still feel they have been used and dumped on for a century, and now it's their turn to get back.

The Persian government attempted to balance one power with another, the British against the Russian, then Germany against both, so as to give themselves a little freedom and independence. This pattern of playing off stronger outside powers against each other continues, a rational response for a weak country trying to preserve its independence.

In 1908 the British first discovered oil in Persia and got an exclusive concession to develop it, paying a paltry 16 percent royalty to Persia. The Anglo-Iranian Oil Company (AIOC) was a state within a state, a company that could call the tune in its host country. Many Iranians hated the AIOC. Early in the twentieth century, many Persians sought democracy and constitutional monarchy. They were ignored by the British and the corrupt rulers of Tehran; this deepened their hatred of the British. In 1925 a vigorous but illiterate cavalry officer, Reza Khan, proclaimed himself shah. Never popular or democratic, Reza Khan ruthlessly modernized his country—which he renamed Iran, Persian for "Aryan," a word later beloved of Nazi ideologists.

When the Hitler regime looked for openings in the Middle East, it found a willing ally in Reza, who thought he could use the Germans to dislodge the British. Instead, the British exiled the shah. When the Soviet Union entered the war in 1941, it invaded the northern part of Iran while the British took the southern, just as the 1907 treaty specified. Iran became a major conduit for U.S. supplies into the Soviet Union during the war. Both agreed to exit Iran within six months of the end of the war. Stalin did not and even set up Soviet puppet states in the north of Iran. Some historians peg Stalin's attempt to seize part of Iran as the opening round of the Cold War.

The power and profits of the AIOC still rankled Iranians. In 1951, a **populist** prime minister, Muhammad Mossadeq, **nationalized** the AIOC and forced the young shah, son of

---

Caspian   Large inland sea between Caucasus and Central Asia.

Shi'a   Minority branch of Islam but Iran's state religion.

Sunni   Mainstream Islam.

Persia   Old name for Iran.

Caucasus   Mountainous region between Black and Caspian Seas.

Central Asia   Ex-Soviet area between Caspian Sea and China.

shah   Persian for king.

sphere of influence   Area where a major power held sway.

populist   A crowd-pleasing politician, claims to represent "the people" against elites.

nationalize   To seize private firms for the state.

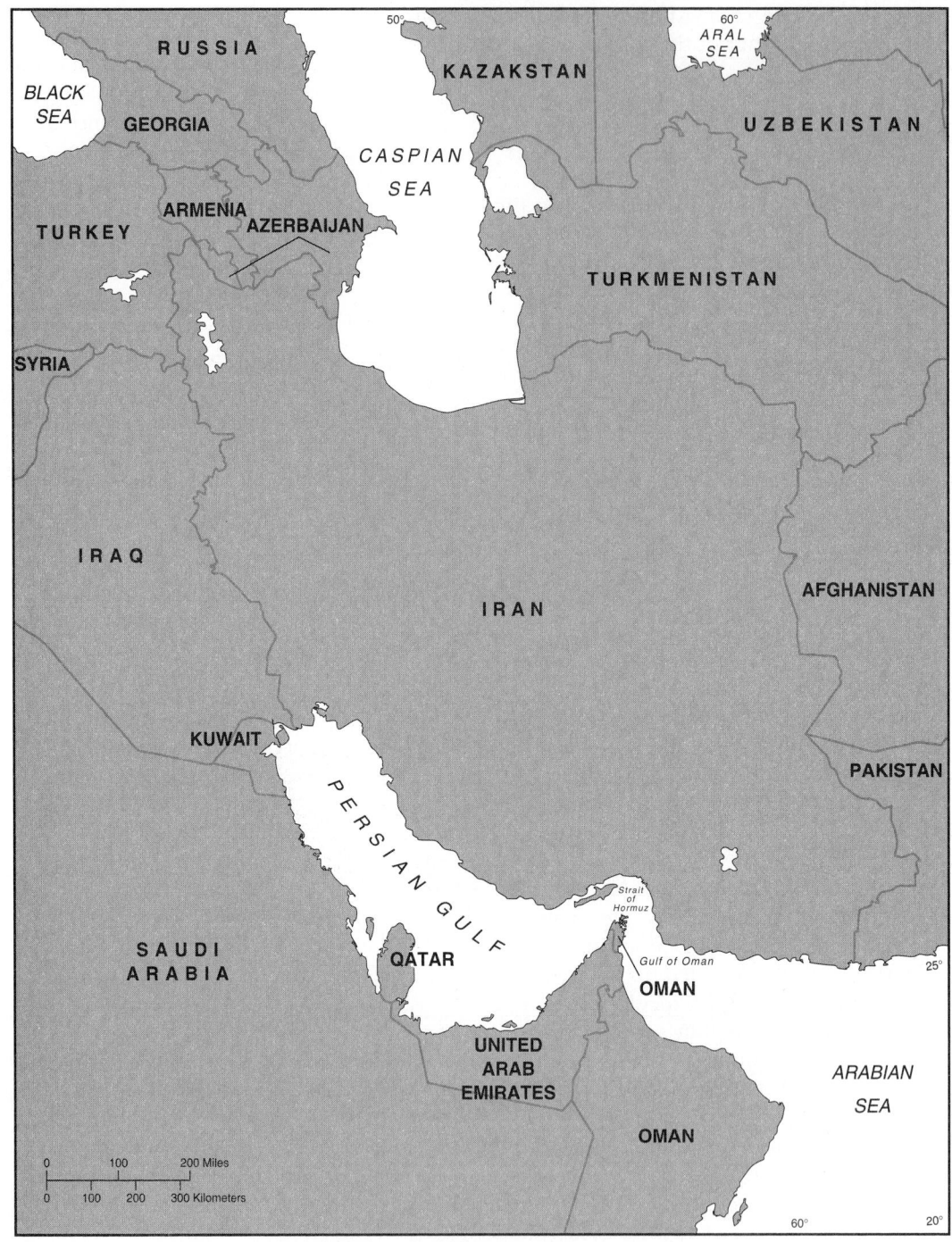

The Persian Gulf and Caspian Sea

Reza Khan, to flee to Rome. Especially hurt were the British, the owners of the AIOC, who turned to Washington for help. President Eisenhower, fearing Communist influence, in 1953 sent Kermit Roosevelt of the CIA to Tehran with $1 million in a suitcase. Hired mobs encouraged anti-Mossadeq and pro-shah protests. Mossadeq fell, and the shah returned but was never very popular.

The shah built a dictatorship. He suppressed both leftists and Islamic fundamentalists. He controlled the parliament and all mass communications. After oil, corruption was Iran's biggest industry. The powerful secret police, the dread SAVAK, arrested and tortured opponents. The United States deliberately did not notice any of this, seeing the shah as a pillar of stability and a friend of America in an important part of the world. The shah was obsessed with military strength, and Washington was happy to sell him weapons. Much of Iran's oil income went for arms, a point that angered many Iranians. Between 1971 and 1977, the United States sold an amazing $12 billion in weapons to Iran, one-third of U.S. overseas military sales. There was a major American presence in Tehran—diplomatic, military, and private business—that rubbed some Iranians, especially devout Muslims, the wrong way. American attitudes on alcohol and sex were un-Koranic and immoral. Khomeini could later play into the feeling that Americans were "unclean."

Both the Americans and the shah believed that petroleum revenues would fuel Iran's modernization. The shah instituted a "White Revolution" (a revolution from the top down, instead of a "red" revolution from the masses up) that divided landholdings and gave them to poor peasants. But many Iranians opposed the land reform, especially Muslim charitable foundations that owned much land. Rioting broke out in opposition. Political development was zero. Economic growth without channels of mass participation in politics—parties, parliament, elections, and so on—means that mass discontent can manifest itself only in violent and revolutionary ways.

One top Muslim cleric, the Ayatollah Khomeini, especially attacked the shah and in 1964 was exiled to neighboring Iraq. Khomeini kept up his drumfire of hatred for the shah and charged that SAVAK murdered his son. The shah put pressure on Iraq, which expelled Khomeini to France in 1978. From his suburban Paris home, Khomeini made bitter anti-shah

Geography

THE STRAIT OF HORMUZ

The entrance to the Persian Gulf at its narrowest is twenty-one miles wide. Two ship channels used by supertankers are one mile wide each, one for west-bound and one for eastbound vessels. Through this strait passes 20 percent of the world's oil supply, much of it to East Asia. Closing the Strait of Hormuz would wreak havoc on the world economy, possibly triggering a depression. It would have been easy for Iran to close, by planting mines in the ship channels or firing missiles. After a few hits, shippers would not be able to pay the insurance premiums. But the Iranians had good reason not to close the Strait: They export all their oil by ship through it; their Arab adversaries could still export by pipeline to the Mediterranean and Red seas. The finger of land on the southern side of the Strait belongs to Oman, a U.S. ally.

OPEC Organization of Petroleum Exporting Countries; cartel aimed at keeping price of oil up.

civilization In Huntington's theory, a major and distinct cultural area, based largely on a religion.

Islamism The Muslim faith used in a political way, sometimes called "Islamic fundamentalism."

---

sermons that were played over long-distance telephone and re-recorded in Iran. Cassettes were then distributed nationwide and played in mosques, overleaping the shah's control of mass communications. Cheap cassette players thus helped bring him down.

What really hurt the shah was too much money. He hammered the Western oil companies for a better deal—eventually getting a fat 75 percent split for Iran—and was a founding member of **OPEC**. The shah took advantage of the 1973 Arab-Israeli war to take over the foreign interests in Iran's oil consortium and quadruple oil prices. The shah did exactly what Mossadeq did but twenty years later. He argued (correctly) that the producing states had been paid too little for their black gold. Now a flood of oil revenue washed into Iran, and the shah went crazy with grandiose visions of Iran, imagining it would soon be a major industrial and military power. Some Iranians—often the more corrupt, including the shah and his friends and relatives—got rich fast; jealousy flared. Poor rural people migrated to the cities in search of work and a better life. Instead, many found unemployment, inflation, and corruption. Religious to begin with, they found sympathy and support at the local mosque, where they also picked up anti-shah messages. By the late 1970s, the shah had little popular support.

Concepts

HUNTINGTON'S "CIVILIZATIONAL" THEORY

The real divisions in the post–Cold War world are not between nations or trade blocs but between **"civilizations"** based largely on religion, argues Harvard political scientist Samuel P. Huntington. In a controversial 1993 article, Huntington saw seven major civilizations: Western (with North American and European branches), Slavic/Orthodox, Islamic, Confucian, Hindu, Japanese (unique), and Latin American. Within a given civilization, nations share much the same outlook and can empathize with each other; conflicts are few and small. Between civilizations, understanding is more difficult and conflicts can be big and nasty.

The greatest source of conflict in the modern world, asserts Huntington, is where Muslim civilization meets other civilizations. "Islam has bloody borders," he argues. Examples: Israel versus the Arabs, Russians versus Chechens, Armenians versus Azeris, Muslim Bosnians and Kosovars versus Serbs, Christians versus Muslims in Lebanon, India versus Pakistan, and Islamic terrorism aimed at U.S. targets.

Furthermore, within Islam there is currently a struggle over who will govern Muslim countries, moderates versus fundamentalists. Already fundamentalists—sometimes known as **Islamists**—impose *sharia* (Muslim law) as the law of the land in Iran and Sudan. If Algeria held free and fair elections, Islamists would win, which is why Algeria cancelled elections in 1992. The Muslim Brotherhood, the father of many Islamist movements, showed they were strong in Egypt's 2005 elections. The radical Hamas (related to the Muslim Brotherhood) won the 2006 Palestinian parliamentary elections. Saudi Arabia and Pakistan could fall to Islamists. In the 2003 war, Muslims worldwide overwhelmingly supported Iraq. The 2003 Iraq war and U.S. occupation stirred Muslim hatred worldwide.

By 1978, major demonstrations shook Iran. Police and troops fired on protesters, enraging them even more. Soldiers began to side with the crowds. The shah, sensing he was doomed (and dying of cancer), departed in January 1979, and two weeks later the Ayatollah returned to the cheers of millions.

secular Nonreligious; separation of church and state.

mullah Islamic cleric.

The Ayatollah's support was a loose coalition of anti-shah groups: Islamic fundamentalists, Communists and other leftists, **secular** intellectuals, and convinced democrats. One by one, sometimes using a firing squad, the Ayatollah got rid of all but his Islamist supporters. The takeover of the U.S. embassy was an internal power play designed to bump Iranian moderates from leadership. Within a year, the **mullahs** had built a dictatorship far bloodier and more thorough than anything the shah had done. One of the last cries of an anti-shah group that had supported Khomeini: "In the dawn of freedom, there is no freedom." Iranians began to discover how revolutions end badly.

Diplomacy

WHAT DID THE UNITED STATES KNOW, AND WHEN DID IT KNOW IT?

Could the United States have warned the shah that his domestic situation was decaying in the 1970s? Perhaps with the right reforms he could have headed off the trouble. We did not tell him because we did not know—in fact, did not want to know. The CIA station in our Tehran embassy agreed to not contact the anti-shah opposition. Such contacts are an important function of any CIA station abroad. SAVAK was supposed to pass on its data to the CIA but did not—the shah's regime refused to admit there were problems—so embassy reports failed to notice the rising tide of anti-shah feeling.

Diplomats are not free agents; they must obey a command structure just like military officers. In 1977 the shah visited Washington, and in 1978 President Carter visited Tehran. The presidential message from both visits: The shah is our friend and is making major improvements. That was the word, enforced by the U.S. ambassador, and American diplomats dared not challenge it. The result was inaccurate and overly optimistic reporting. In

a very important gap, the CIA did not learn the shah was dying of cancer.

Few American diplomats spoke Persian. Only a few Americans in diplomatic missions speak the local language. The U.S. Foreign Service is the only one that does not require fluency in a foreign language. When Iranian radicals seized our Tehran embassy in 1979, only six of the fifty-three hostages could speak Persian, an unusually high percentage because the embassy had already been reduced to a skeleton crew.

The shah's government put on a good public relations smokescreen that made influential Americans think all was well in Iran. Iranian Ambassador Ardeshir Zahedi was famous for showering Washington with lush parties and gifts. Professional PR people—including the wife of one senator—churned out upbeat news and views about Iran for fat fees. Only a handful of U.S. academic specialists saw the decay in Iran and predicted collapse.

The First Gulf War

Iran's neighbor to the West, Iraq (ancient Mesopotamia), is a new country, dating only from 1922. For centuries it was three provinces of the Ottoman Turkish Empire. British forces from India conquered Iraq in World War I and in 1921—owing a debt to the Hashem family of Arabia that had helped Britain oust the Turks—placed a Hashemite prince on the throne of Iraq (and his brother on the throne of newly created Transjordan, carved out of its Palestine mandate). In 1932, Iraq became independent but still under British influence. This rankled nationalistic Iraqi army officers. In 1958 they executed the royal family and its helpers and moved Iraq sharply away from the West and toward the Soviet Union. Saddam Hussein, who began as a revolutionary assassin, became dictator of Iraq in 1979.

There has been bad blood between Iran and Iraq for centuries, especially over the border between the two countries where the Shatt al Arab flows into the Persian Gulf (see box below). In the early 1970s, Iran and Iraq came close to war until Iraq backed down and settled the border in Iran's favor in 1975. Iraq was always unhappy with this settlement, however, and claimed it was coerced into signing.

When Iran turned Islamist in 1979, it encouraged Iraq's Shi'a majority to do something similar. Iran tried to spread its Islamic revolution. Saddam Hussein thought Iran was so weakened by revolution that it would be easy pickings. Iran had no more U.S. protection. In September 1980, Iraq tore up the 1975 treaty and attacked, but the Iraqi invasion roused Iranian nationalism, and the country rallied behind Khomeini. Young Iranians joined the *Pasdaran* (Revolutionary Guards) and threw their lives away in human wave attacks against the Iraqis. Many of them carried little portraits of Khomeini and plastic keys, symbolizing their instant admission to heaven. Losses were staggering. At least a quarter

Geography

THE SHATT AL ARAB

Iraqis proudly note that the 120-mile-long waterway formed by the confluence of the Tigris and Euphrates is called the Shatt al Arab, the River of the Arabs. The lowest forty miles of the Shatt form the boundary between Iraq and Iran. The question is where the border should run. Baghdad claims the whole river, right up to the eastern shore, giving it control of all river traffic. Tehran claims that the border follows the deepest channel of the river, giving Iran direct access to the open sea from its oil ports of Khorramshahr and Abadan.

In an 1847 treaty, the Ottoman Empire got the entire river, but Iran always tried to get more rights around its ports. A 1937 treaty gave Iran a five-mile area around Abadan but otherwise secured the Shatt for Iraq. In 1969 Tehran denounced the 1937 treaty as British imperialism and moved to enforce the middle of the Shatt as its border. To put pressure on Baghdad, Iran helped the rebellious Kurds of northern Iraq. A strong Iran allied with the United States could prevail in those days, and in 1975 Iraq agreed in a treaty to a deepest-channel boundary. Iraq claimed the treaty was forced upon it and broke the treaty by invading Iran in 1980. Another Iraqi war aim: The area on the eastern bank of the Shatt—called Arabistan by Iraq—is partly peopled by Arabs, whom Baghdad felt should belong to Iraq.

The Shatt al Arab forms a boundary between Iraq and Iran. (NYT Graphics)

million died, two-thirds of them Iranians. Iran had the advantage in numbers and courage, but Iraq had the advantage in weapons. Iranians are much more willing to die in combat than Iraqis; they thought that Arabs lacked courage and staying power.

A combination of factors finally ended the war after eight terrible years. Economics slowly tilted against Iran, which could not export nearly as much oil as Iraq. Iraq also received large loans from conservative Gulf monarchies afraid of Islamic revolution. Iraq could buy weapons nearly everywhere; Iran could not. On the battlefield, Iraq's poison gas panicked Iranian troops into retreat. In 1988 Iran finally agreed to UN Security Council Resolution 598, which brought in UN mediation to end the fighting. Khomeini, then 85, said he would rather "drink poison" but had to save the Islamic Republic. Iran nursed its wounds and began a major program of arms purchases.

The Second Gulf War

Washington was so blinded by hatred of Iran that it failed to notice the menace of Iraq under the dictatorship of Saddam Hussein. Washington said a few words against Iraq's use of poison gas—including on its own Kurds—but in 1984 reestablished diplomatic ties with Baghdad on the theory that increased contact, including arms sales, would make Iraq cooperative. During the 1960s and 1970s, Iraq had been a Soviet client state, and we were proud to have "won" Iraq away from Moscow. Some prize. In addition to building the fourth largest conventional army in the world, Iraq quietly purchased equipment from around the world to produce nuclear bombs, poison gas, and medium-range missiles. Germany was the biggest supplier, but some of the technology was American.

Saddam had certain points to complain about. Kuwait and Saudi Arabia, U.S. client states, pumped oil in excess of OPEC quotas, keeping prices down; Iraq wanted prices higher. Iraq had never fully accepted the existence of Kuwait as an independent state; Baghdad claimed that under the Ottomans Kuwait had been part of Basra province. Iraq and Kuwait shared the large Rumaila oilfield, but Iraq charged that Kuwait was pumping far more than its share. Baghdad also argued that Kuwaiti and Saudi loans during the war with Iran should be forgiven; after all, Iraq had turned back Iran's Islamic revolution. But underneath Saddam's complaints was his drive to control the Gulf's oil in order to enlarge

Kurds Nationality inhabiting area where Iraq, Iran, and Turkey meet.

his military machine and make Iraq the regional superpower. Saddam was the new Nasser, the self-appointed hero who would unite and lead the Arabs.

To Saddam's surprise, the United States strongly opposed his invasion of Kuwait on August 2, 1990, ten years after he invaded Iran. Soon U.S. troops arrived in Operation Desert Shield to defend Saudi Arabia from what might be Saddam's next step. In October, President Bush 41, without consulting Congress, ordered the buildup for war. The Bush administration assembled a large international coalition that included Europeans, Arabs, and Asians. U.S. power decided the war, but the allies were politically essential, to show that this was not U.S. imperialism but the will of the UN and the entire civilized world. The Soviet Union backed U.S.-sponsored resolutions in the UN Security Council, and China refrained from vetoing them. Bush lined up the world against Saddam.

The situation was extremely favorable for the United States. Bases, ports, and airfields were ready in Saudi Arabia. The United States had time—almost half a year—to get its forces in place. The U.S. military had always hated the incremental pace of the Vietnam War; the Gulf War was an overwhelming, quick attack. The open terrain left Iraq with few hiding places. In January 1991, Desert Shield turned into Desert Storm. Massive air attacks—many with cruise missiles, stealth jets, and smart bombs—quickly knocked out Iraq's air defenses, communications, electricity, and bridges. Saddam Hussein appeared unfazed and welcomed the upcoming "mother of all battles." He hurled his inaccurate SCUD missiles at Saudi Arabia and Israel, hoping to goad Israel into entering the war, thus breaking the Arab countries from the coalition. After thirty-eight days of air attacks, U.S.-led ground forces sliced into southern Iraq, and in 100 hours of fighting, Saddam's divisions melted away in surrender or hasty retreat. Arab forces were given the honor of liberating the plundered Kuwait City. The United States lost some 150; Iraq lost unknown thousands.

One interesting question about this war is why Saddam did not go chemical. Iraq had used a lot of poison gas against both Iran and Iraqi **Kurds** in the previous Gulf war. Why not in 1991? Some Iraqi SCUDS inspected afterward had chemical-warhead capability. Only one answer fits: Both the United States and Israel would have responded with nuclear

Geography

THE BAB AL MANDAB

Another maritime chokepoint in the region is the narrow southern entrance to the Red Sea, the Bab al Mandab, Arabic for "gate of tears." Here, at the southwestern tip of the Arabian peninsula, is the radical Arab country of Yemen, which gave the Soviets a naval base on its island of Socotra. On the African side of the strait is Eritrea, which broke away from Ethiopia, and the French-run territory of Djibouti. Control of either coast gives radical forces the theoretical ability to close the Bab, cutting off most ship traffic through the Suez Canal. This ship traffic is not as important as it used to be, for supertankers are much too big to pass through the Canal; they have to go all the way around Africa to reach Europe and America.

weapons. President Bush delivered a credible deterrent threat that Iraqi use of poison gas would provoke a terrible U.S. response. Saddam wanted Israel to enter the war, but gas would provoke Israel to annihilate Iraq with nukes. In effect, deterrence took place in the middle of the second Gulf war: A chemical power does not use gas against a nuclear power. Nukes deterred gas. (For more on deterrence, see Chapter 13.)

The real problems came with victory. Should coalition forces keep going to Baghdad and depose Saddam? Many U.S. officers wanted another four days to finish off Saddam. But UN Resolution 678 merely called for expelling Iraq from Kuwait, nothing more. The U.S. military had no appetite for fighting among civilians to "win hearts and minds," another legacy of Vietnam. Better to stop with a clear, finite goal accomplished than to enter into an open-ended commitment in a politically chaotic situation, in Bush's view. Later many Americans regretted that we hadn't finished off Saddam in 1991, saving us a war in 2003.

The White House figured that Iraqis would soon overthrow Saddam anyway. Restive Shiites in the south and Kurds in the north rose against the Baghdad regime, but Iraq's security forces were intact and brutally murdered hundreds of thousands of suspected opponents. Kurds fled to the icy mountains on the Turkish and Iranian borders, barely kept alive by international relief efforts. In vain, Washington pursued a "dual containment" policy of trying to isolate both Iraq and Iran, but America's partners ignored it.

Diplomacy

A GREEN LIGHT FOR AGGRESSION

The United States had trouble grasping the aggressive and dangerous nature of the Saddam regime in Iraq. One suspects that State Department Arabists, trained to promote only good relations with Arab countries, could see no evil in Saddam. When Saddam made threatening demands on Kuwait in July 1990, U.S. Ambassador April Glaspie, fluent in Arabic, had a nice chat with him, urging him to settle things peacefully but adding that the United States would not get involved in territorial disputes. Then she left on vacation. The United States thought the dispute was about borders and oil-drilling rights. But Glaspie did not act on her own; the conciliatory policy came from the White House. Saddam took the message as a green light from Washington to invade Kuwait.

The real problem was Washington's lopsidedly anti-Iran policy that looked the other way when Iraq invaded Iran and used poison gas. Only after the war, when UN inspectors uncovered the magnitude of Iraq's nuclear and chemical weapons programs, did it finally sink in that we had favored a murderous aggressor who planned to seize the entire region.

Would a U.S. warning to Saddam in July 1990 have made a difference? To deliver a credible deterrence threat, we would have needed U.S. forces on the ground in Kuwait and Saudi Arabia, and the two countries would not allow this. Fearful that a U.S. military presence would provoke radical elements—Palestinians and local Islamists—Kuwait and Saudi Arabia want U.S. protection "over the horizon," that is, on ships and not on shore. Only after the invasion, when Saudi princes worried that they would be next, did they "invite" (at Washington's urging) U.S. forces. Kuwaiti and Saudi fears—the fears of spoiled rich kids walking down the meanest block in town—had made it impossible to deliver a credible deterrence warning to Saddam. Even if Ambassador Glaspie had tried, she would not have been believed. You cannot deter aggression with words alone. (For the relationship between diplomacy and military strength, see Chapter 19.)

weapons of mass destruction (WMD) Nuclear, chemical, or biological arms, "nukes, gas, bugs."

A moral dilemma appeared concerning Iraq's children, whom Saddam paraded to visitors as malnourished and without medicines. Actually, Iraq had plentiful revenues to buy food and medicine under a UN-supervised oil-for-food program, but Saddam used the children for propaganda while he bought military equipment and built dozens of luxurious palaces for himself. The UN program faltered in disagreement over what were "humanitarian goods" as opposed to "dual-use technology" that might be used to produce weapons of mass destruction. Iraq played cat-and-mouse with UN weapons inspectors until they left in frustration.

■ The Third Gulf War

As we discussed in Chapter 4, 9/11 gave us a new foreign policy. Within days of 9/11 President Bush 43 decided we must overthrow the fanatic Islamist Taliban regime of Afghanistan for harboring al Qaeda and its chief, Osama bin Laden. In late 2001, using a few U.S. Special Forces working with local anti-Taliban Afghans, we made short work of the Taliban, but Osama escaped to neighboring Pakistan. It was a spectacular U.S. success, one supported by most of the world.

By late 2001 Bush 43 also decided we must oust Saddam in Iraq, and during 2002 he made his decision clearer. This time most of the world opposed us, viewing with skepticism U.S. claims that Iraq had **weapons of mass destruction** and sponsored terrorism. No WMD were found, and that was our main reason for war. Apparently UN weapons inspectors had indeed supervised destruction of Iraq's WMD by the mid-1990s. Saddam's deceptions, however, suggested he had WMD, and U.S. intelligence was flimsy. Bush exaggerated and oversold Iraq's WMD capacity.

In contrast to 1991, Saudi Arabia did not permit us to attack from its soil. Only Kuwait and some small Gulf states let us base there. Only Britain sent troops. Even our old friend Turkey did not help. America was at odds with most of the world. The March 2003 U.S. attack from Kuwait was superbly planned and executed, even better than the 1991 war.

Diplomacy

STATUS QUO ANTE BELLUM

The Latin phrase *status quo ante bellum* (the situation before the war) provided a formula for ending the first two Gulf wars. It means restoring things to the way they were before the war. In 1988, Iraq could accept the border that split the Shatt al Arab, and Iran could agree to ask for no more. In 1991, Iraq had to accept the borders and independence of Kuwait. Every country except Iraq found the status quo ante bellum in the Gulf acceptable.

This time air and ground attacks were simultaneous, and U.S. armor raced up the Tigris and Euphrates valley to take Baghdad in three weeks. In two more weeks all of Iraq was ours, and President Bush declared major combat over on May 1. Iraq,

jihad Muslim holy war to defend the faith.

however, never surrendered or signed a cease-fire; Iraqi soldiers and security police just melted away, some to fight another day.

Monumental looting and lawlessness broke out, something we had not anticipated. Electricity, water, and oil production stopped. So intent were we on combat that we neglected to send military police, civil affairs personnel, and engineers until weeks later. Initially many Iraqis welcomed us, but without security or jobs, many soon resented us. Resistors—most of them Sunni Arabs—shot and bombed U.S., UN, and Shi'a Iraqi targets, trying to make Iraq ungovernable. Far more Americans were killed after the war than in it. Some foreign Islamic terrorists who craved **jihad** against the United States slipped into Iraq. The Middle East was angrier than ever.

Postwar policy in Iraq was initially given to the Defense Department, which supposed that U.S.-sponsored Iraqi exiles would be welcomed and quickly form a federal democracy that in turn would inspire democracy throughout the region. But Iraq, after decades of brutal dictatorship that had crushed all independent voices, was politically fragmented, and its main groups—Shiites in the south (62 percent of the population), Sunni Arabs in the center (under 20 percent), and Kurds in the north—quarreled within and among themselves. We turned nominal sovereignty back to Iraq in the middle of 2004, and Iraq held three elections in 2005—one for an interim government to draft a constitution, a second to approve the constitution, and a third to elect a regular government. Experts warned that Iraq was not ready for democracy, and Iraq's three main groups—Shi'as, Sunnis, and Kurds, who wanted very different things—had trou-

A Marine in front of a Humvee that was destroyed by a homemade bomb in 2005 in Ramadi, Iraq. (Capt. Rory Quinn/U.S. Marines/The New York Times/NYT Photos)

ble forming a stable government. The U.S. dilemma: The longer we stay to do the job right, the more Iraqis dislike us. But if we leave too early, Iraq could slide into civil war.

■ Could Arabia Go the Way of Iran?

Saudi Arabia, with a quarter of the world's proven oil reserves, is the big prize in the Gulf, and it is not as stable as was thought. Until recently, Washington and our news media saw nothing going wrong among the **traditional monarchies** along the Gulf's southern shore.

These countries, however, especially Saudi Arabia, have the same problem that hit Iran: How to modernize the economy without modernizing politics and culture. Monarchies have become fewer over the decades; the more they modernize and educate their citizens, the more they are overthrown.

traditional monarch One who still rules, not a figurehead.

Friendly observers of Kuwait, Saudi Arabia, Qatar, the United Arab Emirates, and Oman used to assure us that citizens of these lands are deeply traditional, their kings and sheiks are caring and legitimate, and rising standards of living make everyone happy. That was true but temporary. With abundant oil revenues, Gulf monarchies were able to buy citizen contentment. But some oil fields have been depleted, oil prices fluctuate, and many of these countries are now in debt. Population has grown sixfold since 1960, and citizens no longer get cushy government jobs and handouts. The behavior of some princes is less than Islamic, undermining legitimacy. Islamist radicalism in Saudi Arabia is large and growing—Osama bin Laden and many of his supporters are Saudis—but little appeared in the news media until terrorist bombings occurred there in 2003. Saudi Arabia could be a bigger problem than Iraq.

Economics

OIL AND US

U.S. motorists hate high gasoline prices and demand the government do something about them. For much of the twentieth century, however, oil-producing countries found prices far too low, which is why they formed OPEC in 1960. By giving each member a quota, OPEC tries to keep petroleum production low enough to keep prices up. Oil-consuming nations like the price of crude oil at well under $30 a barrel, but OPEC likes it at well over $30 per barrel (in the high $70s in 2006).

Americans love cheap gasoline—under $1 a gallon in 1998—but might think twice. Cheap gas encourages people to buy more and bigger vehicles and drive them more miles, producing more air pollution, highway deaths, and traffic jams. Of every seven barrels of oil produced in the world, one is consumed on America's highways. Public transportation is undeveloped. Global warming mounts. The car is a mixed blessing.

America consumes 25 percent of world oil production and imports 60 percent of its oil, a quarter of it from the Persian Gulf. (Our biggest supplier: Canada.) But because oil is one big global market, a disruption anywhere creates shortages everywhere. This is what happened with the 1973 Arab-Israel war and the 1979 overthrow of the shah. It explains why we drove back Iraq in 1991. But should we intervene for oil on a standing basis? It would be trading blood for oil and make us the policeman of the Gulf. Can you imagine us fighting in the Gulf so that we can enjoy our SUVs? A better course would be to kick our "oil addiction." The technology is at hand but will not be developed if gas prices are low.

Things are changing in the region in other ways. Iran is split between those who want reforms that lift the rule of conservative mullahs, and those who veto any reforms and keep themselves in power. In frustration, many boycott Iran's elections, which bar reformists from running. Other Iranians, religiously conservative and resentful of outside influence, still support the Islamic revolution and voted in fanatic President Mahmoud Ahmadinejad in 2005. He accelerated Iran's "peaceful" nuclear program—which could soon build bombs—and wants to "wipe Israel off the map." Iran isolated itself from most of the rest of the world, which fears its nuclear progress. War with the United States is not out of the question.

We should remember, however, that many Iranians are pro-American and staged spontaneous candlelight displays of sympathy with America on 9/11. Both Tehran and Washington know there is money to be made in oil, especially in the pipelines that will bring Central Asia's oil to the world market. (The United States sponsored a pipeline through Turkey, but the best route is through Iran. Russia's pipeline runs through Chechnya—one

Geography

THE MISUSED, ANGRY KURDS

There are twenty-five million Kurds, but they never had their own country. Instead, they live in Turkey, Syria, Iraq, and Iran around where their borders converge. Kurds are mostly Sunni Muslims but are not Arabs, Turks, or Persians and they speak several dialects all their own. They often fight among themselves and do not form a united front. Fierce mountain warriors, the Kurds were first recorded in history for harassing Alexander's invading Greeks. The most famous Kurd was the chivalrous Saladin (1138–1193), who beat the Crusaders.

With nationalism stirring the lands in which they lived in the late nineteenth century, the Kurds too started thinking of their own nation and periodically rising up against Baghdad, Tehran, Istanbul (old capital of the Ottoman Empire), and later Ankara (new capital of present-day Turkey). Turkey brutally crushed the insurgency of the Kurdish Workers party (PKK), a conflict that claimed some 37,000 lives in the late twentieth century. Turkey calls their Kurds "mountain Turks" and urges them to assimilate; many have.

Since the 1960s, the Kurds' struggle has focused on Iraq, where they make up perhaps 20 percent of the population, concentrated in the north around the oilfields of Kirkuk. Baghdad repeatedly tried to crush Kurdish armed resistance, but the tough Kurds held out. In the early 1970s, Iraqi Kurds got help through Iran. The shah, along with Israeli and U.S. covert branches, supplied arms. The shah wanted to put pressure on Baghdad to secure Iran's rights to the Shatt al Arab. The Israelis wanted to weaken an enemy and had stocks of Soviet weapons captured in the 1967 war. And Iraq had become a Soviet client state—which broke relations with Washington in 1967—so the CIA was interested in undermining Iraq.

Then, in a cynical betrayal, when the shah got the border he wanted in a 1975 treaty, he cut off the Kurdish fighters in Iraq and let Baghdad do its worst. With the Iran-Iraq war, Tehran again encouraged Iraq's Kurds to rise up. Some Kurds believed an Iranian victory would give them their best chance for independence. Baghdad used poison gas to kill some 50,000 of Iraq's own Kurdish citizens. In 1991, the United States encouraged Iraq's Kurds to rise against Saddam Hussein but did not help them when they did. Small wonder the Kurds feel betrayed. A Kurdish saying: "The Kurds have no friends."

reason it wanted to crush Chechen rebels.) America and Iran had a common enemy in Iraq. When the United States and Iran were partners, Iraq did not dare attack Iran. Mutual benefit could make us partners again.

■ Lessons of Three Gulf Wars

1. You don't have to be a major power to have a major war. Even Global South countries can build large armies and buy arms.
2. Modern war above all depends on logistics. U.S. airlift capacity, the world's greatest, means it can project power.
3. Money is as important as your army. In the 1980s, Iraq could outlast Iran because it had more money. Massive financial support in 1991 underlay the U.S.-led victory.
4. Arms sellers are happy to supply aggressors. Iraq bought just about anything it wanted on the international arms market.
5. War is increasingly electronic. The ability to paralyze communications and "smart bombs" give us a tremendous edge.
6. Deterrence works. Saddam used chemical weapons on Iran and the Kurds but not on Americans or Israelis. Fear of nuclear retaliation deterred him.
7. Governments control media coverage of wars. We saw essentially nothing in the 1991 war and only "embedded," small-unit coverage of the 2003 war.
8. The aftermath of a war is as important as the fighting. Is a dictator still in power? Are we prepared to run a chaotic country and rebuild it with our dollars? If you cannot follow through, do not go in.
9. The political context of a war is as important as military victory. Does winning make us new enemies, both in the region and worldwide?
10. If you do not understand the culture and complexities of a country, be cautious about occupying it. With little knowledge of Iraq's languages, cultures, and politics, we drastically underestimated the difficulties of Iraq after Saddam.

Classic Thought

THE ENEMY OF MY ENEMY IS MY FRIEND

Of Arab origin, the logical dictum "the enemy of my enemy is my friend" illustrates national-interest thinking. Israel and Turkey, for example, developed cordial ties, even though Turkey is Muslim, and Arab governments howled in protest. But Turkish elites are largely secular, especially top army officers, and Turkey has territorial and river quarrels with its Arab neighbors, Syria and Iraq. Turkey was also given the cold shoulder by the European Union. To whom, then, should Turkey turn? The choice was logical: to another country with the same enemies. National interest can trump ideology and/or religion.

But this does not always work. One country in the region had the same motivation but did not act on it. Iran, along with the United States and Israel, had Iraq as a common enemy. But Iran kept its ideological foreign policy based on Islamic fundamentalism. Logically, Iran should build ties with the United States and Israel. This will be an interesting test case for this Arab insight.

11. The United States, like it or not, is in the Gulf to stay. We may want to clear out of the Gulf but now are in deep. Instability drags us in. The Gulf and its oil is one place we do not walk away from.

Key Terms

Caspian (p. 135)

Caucasus (p. 135)

Central Asia (p. 135)

civilization (p. 138)

Islamism (p. 138)

jihad (p. 145)

Kurds (p. 142)

mullah (p. 139)

nationalize (p. 135)

OPEC (p. 138)

Persia (p. 135)

populist (p. 135)

secular (p. 139)

shah (p. 135)

Shi'a (p. 135)

sphere of influence (p. 135)

Sunni (p. 135)

traditional monarch (p. 146)

weapons of mass destruction (WMD) (p. 144)

Key Web Sites

OPEC
http://www.opec.org/

Handbook of International Economic Statistics, Energy (from CIA)
http://www.odci.gov/cia/publications/

The Republic of Turkey
http://www.turkey.org/turkey/

Royal Embassy of Saudi Arabia
http://www.saudi.net/

Kuwaiti Embassy
http://www.embassyofkuwait.com/index.html

Salam Iran
http://www.salamiran.org/

Bahrain Tribune
http://www.bahraintribune.com/

Kuwait Times
http://www.paaet.edu.kw/ktimes

Planet Arabia
http://www.planetarabia.com

Ayatollah al-Sistani of Iraq
http://www.sistani.org

Further Reference

Beeman, William O. *Iraq, a State in Search of a Nation.* Westport, CT: Praeger, 2005.

Blix, Hans. *Disarming Iraq.* New York: Knopf, 2004.

Bremer, L. Paul. *My Year in Iraq: The Struggle to Build a Future of Hope.* New York: Simon & Schuster, 2006.

Cordesman, Anthony H. *The Iraq War: Strategy, Tactics, and Military Lessons.* Westport, CT: Praeger, 2003.

Diamond, Larry. *Squandered Victory: The American Occupation and the Bungled Effort to Bring Democracy to Iraq.* New York: Times Books, 2005.

Fawn, Rick, and Raymond Hinnebusch. *The Iraq War: Causes and Consequences.* Boulder, CO: L. Rienner, 2006.

Hersh, Seymour M. *Chain of Command: The Road from 9/11 to Abu Ghraib.* New York: HarperCollins, 2004.

Packer, George. *The Assassin's Gate: America in Iraq.* New York: Farrar, Straus and Giroux, 2005.

Phillips, David L. *Losing Iraq: Inside the Postwar Reconstruction Fiasco.* Boulder, CO: Westview, 2005.

Record, Jeffrey. *Dark Victory: America's Second War against Iraq.* Annapolis, MD: Naval Institute Press, 2004.

Roskin, Michael G., and James J. Coyle. *Politics of the Middle East: Cultures and Conflicts,* 2nd ed. Upper Saddle River, NJ: Prentice Hall, 2007.

Shadid, Anthony. *Night Draws Near: Iraq's People in the Shadow of America's War.* New York: Henry Holt, 2005.

CHAPTER 10

THE TROUBLED AMERICAS

OUR NEGLECTED SOUTH

QUESTIONS TO CONSIDER

1. Why do Americans ignore the rest of the Americas?
2. How did Spanish differ from English colonization?
3. Is it fair to call Central America a U.S. sphere of influence?
4. Should we intervene in Colombia? How?
5. Can we stamp out drug cultivation in the Third World?
6. What would be the best way to get communism out of Cuba?
7. Should we turn our attention southward, instead of east and west?
8. Is Mexico becoming democratic? How can you tell?

Americans tend to ignore the countries to our south. Many cannot distinguish among **Latin America**, **South America**, and **Central America**. We pay far more attention eastward across the Atlantic and westward across the Pacific than to our hemispheric neighbors. But they are important both to our future and to world stability in general. One could even propose a U.S. policy that paid more attention to our south (and maybe even a little to our north, to Canada) than to east and west. Latin America is a prime example of the "zones of chaos" that trouble much of the Global South. Drug lords in several Latin American countries buy politicians, judges, police, and the military; the ones they cannot buy they kill.

America is addicted to illegal drugs, most of them from south of its border. (We should actually say "North America," for the rest of the hemisphere is also America, a point that annoys many Latin Americans. They're Americans too.) Marijuana, cocaine, and heroin flow in from the south in ever-shifting patterns. Eradicated in one country, the trade moves to another. Break one drug cartel and others soon take its place. Cut the growing of coca (used by **indígenas** for centuries) and farmers plant opium poppies. With North Americans' appetite for cocaine undiminished and profits enormous, **cocaleros** are happy to grow the leaf (and get $5 a kilo, several times what they get for any other crop) and **narcotraficantes** to process and smuggle it. It is a business, obeying the laws of supply

151

Latin America   All countries south of the United States. (See page 151.)

South America   Continent south of Panama. (See page 151.)

Central America   Countries between Mexico and Colombia (See page 151.)

indígena   Preferred Latin American term for Indian. (See page 151.)

cocalero   Farmer who produces coca leaf. (See page 151.)

narcotraficante   Drug trafficker. (See page 151.)

interdiction   Cutting the flow of something.

statism   Government owns and runs major industries.

entrepreneurialism   Starting your own business; private enterprise.

and demand. Eradication and **interdiction** have not worked. Andean cocaine production has climbed while the U.S. wholesale price of cocaine fell from $100 a gram in 1986 to $38 in 2003, indicating an excess of supply over demand.

We do not know what to do about it. For every kilo intercepted, perhaps twenty get through. Cracking down on U.S. drug users has simply doubled our prison population without denting the problem. Vigorous drug suppression programs in Bolivia and Peru—aerial spraying, crop burning, destruction of processing camps, and paying farmers to grow other crops—temporarily cut drug production there, but it returned. The trade also moved to Colombia, which now produces 90 percent of the cocaine used in the United States and 60 percent of the heroin. Cultivation has branched out into African countries. The real problem is U.S. drug users, found in every walk of life and every town (and on your campus). In the words of Pogo: "We have met the enemy, and he is us."

Should we intervene to stop the trade? In recent years, $3 billion in U.S. aid has gone to Colombia. The U.S. war in Vietnam began with major foreign aid. Analogies can be poor guides—no two situations are exactly alike—but Colombia's jungled *cordilleras* look a lot like Vietnam's Central Highlands and are just as hard to control. Marxist guerrillas, who tax drug traffickers half a billion dollars a year, control wide areas of Colombia as if they had their own little countries. Revolutionary armies have some 20,000 soldiers, better trained, armed, paid, and motivated than the 250,000 government soldiers, who often avoid fighting the rebels. They sound a lot like ARVN (see page 47).

Internal warfare is the norm in Colombia; 300,000 died in *La Violencia* from 1945 to 1965, another 35,000 have died since 1990. The countryside has never been safe

Concepts

STATISM

Spain brought with it **statism** (borrowed from the French kings), the government as number-one capitalist, owning and supervising the big parts of the economy. Railroad, steel mill, or telephone network have to be built? Government will do it, because only government has the ability and money to carry out big projects. Statists argue that they have no capitalists willing and able to do the really big things. Culturally, Latin America had little **entrepreneurialism** and so until recently was largely statist, which led to slow growth, too few jobs, bloated bureaucracies, corruption, and a chronic dependence on foreign capital, thus leading to *dependency*.

from guerrillas and bandits. In Colombia, the two merge, and many "revolutionaries" are in it for the money. Bombings, assassinations, and kidnappings occur daily, some criminal, some political. Right-wing death squads, tied to the Colombian military, murder with impunity. (In Peru, more than 69,000 died in guerrilla warfare from 1980 to 2000 under similar circumstances.) Many of Colombia's judges and journalists have been killed. Colombia is not just a drug problem but exemplifies the weak state that cannot begin to keep law and order. After years of U.S.-sponsored efforts, more drugs flow than ever.

creole Spaniard born in the New World.

mestizo Person of mixed Indian-Spanish descent.

coup Extralegal seizure of power, usually by military.

Spain Colonizes the New World

How did Latin America fall into such a condition? As in Africa, the roots of the problem go back to European colonialism. The Spaniards plunged eagerly into the New World for "glory, God, and gold," in the words of American historian Paul Wellman. Over 80 percent of Indians soon died of smallpox, against which they had no immunity. Spain had just finished eight centuries of pushing out the Moors and they treated Indians the same: Crush their kingdoms and cultures and utterly dominate them. They did not displace the Indians but enslaved and impregnated them, producing a feudal-type hierarchy: a small **creole** class of officials and landowners at the top, a larger class of **mestizos** to do the work, and many impoverished and isolated Indians. The economy was based on extracting gold and silver or on plantations.

Inspired by the U.S. and French Revolutions, the Spanish and Portuguese colonies won their independence in the 1820s. Their idealistic constitutions—modeled on the U.S. and French revolutionary constitutions—flopped almost immediately in the face of the feudal social structures that continued long after independence.

Although modeled on Europe's strong states (see page 16), Latin American countries were weak states. They had the trappings of power: presidential palaces, lots of bureaucrats (far too many), and armies. They did not have the economies or educated citizenries to sustain democracy. A small elite dominated politics. The central government's writ did not extend far from the capital city. Corruption was the norm. Amid frequent instability, army officers pulled **coups** and took over governments. Bolivia has had over 190 coups since independence in 1825.

Central America and the Caribbean

Although little noticed by most Americans, the Caribbean basin is important to the United States: It is weak, near, and strategic. There are many reasons for its weakness. The class structure typically divides the country into a few very wealthy families and many very poor ones. Political institutions are fragile and usually do the bidding of the wealthy

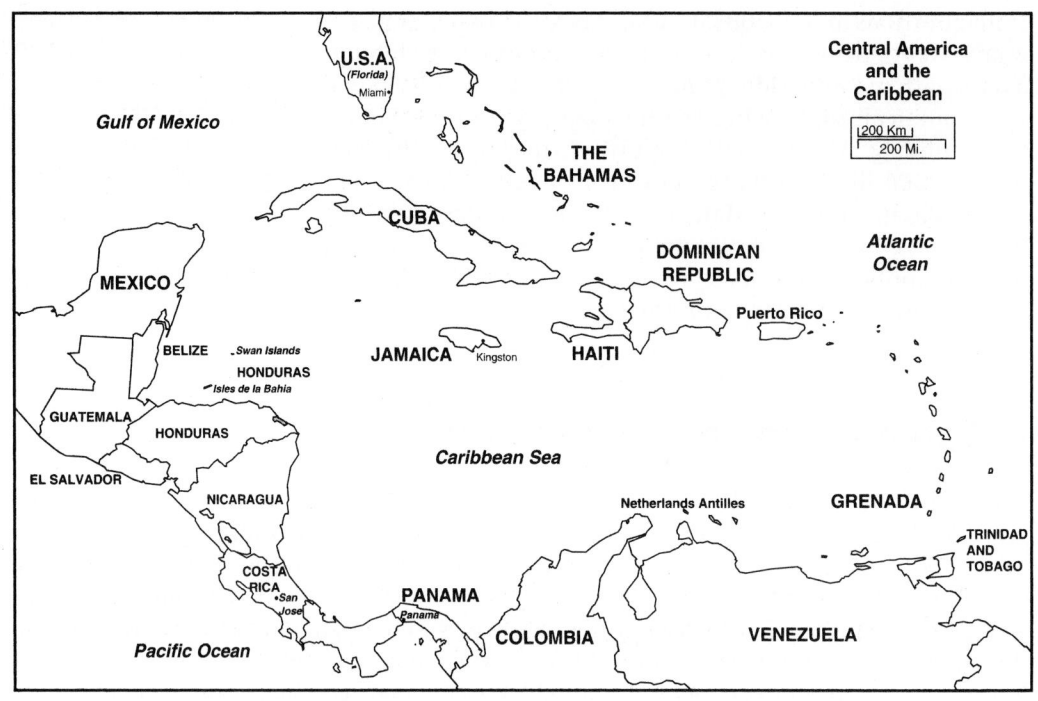

Central America and the Caribbean

class (i.e., make sure they stay wealthy). The economy largely produces raw materials and grows slowly, but populations grow fast—some Central American countries grow faster than 3 percent a year—and the region has far more people than jobs.

The region has been subordinate to the great powers from the first penetration by Europeans in the late fifteenth century. The Europeans saw the strategic and economic importance of Central America and the Caribbean. Imperial competition—by French, Spanish, British, and Americans, and later by Cubans and Soviets—thwarted democracy and economic development. Central America is the victim of its geopolitics. For half a millennium, it has been a magnet for outside forces and controls.

Columbus's discovery of the New World began in the Caribbean (he thought that he was in Asia) and gave Spain dominance in the region. Spain wanted (1) control of trade routes, (2) control of land for settlement, (3) the gold and silver of the New World, and (4) conversion of the natives to Catholicism. Under the Habsburgs, Spain struggled for predominance in Europe and for gold and silver. Mexico was its richest colony.

To control trade and land, Spain established colonies, forts, and harbors. Balboa crossed the Isthmus of Panama to the Pacific in 1513. Six years later, Cortes left Cuba to conquer the Aztec empire in Mexico. The few areas that Spain did not colonize, the English (Jamaica and Belize), French (Martinique), and Dutch (Netherlands Antilles) did. The Caribbean became a battleground among colonial powers. Caribbean piracy got its start

with English letters of marque, royal licenses to capture Spanish gold ships for private profit. (Notice that the U.S. Constitution gives Congress the power to issue letters of marque.) It
was the French fleet in the Caribbean that provided essential
help to the North Americans in their war of independence.
Central America freed itself from Spain in 1821 and tried to
consolidate as the Central American Confederation, which fell
apart in 1839.

dependency   Economic
subordination of poor countries
to rich ones.

intervene   One country reaches
into the affairs of another.

■ Economic Dependency

Under these circumstances, it was only natural that Latin America became economically
tied to outside powers, Britain in the nineteenth century and the United States in the twentieth. During the Cold War, Latin American leftists subscribed to **dependency** theory
(*dependencia* in Spanish) as an article of faith: The big, bad United States keeps Latin
America poor. The United States controls the economies of weaker countries through
local middlemen who do the bidding of U.S. corporations. The poor country is forced
to sell its agricultural and mineral products cheap and buy high-priced U.S.-made goods.
This continually siphons off the wealth of the poor country, which stays poor. Marxists
added a sinister twist to dependency theory: When the United States doesn't get its way
it uses dirty means, such as encouraging rigged elections and military coups. In a pinch,
the United States **intervenes** directly, as in the Caribbean and Central America early
in the twentieth century and in Panama in 1989. If radicals try to break the dependent
relationship—Arbenz in Guatemala, Castro in Cuba, Allende in Chile, or Chávez in
Venezuela—Washington brings great political, economic, and even military pressure to
oust them.

There is some truth to dependency theory, but it overlooks basic economic points. The
Spanish set up extractive economies (mines and plantations) and feudal class structures that

Concepts

INTERVENTION

Earlier (Chapter 4) we defined "interventionism"
from the standpoint of U.S. foreign policy. What is
it like to be on the receiving end? Latin America
provides some case studies. Intervention in this
sense is one country reaching into another to make
or unmake governments. States intervene to control the foreign and sometimes domestic policies of
other governments, and to gain allies for themselves and deny them to their adversaries.

Intervention is usually a lot cheaper and more
subtle than war. It can include bribes to government
officials, foreign aid, secret subsidies to political parties, destabilization campaigns, encouragement to
coup-plotters, arms shipments, proxy armies, and, if
nothing else works, invasion. The United States has
been more likely to send its own troops into the
Caribbean area and to use more subtle means further south.

capital flight   Sending your money out of the country instead of reinvesting it there.

exploitation   Paying producers less than they deserve.

Monroe Doctrine   1823 U.S. proclamation to keep Europe out of Western hemisphere.

Roosevelt Corollary   1905 U.S. warning to Europe not to use local debts to breach *Monroe Doctrine.*

created capital only for export. Now local capitalists, worried about losing their money, stash it abroad: **capital flight** (which we also see in Russia today). Dependency thus occurs naturally because the host country does not generate capital for its own investments; in part this is due to its statist economy, which discourages local capital formation. If local capitalists do not invest, foreign capitalists will.

Economic growth has lessened dependency. And you get growth by participating in the world economy, not by hiding from it. Brazilian sociologist Fernando Henrique Cardoso was a major dependency theorist in the 1960s. By the time he was elected president of Brazil in 1994, he had rejected the theory in favor of capitalism and foreign investment. Many Latin American intellectuals concluded that there is only one thing worse than being **exploited**, and that is not being exploited.

For most of our history, the United States simply paid little attention to Latin America. We seem to have a cultural blind spot for our hemispheric neighbors. Only security concerns prompted U.S. interest: European penetration after Spain's ouster (the **Monroe Doctrine**), German penetration before World War I (the **Roosevelt Corollary**), and Soviet penetration during the Cold War. Security rather than economics is the chief U.S. motivation: no threat, no interest.

Diplomacy

FROM MONROE DOCTRINE TO ROOSEVELT COROLLARY

The United States welcomed Latin America's independence in the 1820s. It removed potentially hostile empires from our hemisphere and reminded us of our own independence struggle. The United States wanted to make sure that other European powers did not try to take Spain's place. In 1823 President Monroe issued his famous Doctrine telling Europe that the United States would not become involved in European affairs, but that "we should consider any attempt on their part to extend their system to any portion of this hemisphere as dangerous to our peace and safety." No European power should recolonize the newly independent lands. Once you're out, you're out for good.

In mathematics, a corollary is a statement that logically flows from a previous proof. The term came with President Theodore Roosevelt's 1905

warning to European powers. If Monroe told the Europeans, "No more colonies in our hemisphere!" we had the right and duty to prevent them from establishing colonies by indirect means. Much of Central America and the Caribbean had become deeply indebted to European banks, and European powers claimed the right to seize the little countries' customs houses and collect tariffs until the debts were paid. This "customs receivership" was a breach of the Monroe Doctrine, Roosevelt reasoned. It would put European (especially German) gunboats in our lake. So Roosevelt told the Europeans: We will collect any debts for you; you keep out. The paternalistic Roosevelt Corollary gave the United States an unlimited right to intervene directly in the region for a generation. To many natives of the region, it looked like U.S. imperialism.

Year	Country	U.S. Action
	MAJOR U.S. INTERVENTIONS IN LATIN AMERICA	
1846–1848	Mexico	Defeat Mexico, take vast territory
1898	Spain	Take Puerto Rico, dominate Cuba
1903	Panama	Break Panama away from Colombia
1912–1933	Nicaragua	Marines occupy to keep order
1915–1934	Haiti	Marines occupy to keep order
1916	Mexico	Pershing pursues Pancho Villa
1916–1924	Dominican Republic	Marines occupy to keep order
1954	Guatemala	CIA overthrows reformist regime
1961	Cuba	Failed invasion by proxy army
1964	Brazil	Encourage coup against leftist regime
1965	Dominican Republic	Occupy to squelch rebellion
1973	Chile	Encourage coup against leftist regime
1981–1986	Nicaragua	Supply anti-Communist rebels
1989	Panama	Invade to capture dictator
1983	Grenada	Invade to oust Communist regime
1994	Haiti	Invade to oust rightist dictator

■ The Pattern of U.S. Intervention

The United States has been intervening in Latin America since before the war with Mexico in 1846–1848, which gained us the southwest and for which we paid Mexico $15 million (remember: force and/or cash). A pattern emerged. Americans came to think of Latin American lands as weak, comical countries. They were not our equals; their sovereignty was nominal. If they threatened U.S. interests and investments, small armed expeditions would correct them. They were like children who needed a spanking from time to time. Earlier, there was great-power rivalry in Central America and the Caribbean. The United States, Britain, and France had a strong interest in building and controlling a canal to link the oceans. In 1846, President Polk signed a treaty with Colombia, which then included Panama, to develop a canal. Competition with Britain for a similar treaty with Nicaragua led to the 1850 Clayton-Bulwer Treaty, which envisioned U.S.-British cooperation in building a Nicaraguan canal.

U.S. investments in the region grew. An American adventurer, William Walker, gathered a private army and took over Nicaragua from 1855 to 1857. He was defeated by U.S. railroad tycoon Cornelius Vanderbilt, a competitor for control of one of the main routes between the two oceans. U.S. investments in the region's coffee, banana, and sugar plantations, and the related docks, railroads, and telegraph lines, steadily grew. Increasingly, the United States saw the Caribbean as an American lake and Central America as a natural sphere of influence. The 1898 Spanish-American War (see Chapter 2) confirmed this attitude for many Americans. Much to American displeasure, a French company under Ferdinand de Lesseps (who had built the Suez Canal) obtained rights from Colombia in the 1870s to build a canal across the Isthmus of Panama. Americans were not too sad that yellow fever and bankruptcy stopped the French effort.

Turning Point

GUATEMALA: THE WORST CASE

Guatemala is perhaps the worst example of U.S. intervention and how it can go wrong. Guatemala was a true "banana republic"; the United Fruit Co. ran much of its economy and owned huge banana plantations and most of Guatemala's infrastructure. United Fruit was a state within a state that no Guatemalan government dared touch but that many Guatemalans resented. In 1944 a coalition of students, liberals, and army officers ousted the dictatorship and set up a democracy dedicated to major reform. Leftists and Communists from all over Latin America—including an Argentine medical school graduate, Ernesto ("Ché") Guevara—came to participate.

A showdown came in 1952 when the government of President Jacobo Arbenz passed an agrarian reform act that targeted United Fruit. Most of the company's gigantic holdings were expropriated for redistribution to landless peasants. In compensation, United Fruit got a paltry $1,185,000—$2.91 an acre—which is what the company had listed its land at for tax purposes. United Fruit cried "communism" and Washington heard.

Secretary of State John Foster Dulles and his brother, CIA Director Allen Dulles, plotted the overthrow of the Arbenz government in 1954. An exiled Guatemalan colonel, with arms and funds from the CIA, recruited a fake "army" of 140 in Honduras. The CIA broadcast imaginary news of battles and rebel victories. Light bombers staged strafing runs to make it look like a big invasion. Arbenz ordered the army to issue weapons to citizens, but it refused and stood aside as the rebel "invasion" ousted Arbenz. With fewer than twenty dead, the United States had toppled a government that had considerable popular support.

The 1954 Guatemalan coup was celebrated as a CIA triumph, but it meant the end of reforms and the beginning of a bloodbath. Leftist guerrillas tried terrorism against the military regime, which retaliated by indiscriminate killing of anyone suspicious. Some 200,000 Guatemalan Indians, priests, teachers, and labor leaders were murdered over the decades. One military regime overthrew another, until finally, in 1985, reasonably democratic elections produced a civilian government. Since then, democracy has gained strength and a peace treaty was signed with the guerrillas in December 1996.

Another consequence of 1954 was the lesson learned by Arbenz's leftist supporters. Some gathered in Mexico City to discuss what had gone wrong. What is needed, they decided, is not reform but revolution, especially replacement of the old army with a new, revolutionary one. One of the discussants was "Ché" Guevara, who then joined Fidel Castro for his 1956 landing in Cuba and three years of guerrilla warfare. When the CIA tried to replicate its Guatemala triumph in Cuba in 1961, it failed.

President Theodore Roosevelt picked up where the French left off. He offered Colombia $10 million plus a quarter of a million a year in rent, but Colombia held out for more. Some Panamanians resented Colombian delay on building the canal, and with support from Washington, they rebelled and seceded from Colombia. Roosevelt sent the cruiser *Nashville* to enforce the breakup of Colombia. A 1903 treaty gave Panama the same deal that Colombia had turned down in return for a canal zone run "in perpetuity" by the United States as "if it were the sovereign of the territory." The United States invented Panama in 1903.

Under the Roosevelt Corollary (see box on page 156), U.S. troops intervened repeatedly throughout Central America and the Caribbean. The governments of the region were "irresponsible," argued Washington, and we had the duty to "preserve order" and keep out other powers. The reasons for U.S. military intervention were many: nonpayment of debts, revolutions, threats to U.S. property, and leaders we disliked. The Marines would land, occupy the cities for a few years to set things right, and leave.

They never, of course, really solved the problems and often left them worse. Typically, the Americans would train a local militia and install its leader as president, confident that he would preserve order and remain friendly to U.S. interests. This led to corrupt military dictatorships but produced an illusory order that was often just a buildup to serious revolution.

Reflections

THE TAKING OF SWAN ISLAND

In late summer 1960, I was an explosive ordnance disposal diving officer on a U.S. minesweeper south of Cuba. Suddenly the Chief of Naval Operations in Washington ordered us to Swan Island, about 125 miles north of Honduras and claimed by both the United States and Honduras. We were to seize the island, capturing or killing the armed "Honduran leftist students" who had invaded hours before.

As our small ship steamed at flank speed toward Swan, the captain called me into his cabin. "When we get there, take your diving team and some explosives and make an underwater attack on the students' ship," he ordered. "Sink it." Our three-man team suited up and readied our explosives.

But as we approached the flat, scrub-pine-covered island, there was no students' ship. An armed landing party went ashore to find that the students had left a couple of hours earlier. They had run up the Honduran flag at the U.S. Steamship Co. communications center—the only installation on the island—drank a case of beer, found the place dull, took down their flag, and left. We guarded Swan for three weeks until relieved by another minesweeper.

Only later did we learn that the "U.S. Steamship Co." was a front for the CIA, a communications center for the U.S.-sponsored Bay of Pigs invasion a few months hence. What did I learn? First, people often play small roles in world events without being fully aware of what is going on. Second, legitimate orders from official authorities make subordinates willing to carry them out. My team was set to blow up that ship and anyone unfortunate enough to be on it, no questions asked.

—N. O. B.

Bay of Pigs   Failed 1961 CIA-backed attempt to invade Cuba and overthrow Castro.

During World Wars I and II, the United States kept German influence out of Central America and during the Cold War fought Soviet influence in the region. The problem was that this pushed the United States to stand by reliable anti-Communist dictators rather than take a chance with democratic reformers who might let Communists in the back door. During the Cold War, a panicky Washington tended to see reformists as Communists and to intervene against them.

Cuba Leaves the U.S. Sphere

Cuba had been solidly in the U.S. sphere since the Spanish-American War in 1898. From then until Fidel Castro rolled into Havana on New Year's Day, 1959, Cuba was a virtual U.S. protectorate, a market for U.S. goods, a place of investment for U.S. capital, and a playground for Americans. Some Cubans resented this status and rallied to Castro's cry "*¡Cuba sí, Yanquis no!*" Castro kept his Communist views to himself as he led a guerrilla war against the corrupt Batista regime in the Sierra Maestra of eastern Cuba. Castro's victory brought a brief period of joy, but soon Castro clamped down his own dictatorship—a far more thorough one than Batista's—and turned to the Soviet Union for arms and financial aid. By nationalizing U.S. industries in Cuba, Castro deliberately angered the Eisenhower administration, which broke diplomatic relations.

Turning Point

THE BAY OF PIGS, 1961

When the Eisenhower administration became aware that Castro was turning Cuba into a Soviet satellite, it had the CIA assemble and train an army of 1,400 Cuban exiles. The model was the 1954 takeover of Guatemala (see box on page 158). But Castro and his helpers had studied the lesson of Guatemala. Castro got completely rid of the old Cuban army—some by firing squad—and replaced it with his own revolutionary army, which he personally headed. Castro's "neighborhood committees" allowed no organized opposition.

The CIA plan called for the exiles to train in Honduras for several months, then stage an amphibious landing supported by U.S. air cover in unmarked planes. The CIA believed the landing would provoke a popular uprising against Castro. After the exiles consolidating a beachhead, the United States would recognize and aid them. Kennedy adopted the plan but canceled direct air support, thinking the world would view it as a U.S. invasion.

Everything went wrong. The landing site was poor, a beach on the island's south called the **Bay of Pigs** that was easy to contain. There was no uprising; Cubans either supported the regime or kept quiet. The invaders of April 1961 were pinned down on the beach; most surrendered. The United States ransomed them back for machinery and medicine. Kennedy was humiliated. He had lost his first tussle with communism in the Third World. The fiasco contributed to his resolve not to lose in South Vietnam.

Castro's aim was the communization of Cuba and the spreading of its revolution. Cuban arms, agents, and influence turned up throughout the region. The entire Cuban upper class and much of the middle class—close to three-quarters of a million Cubans—left for Miami, which suited Castro just fine. Their departure cleared out opposition to his rule and opened up positions for young, loyal revolutionaries. Within two years, Cuba was under a Communist dictatorship.

Fidel Castro visits adoring Cubans in 1964. (Jack Manning/The New York Times)

How did Castro get away with building a Communist satellite a mere ninety miles from U.S. shores? In earlier decades this would not have been possible because U.S. Marines would have been deployed. But the climate had changed. Direct intervention had become unfashionable. The United States thought that it could depose Castro with a small exile army, as we had done with a too-reformist regime in Guatemala in 1954. The attempt went down in the history books as a classic failure.

Castro's revolution and our failure to dislodge him jolted the Kennedy administration into action. Such a thing must never be allowed to happen again. The United

Concepts

SPHERE OF INFLUENCE

Related to hegemony, a sphere of influence is where a major power molds the policies of another state without directly controlling its government. Threats and bribes keep local rulers submissive to the powerful state. Major powers create and maintain spheres of influence for their security, economic well-being, and sometimes for prestige. The term grew up in the China trade, where the European imperial powers divided up coastal areas in the nineteenth century into their "spheres of influence," understandings of who dominated where.

States developed the Green Berets to counter revolutions and an ambitious foreign-aid program called the Alliance for Progress. Castro may have won by stealth in Cuba, but his revolution would not spread, vowed Washington. Johnson applied the Cuba analogy—a poor one—to the Dominican Republic in 1965 and sent in U.S. forces "to prevent another Cuba."

Kennedy understood that reforms were badly needed in order to head off revolution. "Those who make peaceful revolutions impossible will make violent revolutions inevitable," he said. In Central America revolution brewed as some people got rich while others grew poorer. The spread of commercial export crops—coffee, cotton, sugar, tropical fruits—diminished the acreage devoted to foodstuffs such as beans and rice. Commercial farmers made more money, but peasants went hungry. When they got hungry enough, some supported rebels; others flocked northward to work in the United States.

■ Mexico: Drugs and Democracy

American media and academics pay great attention to China and Iraq but little to our number-one problem: Mexico (which, by the way, is a *North* American country). Our cultural blindness to things Latino may underlie the problem. Mexico is the only place on earth where you can walk from the Third World into the First. Poverty and unemployment push

Reflections

OUR CUBA PROBLEM

Long after the Cold War ended and Cuba lost its Soviet patron, the United States still glared at Castro—and he glared back. What to do with this troublesome little island? At the very time that Washington tried to coax Vietnam and North Korea into joining the world, we stayed with a policy of isolating Cuba.

Most of the powerful and passionate Cuban-American voting bloc in Florida opposes anything that appears to be giving in to Castro—from re-establishing trade to allowing Americans to visit Cuba. Knowing how important it is to win Florida, the Republicans generally give the Miami Cubans what they want: no recognition of or trade with Cuba. U.S. laws penalize foreign companies doing business with Cuba, but the rest of the world just ignores the unenforceable laws.

Others—including a growing number of Cuban Americans—think that the way to get rid the regime is to bring Cuba out of its shell by trade and contacts. Exposed to a better, freer life, the Communist dictatorship would soon crumble. Much of Cuba's wretched economy already depends on dollars from relatives in Miami. An uprising is unlikely; Cuba still has secret police, and many Cubans still appreciate the education, jobs, health care, and equality for Cuba's large lower class, many of whom are of African descent. Isolating Castro helped keep him in power.

many Mexicans to make that walk. Mexico's population has grown rapidly—from 20 million in 1940 to 108 million now—but its economy grows only fitfully.

Mexico is a "zone of chaos" on our border, an endless source of drugs, crime, corruption, instability, and undocumented workers. Most of America's illicit drugs flow through Mexico; those who try to stop them are killed. The influence of *narcotraficantes* extends through Mexico's army, police, courts, and even into the presidency.

Mexico had a major revolution from 1910 to 1917. In 1929, the winning generals formed the Institutional Revolutionary party (**PRI**), which won fourteen elections in a row, most of them rigged. Billing itself as a leftish party of the people, PRI became statist, bureaucratic, and corrupt. Mexico's presidents (who hold single six-year terms) until recently simply named their successors, and the party machine delivered their election by suppressing any opposition, handing out gifts, and ordering whole towns to vote PRI. Businesses and banks transferred huge sums to PRI. Until PRI lost free and fair presidential elections in 2000, Mexico was not a democracy.

Mexicans became more middle class, educated, and critical. Many business and government people have degrees from U.S. universities, including Ph.D.s in economics. Much of Mexico's statist economy has been privatized. Pushing in this direction was Mexico's accession to **NAFTA** (see Chapter 18), which opened its borders to free trade with the United States and Canada. **Maquiladoras** near the U.S. border assemble products from many sources for export. (See where your satellite receiver was made.) Mexico's economy—long plagued by unemployment, inflation, currency collapse, and crooked banking—showed 5 percent annual gains in the late 1990s and is now over $8,000 per cap, thus predicting democracy.

Mexico's presidential elections of 2000 showed what happens when a country becomes middle-income and educated. Many Mexicans were fed up with PRI dominance and understood that democracy needs alternation in power. PRI turned from hand-picked candidates to open and hotly contested primaries. Despite PRI's usual tricks—

PRI   Mexico's long-dominant party.

NAFTA   North America Free Trade Agreement that links the United States, Canada, and Mexico.

maquiladora   Assembly plant.

Classic Thought

POOR MEXICO!

¡Pobre México! Tan lejos de Dios, tan cerca de los Estados Unidos. "Poor Mexico! So far from God, so close to the United States," said Mexican President Porfirio Díaz (1830–1915), reflecting the widespread Mexican view that just being next door to us insures U.S. domination. Díaz witnessed the U.S. invasion of 1846–1847 that seized the northern half of the original Mexico in 1848. The sad exclamation also reflects considerable Mexican jealousy of their rich, well-run neighbor. Many Latin American intellectuals share the sentiment.

Mercosur Free trade agreement of southern part of South America.

in Yucatán, they handed out thousands of washing machines (no doubt campaigning for a clean election)—Vicente Fox of the free-market National Action party (PAN) won the election. However, Fox, a former Coca-Cola executive from the more capitalist-oriented north, had to battle the PRI-staffed civil service and state-owned corporations. In 2006, PAN's Felipe Calderón won and continued the trend.

■ What Can We Do?

Practically all of Latin America turned to democracy in the 1980s (exception: Cuba). To be sure, some (Peru and Venezuela) slid back to authoritarianism. With the Cold War over, Central American massacres subsided in favor of elected governments. What can and should the United States do to encourage Latin America's steps to democracy? We should first learn from history that U.S. intervention, even indirect, often makes things worse, leading to dictatorships and bloodbaths. Military intervention can turn long and frustrating. U.S. Marines in Nicaragua hunted nationalist guerrilla Augusto César Sandino from 1927 to 1933 and never caught him. We should think about that before we send U.S. forces into Colombia.

The long-term and only effective solution is economic growth. And one of the best ways to promote growth is free trade. After a few years, NAFTA had a positive impact on the Mexican economy. (And, no, it did not rob Americans of jobs.) The limiting factor in Mexican economic growth—and many other countries—is China, whose labor costs undercut everybody's. Mexico lost factory jobs to China. **Mercosur** (Southern Market) for

Concepts

FREE AND FAIR ELECTIONS

Like most of the Global South, Mexico for a long time had no free and fair elections. The problem goes a lot deeper than secret ballots and accurate counting—the things outside observers look for. The problem is the dominance of the powerful over a population not aware and organized enough to voice its wants and needs. The root cause is a poor country with too few educated people. With few exceptions—India is the biggest one—poor countries do not have democratic elections.

Instead, those who have power use it to make sure they stay in power. They prohibit or hassle

opposition parties—sometimes by murder—until they are ineffective. They deny them access to the mass media, chiefly through government control of television. They distribute gifts, favors, and jobs to their supporters, who vote early and often. They tell the poor and ignorant that they have ways of learning how they cast their ballots. In much of the world (including Russia), elections are rigged well in advance of election day. American efforts to promote electoral democracy in such lands are poorly conceived. The solution: a large, educated middle class. When Mexico got one, it became a democracy.

several years boosted growth in Argentina, Brazil, Uruguay, Paraguay, Chile, and Bolivia (until Argentina's currency collapsed in 2002). One hemispheric vision urges merging NAFTA with Mercosur to make a Free-Trade Area of the Americas (**FTAA**) that would cover almost all the hemisphere. Your generation may rediscover Latin America and participate in its phenomenal growth possibilities. It is, after all, our hemisphere.

FTAA   Proposed Free-Trade Area of the Americas.

Reflections

WE BUILD A HOUSE IN HONDURAS

With a per-capita income of less than $3,000 and its population increasing by over 3 percent a year, Honduras needs all the low-cost housing it can get. As much to learn about Honduras as to help build a house, I joined a Mennonite Church housing team on a demonstration project in a new settlement outside of San Pedro Sula. The Mennonites, including an architect, a mason, and a contractor, concentrated on teaching the Hondurans to build houses themselves using local materials. We built a house in eight days for less than $1,000.

I was surprised to find that even poor Hondurans were far more politicized, energetic, and assertive than I had expected, in spite of massive poverty and malnutrition. Even a squatter shanty town that we visited had an appointed representative who successfully bargained with the local authorities for land for the entire community. There is an awakening in Central America, a growth in civic culture that governments simply cannot ignore.

—N. O. B.

This Honduran family has three generations of rural poverty under one small roof. American volunteers in a Mennonite project built them a new house. Their light-colored hair is not from ancestry but from malnutrition. Over half of Honduran children are malnourished.
(Nicholas O. Berry)

Concepts

"TORN" COUNTRIES

Samuel Huntington (see pages 15 and 138) called countries "torn" when they are pulled between a modernizing elite that wants to join Western civilization and traditional masses that resist. Example: Mexico, where energetic, well-educated younger professionals want to remake Mexico into a modern and capitalistic North American country. Many Mexicans, especially leftists, fight the idea, seeing Mexico's future in socialist help for the poor. Another example: Turkey, torn between secular modernizers who want to join Europe and traditionalists who want to stay Islamic.

Key Terms

Bay of Pigs (p. 160)
capital flight (p. 156)
Central America (p. 152)
cocalero (p. 152)
coup (p. 153)
creole (p. 153)
dependency (p. 155)
entrepreneurialism (p. 152)
exploitation (p. 156)
FTAA (p. 165)
indígena (p. 152)
interdiction (p. 152)

intervene (p. 155)
Latin America (p. 152)
maquiladora (p. 163)
Mercosur (p. 164)
mestizo (p. 153)
Monroe Doctrine (p. 156)
NAFTA (p. 163)
narcotraficante (p. 152)
PRI (p. 163)
Roosevelt Corollary (p. 156)
South America (p. 152)
statism (p. 152)

Key Web Sites

Organization of American States
http://www.oas.org/

Political Data Base of the Americas
http://www.georgetown.edu/LatAmerPolitical/home.html

The National Web Site for the Republic of Cuba—CubaWeb
http://www.cubaweb.cu/

El Universal (Mexico)
http://www.el-universal.com.mx/

La Nacion (Argentina)
http://www.lanacion.com.ar/

Inter Press Service
http://www.link.no/IPS/eng/serv/LA

BBC Americas
http://news.bbc.co.uk/hi/world/americas/

Further Reference

Bowden, Mark. *Killing Pablo: The Hunt for the World's Greatest Outlaw.* New York: Grove/Atlantic, 2001.

Camp, Roderic A. *Politics in Mexico: The Decline of Authoritarianism,* 3rd ed. New York: Oxford University Press, 1999.

Crandall, Russell. *Driven by Drugs: U.S. Policy toward Colombia.* Boulder, CO: Lynne Rienner, 2002.

Hufbauer, Gary Clyde, and Jeffrey J. Schott. *NAFTA Revisited: Achievements and Challenges.* Washington, D.C.: Institute for International Economics, 2005.

Jonas, Susanne. *The Battle for Guatemala: Rebels, Death Squads, and U.S. Power.* Boulder, CO: Westview, 1991.

LaFeber, Walter. *Inevitable Revolutions: The United States in Central America,* 2nd ed. New York: Norton, 1993.

LeoGrande, William M. *Our Own Backyard: The United States in Central America, 1977–1992.* Chapel Hill, NC: University of North Carolina Press, 1998.

Musicant, Ivan. *The Banana Wars: A History of United States Military Intervention in Latin America from the Spanish-American War to the Invasion of Panama.* New York: Macmillan, 1990.

Paterson, Thomas G. *Contesting Castro: The United States and the Triumph of the Cuban Revolution.* New York: Oxford University Press, 1994.

Peeler, John. *Building Democracy in Latin America,* 2nd ed. Boulder, CO: Lynne Rienner, 2004.

Ruiz, Ramón Eduardo. *On the Rim of Mexico: Encounters of the Rich and Poor.* Boulder, CO: Westview, 1998.

Smith, Peter H. *Democracy in Latin America: Political Change in Comparative Perspective.* New York: Oxford University Press, 2005.

Stone, Samuel. *The Heritage of the Conquistadores.* Omaha, NE: University of Nebraska Press, 1991.

CHAPTER 11

ECONOMIC DEVELOPMENT

THE RICH AND THE POOR

QUESTIONS TO CONSIDER

1. What is the relationship between democracy and economics?
2. Is Global South poverty the result of imperialism?
3. How does psychology contribute to backwardness?
4. What factors made the West the first to modernize?
5. What moral case can be made against imperialism?
6. Is the earth's population increasing at a dangerous rate?
7. What explains the massive migrations of our day?
8. Why has the Global South tended to socialism and statism?
9. How does a country get rapid economic growth?

The **"emerging economies," Global South**, or **Third World**—call it what you will—is complicated and contains many exceptions. It is mostly poor, but some oil-producing and newly industrializing lands are not. Still, most Global Southerners get by on less than $1,000 a year per-capita **GDP** (see box on page 169), less than a twentieth of the industrialized lands of West Europe and North America. As countries industrialize, the gap narrows fast.

Some see Global Southerners as nonwhite, but much of Latin America and the Muslim world are inhabited by white people. And some Asian peoples have leaped into the First World (Japan, Singapore) or are about to (Taiwan, South Korea). No peoples are doomed to poverty. Practically all of the Third World was at one time colonized. Some still resent an arrogant and cruel colonial power; some remember an armed liberation struggle. Where that was the case, the country was often anti-Western and pro-Soviet. Most of the Third World, though, liked to call itself "nonaligned," that is, neutral between the capitalist First World and communist Second World.

A strong characteristic of the Global South is its political weakness and instability. Most regimes are weak and subject to overthrow by revolutions and military coups. Most are corrupt and unable to enforce their laws. Colombia's guerrillas and drug lords are an example. Few are democracies. One notable exception is India, which is now scoring rapid economic growth. Neighboring Pakistan, however, is more typical: Military dictatorship alternates with tumultuous democracy, the one leading to the other, and economic growth is slow. The Third World is both economically and politically underdeveloped.

emerging economies/Global South/Third World Asia, Africa, and Latin America. (See page 168.)

GDP Gross Domestic Product; sum total of goods and services produced in a country in one year; measure of prosperity. (See page 168.)

■ The Roots of Poverty

Why are some countries rich and others poor? The richest fifth of humankind take 86 percent of the globe's income; the poorest fifth get 1 percent and live on less than $1 a day. Half the world's population lives on less than $2 a day. There are two broad explanations for this enormous gap, one focusing on external causes, the other on internal.

Among others, Marxists and Third World radicals favor the external explanation. The English economist J. A. Hobson and German Marxist Rosa Luxemburg argued that capitalism's spread around the world, the nineteenth-century empires, had given it a new lease on life. By exploiting their colonies—cheap labor to produce cheap raw materials and captive markets for their products—the capitalist countries were able to last much longer than Marx had expected. Lenin popularized these views in his 1916 pamphlet, *Imperialism: The Highest Stage of Capitalism.* The capitalist empires enrich themselves at the expense of their colonies, which get poorer.

The evidence does not support this view very well. In some cases individual firms got wealthy from the colonial trade but, overall, colonies cost the imperial government more to administer and defend than they earned. Colonialism was more a prestige item than economic calculation. The four richest countries of Europe—Norway, Sweden, Luxembourg, and Switzerland—never had colonies. The fifth richest country, Germany, lost all its colonies in World War I. France enjoyed an economic resurgence after she gave her

Concepts

Per-Capita GDP

The standard way to measure and compare economies is the "per-capita gross domestic product" (GDPpc). Every time a car rolls off an assembly line or you get a haircut, the GDP increases by whatever those items are worth. GDP is not a perfect measure or easy to calculate, for some economic activity is off the books, such as the underground economy and the unpaid work of housewives. Still, it is the best measure of overall economic activity we have. The older expression, "Gross National Product" (GNP), is now used to designate all income, including from overseas, while GDP is considered the more precise measure. The "per capita" is arrived at by dividing the country's GDP by its population. The "per cap," now usually expressed in Purchasing Power Parity (PPP, see page 283), gives the most widely used comparison of how well people live.

neocolonialism   Rich-country dominance by indirect, economic means.

culture   The sum total of a group's learned behavior.

modernization theory   Economic growth modernizes whole society.

colonies their independence in the early 1960s. The poorest country of West Europe, Portugal, was both the first and last colonial empire; its five centuries of empire drained it rather than the other way around. Economists long advised the European powers to get rid of their colonies because they were money-losers.

Even after decolonization, though, the view lingers in updated form. Radicals argue that the poor countries, which have only their raw materials to export, get low prices for them from the rich countries. This drains their wealth from them and keeps them tied to the big capitalist countries and as poor as ever. Instead of colonialism, the Global South now suffers from **neocolonialism** (see box on page 172), say critics. This situation is not necessarily the result of a capitalist plot, however. If a country's chief product is in oversupply, it will earn little from it. One solution is to diversify; Brazil has done this and is now nobody's neocolony. Another solution is to form a cartel like OPEC to limit production and keep up prices. The oil-exporting countries turned the tables on the capitalist oil-importing countries and exploited them. And why did Japan, with no natural resources, ruined and defeated in war, and occupied by the Americans, not turn into a neocolony of the United States?

The internally caused view, often favored by conservatives, argues that **cultural** problems retard the poor countries. Lack of natural resources is rarely the problem. Some of the most resource-poor countries have turned into economic dynamos based on their human resources (Japan and Taiwan), while resource-rich countries have grown poorer (Burma and Argentina). Human resources and sound economic policies are far more important than natural resources. Growth needs a psychology that you can and should work hard to improve your situation. This is weak in traditional societies, where people have for centuries tilled the soil, asked for little, and died young. Political and religious structures often teach obedience to inherited authority and fatalism before God's will.

Concepts

MODERNIZATION THEORY

Economics and politics are clearly related. What is called **modernization theory** has found a dividing line around $5,000 to $6,000 per capita GDP (see box on page 169). Below that, few countries are democratic, and attempts to found new democracies usually fail amidst demagoguery and military coups. Above that level—what are called "middle-income countries"—most countries are democratic and do not slide back into authoritarian rule.

The reason seems to be that poor countries have only a small middle class; societies are generally divided into a few rich and many poor. The middle class, which grows as a country gets richer, is educated and moderate and dislikes dictatorships. As one scholar put it: "No bourgeoisie, no democracy." Taiwan, South Korea, Brazil, and Chile turned from authoritarian dictatorships to democracies after their economies had grown.

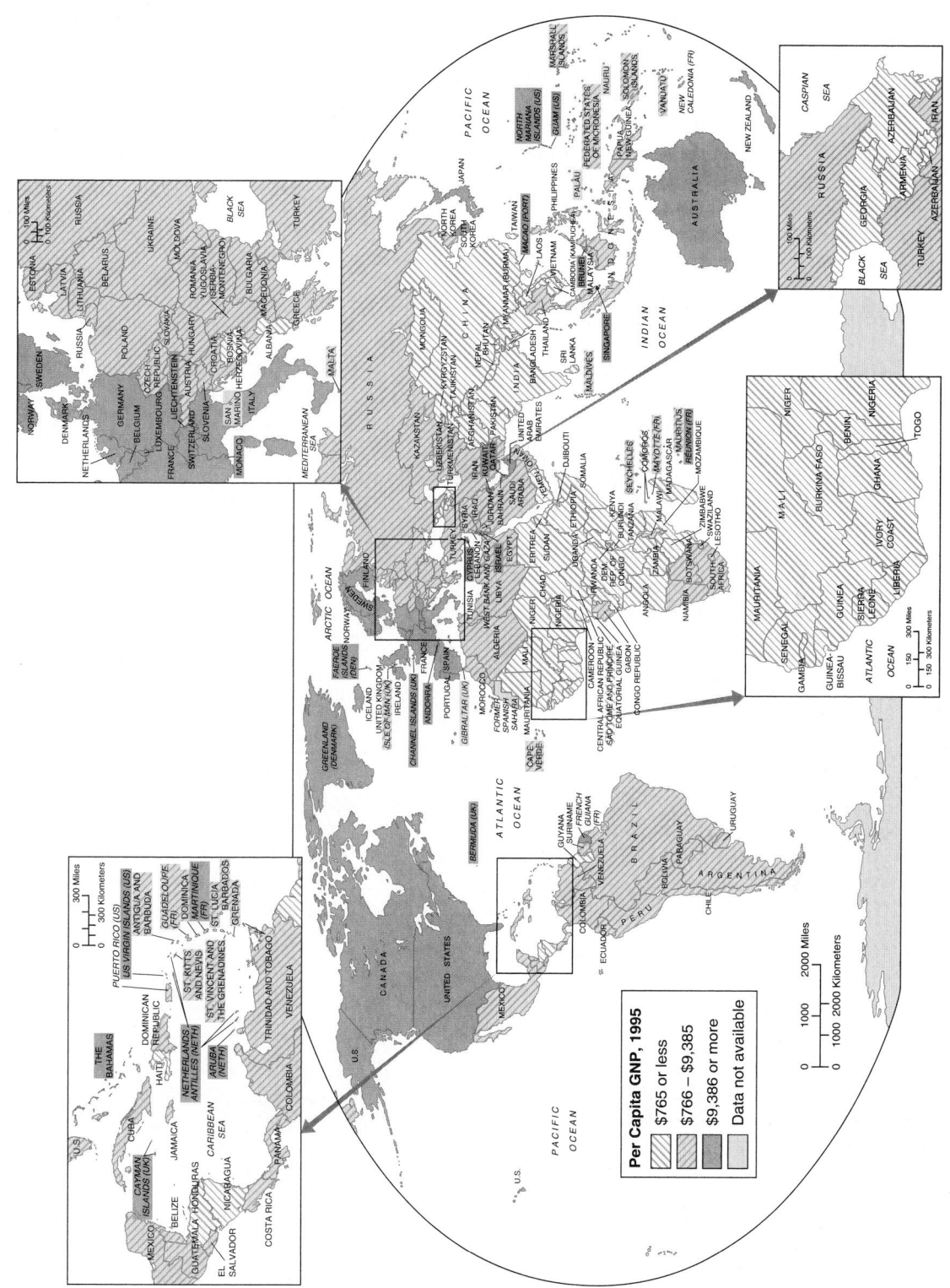

The World by Wealth

Per Capita GNP, 1995

- $765 or less
- $766 – $9,385
- $9,386 or more
- Data not available

"Modern" and "traditional" are heavily cultural. Modern minds do things right, quickly, and often; they adapt to high productivity and high tech. Even if they start poor, modern-thinking people soon produce prosperity. Traditional people see little need to hurry, do things carefully, or grow economically. "Time is money," says modern man. "*Mañana*," says traditional man. Many of these cultures are rapidly changing; witness the rise of several Asian countries from traditional to modern.

Why Did the West Rise?

One approach to the question of economic growth is to ask why some countries began what economist Robert Heilbroner called "the great ascent" first. Europe during the Middle Ages was a traditional society, far behind Arabs, Indians, and Chinese in education, science, and commerce. For most of history, what we now call the Third World produced some 80 percent of global GDP. But by the sixteenth century, certain areas of Europe were starting to grow. For most of the twentieth century, the developed countries were producing some 60 percent of the world's GDP.

The reasons for Europe's modernization are many, but most historians credit the quality of thought that flowed from the Italian Renaissance starting in the thirteenth century. Painting improved as artists discovered perspective and shadow. Leonardo da Vinci bridged the world of art and science; for a renaissance man there was no difference. Galileo discovered laws of physics and engineering that we use today. Printing with movable type opened up learning to much of the population. Commerce increased until trading networks covered most of Europe. People grew restless and oriented to change and improving their situation in life; a new dynamic was unleashed upon the world.

Starting in France, monarchs began to centralize and increase their power, leading to absolutism. Competing with other monarchs, they funded expeditions and imperial expansion to gain territories to exploit. Columbus's discovery took place in a different context from the earlier Viking discoveries of America. The Vikings had no demanding monarch behind them, no desire for an empire, and no printing press to spread news of their find. The voyages of discovery did not trigger the modern age but were an expression of it.

Concepts

NEOCOLONIALISM

In the parlance of radicals, neocolonialism is the indirect continuation of colonialism by economic means. France, for example, freed its many African colonies, but there are more French people in them than ever, helping the African lands with their economy, education, and defense. Radicals call this neocolonialism, but many poor African countries found they needed continued French help. Only France pays much attention to Africa. In Latin America, one version of neocolonialism is called "dependency" (see page 155).

A new culture of money and material progress appeared. In traditional societies, people saw little reason to amass money beyond their immediate needs. Working hard to get rich was impossible and therefore not attempted; wealth and status were inherited. Tradesmen sought a good living for their families but saw no reason to expand beyond that. In certain parts of Europe, however, in about the fifteenth century, a capitalist mentality appeared. It became good and respectable to amass as much wealth as possible, more than you or your family could spend. Instead of steady-state attitudes, people began to think in terms of growth without limit: "Invest and grow; then reinvest and grow some more." This mentality, now abundant in East Asia, is often lacking in the Global South, and without it there can be no self-sustaining economic growth.

Why this shift occurred has never been settled. Some thinkers emphasize technological change and innovation, improved transportation and communication, the consolidation and centralization of kingdoms, and the opening of trade to new parts of the world. The trouble with such explanations is that they were also present in other civilizations—the Roman, Arab, and Chinese, for example—but did not produce self-sustaining economic growth. These empires had the ingredients for takeoff, but they petered out.

Other thinkers emphasize cultural factors, specifically the rise of Protestantism that challenged the steady-state attitudes of the medieval Catholic faith. The Catholic Church was not growth-oriented; it taught people to accept their place in life. Lending money at interest was deemed immoral and was prohibited, a major impediment to economic growth. Protestantism rejected such restrictions and brought economic growth (see box on page 174), especially to England and the Netherlands.

Whatever the causes, the West pulled ahead and conquered or converted the rest of the world. European arms and military organization made short work of Arab, Asian, and African states. Colonial administrators carved up the globe and attempted to remake it to Western tastes. Western dynamism and expansionism—or, if you prefer, greed—took over most of the globe.

A few Global South lands engaged in "defensive modernization"; they tried to adopt enough of the West's technology to stave off the imperialists. Japan adapted European ways wholesale to beat the West at its own game. The Ottoman Turks and Chinese empire adopted European weapons but were picked apart. That's the trouble with halfway modernization.

Reflections

THE PSYCHOLOGY OF BACKWARDNESS

I had studied about transitional countries in the abstract but didn't understand them until I got a pocket calendar in Belgrade, where I was studying. A Balkan country, Yugoslavia at that time (1963–1964) was still partly traditional; that's why I liked it. Many of its people lived in the old ways. The calendar puzzled me for several days until I found the problem.

The calendar was one day off; its makers had made 1963 (and not 1964) a leap year. And then I realized that backwardness is a cultural or psychological problem, a lack of paying attention, of not doing things right the first time. American students are not immune to this problem.

—M. G. R.

Protestant ethic Weber's theory
that religion first ignited
capitalism.

You cannot adopt just one facet of Western civilization—such as the military—and leave the rest of your system traditional. It will not work, for you need Western education, economics, and nationalism to make your military arm work right. You have to become as modern as those who would conquer you.

The Global South resisted—and in some cases is still resisting—becoming westernized. The Global South dislikes the implication that everything they stand for and live by—their religion, values, and culture—is inferior. They usually try to preserve their culture while adopting Western technology. It is a difficult combination. The countries of the Persian Gulf attempted to stay Islamic while building a high-tech, petroleum economy. The result, as we considered in Chapter 9, was instability and breakdown. Islam especially resists Western culture, for Islam sees itself as morally superior to the West's crass materialism.

There are no purely traditional countries left in the world; all are unstable combinations of modern and traditional, creating massive problems that some people would like to fix by returning to a rural idyll where all live as organic farmers. This is not possible; populations are too big and expect growing living standards. It can be a recipe for misery and starvation, as in Cambodia under the back-to-the-village doctrines of the Communists. No, once you have started the "great ascent," you cannot go back. You cannot even pause.

■ The Population Explosion

For most of human history, the population grew very slowly, with high birth rates offset by high death rates. The world's population reached one billion only about 1830. Then, during the nineteenth century, it gradually accelerated, reaching two billion about 1930. Then

Classic Thought

PROTESTANT ETHIC

One of the efforts of the great German sociologist Max Weber (1864–1920) was to refute Marx, who had argued that economic conditions give rise to new thoughts. For example, Marx said the North German princes were already profiting from capitalism when they turned Protestant to escape Catholic restrictions on their profits.

Weber said no, first came Protestantism, then came capitalism; the former gave rise to the latter. Protestants—particularly Calvinists—felt they had to prove themselves in this world, not just wait for their rewards in the next. Consequently, the **Protestant ethic** emphasized hard work and conspicuous individual achievement, explaining why people started amassing capital beyond their immediate needs: "Look at me. I'm a big success." Capitalism, the philosophy of economic growth without limit, argued Weber, has a religious basis.

Weber's theory of a Protestant catalyst for capitalism remains controversial. The earliest capitalists were Catholic banking houses in North Italy and South Germany. And how do you explain East Asia's growth? Some argue that a Confucian Ethic is the functional equivalent of a Protestant Ethic: Work hard and reinvest your money. Any religion can develop such an ethic, but not all have.

it accelerated faster, hitting three billion about 1960 and five billion in 1987. It is now over six billion. On a graph, the line curves upward more sharply every decade, what mathematicians call "exponential growth." The world's population is increasing 1.6 percent a year, but most of this is in the Global South. The population of the First World increases about 0.7 percent a year, but the Third World zips along at nearly 2 percent a year with some countries increasing over 3 percent a year. For a typical Global South country, such growth is devastating. If its GDP growth is 3 percent but its population growth is also 3 percent, it enjoys no per-capita increase and remains as poor as ever. Most Third World countries with slower population growth also show faster economic growth.

How did this debilitating increase happen? It is a kind of overshoot. Traditional societies had high birth rates and high death rates. They needed the former to compensate for the latter and to stay in rough balance. A quarter to half of all babies died soon after birth, as did the mothers, and people lived only to thirty or forty. Simple public health improvements—sewers, clean water, washable cotton underwear—boost lifespans. With inoculations, visiting nurses and midwives, and good diet, people attain near-modern levels of health. Life expectancy in the Third World increased twenty-two years from 1960 to 1995. Their death rate has dropped, but they are used to high birth rates and still expect many babies to die. They like lots of male children, for males earn more to support them in their old age. Their religion may forbid birth control. When their birth rate greatly exceeds their death rate, their rate of percentage increase climbs. Part of the problem, then, is the improvement in health and diet brought by modernization.

Now for the good news. Population growth is slowing nearly everywhere as societies move from traditional to modern. Women have half as many babies as their mothers did.

Economics

MALTHUS WAS WRONG

Two centuries ago Englishman Thomas Malthus, one of the founders of economics, wrote his celebrated essay predicting drastic limits on the number of humans the earth could sustain. Humans increase their numbers "geometrically" (what we today call "exponentially," at a faster and faster rate) while food supplies increase only "arithmetically" (at a constant rate), he wrote. Eventually, people will outstrip food supplies and die from starvation, war, or disease. You can see where economics got its dismal reputation.

Malthus was wrong. Food supplies have increased faster than population growth. There are more than six times as many people as in Malthus's day, and they eat better and live longer. Famines have been local and caused by wars and natural disasters, not overpopulation. India now produces all the food it needs. The problem now is that some Global Southerners lack money to buy food, which is quite another problem, one solved by economic growth.

But growth is the last thing Malthusians want. "Doomsters" on the Malthus model have long predicted shortages of land, food, energy, minerals, or clean air as dooming the human race to declining standards of living. We should, by some of their calculations, have run out of oil a long time ago. Doomsters neglect the possibilities of increased supplies and technological change.

Fifty years ago an average Indian woman bore six children; now it's just under three. The world's population is predicted to peak at about 9 billion around 2100 and then slowly decline. After a while, people recognize that there is no need for so many babies for practically all of them live, and government welfare measures help the elderly. People live in cities, in small apartments, where children are more of a problem than on a farm. Industrialized countries have low birth and population-increase rates. Most of Europe and Japan have shrinking populations. The solution to the world's population explosion is to get the Global South industrialized quickly. The most effective way to curb the number of babies per woman is to educate girls: the more schooling, the fewer babies.

Countries with determined leadership can bring their birth rates down. China, with 1.3 billion citizens, holds its annual increase to 1.2 percent, low for the Global South. The methods for this are not pretty: compulsory abortions, female infanticide, and punishment for parents who produce three children. Saudi Arabia, a strictly Muslim country, had an amazing population growth of 7.9 percent a year in the 1980s, dropping to a still-high 3.3 percent at the end of the century. It is now full of unemployed and angry youths, many of whom turn to Islamic radicalism.

Population growth by itself need not spell doom—if there are enough jobs. But where unemployment is already high, as in much of the Global South, jobless young men turn to violence and revolution. Mexico, Brazil, and Egypt each need to add a million new jobs a year just to keep even. An expanding population may fuel dictators' dreams of aggrandizement: Syria at 3.3 percent a year and Iraq at 3.7 percent.

■ The Great Migration

Jobs are the reason Global Southerners immigrate into the North. Legally and illegally, by planes, boats, and foot, citizens of poor countries seek jobs in rich countries. Hundreds die trying every year. Millions of Pakistanis, Indians, and Caribbean islanders in Britain; black

Economics

THE RULE OF 70

How long does it take a quantity to double, figuring in the effects of compounding? If you know its annual growth rate, divide that into 70 for the number of years it will take to double. West Europe's population increase of a very low 0.2 percent a year means—if that rate holds—it will take 350 years for its population to double in size. The United States, with a moderate 0.7 percent, will double in a hundred years, not counting immigration. Africa, however, with a natural increase of over 3 percent, could double in less than twenty-five years (depending on the impact of AIDS). The average Rwanda woman bore eight children that produced a 3.4 percent annual growth rate and made Rwanda the most densely populated country in Africa, which contributed to the genocide of the 1990s. You can use the same rule going the other way: If a country took eleven years to double its per-capita GDP, it had an average annual percentage increase of 6 percent.

and North Africans in France; Turks and East Europeans in Germany; and Mexicans, Caribbean islanders, and Asians in the United States illustrate the universality and magnitude of the new **migration**. At any given time, an estimated 70 million migrants are on the move, and most rich countries try to keep them out. The United States annually takes in more than one million legal immigrants plus many illegal ones.

migration Resettling from one country to another.

remittance Money sent back home.

fertility rate Average number of babies per woman.

Can you blame the immigrants? Typically, they flee unemployment and dismal prospects. Air fares are cheap, and even the dirtiest, lowest-paid jobs in the First World pay ten or more times what immigrants can make back home. Their **remittances** to relatives are bigger, more efficient, and less corrupt in helping their home countries than foreign aid. And there are jobs in the First World, whose aging work force cannot staff its agricultural and industrial base. Many citizens of rich countries refuse to take low-end jobs; they prefer to live off welfare.

Is there anything wrong with poor immigrants taking the lowliest jobs? Is it not a replay of how many of our ancestors arrived in the United States? They too were in a push-pull situation: Poverty and limited opportunities pushed them out of the old world; wealth and unlimited opportunities pulled them to the new world. In earlier years the immigrants to America were mostly Europeans and they assimilated rather quickly to U.S. culture. After one or two generations, they looked, spoke, and thought like other Americans. The new immigrants are mostly non-European and do not easily assimilate into the host

Economics

UNEVEN POPULATION GROWTH

World population growth is highly uneven, in some places too much, in others too little. In the former countries, generally poor, it means not enough jobs. In the latter countries, generally rich, it means not enough workers to support an aging population on social security. One solution—already being practiced—is migration.

One key measure is the **fertility rate**, the number of babies per average woman. (This is not the same as the birthrate or rate of population increase.) Replacement fertility rate is 2.1—enough to replace both parents plus a little for those who die or have no offspring. If below replacement, a country's population shrinks over time; if higher, it grows. The table on the right shows some UN fertility rate figures.

The average North American and West European woman has between one and two children, the average Global South woman between three and six. (World champ: Gaza Strip, at 7.5.) Citizens of the rich countries also live long on good pensions. Some countries, especially Germany and Japan, are running out of working-age people, whose taxes fuel their retirement systems. Migration from poor to rich countries is therefore not only natural but a fiscal necessity.

Europe	1.7
North America	1.9
Latin America	3.1
Asia	3.2
Middle East	4.7
Africa	6.0

Guatemalans cross into Mexico on their way north for a better life. (Luis J. Jimenez/The New York Times)

country's culture; the gap is too big. Pakistanis in England, North Africans in France, and Turks in Germany may tend to ghettoize themselves and become more religiously Muslim than they ever were in their homelands. Some Spanish-speakers in the United States don't learn English, and parts of the United States have become bilingual Spanish-English—a point that bothers Americans who fear for the nation's unity.

America has it relatively easy, for it is used to immigrants. The European host countries, however, are unused to waves of immigration, especially from outside of Europe. They were never immigrant societies; until recently, they exported people. The result of this meeting of unlike cultures is nasty racism and efforts to choke off the flow of immigration. Most countries of West Europe have anti-immigrant movements or parties, many with fascist overtones, such as the French National Front of Jean-Marie Le Pen and Austrian Freedom party of Jürg Haider, both clever demagogues who whip up racist fears to win many votes. In the high-unemployment areas of Germany, young skinheads take out their frustrations in neo-Nazi movements and foreigner-bashing.

political asylum Permission to remain in host country for those fleeing persecution.

Immigrants have become a global political issue. French, German, and American authorities bundle illegal aliens onto planes back home. Some of them beg for **political asylum**—they say they are persecuted at home—but most countries shrug them off as "economic refugees" and send them back. The United States now looks at them as potential terrorists. If they did not treat the migrants firmly, they argue, it would encourage millions more to come here. The world does not love refugees.

What can be done? The answer is industrialization in the home country, which has at least two demographic effects: It keeps people at home in jobs, and it lowers the birthrate. Instead of trying to prop up its old industries, the rich countries should be exporting them to the Global South, which can use its natural advantage in low labor costs to move into the industrial age. What can we do? Cut tariffs on the products and forgive the debts of the poorest countries. The 17 percent U.S. tariff on African-made textiles and clothing—now repealed—throttled African growth. The Europeans, Japanese, and

Americans lavish nearly $1 billion a day on their farmers in taxpayer subsidies. This floods the globe with cheap crops, which in turn means Third World growers cannot sell their products. What the rich world gives in foreign aid it takes away in the harm done to Global South agriculture. In 2005 the United States proposed a major cut in these odious subsidies, but the Europeans and Japanese refused to consider it.

■ Socialist versus Market Paths

Until recently, much of the Global South approached development with a socialist twist. Many leaders saw colonialism and capitalism as one and the same: unfair, exploitive, and inhuman. If they studied in Europe, they often picked up socialist views and returned to their native lands determined to build a better, more just system by means of state ownership and supervision.

The results were catastrophes. Socialism in the Soviet Union and East Europe merely worked badly. In the Global South it yielded results ranging from genocide under Communist regimes (Cambodia and Ethiopia) to tyranny and economic decline under "third-way" regimes (Tanzania and Burma). The countries that follow a market path, although riddled with problems, generally show more rapid economic growth and greater personal freedom. There are no examples of successful Third World socialist economies.

Eventually, reality hit home. Everything Third World socialists hated—capitalism and world trade—turned out to be the ticket to rapid economic improvement. A new generation of leaders permitted growing market sectors with generally good results: ample food production, a rising standard of living, and fast growth. Socialism was out, free markets in.

Economics

DOES FOREIGN AID WORK?

Some people would like to see a massive increase in foreign aid—with the United States in the lead—to the Global South. True, U.S. foreign aid—about one-tenth of 1 percent of our GDP—is low; West Europe and Canada give about three times as much as a percent of GDP. Much of U.S. aid is in surplus grain, which both supports American farmers and feeds the starving but does little to develop Third World economies. Americans have never liked foreign aid, believing it is a waste of money.

The first big U.S. foreign aid program, the Marshall Plan, lifted West Europe after World War II, but later efforts in the Third World show no connection between aid and economic growth. Some countries received a lot of aid but grew poorer; others received little but grew impressively. Corruption skims off much aid. British economist P. T. Bauer called aid "an excellent method for transferring money from poor people in rich countries to rich people in poor countries." Aid poured into countries without rule of law or sound economic policies drains out like a sieve. With both of those items in place, poor countries attract foreign investment and grow rapidly without aid. No rock concert has ever aided Africa. Self-promotion is not the same as results.

■ Can Capitalism Uplift the Global South?

The collapse of communism in East Europe and the Soviet Union came just as most Global South countries were changing their attitudes on economic development. The socialist and statist presumptions that had been popular in the 1950s and 1960s found few defenders by the late 1980s. Worldwide the new catchword was **"market economics."**

market economics   Capitalism.

But does capitalism work to lift up poor countries? The answer is yes, but only when certain policies are followed. Capitalism sounds like a simple system: Governments step back and let private industry and initiative produce and sell what the market wants. Actually, capitalism is complex and requires government to create favorable conditions. The World Bank has found that the fastest-growing Global South economies generally followed these policies:

1. *Prices:* Let prices find their own level. Subsidies or fixed prices create distortions in supply and demand and retard growth. Free prices are signals, telling producers what and how much to produce. Do not block these signals.

2. *Currency:* Do not print too much money or set fixed exchange rates. One telltale sign: If you can get 20 percent more on the black market for your dollars than you can in a bank, the exchange rate is distorted.

3. *Education:* Invest in people. A healthier and better-educated work force means faster productivity growth and attracts more foreign investment. The real payoff is in good elementary and secondary education, not college.

4. *Trade:* Open your economy to the world economy. Welcome foreign capital and technology and make products for the world market, not just your home market. Says Columbia economist Jeffrey Sachs: "There is not a single example in modern history of a country successfully developing without trading and integrating with the global economy."

Economics

EXPORTING JOBS?

More than any other country, the United States imports clothes, shoes, and other consumer products from the Global South. Now we even import many services. Help with U.S. income taxes and computer support now often comes from India. Economists tell us that both morally and economically, this is the right thing to do, but many Americans denounce it as "outsourcing jobs." Keeping these jobs in the United States would make these goods and services much more expensive.

If we kept these jobs in the United States, many of them would be taken by Global South immigrants willing to work long and hard for low wages. Much of America's sunbelt industry already depends on workers—many of them illegal—from south of the border. By moving some jobs to the Global South, we reorient ourselves to higher-tech, higher-paying jobs, and we give the Global South a chance to climb the economic ladder. Typically, the first rung on this ladder is textiles and clothing. We also turn Global South countries into major trading partners for U.S. goods and services. The flow of trade is never one-way.

5. *Government:* Promote rule of law. Government must not choke off growth by regulations and corruption, but it must enforce contracts, protect private property, and keep dealings **transparent**. Several fast-developing economies tumbled when their "**crony capitalism**" was unmasked.

Some people are unduly pessimistic about economic growth in the Global South. Actually, the emerging economies now account for over half of world GDP and are growing much faster than the now-rich countries did at similar stages of their development. At the early stage of industrialization, it took Britain about sixty years, starting in 1780, to double per capita income, that is, to make its people twice as well off. The United States, starting in 1840, took fifty years to do the same. Japan after 1885 needed only thirty-five years. Turkey, beginning in 1957, did it in only twenty years. Brazil after 1961 took only eighteen years. South Korea, starting in 1966, needed just eleven years. And China, starting in 1977, did it in ten years and continues to double nearly every decade. Why the acceleration? The old industrialized countries had to invent technology; the emerging economies just import it and use it with their cheap labor to undercut the rich countries. Such is the story of China's phenomenal growth of close to 10 percent a year.

> **transparency**   Business and political transactions open to public view.
>
> **crony capitalism**   Corrupt, secretive favors among government officials and business people.

Economics

THE BURMESE WAY TO CATASTROPHE

Burma—which now calls itself Myanmar—serves as a negative model of economic development. Burma, once the world's leading rice exporter, experiences food shortages. With abundant natural resources—rich agriculture, teak forests, and petroleum—Burmese grew poorer. Most of Burma's economy, however, is off the books, in the black market and smuggling. To avoid confiscatory taxes, Burmese smuggle their gems, teak, rubber, and heroin out to Thailand and Malaysia.

How did it get this way? In 1962, General Ne Win (who worked for the Japanese in World War II) seized power in a coup and kept it. A single party, the Burma Socialist Program party, consisting mostly of army officers, preached the "Burmese Way to Socialism" but lived well off corruption and the state-owned economy. Chinese and Indians were expelled, and they were Burma's merchants and technicians. Ne Win also isolated Burma, letting few foreigners in or Burmese out. He waged permanent antiguerrilla campaigns against minority Karens, Shans, Chins, and Kachins who wanted to break away from Burma.

Burmese lived passively with the decline until, in 1988, a jump in rice prices touched off protests. Police and soldiers gunned down thousands. This only enraged Burmese more. Ne Win resigned, but the military dictatorship continues. It liberalized the economy but refused to step down after losing free elections in 1990. Instead, the military put the winning presidential candidate, Aung San Suu Kyi, winner of the Nobel peace prize, under permanent house arrest. Burma was a prime example of the failure of "socialism" in the Global South. With socialism repealed, the Burmese economy has grown, starting in 1993, giving Burmese a per cap of some $1,800 in 2005, a big improvement. Burma may yet see democracy.

demonstration effect   One country copying another's success.

informal economy   Transactions off the books, the black market.

One of the pluses of the post–Cold War system is that two superpowers are no longer competing for clients in the Global South. All manner of horrors and nonsense went on as part of the zero-sum mentality that posed the Third World as a strategic prize. Both superpowers aided and armed dictators, guerrillas, death squads, and political police. They sponsored attention-getting foreign-aid programs that contributed little to economic growth. Much aid was skimmed off by corruption.

The path out of poverty is increasingly understood. Most of the Global South has accepted the above policies for economic development. When one country follows such policies and succeeds, it creates what economists call a **demonstration effect** that encourages copying by other lands. As economist Paul Krugman points out, no one has successfully predicted the next lands of rapid growth; it's always a surprise. India, written off for years as hopeless, in 1991 abandoned its statist economic policies in favor of private enterprise and zoomed ahead, especially in information technology.

As the rapid growth of the emerging economies became clear, a curious reversal took place in the rich countries. From scoffing at poor lands, First Worlders started fearing them: "Hey, they're taking our jobs!" There is little to fear. Ultimately, everyone gains. The Third

Economics

THE BLACK MARKET AS MODEL

In 1987, a book by a Peruvian economist shook Latin America and reverberated through the Third World. Rejecting the standard socialist or statist models for economic growth, Hernando de Soto suggested as a model the most dynamic and innovative sector of Global South economies: the black market. His controversial book, *The Other Path: The Invisible Revolution in the Third World,* said that slow growth in Latin America is the fault of an overlarge bureaucracy that strangles everything in red tape. These societies aren't even capitalist; they are leftovers of a precapitalist colonial system that fosters corruption and inefficiency.

De Soto gave some examples from Peru. It took 289 days to register a small business with the government. A group of minibus drivers needed twenty-six months to get a license. To homestead state land in order to build a small house took three and a half years and cost more than most Peruvians could possibly pay. And Peru wondered why its economy didn't grow faster.

While the official economy chokes on regulations, the **informal economy**—making up from a third to a half of Latin American economies—thrives. Here people simply ignore laws and regulations and work for themselves, producing according to supply and demand. Instead of trying to stamp out the black market, de Soto suggests, countries should encourage it to spread. If you think about it a minute, a black market is just a free market trying to wiggle out from under economic controls.

More recently in *The Mystery of Capital,* de Soto discovered another bar to economic growth: Inability to get loans. The trick to capital growth, he finds, is being able to use your property as collateral for loans. In much of the Third World, squatters do not own the land they build their houses on, so they cannot use their homes to secure loans with which to start and expand businesses. The solution: Give them clear title to their land. De Soto has the gift of looking at things most mainstream economists ignore.

Classic Thought

SOCIALISM WHEN YOU'RE YOUNG

Latin Americans like to repeat this old wisdom: "If you're not a Communist when you're twenty, you have no heart. If you're still a Communist when you're forty, you have no head." They mean that young people are supposed to be idealistic, critical of the present unfair society, and eager to help the poor. After they've been out in the world and learned how hard it is to change things and how great dreams turn sour, people abandon socialist visions. Aging wises you up.

World climbs out of poverty, and First World consumers gain by the cheap products from the Third World. Many Europeans and Americans worry about losing factory jobs, but most of them upgrade their skills and move into higher-paying jobs. And it is much better to have a rich trading partner than a poor one. (For more on this, see Chapter 18.) In terms of percent of world GDP, countries like China and India are just rebounding to where they used to be before the twentieth century. We should not hinder them.

Key Terms

crony capitalism (p. 181)

culture (p. 170)

demonstration effect (p. 182)

emerging economies (p. 169)

fertility rate (p. 177)

GDP (p. 169)

Global South (p. 169)

informal economy (p. 182)

market economics (p. 180)

migration (p. 177)

modernization theory (p. 170)

neocolonialism (p. 170)

political asylum (p. 178)

Protestant ethic (p. 174)

remittance (p. 177)

Third World (p. 169)

transparency (p. 181)

Key Web Sites

Population Reference Bureau
http://www.prb.org

World Bank
http://www.worldbank.org/research/growth/

World Concern
http://www.worldconcern.org

United Nations Development Programme
http://www.undp.org/

U.S. Agency for International Development
http://www.info.usaid.gov/

International Development Research Centre
http://www.idrc.ca/

Further Reference

Bates, Robert H. *Prosperity and Violence: The Political Economy of Development.* New York: Norton, 2001.

de Soto, Hernando. *The Mystery of Capital: Why Capitalism Triumphs in the West and Fails Everywhere Else.* New York: Basic Books, 2001.

Easterly, William. *The White Man's Burden: Why the West's Efforts to Aid the Rest Have Done so Much Ill and so Little Good.* New York: Penguin, 2006.

Harding, Jeremy. *The Uninvited: Refugees at the Rich Man's Gate.* London: Profile Books, 2000.

Harrison, Lawrence E., and Samuel P. Huntington, eds. *Culture Matters: How Values Shape Human Progress.* New York: Basic Books, 2000.

Landes, David. *The Wealth and Poverty of Nations.* New York: Norton, 1998.

Lomborg, Bjorn. *The Skeptical Environmentalist.* New York: Cambridge University Press, 2001.

Naím, Moisés. *Illicit: How Smugglers, Traffickers, and Copycats Are Hijacking the Global Economy.* New York: Doubleday, 2005.

Pinkney, Robert. *Democracy in the Third World,* 2nd ed. Boulder, CO: Lynne Rienner, 2003.

Rapley, John. *Understanding Development: Theory and Practice in the Third World,* 2nd ed. Boulder, CO: Lynne Rienner, 2002.

Sachs, Jeffrey D. *The End of Poverty: Economic Possibilities for Our Time.* New York: Penguin, 2005.

Seligson, Mitchell A., and John T. Passé-Smith. *Development and Underdevelopment: The Political Economy of Global Inequality,* 3rd ed. Boulder, CO: Lynne Rienner, 2003.

Thirlwall, A. P. *Growth and Development: With Special Reference to Developing Economies,* 8th ed. New York: Palgrave, 2006.

PART III

THE ETERNAL THREATS

Alas, wars are still very much with us. Attempts to wish them away leave us unprepared for reality. Technology has historically brought new threats; now weapons of mass destruction proliferate and could be used.

Chapter 12 examines some of the explanations for the causes of war, whether it is inherent in humans, a product of the states they live in, or a result of a chronically insecure international system.

Chapter 13 considers how states seek security. Typically states counter threats by deterrence, détente diplomacy, disarmament, defense, or some combination of these four "Ds."

Chapter 14 discusses why the Bomb is probably here to stay. Nuclear weapons have too many political functions for governments to scrap them, but nuclear proliferation, especially by extremist regimes, suggests that eventually these weapons could be used.

This brings us to the new threat, terrorism, which came to America in a horrifying way on 9/11. We discuss the causes and consequences of global terrorism in Chapter 15.

CHAPTER 12

WHY WARS?

QUESTIONS TO CONSIDER

1. Are humans naturally warlike?
2. What are "micro" and "macro" approaches to war?
3. What did Clausewitz mean by "escalation"?
4. What is the "levels-of-analysis" problem?
5. Could we experience wars based on conflicting cultures?
6. Does capitalism cause wars or peace?
7. Does balance of power lead to peace? Or does a hierarchy of power?
8. What evidence supports the "previous-war" theory?
9. How may analogies be misused in IR?

Thinkers have been pondering the causes of war for centuries, usually with an eye to preventing future ones. Many theories of war have been advanced; none is wholly satisfactory. It is likely that any given war has a mixture of causes, and no two mixtures will be the same. As always in the social sciences, **causality** is hard to prove.

Did humans always practice war? The evidence is mixed, but many scholars think that organized warfare required the founding of cities and their close offshoot, civilization. (The root of "civilization" is the Latin for city.) These produced states, kings, a warrior class, and a reason for fighting other kingdoms: territory. More territory brought a state more food and more people and thus more power to both resist attack and to expand. States, power, and war were likely born triplets. Primitive hunter-gatherers owned no territory and seem to have fought little with other humans. Herders simply used water and pasture and moved on when they were exhausted. They too had no concept of owning land, and their conflicts were generally just raids to steal from other humans. Paradoxically, war seems to have come with civilization.

■ Micro Theories of War

Micro theories are rooted in biology and psychology. They might attempt to explain war as the result of genetic human aggressiveness. Millions of years of evolution have made people fighters—to obtain food and defend their families and territory. From the beginning, extended families formed hunting bands of males, which created male bonding and carried over into fighting other

causality Proving that one thing causes another. (See page 186.)

micro Close ups of individual and small-group behavior.

humans. Novelist (and radical critic) Norman Mailer proposed that Americans' love of hunting caused the Vietnam War, but few accepted the simplistic connection.

The bonding spirit of the football huddle is the same as that of an infantry squad. Thus one cure for war, some suggest, is getting young males to bash themselves silly on the sports field, and that will slake their thirst for violence. No evidence supports the notion that sports can replace war. In the biological view, humans are essentially animals. As Hobbes put it: "Man is to man a wolf." Actually, that is unfair to wolves, who are usually pretty nice to other wolves.

Are humans genetically programmed to be aggressive? Animals are not uniformly aggressive, but they may become so when attacked. Carnivorous mammals such as lions have to be trained by their mothers to hunt and kill. Man's closest relatives, the primates, are mostly peaceable and sociable. Recent research suggests that young soldiers, far from being natural killing machines, have to be carefully trained and encouraged to kill. The natural instinct in battle is to run away. To prevent this, armies invented sergeants. Police officers who have killed in the line of duty must go to mandatory psychological counseling; without it, they may have breakdowns. Warfare does not come naturally. Aggressive behavior on the football field does not necessarily transfer to killing others.

Most anthropologists reject biological determinism, arguing that primitive peoples exhibit a wide variety of behavior—some are aggressive and some are not—that can be explained only by culture. Primitive hunter-gatherers—such as the San people of Southern Africa, whom DNA reveals to be the ancestors of us all—are quite amiable. When they encounter other bands in their perpetual search for food, they share information about game and water and arrange marriages (to guard against inbreeding) and go on their way. Fighting is rare.

Writers with a psychological orientation explore the personalities of leaders, what made them that way, and how they obtained their hold over the masses and brought them to war. Studies of the 2003 Iraq War are incomplete if they do not include the state of mind of Saddam Hussein and of America after 9/11, a psychological shock that had to be avenged. What made Osama bin Laden and his followers Islamic fundamentalists? Why do some radical Islamists hate us more than they love life?

Biological and psychological theories offer some insights but fall far short of explaining wars. If humans are naturally aggressive, then all nations should be constantly at war. But most nations most of the time are at peace. How is it that countries can fight a long series of wars—the ten Russo-Turkish wars over two hundred years around the Black Sea or the half-century of Arab-Israeli wars—under different leaders who surely must have been psychologically distinct? Biological and psychological approaches may offer insights into some of the *underlying* causes of war but not the immediate causes. For this we turn to state-level and macro theories.

■ State-Level Theories of War

Here we move the camera back from the close up of micro-level analyses of individuals and small groups to the wider view of state-level analysis, which looks at whole countries, their political structure, economy, and culture. Marxists argued for decades that a capitalist economy inclines a country to war. The very rich and their helpers invariably control the government and dictate policy. When the capitalists run out of markets in one country, they expand to others, giving rise to empires and wars as the several capitalist powers bump into each other around the globe. This, wrote Lenin, was the cause of World War I. Evidence shows that competition for colonies played little or no role in the march to war. In 1885, for example, the European powers met in Berlin to amiably carve up Africa.

classic liberalism   Original liberal theory of Adam Smith, that free markets with minimal state intervention are best. (Note: This view has been taken over by U.S. *conservatives*.)

level of analysis   Where you suppose causality resides: in individuals, states, or the international system.

Classic liberals such as Norman Angell argued that it is precisely the free market of capitalism that leads to peace. The economies of most countries become so prosperous and interdependent that they cannot go to war with each other. This view made good sense during most of the nineteenth century, when world trade grew and peace prevailed. World War

Classic Thought

WALTZ'S THREE LEVELS OF ANALYSIS

In 1959 Kenneth Waltz published a minor classic, *Man, the State, and War*, which delineated three **"levels of analysis"** that are often confused but should be separated for the sake of clarity. The first level, "man," supposes individual humans cause wars. Evil, mentally ill, or power-hungry people, especially national leaders, may start wars to enhance their powers or their egos. Some posit humans as biologically aggressive. Studies of Hitler as the cause of World War II are first-level analyses. They are often popular but lack rigor. How could one man start a giant conflagration? Only if he had control of state power. How did he get such power, and why did the state, say, Germany, follow him?

This bumps the level of analysis up to the "state" level in which we look at whole countries, their societies and economies. Here it is bad states that cause wars. The particular form of "bad" varies from thinker to thinker. Marxists see capitalists as the problem. Economic slowdowns force capitalist states into overseas expansion and war with other lands. During the Cold War, many

Americans blamed Communist states for causing wars such as Korea, Vietnam, and Afghanistan. Always insecure, they were driven to expand and wipe out their capitalist rivals. Woodrow Wilson saw non-democratic governments as the problem, such as Kaiser Wilhelm's Germany, a state that was geared up for World War I. Replace these with democracies, and peace will prevail.

Any explanation offered in these first two levels, Waltz argued, is incomplete. We really have to take it up to the third level of analysis, the international system. Most of these systems (which we explored in Chapter 1) are anarchic; that is, there is no overriding force or power to make countries obey. Simply put, there are wars because there is nothing to stop them. Evil personalities or expansionist states may be the specific cause of a war, but this cause becomes operative only in a context of international anarchy. Studies become muddy when they use the insights of one level of analysis to explain something at another level. IR thinkers have been using Waltz's "levels of analysis" ever since, and so shall we.

I then busted both to pieces. Globalization (see Chapter 18) is an updated version of the view that capitalism encourages peace.

For Woodrow Wilson it was undemocratic regimes that cause war, specifically the **reactionary** monarchies of Germany and Austria-Hungary in 1914. Once they were destroyed and replaced with democracies, there would be peace. This is an early version of the "democratic peace" theory (discussed on page 345): Democracies do not go to war with other democracies. It seems to be true, but getting democracy to grow where it has never grown before is no easy matter. Germany's democracy of the 1920s collapsed into Hitler's hands in the 1930s. The fall of the Soviet Union led to the authoritarianism of Putin.

State-level analysis can also include the country's culture. Are some inherently hostile? (See box below.) Did Germans and Japanese have a national superiority complex

reactionary Extremely conservative; favors returning to old ways.

Concepts

ISLAMIC WARS?

Cultural explanations of war and conflict got a boost with Huntington's 1993 article, "Clash of Civilizations" (see pages 15 and 138). Several analysts of turmoil in the Middle East hold that its underlying element is a broad and deep Muslim cultural antipathy toward the West. Even a Danish cartoon could set off Muslim riots in 2006. Nearly all Muslim countries opposed our 2003 war against Iraq. The cultural approach argues that Islam and Christianity were born enemies, for Islam teaches that it is God's successor to Christianity and will triumph worldwide.

In the seventh century, Islam's first conquests and conversions were of the Christian lands of the Byzantine Empire and North Africa. Islam and Europe have been enemies for centuries—the Moorish conquest of Spain (and invasion of France), the Crusades, the Ottoman conquest of the Balkans (and two sieges of Vienna), and European imperialist takeovers of the Middle East.

For several and complex reasons, Muslim civilization stagnated while an energized Europe, starting around 1500, moved ahead. Russia and Austria slowly pushed back the Ottoman Empire in the Balkans in a series of wars. Be careful of calling Muslim-Christian wars religious or cultural. Motivation was usually heavy on the material side—fighters seeking lands and booty and emperors seeking to expand their empires—with religion as

the excuse. A possible exception to this might be the First Crusade (1095–1099), which was motivated by Christianity but did many un-Christian acts along the way.

War seen in this way is a grudge match between cultures in which the loser of one century seeks revenge the next. This theory is much too simple, because at any given time many Muslim lands are at peace and even aligned with Christian countries, while many Muslim lands fight bitterly among themselves. In 1991 some Muslim states supported the U.S.-led war against Iraq. Why? In 1991 we were liberating a Muslim country, Kuwait; in 2003 we weren't. Muslim countries, like all countries, form their policies according to their national interests at that moment. Change the situation and their policies change even if their "culture" stays the same.

If Muslims hate the West, why do so many of them try to immigrate to Western countries? Some analysts point to specific issues—for example, the U.S. occupation of Iraq and support for Israel and for local authoritarian regimes such as Egypt and Saudi Arabia—as the root of Muslim opposition. If Washington changed its policies, they argue, Islamic hatred would subside. One big danger: If we act on the "culture war" theory, we make it come true, possibly creating enemies where we had none.

escalation   Tendency of wars to get bigger and fiercer.

that encouraged them to conquer their respective continents? Are Americans domineering and self-righteous "cowboys" who think they can remake the globe in their image? One problem with "culture" as an explanation is that it can change quickly and thoroughly in response to events. Germans and Japanese are now pacifistic, unwilling to support the United States in Iraq or send troops into any kind of combat. Before World War II people said Jews cannot fight and make poor soldiers. Now some complain that Israelis automatically turn to military solutions and oppose peace. Many top Israeli political leaders have been retired generals.

Classic Thought

THE CRUX OF CLAUSEWITZ

The Prussian philosopher of war, Carl Maria von Clausewitz (1780–1831), has been widely ignored in our time. Although his massive *On War,* essentially his notes edited by his widow, is difficult to read and full of seeming contradictions, we think Clausewitz's lessons are worth learning. At the risk of oversimplifying, we think this is the crux of his thinking:

1. Wars tend to **escalate**. Why? Both sides want to win, so they continually increase their efforts. The war takes on a life of its own, growing bigger and more ferocious. Don't suppose you can always keep wars small and under rational control.

2. A war that escalates to "absolute war" would have no purpose, so put limits on how far a war can escalate.

3. Restrain war by making sure it has clear and doable political goals. Thus Clausewitz's famous dictum, "War is the continuation of policy by other means." If you don't have such goals, don't go to war.

4. Politics is in command. The general must advise civilian authorities, especially on questions of feasibility, but the setting of political goals is not his job. He should make sure there are feasible political goals and that the civilian authorities understand the heavy costs involved.

5. Win the war by breaking the enemy's "center of gravity," without which he cannot resist. That probably means destroying his main forces.

6. Territory is not so important. If, say, you capture the enemy's capital but his main

forces are intact, you are still in trouble. (Example: Napoleon takes Moscow, but the Russian army is unbroken.) Terrain matters only if it helps you crush the enemy. Don't take a hill for the sake of taking a hill.

7. Don't think you can get away cheaply or easily. If you hold back in intensity, you merely give the enemy a better chance.

8. Likewise, don't think you can get away without the horror of the Battle (*die Schlacht,* cognate to slaughter). Don't kid yourself that you might win by clever maneuvers and bluff.

9. Therefore, "First, be very strong." It sounds obvious, but many in the White House, State Department, and Congress think a "show" of force will suffice.

10. A "remarkable trinity" of people, government, and army makes the enterprise work. Weakness in one element may doom the effort. (Example: A U.S. public that no longer supported the war in Vietnam.) Don't go to war unless you're solid in all three.

11. To remember Clausewitz's points, think of all the things we did wrong in the Vietnam War. Clausewitz warned against every one of them. Political goals? Feasibility? Costs? Enemy's center of gravity? Escalation? Trinity?

12. Clausewitz was no bloodthirsty warmonger. His detractors have misread him as such. He is saying that war has a logic of its own that you ignore at your peril.

■ Macro Theories of War

Moving the camera back until it takes in the entire globe leads us to **macro** theories, which are rooted in history and political science. They concentrate on the power of states without looking too much into state structures, economies, and cultures the way state-level analysis does. Instead, it tends to treat states as billiard balls colliding on a pool table. The internal structure of the balls is presumed to be more or less the same; they move according to the external forces that bump them. The first thing states do, as we shall explore in the next chapter, is defend themselves. A state can be democratic, dictatorial, Islamist, or vegetarian, but almost axiomatically, if attacked it will fight back. A possible exception here might be Czechoslovakia in 1938 and 1939, which allowed itself to be taken by Hitler without a shot fired. But Britain and France had abandoned a brother democracy at Munich in 1938, leaving Czechoslovakia alone and dispirited.

macro Big, panoramic view of state interactions.

Another rather basic tendency of states is to expand when and where they can. If they have little power, of course, they do not attempt to expand but hunker down and try to avoid trouble. States with considerable power, however, tend to use it, as in the Germans' medieval push to the east, the Americans' "manifest destiny," the growth of the British empire, and the Soviets' takeover of East Europe. Only countervailing power may stop the drive to expand. One country, fearing the growth of a neighbor, will strengthen its defenses or form alliances to offset the neighbor's power. NATO forming to stop Soviet power is an example. Likewise, the more recent tendency of many countries to oppose U.S. policies (the "counterweight" system discussed in Chapter 1) is a natural reaction against a superpower that tells others what to do. Notice that such foreign-policy moves have little to do with leaders' psychologies or cultural differences, and macro approaches do not much bother with them.

Why should states wish to expand? Why do they not simply build sufficient power to keep away invaders but stay home? That would be the ideal, extolled by realist thinkers such as Hans Morgenthau (see page 27). Unfortunately, states are plagued by insecurity. States survey the world around them and often perceive threats or opportunities. They might behold a weak neighbor who could soon be taken over by a stronger state, bringing a hostile power to their own borders. So they adopt the (flawed) reasoning, "If we don't take it, someone else will." The United States expanded from sea to shining sea on that basis and then took the Philippines and Hawaii. States may practice outright conquest or merely gain hegemony (see page 86). Either way, expansion often leads to collision with other powers that are also expanding. In Manchuria in 1904 an expanding Russia bumped into an expanding Japan and started the Russo-Japanese War. Later, U.S. power collided with Japanese power in Asia and the Pacific.

Much international behavior can be explained by the aphorism *Si vis pacem para bellum* ("If you want peace, prepare for war"), which underlay U.S. policy during the Cold War. Better an arms race than military weakness, which would tempt an aggressive adversary and thus lead to war, was the thinking in Washington. Another aphorism is "The enemy of my enemy is my friend" (discussed on page 148). Within five years of the end of World War II, recent-enemies Germany and Japan were U.S. allies, because all faced expansionist Communist power. Typically, when the threat ends, the alliance fades (see Chapter 16). Political leaders, claim macro theorists, have an almost automatic feel for national interest and power and move to enhance them.

■ Power Asymmetries

Most countries seek sufficient (sometimes excessive) power, but does this lead to war or peace? There are two macro theories about this. The balance-of-power theory (discussed in Chapter 1), the oldest and most commonly held theory, says that peace results when several states, improving their national power and forming alliances, balance one another. Would-be expansionists are blocked. Under **asymmetric** conditions, war is more likely. According to balance-of-power theorists, the great periods of relative peace—between the Peace of Westphalia in 1648 and the wars that grew out of the French Revolution (1792–1814), and again from 1815 to the start of World War I in 1914—have been times when European alliances balanced each other. When the balances broke down, there was war.

asymmetric   Out-of-balance, as when one country has more power than another.

misperceive   To see things wrongly.

Fighting in Bosnia calmed in 1995 only after power there roughly balanced. When the Serbs were ahead, they had no incentive to settle; when they were on the defensive, they had a strong incentive to stop the fighting. Many thinkers consider the Cold War a big and durable balance-of-power system that explains why there was relative peace—at least no World War III—for more than four decades.

Other analysts reject the balance-of-power theory in favor of a hierarchy of power theory (also discussed in Chapter 1). First, because calculations of power are so problematic, it is impossible to know when power balances. Second, the periods of peace, some writers note, occurred when power was asymmetric, when states were ranked hierarchically in terms of power. Then every nation knew where it stood on sort of a ladder of relative power. It is in times of transition, when the power hierarchy is blurred, that countries are

Concepts

MISPERCEPTION

How do we know in IR that what we perceive is accurate? The world "out there" is extremely complex, often defying our attempts to simplify it into intelligible form for our limited brains. News and intelligence reports are often skewed. Thus we often **misperceive** what is happening in other countries, seeing them as either better or worse, more aggressive or more peaceful, weaker or stronger, than they actually are.

Often we learn only later that we have been mistaken. Chamberlain in 1938 at Munich misperceived Hitler as a reasonable man who wished peace. The United States misperceived Iraq in 2003, supposing that it had weapons of mass destruction.

Many specialists on the Soviet Union misperceived it as being a strong, stable system; they were surprised at how fast it collapsed. Anyone, including experts and top decision makers, can be caught up in misperceptions.

Wrote Catholic theologian Thomas Aquinas in the thirteenth century: "That which is perceived, is perceived according to the nature of the perceiver." (You get extra credit if you learn it in the original Latin: *Quisquid recipitur recipitur secundum modum recipiensis.*) You see what you are trained to see. St. Thomas's insight is old but still valid, especially in IR.

tempted to go to war. After a big war with a definitive outcome, there is peace because then relative power is clearly known. If this theory is correct, then trying to achieve an accurate balance of power is the wrong thing to do; it will lead to war because obstreperous states will think they have a good chance to win.

Misperception

Weaving micro and macro approaches together, some thinkers have focused on "image" or "perception" as the key to war. Both psychological and power approaches have something to contribute, but they are incomplete. It's not the real situation (which is hard to know) but what leaders perceive that makes them decide for war or peace. They often misperceive, seeing hostility and development of superior weaponry in another country, which sees itself as acting defensively and as just trying to catch up in weaponry. John F. Kennedy misperceived the Soviets as enjoying a "missile gap" over us; he greatly increased U.S. missile efforts. It turned out that the Soviets were actually behind us, and they perceived the new American effort as a threat that they had to match. The misperceptions led to the 1962 Cuban missile crisis, the closest we came to World War III.

The history of U.S.–China relations (see Chapter 17) was a rollercoaster of exaggerated images alternating between a "little brother" China that we had to save from the Japanese, followed by an aggressive Communist China that had to be stopped by war in Korea and Vietnam, and then a friendly China and ally against Soviet power. Korea in 1950 offers two good examples of misperceptions. As UN forces under General Douglas MacArthur pushed back the North Koreans to their border with China, Beijing became convinced we intended to keep going into China. That was never our intention. Beijing put out clear warnings to keep well back from the Yalu River, but MacArthur could not imagine China would enter the war and was taken by surprise when China did and pushed back UN forces. When the Communists built the Berlin Wall in 1961, we misperceived it as a first Soviet step to take all of Berlin. We thundered back that we would not let them take West Berlin,

Classic Thought

THUCYDIDES ON FEAR

One of the earliest thinkers on the cause of war was a cashiered Athenian general who had time to reflect and write about the Peloponnesian War that devastated ancient Athens. Thucydides's insight still has not been topped: "What made war inevitable was the growth of Athenian power and the fear this caused in Sparta." Athens had become an imperial power, gaining hegemony over many other Greek city-states. Sparta and some other city-states grew worried. Sparta wished no war but observed the growth of Athenian power and how they used it ruthlessly; for example, they massacred the defiant Melians who refused to submit to Athenian domination. "We could be next," thought the Spartans, so they organized an alliance against Athens. The Athenians, in turn, feared this alliance as a threat. In a climate of mutual fear against the other side's presumed—or possibly real—drive for hegemony, war became inevitable.

which the Soviets perceived as a first U.S. step to invading East Berlin. Both sides were extremely nervous. Some scholars argue that the 1961 Berlin crisis was actually more dangerous than the 1962 Cuban missile crisis (see pages 88–90). A Soviet or American tank gunner at Checkpoint Charlie in August 1961 could have started World War III.

In misperception or image theory, the psychological and real worlds bounce against each other in the minds of political leaders. They think they are acting defensively, but their picture of the situation may be distorted. For a long time, it is interesting to note, no country has ever called its actions anything but defensive. The Americans in Vietnam saw themselves as defending the free world; the Russians in Chechnya see themselves as defending their country. In its own eyes, a nation is never aggressive. A country—under the guidance of its leaders, its ideology, and its mass media—may work itself into a state of fear and rationalize aggressive moves as defensive. Under rabidly nationalistic leadership, most Germans and Japanese in World War II saw themselves as defending their countries against hostile powers. Serbian dictator Slobodan Milosevic played the Serbian nationalist card and got most Serbs to believe they were threatened with subjugation or even genocide. Once convinced that they are being attacked, normally peaceful people will commit all manner of atrocities.

North Korea, locked in isolation and hysteria, looked at the U.S. conquest of Iraq and feared it would be next. Bush 43 had indeed called Iraq, Iran, and North Korea the "axis

Concepts

THE PREVIOUS-WAR THEORY

What causes war? The previous war. This answer is simple, but is it too simple? Actually, it is a shorthand way of stating something more complex: Any given war leaves behind regional imbalances, thirsts for revenge, and elite calculations that often lead to another war. Other factors, to be sure, help determine if a new round of war actually takes place. As Geoffrey Blainey points out, a really thorough, crushing defeat tends to keep the losing power in its (lowly) place for a long time. Examples are Paraguay following the War of the Triple Alliance (1865–1870), Bolivia following the Chaco War (1932–1935), and Germany and Japan following World War II. Nothing aggressive—or even much defensive—has been heard from then since.

The Arab-Israel wars are examples of the opposite, as none of their wars was definitive. In reverse historical order: Israel's 1982 Lebanon incursion and subsequent intifadas grew out of the business left unfinished by the 1973 war, which grew out of the imbalances left by the 1967

war, which was a bigger version of the 1956 war, which was an offshoot of the 1948 war, which was a direct result of the Holocaust during World War II, which was just a continuation of World War I, which grew out of the wars of German unification, which were a result of the Napoleonic conquests. . . . Schematically, it looks like this:

WWI » WWII » 1948 » 1956 » 1967 » 1973 » 1982

The previous-war theory leads to a couple of conclusions: (1) There are few really decisive wars that settle things once and for all. A war may settle it for the losing country for a while—Germany and Japan after World War II—but regional power vacuums left by their defeats brought Communist power into East Europe and East Asia, which led to the Cold War, Korea, and Vietnam. (2) Preventing one war may also prevent a string of subsequent wars. You will not know, of course, which wars you have prevented.

of evil." Careful what you say to a domestic audience; it goes around the globe within minutes and is heard as something quite different. What most Americans dismissed as a figure of speech to rally domestic opinion, Pyongyang perceived as a real threat. In turn, Pyongyang tested a nuclear bomb and long-range rockets, thinking that would deter the Americans. Washington, in turn, perceived North Korea as threatening to attack America. Wars have started over mutually reinforcing perceptions such as these.

arms race Competition between rival countries to build more weapons.

Mutual misperceptions of Muslims and Americans have reached dangerous heights. Many Americans perceive Muslims as fanatics and terrorists. Most Muslims perceive Americans as arrogant and imperialistic. We saw ourselves as liberating Iraq, whereas Muslims saw us as conquering Iraq, intending to keep it for its oil. There is no quick fix for these misperceptions. U.S. programs to improve "communications" with the Arab world have little impact. Arabs now get much of their news from independent satellite stations such as Al Jazeera, which are highly critical of U.S. policy. Arabs and Americans utterly misunderstand each other, making U.S. leadership in that part of the world unlikely.

A subset of misperception theory might be termed "the fear factor." Depending on their geographical and political situation, many countries are dominated by fear, sometimes justified, sometimes exaggerated. They believe other nations are out to harm them, possibly to conquer them. Hence they arm and form alliances in ways that often increase tensions and fear. The United States feared Iraq had weapons of mass destruction and was building more when we invaded in 2003. Command pressure reached down into the working levels of U.S. intelligence agencies, requiring them to produce intelligence data confirming the leaders' worst fears. Rumors were accepted as facts.

Misperception and fear can go the other way too. Sometimes states are not sufficiently attentive and fearful. They love peace so much they shrug off threats. British and French leaders between the two world wars were timid. With their staggering losses in World War I in mind, they failed to see the Hitlerian threat until it was almost too late. The United States did no better; it took Pearl Harbor to jolt America into realizing that we could not isolate ourselves. Israel in 1973 convinced itself that Egypt could not and would not strike across the Suez Canal.

■ The Power Dilemma

All except pacifists agree that a state must have sufficient power. The world is dangerous, and going unarmed invites attack. But if you have too much power, you create fear among other states, who themselves arm and ally to offset your power. Some call this the "security dilemma," in which your search for security ends up making you less secure (see Chapter 13). At a minimum, an **arms race** ensues, sometimes ending in war. The trick is to get the "right" amount of power, but this is exceedingly hard to calculate. Because many states are chronically insecure, they "worst-case" (see page 85) and build more military power than they really need. Better too much than too little, they reason. As we discussed in Chapter 5, such was the case with the chronically insecure Soviet Union, which unintentionally created a ring of enemies around itself, thus making it more insecure.

legitimate   In Kissinger's theory, IR system in which states accept each other's right to exist.

revolutionary   In Kissinger's theory, IR system in which major state seeks to overthrow others.

Many students of IR detect the origin of the problem not in power but in the type of international system that prevails at a given time. If it is tense, countries will arm. If it is relaxed, countries will keep few arms. After Napoleon, Europe faced no threats from other European powers until Germany unified in 1871 and turned expansionist late in the nineteenth century. With no threats, Europe generally relaxed and enjoyed three generations of peace and prosperity. Now, after the collapse of the Soviet Union, Europe again faces no threats from another European power. (It still has to contend with terrorism that originates in the Middle East and North Africa.) Europe shrinks its armies and chastises the United States for being trigger-happy. The context creates the psychology.

The trick then, as Henry Kissinger realized at least since his 1954 Harvard doctoral dissertation, is to artfully construct a **"legitimate"** world system—one in which no country threatens another. Metternich did this in Europe after Napoleon was finally packed off to a remote island in the South Atlantic. A **"revolutionary"** world system—one in which types like Napoleon and Stalin threaten everybody—automatically brings tensions and wars that cannot be wished away by good will. In these conditions, states are driven to accumulate power, sometimes too much.

Turning Point

"NO MORE MUNICHS"

One of the most overused and misleading analogies of all time has been "Munich," the 1938 meeting in which Britain and France tried to appease Hitler by giving him a piece of Czechoslovakia. "No more Munichs" was used for decades in Washington and contributed to U.S. intervention in Vietnam. Even Secretary of State Madeleine Albright, the daughter of a Czech diplomat, said in the late 1990s that the formative experience of her life was Munich, and she continued to apply its lessons.

The Munich analogy was seriously misapplied to Vietnam in the 1960s. In the first place, the United States did not even participate in the Munich conference and did not give Hitler anything. London and Paris take the blame for the Munich fiasco. More importantly, communism was a far more complex foe than Hitler, requiring very different strategies. Communist countries were divided among

themselves, and after 1953 there was no Stalin to hold them together. China was not a puppet of the Soviet Union, and Vietnam was not a puppet of China. Third, Hitler was in a hurry; Communist leaders, believing history was on their side (it was not), took their time. Fourth, in 1938 Britain and France were militarily weak and dominated by war-weary leaders, very unlike Washington in the 1960s.

Few now admit to ever having used the Munich analogy, but the one that replaced it may be no more accurate: "No more Vietnams." Vietnam provides faulty analogies for very unlike situations in Colombia, ex-Yugoslavia, Afghanistan, and Iraq. Vietnam was like Vietnam, unique, one of a kind. Be skeptical when someone tells you a current situation is "like" an earlier one. Ask: "Do the elements of analogy outweigh the elements of dysanalogy?"

■ The Danger of Analogies

Human intelligence is finite; it cannot start every thought from scratch. Instead, we rely on **analogy**, even though analogies can be terribly mistaken. Analogies pervade our thinking, structure our organizations, and are drummed into us in school. Indeed, in studying IR you are in effect assembling a "tool kit" of analogies to apply to present situations. Unfortunately, no two cases are identical; the elements of *dysanalogy* often outweigh those of analogy.

analogy   A previous situation that (you think) explains a present one.

The history of IR is replete with analogies, often false ones. The Germans in 1914 marched happily off to war, thinking it would be like their quick victory of 1870–1871 in the Franco-Prussian War. Indeed, almost everyone thought conflict in 1914 would be short, because they made an analogy with the most recent conflict, the Russo-Japanese War of ten years earlier. Only a few predicted that machine guns and barbed wire would force armies to dig trenches, and fighting would stall for years. Generals, it is often said, tend to refight the last war. Dean Rusk in 1951 used an analogy of the Japanese puppet state of Manchukuo (see page 269) to explain to Congress why we had to fight Communist China in Korea: "The Peiping [Beijing] regime may be a colonial Russian government—a Slavic Manchukuo on a larger scale." We now see that China was not a Soviet puppet state. Two analogies now currently offered: (1) 9/11 was like Pearl Harbor, and (2) we have entered into a conflict with radical Islam that is like the Cold War: long, ideological, and requiring numerous U.S. military interventions. Are either good analogies?

Key Terms

analogy (p. 197)

arms race (p. 195)

asymmetric (p. 192)

causality (p. 187)

classic liberalism (p. 188)

escalation (p. 190)

legitimate (p. 196)

level of analysis (p. 188)

macro (p. 191)

micro (p. 187)

misperceive (p. 192)

reactionary (p. 189)

revolutionary (p. 196)

Key Web Sites

Naval Postgraduate School Library
http://web.nps.navy.mil/~library/

College Course
http://www.nd.edu/~dlindley/govt491/govt491maincoursepage.html

Culture of Violence
http://www.abolithwar.org.uk/causes.shtml

1899 Essay on Causes of War
http://www.wku.edu/~smithch/wallace/S567.htm

Further Reference

Blainey, Geoffrey. *The Causes of War,* 3rd ed. New York: Free Press, 1988.

Bobbit, Philip. *The Shield of Achilles: War, Peace, and the Course of History.* New York: Knopf, 2002.

Gabriel, Richard A. *Empires at War: A Chronological Encyclopedia,* 3 vols. Westport, CT: Greenwood, 2005.

Kagan, Donald. *On the Origin of War and the Preservation of Peace.* New York: Doubleday, 1995.

Kahler, Miles. "Rumors of War: The 1914 Analogy." *Foreign Affairs* 58 (Winter 1979/80): 2.

Kissinger, Henry A. *A World Restored: Castlereagh, Metternich and the Problems of Peace, 1812–1822.* Boston, MA: Houghton Mifflin, 1973.

Mandelbaum, Michael. *The Fate of Nations: The Search for Security in the Nineteenth and Twentieth Centuries.* New York: Cambridge University Press, 1989.

Michalak, Stanley. *A Primer in Power Politics.* Wilmington, DE: Scholarly Resources, 2001.

Volgy, Thomas J., and Alison Bailin. *International Politics and State Strength.* Boulder, CO: Lynne Rienner, 2002.

Waltz, Kenneth N. *Man, the State, and War: A Theoretical Analysis,* rev. ed. New York: Columbia University Press, 2001.

CHAPTER 13

NATIONAL SECURITY
HOW STATES PROTECT THEMSELVES

QUESTIONS TO CONSIDER

1. Why is there still so much international insecurity?
2. What is the relationship between technology and security?
3. If deterrence worked during the Cold War, could it work now?
4. Under what circumstances can détente diplomacy work?
5. How did "appeasement" become a dirty word?
6. Is disarmament really impossible?
7. What is the difference between deterrence and defense?
8. Would a national missile defense make America secure?

At first, the end of the Cold War seemed to lessen the **security** problems of the major powers, but in a decade 9/11 brought new threats in unexpected ways and demonstrated that countries, even rich and powerful ones, must always be on guard. For some states, security problems have actually gotten worse after the Cold War bipolar system ended. With bipolarity, the two superpowers tried to supervise much of the globe and keep their client states on a leash. Now the leashes are broken, and many states seek weapons of mass destruction.

There are some good signs. International wars diminished in number after the Cold War, as Moscow's client states no longer got generous loans for massive shipments of Soviet arms. Russia is still happy to supply weapons, but now the buyers have to pay for them. Unfortunately, internal wars did not decline but grew when the Cold War ended. Internal wars peaked in 1993 and still number over a dozen. As we will analyze at the end of this chapter, internal security depends on good government with lots of foreign assistance. Internal wars are usually the fight of a minority that feels discriminated against to break away and become a separate country.

International wars still present the greatest danger to national security. In an age where nuclear, chemical, and biological WMD proliferate and where disputes still smolder over boundaries, ethnic and religious power, resources, refugees, human rights, and

security   What a country does to safeguard its sovereignty. (See page 199.)

defense   Blocking an enemy's attack.

deterrence   Dissuading attack by showing its high costs.

détente diplomacy   Attempts to relax tensions between hostile countries.

disarmament   Elimination of existing weapons.

trade, security will remain high on every state's agenda. Virtually all states try to get international organizations, such as the UN, the African Union (AU), the Association of Southeast Asian Nations (ASEAN), or the Arab League, to resolve disputes that endanger security. If the causes of the conflict are deep and serious, however, international forums are of little help. (See Chapter 21 for the UN role in national security.)

Some states form alliances to help with their security problems. As we shall see in the case of NATO, alliances rise and fall with the security threat (see Chapter 16 for more on this). Alliances pool the resources of members to gain strength either to defend against an attack or, even better, to deter an attack before it happens. Thus of four basic strategies to preserve security, **defense** and **deterrence** rank first and second, followed by **détente diplomacy** and **disarmament**. Alone or in combination, states utilize these four strategies. Technology has always influenced their strategies.

Concepts

SECURITY

Since the first organized states came into contact with other states, security has been the chief interest of rulers and remains the overall prime national interest. Governments go to great lengths to protect their people and preserve their territories and themselves. Security—closely related to sovereignty—means keeping the state whole—its government, its people, and its territory. There are at least six general approaches states adopt:

1. *Live and let live.* This is the best way, provided you live in a peaceful world and have nice neighbors. Small island nations sometimes pursue this strategy.
2. *Bystanding.* If you have aggressive neighbors, you may try to stay neutral, as Sweden and Switzerland did in both World Wars.
3. *Bandwagoning.* A weak country may decide the safest path is to join a stronger country and let it lead. Thailand joined Japan in World War II, and Saudi Arabia

for a while followed the lead of Egypt's Nasser in the 1960s.

4. *Buck-passing.* Similar to bystanding, a buck-passing country passes responsibility to a powerful hegemon, the way most of West Europe let the United States bear the heavy Middle East burdens.
5. *Balance of power.* As we discussed in Chapter 1, nations often decided to pool their power to offset a threat, as NATO did toward the Soviet Union.
6. *Hegemony.* A strong country becomes the dominant power, arranging things as it sees fit and letting weaker powers bystand or buck-pass. The United States may have moved into this strategy after 9/11.

Remember, there are no sure-fire strategies. Much depends on your relative strength and the situation you face. Whatever you do can become obsolete or make things worse. Flexibility is the key.

Technology and Security

A nation's security has always depended on the type and level of military technology existing at a given time. Change the technology and you change what a country must do to secure itself. (See box on the fall of Constantinople below.) In fifteenth-century

revolution in military affairs
Electronic, high-tech warfare.

Europe, cannons meant that large, sovereign kingdoms absorbed small, medieval principalities. Castle walls no longer protected. Gunpowder (among other ingredients) ushered in the modern age and brought fourth two new military branches, artillery and infantry. State power now depended on a large population and a robust economy. Rivalries between monarchs stimulated expansion and conquest abroad, including the New World.

In our own age, nuclear weapons and technologies of communications and transportation have had profound effects, especially on wars. It is called the **revolution in military affairs** (RMA). War is increasingly electronic—precision guided munitions, global positioning systems, communication networks, computers—as was shown in two wars in the Persian Gulf and in Kosovo. Some argue that all the United States has to do is keep about a twenty-year technological lead and it will never be attacked, a dangerous assumption. We learned on 9/11 how our own technology—fuel-laden jetliners—could be used against us.

Technologies also drive the strategies that states use to protect themselves. As with the walled city, the existence of the nation-state depends on its ability to protect itself. When it no longer can, the nation-state could slide into history, like the walled city. Protection in the nuclear age means integrating into the global system and establishing good government at home. The four strategies mentioned earlier—defense, deterrence, détente diplomacy, and disarmament—are based on certain assumptions about the relations between states. Each has evolved along with technology. Each uses a different process to secure the state, and none is totally effective. Some measure of insecurity is normal in international politics.

Turning Point

THE FALL OF CONSTANTINOPLE

The famous battle of Agincourt was fought in 1415 without firearms, but the technology of war quickly changed. In 1453, Sultan Mehmed II of the Ottoman Empire, then twenty-one years old, eradicated the last vestige of the old Byzantine Empire, the city-state of Constantinople, with a new weapon, seventy large cannons or bombards, the heaviest weighing 19 tons and capable of firing a 1500-pound stone ball over a mile. Forty days of bombardment leveled enough towers and penetrated enough of the city's walls to allow a successful land and sea assault. Emperor Constantine XI died defending his city. Walls that had protected the Byzantine capital for centuries fell before a new technology of war. Cannons were the beginning of the end of impregnable fortifications. Quickly, all of Europe's monarchs acquired their own cannons and began building new types of fortifications.

Defense

The assumption behind defense is that there are hostile powers that might like to attack you. Agreements are unlikely to restrain them. Deterrence may not be credible. Diplomacy works only when backed up by arms. If an aggressor thinks he'll win, the chances of war are high.

Defense first serves as a deterrent warning: Attack me and you'll pay for it! If that fails, it preserves the state by blunting the attack and then possibly counterattacking to overthrow the attacker, as the Allies did to Nazi Germany and Imperial Japan in World War II. The difference is that deterrence prevents an attack by threatening high costs from retaliation whereas defense prevents an attack by showing the attacker he won't win. Defense and deterrence overlap.

At least two problems come with every country's defense strategy: (1) Do you have enough? (2) Is it the right kind? Terrible mistakes are made on both counts. For the first question, you must ask, "What is my strategic situation?" West Europe today, facing few security threats (but one of them is terrorism), can spend little on defense and have small armies. To counter terrorism, you need good police work rather than large armies. Indeed, West Europe long depended on the United States to defend it during the Cold War; now Europe has to do even less. At least that's the way most European saw it. (They were recently rudely awakened.) Canada, decades ago, decided that maintaining a large army was infeasible and unnecessary—the United States would always defend it—so it has only a small (but well-trained) army dedicated chiefly to peacekeeping operations, which it does well. Canada's choice is rational for its circumstances and has won Canada much international respect.

If you face a serious threat with no major ally to protect you, however, you'd better arm. France waited until too late to rearm and was overrun by German forces in 1940. Britain was barely saved by the English Channel. Goering talked Hitler into first smashing Britain with air power before a German amphibious invasion, and this gave the British time to rebuild and gain a powerful ally, the United States. The British also had a new technology, radar, which gave them time to scramble their Hurricanes and Spitfires to meet German bombers.

Second, you must constantly ask if your troops and weapons are of the right kind to meet a likely attack. Generals, it has long been said, prepare to fight the last war. In one or two decades, technology can totally change the battlefield. The tank, used at the very end

Concepts

DEFENSE

Defense makes an opponent's offense ineffective. Offense seeks to weaken a state and break its political will; defense strengthens a state and upholds its will. Whatever military technique the offense uses, the defense tries to counter. If a defense is strong and an aggressor knows it beforehand, defense may also serve as a deterrent.

of World War I, attracted little attention in the British and French armies. A British strategist, Basil Liddel Hart, and a French colonel, Charles de Gaulle, wrote on armored warfare, but mostly German officers read them. By 1939 Germany had totally reconfigured its forces around armor and the **Blitzkrieg** doctrine. Its neighbors, who did not, were quickly smashed. Polish cavalry heroically charged German Panzers in 1939 with predictable results.

Blitzkrieg   German for "lightning war"; quick armored attack.

Strategic Defense Initiative Defensive shield in space to protect the United States from rockets; proposed by Reagan but never built.

Maginot Line   French fortifications facing Germany before World War II, easily circumvented.

One key question strategists must ponder: Does current war technology favor the offense or the defense? Mistakes here can be catastrophic. As we discussed in Chapter 12, Europeans before World War I, looking at recent wars (Franco-Prussian and Russo-Japanese), thought war now favored the offense: Attack quickly with bold thrusts, and you'll win a short war. Instead, the machine gun and barbed wire gave the advantage to the defense, and the war bogged down into trenches for four horrible years. The tank then gave the advantage to the offense in World War II; it went around or smashed through fixed fortifications (see box below).

Currently, most suppose technology favors the offense, as U.S. forces demonstrated in two wars against Iraq. But a foe with good electronic countermeasures could turn the tables on a high-tech offensive. Furthermore, guerrilla warfare and terror tactics work around high-tech armies, as we saw in Vietnam and Iraq. Do not count on technology to solve all security problems.

In the early 1980s, some U.S. scientists and strategists argued that a defense against missiles could soon be developed. They did not trust the Soviets to keep their arms control agreements. This was the beginning of the **Strategic Defense Initiative** (SDI) or "Star Wars," announced by President Reagan in 1983. Critics charged that the complex system— which would have to hit missiles and their warheads in flight—either wouldn't work or, if it did work, would destabilize nuclear deterrence by giving one side a shield to hide behind while it launched a first strike.

Turning Point

THE MAGINOT LINE

Germany trounced France in 1871 and nearly won again in World War I. In 1929, France began constructing a series of fixed fortifications running from the Swiss to the Belgian borders. Called the **Maginot Line** after the French War Minister André Maginot, its elaborate concrete bunkers and tunnels made France feel secure with only a small army.

The Maginot Line failed in 1940 and discredited defensive weapons and strategies for over four decades. Germany outflanked the Line by its *Blitzkrieg* attack through Belgium and Luxembourg and penetrated weak points. Moral: Fixed fortifications don't work (a point Israel relearned when Egyptian forces breached its Bar Lev Line on the Suez Canal in 1973).

The end of the Cold War took the urgency out of SDI, but research continued. Iraq's Scud missile attacks in the Gulf War reawakened concern, and in 1993 President Clinton ordered research on theater missile defense (TMD), protecting our forces from short-range missiles. Republicans in Congress pressed for **national missile defense** (NMD) protecting all fifty states, and Clinton ordered NMD research. Proponents of NMD in the Bush 43 administration argue that "axis of evil" states with missiles and nuclear warheads—North Korea and Iran—will soon be a threat.

Critics charge NMD would set off a new arms race. Russia, China, and even U.S. allies in Europe denounce NMD. It broke the 1972 ABM Treaty, which prohibits defense against missiles, a U.S.-inspired idea that mutual vulnerability keeps nuclear deterrence stable. At first Moscow was skeptical of this idea, but Nixon and Kissinger sold them on it. Breaking a treaty is a serious matter, but the Bush 43 administration said the treaty was obsolete and U.S. security concerns had changed. An NMD shield could also protect Japan, North Korea's close target. Russia and China warned of a "spiraling arms race."

NMD has weak points; early tests failed. Critics accuse proponents of missile defense of having a "Maginot Line mentality," building a false sense of security. Simple mylar decoys would confuse and overwhelm NMD. A rogue state or terrorists would more likely deliver a nuclear device by shipping container.

Concepts

DETERRENCE

To deter is to stop someone from doing something that he or she is not yet doing. A can deter B from doing X by issuing this threat: "If you do X, I will do Y." B must perceive the costs of A doing Y as far greater than the benefits that might come from doing X. Deterrence presumes that B is rational. No rational animal will do X if it brings more costs than benefits. It also presumes that A can see B's cost-benefit calculations accurately.

A homey illustration: When Nick Berry's wife drops a sausage on the kitchen floor, she yells "No" as their dog rapidly approaches the sausage. The dog is not deterred; she grabs the sausage and runs. The dog knows that the wife does not strike animals or anything else. The only cost the pet will incur is a vocal "Bad dog!" The sausage is worth far more than that. However, when Nick drops a sausage, his "No!" stops the dog short. She knows that he does strike, a cost not worth the sausage.

Deterrence depends on four Cs:

1. Communication: A must deliver the threat before B decides to act.
2. Capability: A must be perceived as able to carry out its threat and inflict costs.
3. Credibility: B must perceive A as actually doing Y if B does X. A must not be seen as bluffing.
4. Calculation: B must reckon the benefits of X as less than the costs on itself if A does Y.

Deterrence

Deterrence is based on the assumption of rationality and making cost-benefit calculations. An enemy will not attack if the costs outweigh any benefits. Deterrence is the ability to impose costs and let the enemy know it in advance. Such capability comes from the size, skill, and weaponry of one's armed forces. Britain, for example, deterred all serious plans of invasions after 1066—except for the Spanish Armada—by having the naval capability to destroy the invasion fleet. That Spanish Armada disaster in 1588, due partly to storms, added **credibility** to British deterrence.

credibility Being considered trustworthy, believable; the crux of deterrence.

The problem with conventional deterrence is that if a state can defeat an attack, why not attack the threat first and knock it out before it can hurt you? In this way, a deterrent capability can lead to war. It is expensive to maintain the military superiority necessary for deterrence over a long time. Why not use it? The English, for example, both before and after the Armada, raided and plundered the Spanish empire and its ships. Spain couldn't deter them. Conventional deterrence depends on superiority and restraint. Nuclear deterrence depends on the ability to inflict huge damage by unrestrained retaliation.

Concepts

Do WMD Deter or Provoke?

Countries acquire arms to defend or deter, but the 2003 Iraq War demonstrated that weapons of mass destruction may be worse than worthless. Under what circumstances would you really use them? Do they deter an attack or provoke one? If the Iraq War forces countries that have been developing nukes, bugs, and gas to rethink and abandon these programs—as Libya did—it may have served a worthwhile purpose. (Libya, internationally isolated since its agents blew up Pan Am 103 over Lockerbie, Scotland, in 1986, was also under severe economic pressure to mend its ways.)

Saddam clearly had WMD in the 1980s—he used them against Iran—but concluded (rationally) in the 1990s that they were useless against the United States. If Saddam used them he would have confirmed to the world the Bush accusations, and Iraq would suffer horrifying damage in return. Iraq's WMD were a multimillion-dollar program that had to end with disposal of them.

The Iraq experience suggests that less-powerful countries lose security by trying to catch up with a superpower in WMD. Whatever their programs yield in terms of warheads, they are still vastly weaker than the United States and are unlikely to use their bugs and gas and certainly not their nukes. If they use them, they risk destruction. Making a hole in Manhattan is simply not worth losing your entire country.

Any indication of WMD in the hands of aggressors likely provokes other countries more than it deters them. That is precisely what happened with Saddam—even if he didn't have WMD. With every fragmentary (and, it turns out, inaccurate) evidence of Iraqi WMD, Bush became firmer in his resolve to eliminate them. Bush was not afraid; he was enraged. WMD can get you into precisely what you were trying to deter: a hopeless war and overthrow of your regime.

coercive disarmament   Methods of compelling a foe to give up weapons.

Nuclear weapons allow even the weaker side to impose unacceptable costs and thus deter attacks. World War III was prevented, even during the worst crises of the Cold War, because no one could rationally calculate that it would bring benefits greater than costs. Protecting a state by deterrence relies on preventing a potential aggressor from beginning policies that lead to war. The logical conclusion that nuclear war is obsolete is one of the revolutionary effects of nuclear weapons. Nuclear technology produced a major turning point in world history. (See Chapter 14 for more on nuclear proliferation.)

Deterrence really hit its stride in the nuclear age, because no one could make a rational calculation in favor of starting a nuclear war. Nuclear deterrence carries an inherent credibility. Governments will likely use any weapon to prevent their state's extinction. Nuclear weapons also cost less than large numbers of conventional armaments. They induce caution in even the most aggressive leaders. States with nuclear weapons or those under another state's nuclear umbrella through a military alliance seem almost immune from attack.

These advantages of nuclear deterrence, paradoxically, are also its weaknesses. If a government that is attacked by conventional forces engages in nuclear retaliation, does it not invite a nuclear attack on itself? This is called "counterretaliation." A conventional attack puts the onus of making the war nuclear on the victim. Since the use of nuclear weapons risks the survival of the state, would "first use" of the weapon be credible? Some theorists say no. They advocate sufficient conventional forces to repel an attack. But, as we considered, large conventional forces sufficient to defeat an attack can tempt a country to use them. Like the English navy against Spain, large conventional forces could be used to attack without the fear of nuclear retaliation.

In recent years international peacekeeping forces seek to deter both sides in regional conflicts. U.S. peacekeepers, for example, were in ex-Yugoslavia for several years to deter Serbia from forcibly annexing what it regards as its provinces. (For the growth of peacekeeping, see Chapter 21.)

Can deterrence work after the Cold War, this time against "rogue" states? Some say it already did, in both Gulf wars. In 1991 Iraq had chemical warheads but chose to fling only its ineffective high-explosive warheads at Israel and the U.S.-led coalition forces. Saddam knew what would hit Iraq if he went chemical. The Bush 43 administration feared Saddam would use WMD in 2003, but it turns out he didn't have any. Saddam had let us think he did, apparently to deter Iran from attacking Iraq. Instead, Bush became more and more convinced that we had to invade Iraq in order to take out Saddam's (nonexistent) WMD. Actually, we had deterred Iraq into giving up its WMD before the 2003 war, but we did not know we had succeeded. This type of deterrence—called **"coercive disarmament"**—might in some cases make invasion unnecessary.

The RMA has enhanced U.S. deterrence capability. Powerful computers and sensors can find targets and guide munitions. New, high-tech weapons systems give the United States—whose military spending rivals the rest of the world combined—a distinct advantage, as Iraq learned in both Gulf Wars. It is bad news for potential foes; therefore it deters.

Nuclear or conventional deterrence rarely stands alone as the strategy to preserve security. Even during the height of the Cold War, from 1947 to the late 1960s, the two enemy blocs talked to each other. Arms control, trade, and cultural and educational exchange agreements helped calm things. Détente diplomacy eventually created and confirmed the end of the Cold War and could do the same in current regional conflicts.

■ Détente Diplomacy

As we considered in Chapter 6, détente means a lessening of tensions, a backing away from warlike positions held by hostile nations. The word originated in medieval warfare, when the crossbow was a fearsome weapon. Once tensioned, its bolt (small arrow) could penetrate a knight's armor. If it wasn't fired, though, it had to be "detensioned," or cranked down. *Détente* is simply French for detension. It does not mean the two countries have reached an *entente* (see page 91) with each other; it just means war is less likely.

Two things are needed for détente diplomacy. First, the parties to the dispute must have more interests in common than in conflict. This means that a negotiated settlement will bring more benefits than costs compared to other alternatives. Some of the other alternatives are unpleasant: continued deadlock, submission, escalation of threats, and use of force aiming at military victory. The parties may find détente a much better alternative, as did the United States and Soviet Union.

Détente diplomacy depends on the parties' abiding by the terms of their agreements. States generally comply with agreements that are in their interests. Why else would they enter into agreements in the first place? If a state customarily violates its agreements, few do business with it. Serious violations by one side bring serious violations by the other, and soon there is no agreement left. Collapse of the agreement probably means renewed tensions, something the signatories

President Reagan and Secretary Gorbachev meet for the first time in Geneva in 1985. Their good relationship made détente possible. (Terry Arthur/the White House)

may wish to avoid, so most states keep their agreements. When North Korea abandoned its agreement to not build nuclear weapons, its hopeful trade, aid, and technical agreements with South Korea, Japan, and the United States shriveled.

Three tendencies have spurred the use of détente diplomacy. First, nuclear weapons and their rapid delivery systems have made the use of force dangerous as a direct method of

appeasement   A concession to satisfy a hostile country; in disrepute since Hitler.

ending conflict. India and Pakistan, contending over Kashmir, conduct occasional détente diplomacy under the shadow of mutual nuclear deterrence.

Next, world trade is growing and most countries want to participate in it. Lower tensions between states lead to more trade, and détente diplomacy is the way to do this. Starving North Korea needs détente to save its economy.

Finally, spy satellites, electronic eavesdropping, and seismology—euphemistically called "national technical means of verification"—make violations of agreements, especially on arms control, difficult to hide. In 2006, North Korea's first test of a nuclear device could be heard through earth rumbles. Technology provides more confidence that treaties will be observed.

How do diplomatic agreements enhance a state's security? All agreements have a similar format: Party A will do X (or not do Y), and in exchange party B will do S (or not do T). Agreements promote stability and ban aggression. Most spell out procedures for resolving conflicts over the interpretation of the agreement. Agreement can create momentum for more agreements. They become "confidence-building measures." Since diplomacy, compared to threats and military measures, is inexpensive, benefits relative to costs are usually exceedingly high.

Détente diplomacy does not always work. If common interests are actually far less than conflictual interests or one side has no intention of keeping its word, making agreements would be a major mistake. Agreements would not restrain the behavior of the other party. One side is duped into a false sense of security, which leads to unpreparedness for attack or threats. Hitler was clever with fake détente diplomacy (see box below). A country like North Korea, self-isolated and paranoid, is difficult to coax into mutually beneficial compliance.

Faced with a threat, most countries will try détente diplomacy along with defense and deterrence. It does not come with a guarantee, but India and Pakistan, Russia and Japan,

Turning Point

APPEASING HITLER

The prototypical failure of détente diplomacy was that of Britain and France toward Germany in the 1930s. British and French leaders thought that Hitler had plausible claims against the inequities of the Versailles Treaty and to incorporate Germans outside Germany into the Third Reich. They thought that **appeasement** would bring peace and stability to Europe. Hitler said he only wanted justice and national self-determination and hid his real goals—German power and control of Europe.

British Prime Minister Neville Chamberlain and French Premier Edouard Daladier accepted Hitler's takeover of the German-speaking area of Czechoslovakia at the Munich summit in 1938. The next year, Germany took all of Czechoslovakia and then attacked Poland, exposing the enormity of Hitler's deception. Britain and France would have actually enhanced their national security by standing firm in 1938. Ever after, appeasement has been a synonym for weakness in the face of aggression. The real lesson is that détente needs two sides to work.

Turkey and Greece, and other historic rivals have sometimes been open to détente diplomacy (see Chapter 19). If a détente process works really well, it could lead to disarmament to provide states with security.

■ Disarmament

The assumption behind disarmament is that "arms cause wars." Proponents of disarmament agree with anthropologist Margaret Mead that war is learned behavior and can be unlearned. And arms are the centerpiece of war behavior and of the whole military mentality.

True, those who manufacture arms and those who are skilled in their use have a vested interest in war. Both occupations would disappear if war did not exist. The mere presence of arms creates the possibility of war. Arms repress humans' cooperative nature. Arms in the hands of one state are seen as threats by other states, so they too will arm. Arms races lead to war. Nuclear weapons make war too devastating to contemplate. Disarmament, by eradicating the expectation and tools of war, prevents wars. Humanity will turn to peaceful methods, preferably multilateral diplomacy in the United Nations and international law. Military spending can go for human needs. So goes the theory of disarmament.

The weaknesses of this theory are evident. To paraphrase James Madison, who said that if people were angels, governments would not be necessary, we add that neither would wars. Common views of human nature are pessimistic for good reason. There's always a North Korea. Humans tend to resort to fighting. In a situation where both A and B want X and only A is armed, who will get X? If both A and B are disarmed, what about C, D, and E? Since armed states have an advantage over disarmed states, and there are vital interests that can be attained only by armed force, disarmament would only lead to insecurity, especially in the nuclear age.

Accordingly, there have been no general disarmament treaties. More modest attempts at disarmament have been more successful. Treaties focusing on the elimination of weapons in a particular geographical area are common and effective. These include the U.S.-British (for Canada) 1817 Rush-Bagot Treaty that essentially demilitarized the Great Lakes (the first successful disarmament treaty), the 1967 Latin America Nuclear-Free Zone Treaty, and international treaties that ban weapons in space (1967), in Antarctica (1960), and on the ocean floor (1971). Other treaties ban particular weapons, such as the 1972 Biological Weapons Convention, and the 1997 Chemical Weapons Convention. The 1987 Intermediate Nuclear Force (INF) Treaty eliminated the U.S. Pershing II and Soviet SS-20 missiles.

Other attempts to bar weapons have not been as successful. The 1970 Treaty on the Nonproliferation of Nuclear Weapons (NPT) included a pledge by the five "official" nuclear weapon states to negotiate a treaty "on general and complete [nuclear] disarmament," but they found nuclear weapons still useful and did not follow through. Cuba, India, Israel, and Pakistan never signed the NPT. Iraq, Iran, and North Korea signed it but ignored it. No one expects nuclear disarmament soon. As a U.S. Defense Department official said, "Nuclear weapons are still the foundation of a superpower."

General and complete disarmament, alas, is either a utopian dream or a fraud as long as security threats exist. Eliminate all security problems and states will disarm. Until then, don't expect states to go defenseless in this world.

■ A Combination

States use defense, deterrence, détente diplomacy, and disarmament, often in combination. Defense, deterrence, and détente can be combined. Defense and deterrence make the costs of aggression too high, and détente makes the benefits of cooperation enticing. President Nixon emphasized the reinforcing effects of deterrence and détente.

Disarmament conflicts with deterrence and defense. If states are truly disarmed, they can neither deter nor defend. Disarmament also conflicts with détente, as détente presupposes that arms will always exist but that diplomacy can reduce tensions. Disarmament can happen only in a pacific, congenial world.

Mutual deterrence and comprehensive defense may also be incompatible. The opponent's deterrent threat—"If you attack me, then I will retaliate and impose huge costs on you"—becomes incredible if you have an effective defense. This was the problem with SDI and NMD. If they really work, they undermine deterrence stability.

Defense and détente can sometimes be compatible. Well-defended states, feeling secure, can reduce tensions by diplomacy. Détente, however, may undermine one's defenses. Nixon and Carter thought they had a general détente with Moscow and reduced defense spending. When Moscow's expansionist aims became clear with the invasion of Afghanistan in 1979, Carter had to abruptly increase U.S. defense spending. (The Reagan arms buildup actually began under Carter.)

So what is the best way for a state to protect itself? The answer depends on the assumptions you make about the nature of your international rivals. Disarmament works if they are angels. Deterrence and détente work if they are rational and generally keep their agreements. Defense is necessary if they can never be trusted.

Key Terms

appeasement (p. 208)

Blitzkrieg (p. 203)

coercive disarmament (p. 206)

credibility (p. 205)

defense (p. 200)

détente diplomacy (p. 200)

deterrence (p. 200)

disarmament (p. 200)

Maginot Line (p. 203)

national missile defense (p. 204)

revolution in military affairs (p. 201)

security (p. 200)

Strategic Defense Initiative (p. 203)

Key Web Sites

Department of Defense
http://www.defenselink.mil/

Defense Intelligence Agency
http://www.dia.mil/

National Security Agency
http://www.nsa.gov:8080/

NATO
http://www.nato.int/

War, Peace & Security Guide
http://www.cfcsc.dnd.ca/links/

Arms Control and Disarmament Agency
http://www.acda.gov/

Center for Defense Information
http://www.cdi.org

Federation of American Scientists
http://www.fas.org

Further Reference

Bateman, Robert L., ed. *Digital War: A View from the Front Lines.* Novato, CA: Presidio Press, 1999.

Carter, Ashton B., and William J. Perry. *Preventive Defense: A New Security Strategy for America.* Washington, D.C.: Brookings, 1999.

Cimbala, Stephen J. *Shield of Dreams: Missile Defense and Nuclear Strategy.* Westport, CT: Praeger, 2002.

Cirincione, Joseph, ed. *Repairing the Regime: Preventing the Spread of Weapons of Mass Destruction.* New York: Routledge, 2000.

Clark, Gen. Wesley K. *Winning Modern Wars: Iraq, Terrorism, and the American Empire.* New York: PublicAffairs, 2004.

Croft, Stuart. *Strategies of Arms Control: A History and Typology.* Manchester, UK: Manchester University Press, 1996.

Crowley, Roger. *1453: The Holy War for Constantinople and the Clash of Islam and the West.* New York: Hyperion, 2005.

Gray, Colin S. *Strategy for Chaos: Revolutions in Military Affairs and the Evidence of History.* Portland, OR: Frank Cass, 2002.

Macgregor, Douglas A. *Transformation under Fire: Revolutionizing How America Fights.* Westport, CT: Praeger, 2003.

Nichols, Thomas M. *Winning the World: Lessons for America's Future from the Cold War.* Westport, CT: Praeger, 2003.

Owens, William A. *Lifting the Fog of War.* New York: Farrar, Straus, and Giroux, 2000.

Payne, Keith B. *Deterrence in the Second Nuclear Age.* Lexington, KY: University Press of Kentucky, 1996.

Smoke, Richard. *National Security and the Nuclear Dilemma,* 3rd ed. New York: McGraw-Hill, 1992.

CHAPTER 14

NUCLEAR POLITICS

THE BOMB IS HERE TO STAY

QUESTIONS TO CONSIDER

1. Is nuclear nonproliferation dead, or can it be restored?
2. How do nuclear weapons confer international prestige?
3. What was "massive retaliation" and what was it designed to do?
4. Which countries have nuclear weapons? Why do others seek them?
5. Why did Iraq resist international inspections of its weapons of mass destruction?
6. Are political uses of nuclear weapons more important than military uses?
7. Which countries abandoned their nuclear-weapons programs? Why?
8. What is Clausewitz's theory of escalation?

Several countries have acquired nuclear technology that is being turned into bombs. Iran and North Korea, for example, bought tons of nuclear technology from our alleged ally, Pakistan. (Iraq was not one of Pakistan's customers and in fact had no nuclear program when we invaded in 2003.) The attacks of 9/11 turned the nearly forgotten issue of **proliferation** into an urgent concern. According to one expert, forty countries could, if they wished, develop nuclear warheads. How many will? And how will they use them? Could the next terror attack be nuclear?

The atomic bomb was developed as a war weapon but evolved into a political weapon. Its political functions appeal to states under threat (Israel, India, Pakistan, North Korea) and those with major-power ambitions (India and Iran). Nuclear proliferation continues. Attempts by the first five nuclear states (the United States, Russia, Britain, France, and China) to stop other states from acquiring "the ultimate weapon" have largely failed. Sooner or later, there's a good chance that some state with deep hatreds will use a nuclear weapon. Concern now focuses on North Korea, but others could use a nuke first.

■ Weapon of War

Just before World War II, Einstein and others advised President Roosevelt that an atomic bomb could be built. During the war, the Manhattan Project—which consumed 30 percent of U.S. electricity during that time—built three. To check that it would work, the first was detonated at Alamogordo, New Mexico, on July 16, 1945. The second and third destroyed Hiroshima and Nagasaki in early August. Tru-

proliferation More states acquiring nuclear weapons. (See page 212)

man always said that the decision to drop the bomb was easy. Invading the Japanese main islands would be bloody, and we had spent massive sums to develop the bomb. Truman also believed that in war you can use any weapon not specifically outlawed.

The spectacular new weapon heightened U.S. confidence. Along with the Soviet entry into the war against Japan two days after Hiroshima, it produced the Japanese surrender.

But Truman did not order its mass production. He saw no explicit political function for the bomb, such as making the British dismantle their empire or making the Soviets comply with their agreements on East Europe.

Truman in 1946 even proposed internationalizing the bomb: The UN would control all fissile material and limit it to peaceful purposes. This "Baruch plan" also said that a Soviet veto in the Security Council could not block UN nuclear policy. The Soviets rejected the American plan because it meant an end to their nuclear program before they got their own bomb and gave the United States a permanent lead. Even if it gave up all its nuclear weapons, the United States could make them quickly because it knew

The first atomic bomb was tested at the Trinity test site in Alamogordo, New Mexico, on July 16, 1945. (The New York Times)

how. Furthermore, for the Kremlin, weapons were political tools. The Soviets were right, and soon the Americans came to the same conclusion.

The onset of the Cold War created several political functions for nuclear weapons: nuclear deterrence, alliance building, and international prestige. Others would come later, including those that appealed to nuclear powers of the second rank.

◼ Nuclear Deterrence

Once the Cold War began, the Truman administration saw the deterrence effect of the atomic bomb, which until 1949 we alone possessed. The Soviets would not attack West Europe, their obvious first target, because that would bring war with the United States and huge costs. But Truman and Dean Acheson (later secretary of state), thought deterrence would end when the Soviets acquired their own bomb. Then they could deter the U.S. deterrence, and West Europe would become vulnerable.

After the Soviets detonated their own bomb in 1949, the Truman administration authorized development of the hydrogen (thermonuclear) bomb and long-range bombers and groped for a way to restore deterrence. In 1950 the famous National Security Council

Reflections

HIROSHIMA

In Peace Park stand memorials to the bombing of August 6, 1945. A museum shows what residents were doing that morning: working, eating breakfast, going to school. It describes the B-29 bomber, the "Little Boy" bomb, and the attack. A model shows "ground zero." Most of the museum shows the effects of the blast and the radiation on people and objects. There is no politics, just understated horror. Don't miss it if you visit Japan.

—N. O. B.

Hiroshima's Peace Park diorama shows what the city looked like shortly after the 1945 nuclear blast—burnt flesh melted off bones. (Michael G. Roskin)

In Hiroshima's Peace Park this municipal building, which partially withstood the world's first nuclear attack in 1945, was reinforced to stand as a memorial to war's ravages. (Michael G. Roskin)

Report 68 (NSC-68) recommended increasing **conventional forces** at home and in West Europe. U.S. divisions under the prestigious General Dwight D. Eisenhower would reassure Europe, which we also pressured to increase their own conventional capabilities. Deterrence, based on conventional forces, would be restored.

conventional forces Non-nuclear military strength.

thermonuclear Powerful release of energy from fusion of hydrogen atoms.

Critics said this was a mistake. Huge conventional forces were expensive and unpopular. Nuclear weapons could still deter a nuclear-armed Soviet Union. Strategic theorist Bernard Brodie made this point in 1946, and John Foster Dulles promoted it. At this point in the history of the bomb, it is necessary to explore its other political functions.

■ Alliance Building

Power in international politics comes from many sources, not just from weapons. More important are alliances (see page 248). States form alliances because individually each is weak; together they are strong. Rome's long-lasting power came from its ability to make allies. Nazi Germany was unable to make and keep allies. The United States remained the premier power in the Cold War because it attracted more allies than the Soviet Union.

Concepts

NUCLEAR AND THERMONUCLEAR WEAPONS

A nuclear weapon, like the ones dropped on Hiroshima and Nagasaki in 1945, operates on the principle of fission, the splitting of uranium atoms. Specifically, tiny quantities of the unstable isotope U-235—which gives off plentiful neutrons—is refined and separated from the more plentiful U-238, to a purity of 90 percent or higher, called "weapons grade" uranium. Refined to 20 percent of U-235, "highly enriched" uranium can be used to generate electricity but not to make bombs. It can, however, be further enriched until it reaches weapons grade, which is what we fear Iran will do. In a bomb, a conventional explosion concentrates the U-235, the free neutrons of which smash into and split more atoms, freeing more neutrons and creating enormous heat and energy.

Instead of uranium, modern nukes are made with plutonium, which comes from reprocessing spent uranium from power plants. Plutonium bombs are cheaper than U-235 bombs. A hydrogen or **thermonuclear** weapon uses the heat of a nuclear explosion to fuse deuterium or heavy hydrogen atoms into helium atoms. As the atoms fuse, they release vast amounts of heat and energy. A uranium or plutonium bomb is the starter motor of a hydrogen bomb. Miniaturization technology has so reduced thermonuclear weapons that three or four could fit on a small desk. Most nuclear weapons of the major powers are thermonuclear.

extended deterrence Covering allies with your nuclear capacity, as in U.S. promises to NATO.

second-strike capability Ability to hit back after a first strike; if credible, promotes deterrence.

Both major powers realized early that nuclear weapons helped them build alliances. The Cold War and its arms race increased the threats to medium and small powers, especially those strategically located in Europe and Asia. The major nuclear powers could offer allies **extended deterrence**, protection under the big power's "nuclear umbrella." In addition to NATO, the United States made security treaties with Japan in 1951,

Concepts

NUCLEAR STRATEGIES

Second-Strike Capability State A has **second-strike capability** if it can absorb a first strike from B and have enough nuclear weapons to retaliate and inflict "unacceptable damage" on B. In the early 1960s Secretary of Defense McNamara estimated that destroying 50 percent of the Soviet economy and 25 percent of its population would be unacceptable to the Soviets. Therefore, the force posture of the United States, after being attacked, had to be able to cause that much damage.

There are four basic ways A can protect its second-strike capability. It can hide it (submarines), harden it (concrete silos), move it (on trucks), or protect it (anti-missiles). The United States still protects its second-strike capabilities by a "triad" of deterrent forces: land-based intercontinental ballistic missiles (ICBMs), submarine-launched ballistic missiles (SLBMs), and air-launched cruise missiles (ALCMs) from long-range bombers. A credible second-strike capability is the crux of deterrence.

First-Strike Capability State A thinks it can attack B first and destroy B's second-strike capability, a "disarming" attack that removes B's deterrent capability. No one can be confident that a nuclear foe can really be "disarmed" in a first strike; he will still have some second-strike capability. A first strike on a nuclear power would simply invite one's own destruction. It is an unlikely strategy.

Countervalue Attack Targeting the economy and population of the foe, "city busting," common in World War II, is a countervalue strategy.

Early Soviet and American strategies emphasized countervalue attacks, but the doctrine faded as too horrible to use.

Counterforce Attack Targeting a foe's troops, bases, and especially missile sites is called a "counterforce" strategy. With more and more-accurate missiles, the superpowers decided to protect their now more vulnerable second-strike capabilities and societies by shifting to counterforce doctrines. It is also more "humane," killing fewer people and cutting the risk of a "nuclear winter." The catch is that counterforce targeting is more likely to be used, precisely because it entails less chance of losing one's own cities to retaliation.

Extended Deterrence A nuclear superpower protects its allies by treating an attack on them as an attack on itself and retaliating on those who attacked them. West Europe was under the U.S. nuclear umbrella during the Cold War, and Japan and South Korea, facing an unpredictable North Korea, remain under it today.

Minimum Deterrence Having even a few nukes for a credible second-strike capability is called "minimum or finite deterrence." This strategy presumes that arms control agreements would stabilize deterrence. Recent Russian and U.S. strategic arms reduction talks and unilateral cuts have moved both states toward a minimum deterrence posture. China and India claim they seek only minimum deterrence.

Australia and New Zealand (ANZUS) in 1951, and Southeast Asian states (SEATO) in 1954. Nukes gave both superpowers **access** into the foreign policy processes of their allies.

access   One country's ability to get listened to by another.

Washington's offer of extended deterrence to its allies was credible for most of the Cold War but started to erode when President Kennedy introduced "flexible response" into NATO strategy. This said NATO will first make a conventional (non-nuclear) response to a Soviet attack and go nuclear later only if absolutely necessary. Kennedy offered it as a way to avoid nuclear war, but it raised doubts in the mind of French President Charles de Gaulle whether the United States would really come to Europe's defense with its nuclear weapons. For de Gaulle, flexible response was a way for the Americans to chicken out. It weakened the credibility of NATO's nuclear deterrence, so he stepped up France's own nuclear program.

■ International Prestige

Nuclear weapons also enhance prestige. In facing a prestigious state, governments are cautious, accommodating, and respectful. Prestige then increases foreign policy accomplishments, producing even more prestige. Security and economic well-being are the most important national interests, but prestige is not far behind. Every major power jealously seeks prestige. De Gaulle practiced the "politics of prestige" to restore France to the front rank. A word from a prestigious state carries a lot of weight. States automatically gain respect when they explode their first nuclear warheads, a major reason countries develop them.

On the home front, a policy of prestige can be relatively low-cost and keep leaders and regimes in power. Average Soviets enjoyed the prestige of the Soviet empire and the accomplishments of Soviet science, such as *Sputnik*. They could look beyond their shabby economy and say, "We are equal to the Americans and even ahead in some things." The collapse of the Soviet system left them psychologically impoverished and bitter. The Putin regime is doing what it can to restore Russian prestige.

Concepts

ACCESS

Alliances give nuclear powers access to the political systems of their allies. A has "access" to B if A can influence the formation of B's policies and affect its foreign-policy decisions. Access is a foot in the door. The major nuclear power finds it easier to talk to officials of the dependent non-nuclear country. Access leads to the *responsiveness* of B to A's suggestions and requests. By the same token, a country that develops its own nuclear bomb, such as France and China, can ignore its former protector, the United States and Soviet Union, respectively. For some countries, this is a powerful motive to acquire nuclear weapons.

■ Deterrence Reconsidered

Let us take another look at deterrence, discussed in the previous chapter, and its transformation. In 1952, John Foster Dulles expounded "A Policy of Boldness." The Soviets would not consider attacking, Dulles believed, if the United States "was willing and able to respond vigorously at places and with means of our own choosing." It did not matter that the Soviets also had nuclear weapons. The United States would inflict horrible devastation on the Soviet Union if it attacked the West. Dulles played down what the United States would suffer. If the Soviets were convinced that the United States had such a capability and doctrine, they would be deterred.

Eisenhower named Dulles secretary of state and accepted Dulles's nuclear strategy of "massive retaliation." Ike ordered a rapid increase in the production of nuclear weapons and bombers and stepped up the development of missiles to make massive retaliation credible. Ike also shelved the huge conventional-force buildup recommended by NSC-68 and approved a nuclear-deterrence strategy. Large conventional forces were unnecessary and too expensive. Keeping them small would actually enhance deterrence, because we'd have no choice but to go nuclear, and the Soviets would know that. American troops in Europe would be only a "trip wire"; an attack on them would set off U.S. nuclear retaliation. Europe would be safe at relatively low cost. It's hard to prove why something did *not* happen, but the Soviets did not invade West Europe, and the 1950s were relatively peaceful. Deterrence, although scary, worked.

■ Nuclear Proliferation

Other states soon noticed the political benefits that come with nuclear weapons, and they began to proliferate. Britain independently developed nuclear weapons and exploded its first bomb in 1952. Britain's forces alone were too small to deter the Soviets, but London

Concepts

PRESTIGE

Prestige is the reputation for being successful. A has prestige if B believes A usually gets what it wants. Prestige develops as states obtain their foreign policy goals over time. The immense British Empire brought it vast prestige in the nineteenth century. The explosion of the first atomic weapon added to U.S. prestige, while the launching of the first earth satellite, *Sputnik,* in 1957 dramatically enhanced Soviet prestige. States that habitually fail in their foreign policies, such as the Ottoman Empire long before its collapse during World War I—the "sick man of Europe," it was called—see their prestige vanish.

saw political benefits from nukes. The prestige of having nuclear weapons kept Britain a world power. Being a member of the nuclear club gave Britain access to any negotiations by the superpowers on nuclear arms and to U.S. nuclear policy decisions. France under Charles de Gaulle and China under Mao Zedong came to exactly the same conclusions as Britain. Both leaders sought to break away from their dependence on their respective superpower patrons, to be their own masters.

De Gaulle, as we noted, saw President Kennedy's "flexible response" as weakening deterrence and increasing the chances of war. Accordingly, de Gaulle needed his own nukes so he could make a war nuclear without asking Washington. In 1960 France exploded its first nuclear bomb and then created the *force de frappe* (strike force). De Gaulle argued that his independent nuclear capability strengthened deterrence and pulled France out of NATO's integrated command in 1966. Presidents Kennedy and Johnson opposed de Gaulle's independent nuclear course, which they saw as dividing and weakening the West. They also saw it as eroding their roles as "leaders of the free world."

Chinese motives parallel those of France. Mao had major disagreements with the Soviets over nuclear strategy and other foreign policies. In the late 1950s, China wanted the Soviets to exploit their space triumphs by getting tougher with "U.S. imperialism." China also wanted to accelerate its own nuclear program. The Soviets refused both demands. China's policies were far too risky and radical, reasoned Moscow. Angry polemics increased between the two Communist lands, and in 1960 the Soviets withdrew their aid funds and personnel, taking their blueprints with them.

In 1964 China exploded its first bomb and joined the nuclear club. Nuclear weapons, along with the world's largest standing army, deterred any U.S. or Soviet attack and gave China the status and prestige to attract Communist states and parties to its side of its split with Moscow. Nuclear weapons provided considerable political benefits to China. Khrushchev and Brezhnev opposed Mao's independent nuclear course. They saw it as dividing and weakening the international Communist movement and eroding their roles as leaders of that movement. The Soviets sought to depose Mao and even considered a conventional attack on China's nuclear facilities in 1969. When the Soviets probed President Nixon for the U.S. reaction to such an attack, Nixon replied that it would drive the Chinese into alliance with a very receptive United States. The Soviets abandoned the military option.

Concepts

ARMS CONTROL

Disarmament, discussed in Chapter 13, aims at having countries get rid of their weapons, a generally unrealistic goal. Arms control is less ambitious but more realistic. It aims at limiting arms—their type, numbers, testing, deployment, concealment, and transfer. Arms-control treaties aim to slow down arms races and often are part of détente diplomacy.

■ Arms Control

In sum, there are good reasons why countries want nuclear arms. Faced with nuclear proliferation in the 1960s, Washington and Moscow had a common interest in stopping it, to preserve their deterrent capability, alliance leadership, and prestige. A **non-proliferation treaty** and other **arms control** agreements do four good things:

1. They decrease threats and increase cooperation. Uncontrolled arms races can lead to a surprise attack and prevent cooperation. Agreements that control or slow the arms race can lead to other agreements. The Antarctic Treaty of 1960, the Outer Space Treaty of 1967, and the Seabed Arms Control Treaty of 1971 kept those places demilitarized. The Strategic Arms Limitation Talks (SALT I) of 1972 froze the number of Soviet and U.S. strategic missiles until Bush 43 abandoned it in favor of a national missile defense. SALT II of 1979 sought to cut to 2,250 the nuclear-weapon launchers of each side. The Intermediate Nuclear Force (INF) Treaty of 1987 eliminated all Soviet SS-20 and U.S. Pershing II intermediate missiles. With tensions lower, cooperation increased.

> **non-proliferation treaty (NPT)**
> 1968 agreement that nuclear powers will not transfer nuclear-weapons technology and non-nuclear powers will not acquire it.
>
> **arms control**   Limiting weapons systems, a lesser goal than disarmament.

2. They enhance deterrence. If offensive weapons are limited, then neither side has enough for a first strike and both preserve their second-strike capabilities, the crux of deterrence. SALT I and II precluded Soviet and U.S. first-strike capabilities, and deterrence got more stable.

3. Reduced costs: In total, nuclear weapons cost the United States an estimated $1 trillion. After the 1979 Soviet invasion of Afghanistan, Washington put arms control agreements on hold and increased defense spending. This strategy bled the Soviet economy.

Turning Point

THE NUCLEAR NON-PROLIFERATION TREATY

In the mid-1960s, Washington and Moscow feared that many more states would join the nuclear club. According to one U.S. estimate, in twenty years, "peaceful" nuclear reactors would produce enough plutonium to make twenty bombs daily, greatly increasing the risk of nuclear war.

In 1967 both superpowers submitted identical texts of a draft NPT treaty to the UN. Opened for signatures in 1968, it prohibited the transfer of nuclear material for weapons use, obliged signatories to follow International Atomic Energy Agency (IAEA) safeguards in their peaceful nuclear programs, and committed states without nuclear weapons not to develop them and those with nuclear weapons to make further progress in nuclear arms control negotiations. IAEA inspections are the crux of NPT.

NPT was signed by 170 nations, but not by India, Pakistan, Israel, and Cuba. The five big nuclear powers committed themselves to eliminate their nukes and to not test them after 1996. Testing is important; without tests you cannot know for sure if they work. Stopping testing worldwide would mean no new members to the nuclear club. Most countries signed a Comprehensive Test Ban Treaty in 1996, but the U.S. Senate rejected it, saying it couldn't be verified and would block further U.S. nuclear weapon development.

Moscow could not intervene abroad or sustain domestic consumption. Gorbachev's détente policies—withdrawal from Afghanistan, abandonment of the Brezhnev Doctrine
in East Europe, and reforms at home—led to both Soviet and U.S. defense cuts. The
Soviet military burden—some 25 per-
cent of its GDP—was a major factor in
its collapse. The Strategic Arms Reduction Talks (START I and START II)
brought down the number of nuclear
warheads to 3,500 for the United
States and 3,000 for Russia.

4. They stabilize the distribution of
power. Early Soviet-U.S. arms control
agreements were designed to keep the
superpowers in control. In particular,
the 1968 NPT (see box on page 220)
sought to keep the world bipolar and,
it was thought, more stable. Nuclear
proliferation brings unpredictable
shifts of power and the increased danger that an unstable leader will use a
nuke. No other country wants Iran or
North Korea to acquire nuclear
weapons.

5. They try to keep nuclear weapons and
materials out of the hands of terrorist
groups. Before 9/11 this seemed to be
an unreal issue but now is very real.
Pakistan now has the world's first and
so far only Islamic bomb. Powerful Islamist forces inside Pakistan support al
Qaeda in a jihad against the West. Pakistan has sold or traded nuclear technology with Iran, Libya, and North
Korea. The more countries with
nukes, the sooner terrorists will get
them. Careful International Atomic

*President Bush and Russian President Vladimir Putin exchange copies
of the 2002 treaty they just signed, which calls for reduction in their
countries' nuclear warheads.* (Stephen Crawley/The New York Times)

Energy Agency (IAEA) control of all fissile materials (highly enriched uranium and plutonium) could stop this, but Iran and North Korea block IAEA inspections.

■ The Nuclear Proliferators

Conspicuous among those not signing the NPT were Cuba, South Africa, Israel, India,
Pakistan, Brazil, and Argentina. In 1998, India and then Pakistan tested bombs to the
cheers of domestic crowds. With them, it's not just prestige; they were born enemies and
have fought three wars. Their next, probably starting over Kashmir, could be nuclear.
President Clinton visited both countries in 2000 and called the Indian subcontinent "the

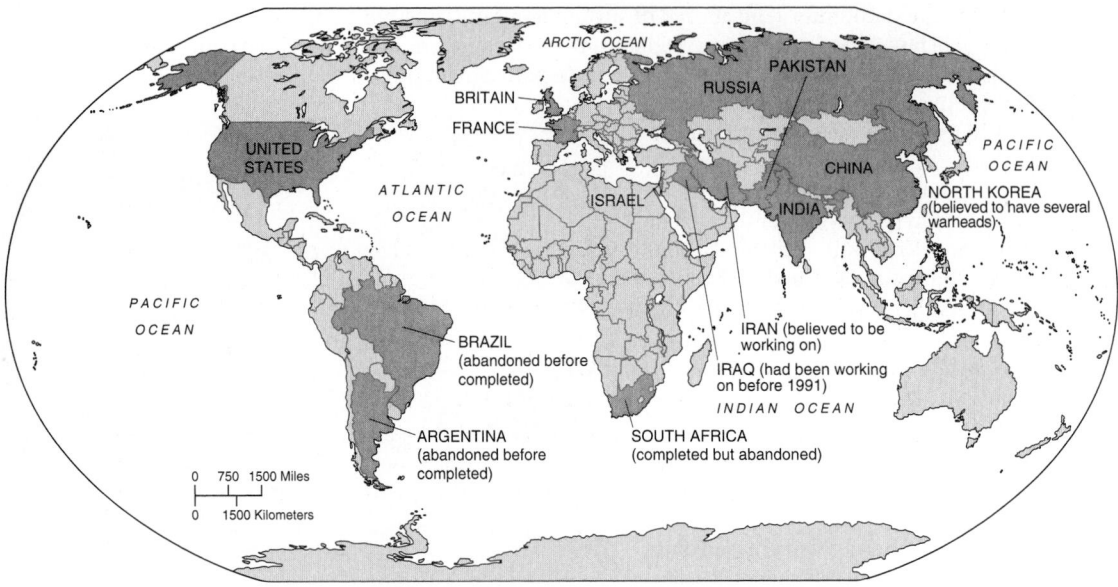

Countries with Nuclear Weapons

most dangerous place on earth." He urged both governments to give up nuclear weapons. They demurred. Israel's nuclear program, officially denied, also gives it prestige and the capability to deter an attack.

Argentina and Brazil were in a prestige race to become South America's first nuclear power. In 1991, civilian regimes in both countries recognized that their nuclear programs were expensive and served no purpose, and they ended them. South Africa secretly began a nuclear-weapons program in 1974, facilitated by abundant local uranium and Israeli scientists, and tested devices on an island in the South Indian Ocean and in deep abandoned mineshafts. But the end of the Soviet threat and withdrawal of Cuban troops from Angola removed any South African use for nukes. And the white South African government did not wish to pass on nukes to its black successor regime, so South Africa became the first and only state to give up nuclear weapons. By 1991 they dismantled their six nuclear devices and destroyed related technology. South Africa then signed the NPT.

Signing the NPT has not kept some states from building nukes. North Korea exploded a nuclear device in 2006, and Iran is not far behind. After the 1991 Gulf war, an IAEA team in Iraq was astonished at how far along its nuclear program was. Iraq might have had a warhead in another year or two. As part of the 1991 cease-fire, Iraq was supposed to lose its ability to develop any WMD but played so deceptively with UN inspectors that the Bush 43 administration believed Iraq had or was working on WMD. If Saddam had cooperated with UN inspectors, he would still be in power today.

There is also a great temptation to sell nuclear technology. The United States, Russia, Germany, France, Argentina, China, and others have sold "dual-use" technology and fissile material. Peaceful reactors can slowly produce weapons-grade material. Russia sold nuclear reactors to Iran that complied with NPT provisions, but IAEA inspectors in 2003 found traces of weapons-grade materials at the Iranian reactors.

The 1991 Gulf War and disintegration of the Soviet Union in 1991 showed the real dangers of proliferation. China was the last big holdout in limiting and putting conditions on nuclear sales. In the 1990s, China sold nuclear material and technology to Algeria, Argentina, Brazil, India, Iran, Iraq, North Korea, Pakistan, South Africa, and Syria. China now says that buyers must submit to IAEA inspection and pledge not to transfer anything to another country.

Small amounts of nuclear material, mostly from Russia, are smuggled out to the world market. German and Czech police have seized many kilograms of uranium. A "nonproliferation center" tries to track such trade worldwide. The U.S. Nunn-Lugar program pays Russia to reduce its stockpile of nuclear weapons and employ its nuclear scientists in non-military occupations. Another ominous trend is the proliferation of missiles. Some thirty-five states now have long-range missiles. North Korea is developing both nukes and long-range missiles and could one day use them.

■ What Would Happen if Nukes Were Used?

1. The political functions of nukes would end. Deterrence would have failed. Alliances would shatter because a non-nuclear ally in a nuclear war would make the most risk-free target for the enemy. Small allies would bail out. Many nonaligned states would

Classic Thought

CLAUSEWITZ ON ESCALATION

Carl von Clausewitz (1780–1831), a Prussian general with no battlefield victories to his credit, was the first to use "escalation" in its modern military sense. In his *On War* (German: *Vom Kriege*), he saw escalation as a tendency built into the nature of war: "As one side dictates the law to the other, there arises a sort of reciprocal action, which logically must lead to an extreme." He called this *eine Steigerung bis zum Aüssersten,* an escalation to the extreme. The war tries to become absolute or total. The Napoleonic wars, in which Clausewitz fought

(against the French), approximated absolute war.

Far from being a lover of such horror, Clausewitz repeatedly cautioned against letting war escalate to an extreme. That would serve no purpose; it would be destruction for its own sake. Civilian authorities, "the Cabinet," must block this tendency by making sure the war serves limited, political objectives. Is escalation automatic or controllable? Clausewitz never came up with an answer, but his book is a warning that escalation can easily spin out of control.

decapitation   The removal of a country's leadership and ability to direct its war effort.

invasion insurance   Ability to deter invasion by possessing even a few nuclear weapons.

treat the combatants as pariahs and not give them access to their markets or their halls of government. There would be no prestige from massive civilian devastation.

2. Disarming attacks would become more likely. Why wait until the other guy is ready? A bit of this already happened with Israel's bombing of Iraq's Osirak reactor in 1981. The raid spurred Iraq's nuclear program, which set the stage for two Gulf wars. Bush 41 and 43 cited the removal of Iraq's nuclear capabilities as one of the prime reasons for invasions. This motive would become standard once nukes are used.

3. Economies would collapse. A nuclear war involving Israel, for example, would target Gulf oil facilities, producing a sudden 40 percent shortfall in world oil supplies. The world has never experienced anything like that. It could be worse than the Great Depression.

4. The war would escalate, becoming wider and fiercer. One conflicts triggers others. A world war is actually several smaller wars strung together. Suddenly seeing new opportunities, other countries join in. Without World War II well underway, Japan would not have seized Southeast Asia from a weakened Britain and France or struck Pearl Harbor. Whoever wins becomes a security threat to other states. If India and Pakistan went to war over Kashmir, China could back its Pakistani friend and Russia its Indian friend.

5. Nuclear **decapitation** would early knock out a country's political leadership and C4I (command, control, communications, computers, and intelligence). Liddel Hart called it "the shot in the brain." Control of people, defenses, and territory would weaken. Anarchy could break out.

6. Nuclear winter could produce a climatic disaster. Some scientists say detonating many nukes would kick millions of tons of soot into the upper atmosphere, darkening and cooling the earth and cutting photosynthesis, the basis of the food chain. Other scientists dispute the nuclear-winter model, but in geologic time at least three such disasters wiped out most life on earth.

7. The war would be hard to end. With a few nukes in reserve for **invasion insurance**, the horrible costs already absorbed, the burning national hatreds, and the breakdown of international law and organizations, the war could go on for years, even decades. After decapitation, who could negotiate the war's end?

Concepts

INVASION INSURANCE

States believe that with even a few nukes they will not be invaded. Invasions require the massing of forces, and they become a prime target for nukes. This does not necessarily work, however. Egypt and Syria were not deterred from attacking Israel in 1973, even though they knew Israel had nuclear weapons, which, in fact, Israel contemplated using.

Likewise the possibility that Iraq had nuclear weapons did not deter the 2003 U.S. invasion; indeed, it provoked an invasion that aimed at knocking out Iraq's nuclear program before it actually produced bombs. North Korea supposes it gets invasion insurance by building nukes, but it may be provoking a regional arms race or even a preemptive U.S. strike. Under the threat of North Korean nukes, Japan is reconsidering its nuclear phobia. Ironically, nuclear weapons may make their possessors less secure.

◼ Nuclear Doom?

Do nuclear weapons automatically mean catastrophe? Early in the nuclear age British Lord Bertrand Russell, a pacifist, predicted humankind would soon be either annihilated or forced to live under a world dictatorship. About the same time, Albert Einstein said: "Nuclear weapons have changed everything except our way of thinking, and thus we drift toward unparalleled catastrophe." But our thinking has changed. There is a widespread recognition that nuclear war would be far more dangerous than any conventional war and should be avoided. Slowly, the world gropes to restrain war.

And there are hopeful signs. There is concerted opposition to any state, even the United States, first using nuclear weapons. Nuclear weapons have made deterrence a strong strategy, one that may have made unnecessary the 2003 invasion of Iraq. The prospect of nuclear retaliation so far has inhibited anyone from pressing the button. Rationally, major nuclear war is now an obsolete strategy, a realization that will forever alter the conduct of international politics.

The United States has no intention of giving up nuclear deterrence. To be sure, the U.S. nuclear budget is way down, from 24 percent of defense spending in the 1960s to less than 3 percent now. U.S. forces no longer deploy nuclear weapons abroad. Only submarines and land silos have nuclear-tipped missiles. Many tactical nuclear weapons have

Concepts

AN ISLAMIC BOMB

Pakistan's testing of a nuclear device in 1998 was the world's first "Islamic bomb." Iran could have the second one in a few years. Are both of them sufficiently stable and rational to refrain from using a nuke? Many had doubts. If they did not use nukes themselves, could they quietly transfer them to Islamist terrorists for strikes against Israel, the United States, or India? Such an attack would be difficult to deter because it would not come from a clearly identifiable country. Whom would we nuke in retaliation?

In 2004 the story came out that Pakistan had been selling nuclear-bomb technology to Iran, North Korean and Libya (but not Iraq) for years. (Libya abandoned its nuclear program and opened it to inspection.) Muhammad ElBaradei, head of the IAEA, called the revelation "the tip of an iceberg" of a "global black market" and feared nuclear proliferation was accelerating.

Pakistan's military dictator, General Pervez Musharraf, who seized power in a 1999 coup, could be overthrown by radical Islamists, including people who aid al Qaeda. Osama bin Laden is likely hiding among sympathetic tribes in Pakistan's untamed northwest, along the Afghan border, where government writ does not run. Pakistan's small nuclear arsenal (of perhaps fifty warheads) could fall into the hands of fanatics who urge Pakistanis to riot against Danish cartoons.

Iran, swearing it is developing nuclear technology for the peaceful generation of electricity, barred IAEA inspectors and restarted its uranium enrichment program. No one trusts Iran. Its president, Mahmoud Ahmadinejad, elected in 2005, at times seemed irrational, as when urging Israel be "wiped off the map." Israel could be tempted to bomb Iran's nuclear facilities, as it did to Iraq's in 1981. Asked how far he would go to prevent an Iranian bomb, Israel's top air force general, whose parents were from Iran, replied, "2,000 kilometers." Israel does not kid about these things; it preempts.

been destroyed. Most nuclear missiles have been "de-alerted" (by removing their warheads) or "de-targeted" (by not inputting any target coordinates).

Nevertheless, the Pentagon gives three reasons to maintain nuclear deterrence: (1) Threats to U.S. and allied security can arise "suddenly and unpredictably." We must be able to counter them. (2) Nuclear weapons remain a "hedge" against a Russian "reversal of reforms" and renewed hostility. (3) Rogue states with WMD and missiles must face nuclear retaliation to "give them pause."

Deterrence worked during the long Cold War. It really was, in Churchill's words, the "sturdy child" of the balance of terror. Granted, it could have broken down during the 1961 Berlin Wall and 1962 Cuban missile crises. You don't want to test it too many times like that. But even in times of great stress, nuclear annihilation wonderfully concentrates the mind.

Critics rejoin that mutual deterrence might have worked between the United States and Soviet Union, but they were governed by rational people. Proliferation will eventually put the bomb into the hands of irrational leaders, people so consumed by nationalistic, ideological, or religious hatred that nothing deters them. Your generation will find out if this is the case. A nuclear war in the Middle East, South Asia, or Korean peninsula is quite possible. The paradox of the post–Cold War age is that now nuclear war—albeit not between the superpowers—is more likely than ever.

Key Terms

access (p. 217)

arms control (p. 220)

conventional forces (p. 215)

decapitation (p. 224)

extended deterrence (p. 216)

invasion insurance (p. 224)

non-proliferation treaty (p. 220)

proliferation (p. 213)

second-strike capability (p. 216)

thermonuclear (p. 215)

Key Web Sites

Nuclear Weapon Systems Sustainment Programs
http://www.defenselink.mil/pubs/dswa/

The High Energy Weapons Archive: A Guide to Nuclear Weapons
http://www.fas.org/nuke/hew/index.html

Center for Defense Information
http://www.cdi.org

Federation of American Scientists
http://www.fas.org

Arms Control Agreements
http://www.fas.org/nuke/control/index.html

U.S. Strategic Command
http://www.stratcom.af.mil/

Further Reference

Beckman, Peter R., Paul W. Crumlish, Michael N. Dobkowski, and Steven P. Lee. *The Nuclear Predicament: Nuclear Weapons in the Twenty-First Century.* Upper Saddle River, NJ: Prentice Hall, 1999.

Cimbala, Stephen J. *The Dead Volcano: The Background and Effects of Nuclear War Complacency.* Westport, CT: Praeger, 2002.

Feldman, Shai. *Nuclear Weapons and Arms Control in the Middle East.* Cambridge, MA: The MIT Press, 1997.

Freedman, Lawrence. *The Evolution of Nuclear Strategy,* 3rd ed. New York: Palgrave, 2003.

Gray, Colin S. *The Second Nuclear Age.* Boulder, CO: Lynne Rienner, 1999.

Reiss, Mitchell. *Bridled Ambition: Why Countries Constrain Their Nuclear Capabilities.* Washington, D.C.: Woodrow Wilson Center Press, 1995.

Sagan, Scott D., and Kenneth Waltz. *The Spread of Nuclear Weapons: A Debate.* New York: W. W. Norton, 1995.

CHAPTER 15

THE CHALLENGE OF TERRORISM

QUESTIONS TO CONSIDER

1. Is terrorism a new threat?
2. How do you tell a terrorist from a freedom-fighter?
3. How does terrorism relate to guerrilla warfare?
4. Can a few terrorists really overthrow a government?
5. Why is terrorism so connected to the Middle East?
6. What is "blowback" and how has it hurt us?
7. What is *salafiyya* and how does it underpin Islamic terrorism?
8. Is the United States equipped to stop terrorism?

With 9/11 America entered into what the Pentagon called the Global War on Terror (GWOT), a long struggle against chiefly Islamic **terrorism**. The new struggle resembles the Cold War: long, ideological, and focused on gaining and keeping allies.

Keeping allies is not easy. All Muslim countries have sizeable Islamist movements that hate America. In some cases—Pakistan and Saudi Arabia, two countries that had sponsored Muslim fundamentalism—these movements could overthrow wobbly governments with devastating consequences. The fall of Saudi Arabia to Islamists could disrupt world oil supplies and plunge the globe into a new Great Depression (see page 279). If Pakistan falls, it would deliver nuclear weapons into the hands of the same people who destroyed New York's World Trade Center. Our European allies counsel caution, and most parted company with us over the invasion of Iraq in 2003. We lost allies.

Global War on Terror is probably not a good name. Few suggest doing anything about Irish, Basque, or Sri Lankan terrorists. There is no general wave of terrorism washing over the world or the United States. There are specific Islamic extremist groups with specific goals: Get the United States out of the Middle East, destroy Israel, and take over Muslim lands. Islamists had already taken over Iran, Sudan, and Afghanistan. Terrorists are not

crazy. Osama bin Laden and his organization, al Qaeda (The
Base, so called after the computer database he kept of volun-
teer Muslim fighters against the Soviets in Afghanistan), is
composed of militantly committed people, not psychopaths.

The struggle is really over the future of Muslim countries,
whether they become modern and moderate or traditional and fanatic. A better name
might be the "war over Islamic modernization." If we fail, if these lands fall to hate and
violence, we may speak of the "Islamic Wars," and they could be quite nasty.

Success in this war will come if Muslim lands reject bin Laden and his message of hatred and grant him and his kind no succor. Stability will come when Muslim countries
discover how to combine Islam with modernity, a difficult but feasible project. Failure in
this war will come if Muslim governments fall into the hands of religious extremists,
which is exactly their goal. Then Huntington's "clash of civilizations" (page 138) could
become a ghastly "war of civilizations." We must tread carefully; pushing too hard on a
shaky Muslim government could topple it.

The search for terrorists in the United States is interesting for what it did *not* turn up.
It found no network of Arab or Muslim Americans involved in the plot: all the perpe-
trators were inserted from abroad. (Scattered Muslim Americans were found to have Al
Qaeda or Kashmiri connections, but none were involved in 9/11.) None of the 9/11 ter-
rorists were Iraqis, Palestinians, or Afghans. Fifteen of the nineteen hijackers were from
Saudi Arabia; their leader was Egyptian. Years ago al Qaeda merged with Egyptian Islamic
Jihad, the group that assassinated Egyptian President Anwar Sadat in 1981.

Earlier profiles of terrorists—taken from Israeli composites—no longer fit. The 9/11
suicide hijackers were not poor and ignorant; many were middle class and educated.
Most had lived or studied in West Europe and seemed to have turned into Muslim fanatics there rather than in their homelands. To get a handle on this complex, confusing situation, let us divide our consideration into past, present, and future of the Middle
East.

■ The Middle East Past

The great problem the Middle East inherited from the past is that its great Islamic civilization was brought low, partly by outside forces, and never recovered. Remembering
the glories of bygone centuries, some Muslims look at the West as the force that brought
them down and keeps them down—an exaggeration but not without some foundation.
Next to oil, resentment could be the Middle East's greatest export product.

Historically, Islamic civilization was for centuries far advanced over Christian Europe in science, philosophy, medicine, sanitation, architecture, steel making, and just
about anything you can name. It was through translations from the Arabic that Europe
got reacquainted with classic Greek thought, especially Aristotle, which helped trigger the
Renaissance and Europe's modernization. Go back a millennium and you would find
Muslims wondering if it wasn't Christianity that kept Europe backward.

Concepts

WHAT IS TERRORISM?

Terrorism is a strategy to weaken a hated political authority. It is a security threat but almost the opposite of the nuclear one: little pinpricks instead of a huge bang. Related to guerrilla or irregular warfare, it is not a new thing. The Irish Republican Army and Internal Macedonian Revolutionary Organization (IMRO) go back more than a century. The ethnic, nationalistic, religious, and ideological grudges of the twentieth century expanded terrorist activity. Wherever there are groups with grudges, terrorism can start. They are especially prevalent in the "zones of chaos" of the Third World.

We look at terrorists as irrational, but they see themselves as rational. Their steps are calm, calculated, and purposeful. They pursue their political goals by gruesome means because the occupier or enemy is much stronger. A "fair fight" means certain defeat, so they must use indirect means. Basques, Kurds, Palestinians, and Tamils desire their own state. Spain, Turkey, Israel, and Sri Lanka, respectively, do not want them to have their own state and repress their movements. Thus were born, respectively, ETA, PKK, PLO, and Tamil Tigers (who do the most suicide bombings). There is always a reason behind every terrorist movement. In these cases, it's national liberation.

Terrorism is a group activity, the work of committed believers in political causes. Lone gunmen operating outside of groups, such as John Hinkley, are simply deranged. Osama Bin Laden's al Qaeda, our chief concern these days, bombed U.S. embassies in Africa and warships and then flew jetliners into the World Trade Center and Pentagon. Al Qaeda recruits Muslims everywhere for political and religious goals (in Islam, the two are intertwined), to make all Muslim countries fundamentalist and remove U.S. influence from the Middle East. Terrorism today is inseparable from the stresses and strains of politics in the Middle East.

All states officially treat terrorism as criminal but some—such as Syria, Pakistan, Iran, Libya, and North Korea—quietly engage in "state-sponsored terrorism." The 1981 attempt to kill Pope John Paul II clearly traces back to the Kremlin. The Turkish gunman, an escaped convict, got his money, forged passport, and gun from Bulgarian security police, who were supervised by the Soviet KGB. Terrorists need bases, money, arms, and bombs, and these are sometimes supplied by the intelligence services of one country that wants to undermine another. Pakistan, although steadfastly denying it, tries to undermine Indian rule in Kashmir by secretly training and arming Muslim infiltrators.

Does terrorism work? Rarely and seldom alone. It is usually one pressure among several. **Hezbollah** bombings helped persuade both the United States (in 1983) and Israel (in 2000) to leave Lebanon, but those attacks on soldiers were more guerrilla warfare than terrorism. Often terrorism is entry-level warfare, a first stage of an effort to start mass resistance and guerrilla warfare. Like other types of warfare, terrorism aims to change the enemy's mind. A touch of violence on top of massive political and economic pressures persuaded whites to abandon their monopoly on power in Rhodesia in 1980 and South Africa in the early 1990s.

In most cases, however, especially after terrorists have killed innocent civilians, it just stiffens the resolve of the target country. Suicide bombings of Israelis persuaded many to support a giant fence to wall out Palestinians. The horrors of 9/11 convinced most Americans to use our armed forces to overthrow any regime that might sponsor terrorism against us. Bombings in Europe unified and stiffened the resolve of Europeans. And terrorists want this anger, arguing that the more the target strikes back, the more recruits they will gain, Lenin's revolutionary idea of "the worse, the better."

But Islamic civilization stalled and European civilization modernized. By the sixteenth century, when European merchant ships arrived in the Persian Gulf, the West was ahead of Islam. Why did Islam get stuck? First, there are some specific historical causes. The Mongols in the thirteenth century conquered the great Abbassid **caliphate**, massacred the inhabitants of its capital, Baghdad, and destroyed the region's irrigation systems, something the Arab empire never recovered from. (The Mongols' impact on Russia was also devastating.) Possibly because of the Mongol devastation, Islam turned to mysticism. Even earlier, Islamic teaching had turned

Hezbollah ("Party of God") Militant Shi'a movement. (See page 230.)

caliphate Muslim dynasty ruled by *caliphs*, successors to the Prophet Muhammad.

Baath Arab Social Renaissance party, secular and nationalist party that ruled Iraq under Saddam and still governs Syria.

Concepts

TERRORISTS OR FREEDOM-FIGHTERS?

It has long been said that "one man's terrorist is another man's freedom-fighter." If you like the cause, you call him a freedom-fighter. If you dislike the cause, you call him a terrorist. The British regarded American patriots and even General Washington as terrorists. Many old Canadian families are descended from Tories who fled the terror inflicted on them by the American Revolution. Northern Irish Protestants call Gerry Adams a terrorist; Northern Irish Catholics do not. Two prime ministers of Israel, Menachem Begin and Yitzhak Shamir, were hunted as terrorists by the British in Palestine before 1948. Unbelievable as it sounds, millions of Muslims cheered 9/11 as a blow for freedom.

Some thinkers argue that the targets of terrorism separate it from a struggle for freedom. Targeting innocent civilians is terrorism; battling armed soldiers is an act of war. Thus blowing up a bus of Israeli civilians is terrorism, but, argue Israelis, Israeli retaliation on the Hamas perpetrators is legitimate self-defense. By this standard, al Qaeda's bombing of U.S. embassies in East Africa (which killed mostly local pedestrians) was terror, but its bombing of the U.S.S. *Cole* was legitimate war-fighting.

Such distinctions are irrelevant, and terrorists themselves usually shrug them off, arguing that they, the underdog, must hit the enemy wherever he is vulnerable, and that includes civilians. Chechen terrorists repeatedly hit Russian civilian targets. They once held hostage a crowded theater in Moscow. (Russian police used gas to put the entire theater to sleep, and many died.) The French Resistance in World War II learned to assassinate French officials who collaborated with the Germans rather than take on the German army. The Germans called them terrorists. The Vietcong terrorized many South Vietnamese villages in the name of their liberation struggle. We called them terrorists but roasted whole villages with napalm in the name of a struggle against communism. Remnants of Saddam's **Baath** now kill both U.S. soldiers and Iraq civilian We call them terrorists. For terrorists, no one who cooperates with the occupier is innocent.

The methods of terrorism help define it. Car and truck bombs, hijacking ships and jetliners, and suicide bombers are the hallmarks of terrorism. Terrorists argue that the enemy is unfairly equipped with artillery, planes, and tanks, so they must use whatever weapons they can devise. With terrorism, expect the unexpected.

---

blowback Negative unforeseen consequences of your policy.

from independent and flexible interpretations of the Koran to a single, set interpretation. Instead of an open, flexible, and tolerant faith that was fascinated by learning and science, Islam turned sullen and rigid. When the Portuguese first rounded the southern tip of Africa in 1488, they opened up direct trade routes between Europe and Asia, bypassing the Islamic middlemen. Trade through the Middle East declined sharply and with it the region's economy.

But more important was the domination of European (chiefly British) imperialists starting in the nineteenth century. Between the two world wars, Britain ruled a broad swath from Palestine (now Israel and Jordan) across Iraq and had major influence all around the Persian Gulf. Pakistan (then part of India) was a British colony. Imperialism created the same resentment we see in China, the resentment of a proud civilization brought low by upstart foreigners: "You push in here with your guns, your railroads, and your commerce and act superior to us. Well, culturally and morally we are superior to you, and eventually we'll kick you out and restore our civilization." With this type of thinking comes hatred of anything Western and therefore opposition to modernity, because that means admitting the West is superior.

How to Modernize the Middle East

Many see the present-day Middle East as a failure of modernization. Most Middle Eastern countries have halfway modernized, but this has created big economic, political, and social problems. The trick will be to get them to modernize all the way, but many

Concepts

BLOWBACK

One consistent pattern emerges from helping Islamist groups: They turn on their sponsors. Some, including the CIA, call this "**blowback**," an action that blows back into your face. Israel, for example, thought it was clever in the 1980s to help Hamas, a charitable religious group that was supposed to offset Yassir Arafat's secular Palestine Liberation Organization. But Hamas always aimed to destroy Israel and has pushed aside the PLO.

Saudi Arabia, founded in 1932 on the puritanical Wahhabi brand of Islam, used its oil wealth to spread this rigid creed through religious schools in poor Muslim lands, including Pakistan. Now its Wahhabi adherents want to overthrow the House of Saud for drifting away from true Islam and depending on the Americans. Pakistan's Inter-Service Intelligence agency (ISI) actually invented the Taliban by organizing Afghan refugee students in fundamentalist Koranic academies in Pakistan. Pakistan, with U.S. approval, promoted a Taliban government in Afghanistan to overcome the chaos and lawlessness on its northern border. Pakistan also used Islamist fighters in its own terror campaign to wrest Kashmir from India. Now the Taliban vows a *jihad* against both the Pakistani and U.S. governments. Careful whom you help in this part of the world.

resist on cultural and religious grounds. To oversimplify the situation in the Middle East today:

$$\text{Islam} + \text{imperialism} + \text{unemployment} + \text{corruption} = \text{Islamism.}$$

A subset of the equation is:

$$\text{fast population growth} + \text{slow economic growth} = \text{unemployment}$$

A Muslim country that has tasted Western imperialism and has many unemployed and a corrupt government will likely develop a Muslim fundamentalist movement. Unemployment is predictable from the extremely high birthrate with an economy that is growing only slowly, the case in every Muslim country. As we considered on page 177, Middle Eastern women bear three times as many children as European women. Until recently, Saudi women bore an average of eight children, making the Saudi population triple in a generation. Unemployed or underemployed young men are often drawn to extremist politics. The ruling elites' vast corruption demonstrates to the poor masses that the government is illegitimate. Islamist preaching takes full advantage of this.

The long-term solution is to get these countries modern, with growing economies, jobs, education, small families, and clean government. Vast obstacles stand in the way.

Concepts

IS ISLAM THE CAUSE?

University of Chicago political scientist Robert Pape vigorously dissents from the widely held view that the prime cause of terrorism in the modern world is Islam. Pape studied suicide bombers worldwide and found little religious influence. The originators and chief perpetrators of suicide bombings are Tamil Tigers, Marxist separatists who demand a Tamil state in the north and east of Sri Lanka (formerly Ceylon).

The commonality in suicide bombings in many lands, found Pape, was the desire to rid a country of foreign occupiers, be they Soviets, Americans, Israelis, or Sinhalese (the main nationality of Sri Lanka). The solution, says Pape, is for the foreigners to get out. If Pape is correct, the only solution to the Israel-Arab struggle is for Israelis to leave Israel, which is precisely Hamas's goal. Israel is unlikely to cooperate.

Pape's theory explains suicide bombings of Americans in Iraq but not of the Shi'a majority in Iraq, who are not foreign occupiers. Many more Iraqi Shi'a are now killed than Americans. Pape's theory does not explain the 2004 Bali bombings unless you define Australian tourists as an occupying force. This theory does not explain the 2005 suicide bombings of three hotels in Amman, Jordan, which killed Arabs. It is also a stretch to say the young Muslims in Madrid (2004) and London (2005) who blew up trains did it to protest the Iraq situation. If Muslims anywhere can commit these acts in support of distant co-religionists, we return to religious and cultural explanations of terrorism. In the Spain and England cases, it is the inability of Europe to assimilate Muslims and the resultant alienation of unemployed Muslim youth.

Many economies are "statist" and block the rapid growth that free-market economies can deliver. The oil-producing countries around the Persian Gulf have become dependent on petroleum revenues, many of which they have squandered without provision for long-term growth. Besides, the oil industry requires few workers. Some Arab intellectuals call their oil a "curse" for the way it has skewed economic development and made rulers rich and unaccountable. The biggest problems, however, are the cultural and religious attitudes that reject modern life. These factors combine to turn the Middle East into a "zone of chaos" (see page 13) that threatens the entire world.

Most Middle East experts deny there is anything inherent in Islamic doctrine that keeps Muslim societies from modernizing. Looking at cases, though, one finds no Islamic countries that have fully modernized. Under Atatürk, Turkey made great strides between the two World Wars, but Islamic militants always tried and still try to roll back his reforms. The shah tried to modernize Iran but was overthrown by Islamists (pages 137–138). Sadat tried to modernize Egypt but was assassinated by Islamists. Oil brought some Muslim countries outside revenues; they are rich but not modern.

Does Islam cause backwardness? By itself, probably not. Islamic cultural antipathy toward the West—emphasized by Samuel Huntington (see page 138)—and to modernity in general slows and often reverses progress in Muslim lands. But there are currents stirring in Islam that could reorient it to modernity. As is often the case with religious reforms, going back to the original source can produce a reformation. Some Muslim scholars note that there is nothing in the Koran about suppressing women or denying progress. The Koran, to be sure, prohibits loaning money at interest, but Muslims already work around that by taking equity positions—stocks instead of loans. Eventually, we could see societies that are both modern and Muslim. One of the best ways to promote this: Educate women. Ironically, this has gone farthest in Iran, where the fundamentalist regime has educated more women than in other Muslim lands (in separate schools and colleges, of course). These educated Iranian women are now demanding the equality they say is part of the Koran.

In Huntington's terms (see page 166) most Muslim lands are "torn" countries, pulled between Western and Islamic cultures. Many of the educated elite are open to Western values, but most people cling to traditional and even fundamentalist Islamic values. Pakistan's military president, a man who knows and understands the West and modernization, took a big chance in supporting America in overthrowing the Taliban in Afghanistan. Most Pakistanis wanted it the other way around; some vowed to join a *jihad* against the United States. (General Musharraf also hedged his bets by not cracking down on Islamic radicals.) The governments of Pakistan, Algeria, Egypt, Saudi Arabia, and other Muslim lands are sitting atop rumbling volcanoes of Islamic fundamentalism; they could be overthrown.

Two specific and ongoing causes inflame many Muslims: (1) The existence of Israel and U.S. support for it; and (2) the presence of U.S. forces in Muslim lands. They see Israel as a new type of Western crusader state that seized holy land and must be expelled. They are not interested in compromise. Jerusalem is also holy to Muslims. Israel, however, is but a step to the bigger goal. If Israel did not exist, the region would still be a zone of chaos.

This brings us to Osama bin Laden, seventeenth of fifty-two children (by multiple and rotating wives) of a Saudi Arabian construction billionaire. Osama bin Laden organized and helped fund **jihadis** to expel the Soviets from Afghanistan in the 1980s. He never liked and did not work with Americans in this effort and strongly opposed U.S. forces in Saudi Arabia to defend it against Iraq in 1990 and 1991. To them, all of Saudi Arabia (not just the holy cities of Mecca and Medina) is sacred Muslim ground that was defiled by the U.S. troops. He became furious when a small U.S. force stayed after the 1991 war (removed, at Saudi request, in 2003) and denounced the House of Saud for allowing it. Saudi Arabia revoked his citizenship in 1996, but he had earlier cashed out his estimated inheritance of $300 million and hid it in many places. He also continues to get money from relatives, supporters, and Muslim charities in Saudi Arabia. Osama is likely hiding in Pakistan's wild Northwest Frontier Province, where tribal inhabitants praise him. Just killing bin Laden won't be enough, as trusted helpers will replace him.

U.S. Marines board a helicopter in search of Osama bin Laden along the snowy Afghan-Pakistan border in 2004. (Lt. Patrick Keane, USMC)

■ Which Way for U.S. Policy?

Bush 43 repeatedly rationalized the attack on Iraq by saying, "We are fighting them over there so that we won't have to fight them here." Critics have charged that the war in Iraq has made things worse and has also been a distraction from getting al Qaeda, which is still in operation. The U.S. invasion stirred up Islamic hatred worldwide. The insurgents in Iraq were mostly homegrown Sunni chauvinists and Islamists divided into dozens of small and hard-to-catch groups. A few foreign jihadis (mostly young Saudis) entered Iraq but soon fell into conflict with Iraqi Sunni groups. They had totally different aims: The Sunnis sought to restore the power they held under Saddam, and the foreigners wanted a jihad against Americans, Shi'a, and anything secular. A Jordanian fanatic (killed in 2006) set up one group and called it "al Qaeda in Iraq." So al Qaeda did come to Iraq, but only during the U.S. occupation.

jihadi Muslim holy warrior, also called *mujahad* (plural: *mujahadeen*).

The Bush administration wanted a war in Iraq because wars have clear goals and methods. But the situation was trickier. Al Qaeda was no single enemy country but loosely linked cells in many lands, cells that invented themselves as al Qaeda with little help

salafiyya   "The way of the founders," reactionary Islamic puritanism and the basis of current Islamism. Adjective: *salafi.*

shari'a   Islamic law, drawn from the Koran.

umma   The community of all Muslims.

or guidance from Osama bin Laden. Getting al Qaeda was like trying to grab fog.

What then should we do in the face of Middle East terrorism? First, we must remember that Osama bin Laden wants us to overreact, to use our strengths against us, just as his hijackers used our technology against us. The military option is tempting but must be used sparingly, as it tends to provoke Islamism rather than calm it. Few Muslims liked the secular Saddam regime in Iraq, the least Islamic in the Arab world, but most strongly objected to the U.S. invasion of a brother Arab land. Osama despised Saddam Hussein as a hypocrite and idolater but portrayed the U.S. invasion as a crime against all Muslims.

Osama's immediate target is his homeland of Saudi Arabia, whose royal house was based on the puritan Wahhabi faith but now lives quite differently. For decades Saudi officials denied any problems in the Kingdom—they even denied that most of the 9/11 hijackers were Saudis—but now worry that thousands of young salafis are ready to overthrow the regime. Saudi Arabia is indeed the real prize. Not just the United States but the world depends on the flow of oil from the Persian Gulf. Some object that oil is a

Concepts

SALAFIYYA

The religious root of much Islamic terrorism traces back to the thirteenth-century Damascus religious leader Ibn Taymiyya, who devised the doctrine of **salafiyya** to combat the terrible Mongol invasion. Although these Mongols converted to Islam, Ibn Taymiyyah argued that they were fake Muslims, for they replaced **shari'a** with their pagan Mongol laws. Accordingly, they were to be resisted and killed as hypocrites. In the eighteenth century, an Arabian salafi preacher named Ibn Wahhab made a religious alliance with the House of Saud, a combination that took over the peninsula in the 1930s. Saudi Wahhabism and Osama's al Qaeda today are forms of salafiyya.

Salafis condemn anything suspicious or modern as hypocrisy or idolatry. Muslim rulers who seek wealth and power are hypocrites. Setting up Western-type states and governments is a form of idolatry. Islam must not be chopped up into separate nation-states—which are idols—but must be preserved as one giant **umma**, as the Prophet Muhammad intended. Salafiyya is an international pan-Islam movement and a permanent undercurrent in Sunni Islamic thought. (It is not found in the Shi'a branch of Islam, which salafis denounce as pagan and idolatrous.) Salafiyya can turn its followers into fanatics who seek Islamic purity, reject compromise, and are happy to die as "martyrs" to the faith. Salafis long to destroy Israel, America, and insufficiently pure Muslim rulers, which means most of them, including the House of Saud. Al Qaeda, a salafi movement, never supported Saddam's secular regime in Iraq or Palestinian nationalism except as ways to arouse Muslims to join a jihad.

selfish or greedy cause, but if it is seriously disrupted the entire world will suffer. Anything we do with Saudi Arabia can blow back in our faces. Keeping U.S. troops there aroused

radiological Gives off dangerous radiation.

Concepts

TERRORISM PLUS WMD

We earlier discussed weapons of mass destruction—nukes, gas, and bugs. Could terrorists get hold of WMD and use them in spectacular strikes? Some say they already have, that the 9/11 attacks, which killed more than 3,000, were in effect WMD. But what if an organization like al Qaeda gets something far more powerful? America is not safe from nuclear terrorism.

Many experts now fear it's only a matter of time before terrorists buy a nuclear device or fissile material from North Korea, Pakistan, or Russia. When they get a nuke, they'll use it. Worldwide, there are already more than 30,000 nuclear warheads plus fissile material (highly enriched uranium or plutonium) for another 240,000. Much of this material, especially in ex-Soviet lands, is poorly secured and easily stolen and smuggled by gangsters in league with crooked officials. A nuclear device would not have to be an advanced or compact model to blow up a major city.

Would a U.S. deterrence threat (discussed in Chapters 13 and 14) be sufficient to persuade potential suppliers to not give or sell nukes to terrorists? Some suppliers might think the bombs could not be traced back to them. Should the United States announce that, in cases of uncertainty, it would bomb the three most likely countries? And if we're wrong, we'll apologize. Would that be an effective deterrent? North Korea in the past did terrorism with conventional explosives and did not care when they were exposed. The more nuclear-armed nations, the greater the likelihood of one or more warheads falling into the hands of terrorists. Part of the U.S. war against

terrorism, therefore, must include strengthened safeguards against nuclear proliferation, which has not been a U.S. priority until recently.

Not the same as a nuclear blast, a **radiological** weapon or "dirty bomb" would spew out radioactive dust and contaminate a wide area, such as Wall Street. A radiological weapon is simply waste uranium or plutonium (from hospitals, industries, or power plants) packed around a few sticks of dynamite. It would kill few but might take months to decontaminate. What would be the economic effects of shutting down lower Manhattan?

Just after 9/11, letters containing anthrax were mailed out, some to Capitol Hill. Five Americans died from the first instance of bioterrorism, whose origin is still a puzzle. Initial suspicion focused on al Qaeda, possibly supplied with anthrax by Iraq, but no evidence was found after the 2003 war. Anthrax is not that hard to brew and pulverize and could fall into terrorist hands. Smallpox is even easier to produce and disseminate—just infect a few dozen volunteers and put them on planes to the United States with instructions to sneeze in crowded places. No Americans have been immunized against smallpox since the early 1970s, but we could quickly crank up an immunization program.

Gas is the least likely WMD for terrorists, as it requires large quantities and could quickly be traced to the country that supplied it. As we found in the 1991 Gulf War, nukes deter gas. Is a terrorist attack with WMD likely? You may have an answer by the time you read this.

much local opposition. Saudi Arabia did not let us attack from their soil in 2003 and asked us to pull out U.S. forces shortly after the war, which we did. Only Saudis can handle the al Qaeda underground in Saudi Arabia.

Our first line of defense is at home—using methods such as improving border and airport controls—and it has worked. It is now much harder for terrorists to enter and operate in the United States, although they are certain to keep trying. Credit goes to our front line, the newly renamed Immigration and Customs Enforcement (ICE), which watches U.S. borders and airports and is now a part of the new Department of Homeland Security.

Much work remains, especially in communication among agencies and a central clearinghouse for information on possible terrorist activity. ICE, the Coast Guard, FBI, and CIA still do not quickly communicate with each other or with local police. A major problem: By law and by corporate culture, the CIA shares information with no other agency. There is still not a single computer system or data base to link agencies. If all

Concepts

WHAT WILL BE TERROR'S NEXT TARGET?

Terrorism, by its very nature, aims at vulnerable targets, often ones little considered beforehand. With terrorism, expect the unexpected. Few critics praised Tom Clancy as a writer, but many respected his ability to write scenarios such as these:

- Tens of thousands of huge shipping containers arrive in U.S. ports daily, and we check only 5 to 7 percent of them (up from 2 percent). A primitive nuclear device could be set up in one and staffed by a few martyrs, who would complete final assembly and detonate just as the ship docked in any of dozens of U.S. ports.

- The new expressway under Boston is a natural target. A large truck with conventional high explosives or gasoline—to say nothing of a nuclear device—could detonate in the middle of it and make a big hole in downtown Boston.

- A concerted attack on oil refineries with homemade or smuggled mortars and rocket launchers could knock out an appreciable fraction of America's gasoline supplies and double gas prices, as Katrina did in 2005.

- A really clever computer virus could disable most of America's information technology, on which we are now highly dependent.

- A "dirty bomb" of radioactive waste, cheap and easy to make, could contaminate an important area such as Wall Street for weeks, shutting down much of America's finance industry.

- America is not the only target. Starting fires in Saudi Arabia's oilfields could produce a shortfall of several percent in global supply and trigger a worldwide recession. And the Kingdom has many salafi extremists who are familiar with its oil industry.

the fragmentary warnings of 9/11 had been put together on a single desk, we might have been able to stop it. The FBI in Washington ignored field reports that young Arab men were taking suspicious flying lessons in which they told instructors they did not wish to learn to take off or land.

Patient police and intelligence work rather than military invasion is the better way to find terrorists overseas. We need a sort of international SWAT team with language skills. TV dramas show such teams in action, but they are years ahead of reality. The FBI does not operate overseas; the CIA has no law-enforcement powers; and neither is part of the new Department of Homeland Security, which simply shuffled together some existing bureaus of other departments. We are still organizationally unprepared to stop terrorist attacks or deal with their aftermath. The Federal Emergency Management Agency (FEMA), part of Homeland Security, did not inspire confidence in its handling of Hurricane Katrina.

Next, the only way that U.S. law enforcement can operate in other countries is through their police and intelligence agencies, many of which are not completely cooperative or trustworthy. Saudi Arabia and Pakistan, for example, have never come clean about al Qaeda activity on their soil; they are scared of Islamists and are reluctant to crack down on them. We must make allies out of moderate Muslim governments by offering them a choice: It's us or the Islamists. Cooperating with U.S. intelligence is better than cooperating with Islamist terrorism, which brings only violence and poverty.

Domestically, we have much work to do. U.S. computer networks, oil refineries, and nuclear power plants are serious vulnerabilities. U.S. controls are lax; an estimated four million people are in the United States on expired visas. At least two of them were among the 9/11 hijackers, who had no trouble entering and living in the United States with no one asking them what they were up to or how they got their money. The hijackers laughed at how open and easy everything is here. Some of this openness has got to be tightened. A national identification card should be considered. Both civil libertarians and gun owners cry "police state," but you already carry the equivalent: a photo driver's license with bar code plus a social security card. Just combine the two. (Students object, fearing bartenders would ask to see it.) Too complex? Just such a national ID card has been issued to thousands of Mexican workers who daily cross the U.S. border.

Very importantly, this is not the end of the world. There is a tendency toward panicked overreaction and a human need to "do something, anything!"—and this is not always to good effect. After 9/11 some Americans bought gas masks and dubious pills. Law-enforcement agencies rounded up anyone with olive complexions or droopy mustaches. To give in to excessive fear means to give one round to the terrorists, which is exactly what they want. America's enemies have always assumed that we are a weak and decadent society, one with no deep or spiritual values, dedicated only to money and luxuries and unwilling to sacrifice or sustain casualties. They have failed to understand that America is a highly resilient and adaptive society with great internal strengths.

■ Lessons of Terror

1. Security is a permanent problem. Neither the end of the Cold War nor isolationism gives us security. They'll come and get us in our homeland.

2. The Middle East is an inexhaustible source of violence, and we cannot totally withdraw from it or ignore it.

3. Terrorism is rarely an effective strategy. America was enraged but not seriously wounded by 9/11.

4. Huntington's "clash of civilizations" theory looks more plausible (see Chapter 1 and Chapter 9).

5. Rapid population growth is a factor in world politics (see Chapter 11). Countries with high unemployment breed terrorists.

6. Deterrence doesn't work if your enemy is unafraid of dying. Militant salafis wish to die as martyrs.

7. Invading countries in order to combat terrorism can breed even more terrorism.

8. Allies count, both in Europe and the Middle East. The 2003 Iraq War, pursued without regard to the views of allies, made America partially isolated.

9. Terrorist attacks could use weapons of mass destruction. Watching for WMD must be a major objective, but it takes allies.

10. The United States is so free and open it allows terrorists to enter and use our own technology against us. Some calm tightening up is overdue.

Key Terms

Baath (p. 231)

blowback (p. 232)

caliphate (p. 231)

Hezbollah (p. 231)

jihadi (p. 235)

radiological (p. 237)

salafiyya (p. 236)

shari'a (p. 236)

terrorism (p. 229)

umma (p. 236)

Key Web Sites

U.S. Defense Department War on Terror
http://www.defendamerica.mil

Terrorism Research Center
http://www.terrorism.com

Israel Counter-Terrorism Center
http://www.ict.org.il

Central Intelligence Agency
http://www.cia.gov/terrorism

Department of Homeland Security
http://www.ready.gov

United Nations
http://www.un.org/terrorism

State Department Patterns of Terrorism
http://www.state.gov/s/ct/rls/pgtrpt

Further Reference

Art, Robert J., and Louise Richardson, eds. *Democracy and Counterterrorism: Lessons from the Past.* Herndon, VA: U.S. Institute of Peace, 2006.

Benjamin, Daniel, and Steven Simon. *The Next Attack: The Failure of the War on Terror and a Strategy for Getting It Right.* New York: Henry Holt, 2006.

Carr, Caleb. *The Lessons of Terror: A History of Warfare Against Civilians.* New York: Random House, 2004.

Esposito, John L. *Unholy War: Terror in the Name of Islam.* New York: Oxford University Press, 2002.

Gerges, Fawaz A. *The Far Enemy: Why Jihad Went Global.* New York: Cambridge University Press, 2005.

Gurr, Nadine, and Benjamin Cole. *The New Face of Terrorism: Threats from Weapons of Mass Destruction,* rev. ed. New York: Palgrave, 2002.

Hafez, Mohammed M. *Why Muslims Rebel: Repression and Resistance in the Islamic World.* Bounder, CO: Lynne Rienner, 2004.

Hoffman, Bruce. *Inside Terrorism,* rev. ed. New York: Columbia University Press, 2006.

Kepel, Gilles. *The War for Muslim Minds: Islam and the West.* Cambridge, MA: Harvard University Press, 2004.

Lawrence, Bruce, ed. *Messages to the World: The Statements of Osama bin Ladin.* London: Verso, 2005.

Musalam, Adnan A. *From Secularism to Jihad: Sayyid Qutb and the Foundations of Radical Islamism.* Westport, CT: Praeger, 2005.

National Commission on Terrorist Attacks Upon the United States. *The 9/ll Report.* New York: St. Martin's, 2004.

Pape, Robert A. *Dying to Win: The Strategic Logic of Suicide Terrorism.* New York: Random House, 2005.

Roy, Olivier. *Globalized Islam: The Search for a New Ummah.* New York: Columbia University Press, 2004.

Scheuer, Michael. *Through Our Enemies' Eyes.* Dulles, VA: Potomac Books, 2006.

Stern, Jessica. *Terror in the Name of God: Why Religious Militants Kill.* New York: HarperCollins, 2003.

Whittaker, David J. *Terrorism: Understanding the Global Threat,* rev. ed. New York: Longman, 2007.

PART IV

THE ECONOMIC BLOCS

International political economy (IPE) is the interface between governments and the world economy. IPE underlies much of IR and helps determine what kind of IR system exists. Does the world now have a new IPE? Are globalization and the Internet transforming the globe? Or are economic blocs forming—Europe, Asia, and North America, each already producing roughly one-third of the world's economic output—that are less than open? Is the new system likely to be stable? One thing is clear: The IPE does not run itself but requires major-power leadership.

Chapter 16 considers how Europe has gone from U.S. dependency to rival. It explains why the new common currency, the euro, symbolizes the growing power and assertiveness of a united Europe. What will be Europe's relationship with the United States? The EU is going its own way, ignoring Washington's pleas to open its markets and follow America's lead in places like Iraq. NATO, the foundation of Europe's postwar security, has faded in the absence of the Soviet threat. Europe now builds its own rapid-reaction force outside of NATO and has little interest in supporting the United States in the Middle East. The United States and EU have parted company in many areas.

Chapter 17 looks at the amazing changes in Asia since World War II, the entrance of China onto the world stage and the rise of Japan from the ashes of defeat. Along with the other rapidly growing economies on the Pacific Rim, they could form a trading bloc with greater production than either NAFTA or the EU. How did this economic miracle happen and then falter? And, the biggest question of all, will China turn capitalist and democratic or nationalistic and hostile?

Chapter 18 considers globalization theory in relation to the U.S. economy. What are the complaints of anti-globalists, and are they choking off this system? Can world trade expand without U.S. leadership? Is the United States really interested in an open world economy or does it too practice trade protectionism? Is U.S. prosperity vulnerable to world shocks that could tumble the dollar and lead to a new Great Depression?

CHAPTER 16

EUROPE DIVORCES AMERICA

QUESTIONS TO CONSIDER

1. What are the "politics of resentment"?
2. What two tracks do NATO and the European Union represent?
3. What did Yugoslavia show about European unity?
4. What areas does NATO cover? Who is a member?
5. Who were the first six members of the Common Market? Who joined later?
6. What is the EU common currency? Is it working?
7. What is the difference between Slovenia and Slovakia?
8. What political differences have Europe and America developed?
9. What are the dangers of expanding NATO? What new members are to be added?

Europe and America got divorced. With the Cold War long over, many Europeans resent America as the new hegemon that tries to remold the world in its image. The resentments had been building for years but came to a head with European opposition to the 2003 Iraq War, which they saw as an example of President Bush's "unilateralism." Europeans seriously disliked Bush 43, and he returned the favor. Paris calls America the *hyperpuissance* (hyperpower, stronger than superpower) and vows to resist it. U.S. military power is unmatched, but some of its other forms of power are quite limited. Power, remember, is one country's ability to get another to do its bidding, and most of Europe—with France in the lead—rejects U.S. advice, pressure, warnings, and demands. Europe forms a weak and divided "counterweight" to U.S. power (see pages 12–13).

Paris is actually expressing the resentment—shared by many other countries—that is part military, part economic, part cultural, part political, and heavily psychological. Europe fears a U.S. "cowboy mentality" that rejects the UN and international law in favor of military solutions. Europe, after bashing itself bloody in two world wars, has turned strongly anti-war and favors negotiations and treaties. Europe is jealous of America's prosperity and abundance of jobs and in response, says it will not adopt "savage" U.S. capitalism, with its growing wealth gap, but will build humane (and expensive) welfare states. In health, welfare, and education standards, Europeans note, Europe is ahead of America.

soft power Influence through cultural, legal, and moral example.

Culturally, some Europeans—especially elites—resent U.S. movies, TV shows, fashions, and music. They fear American junk is drowning out their classical and creative culture, although ordinary Europeans happily consume American movies and fast food. Almost all Europeans think America's gun laws and capital punishment are primitive. America is religious; Europe is irreligious (exception: Poland) and suspects Bush 43 of pursuing a Christian fundamentalist agenda. So-called **"soft power"** is not a trivial element in IR; it drives long-term shifts of attitude.

Europe tired of depending on the United States for security and always following the U.S. lead. We want to be equal to the Americans, say Europeans, the EU equal to the U.S. We want our own means of defense instead of relying on U.S.-led NATO. Our foreign policy will not obediently follow Washington's. And we want our own currency, information technology, major industries, and anything else that gives us independence from the United States. Well before the Cold War ended, the politics of resentment began pulling Europe and America apart. America sees itself as the senior partner and natural leader, the

Geography

LABELING EUROPE

During the Cold War Europe was divided into an East and a West. There were some neutrals that were neither in NATO nor the Warsaw Pact (Sweden, Finland, Switzerland, Austria, Ireland, and Yugoslavia). Within East Europe, however, there are two historically and culturally distinct regions, Central Europe and the Balkans.

For our purposes, West Europe is made up of countries that touch the Atlantic, plus Switzerland and Italy. Central Europe is from Croatia north—Croatia, Slovenia, Hungary, the Czech Republic, Slovakia, and Poland, plus Austria. (Do not confuse Slovenia and Slovakia. Slovenia is the northwestern part of old Yugoslavia, next to Austria and Italy. Slovakia is the eastern half of old Czechoslovakia, between Poland and Hungary.) Central Europe is basically the old Habsburg or Austro-Hungarian

Empire (which included southern Poland) and is largely Roman Catholic. This area is more advanced than the Balkans and turned quickly to democracy (Croatia and Slovakia were a little slow) and market economies. Most Central European countries joined the EU in 2004, so that now when we say "Europe" we generally mean West plus Central Europe.

The Balkans (named after the Turkish word for mountains), long a part of the Turkish Ottoman Empire, is south of Croatia. It includes Serbia, Bosnia, Macedonia, Albania, Greece, Romania, and Bulgaria. The Balkans, largely Eastern Orthodox in faith, are poorer and less democratic than Central Europe and took longer to join the EU. Note how Yugoslavia's attempt to meld its Central European and Balkan elements into one country ended in bloody breakup.

European Union (EU)
Confederation of most of Europe;
began as Common Market in
1957.

UNPROFOR 1992–1995 UN
Protection Force supposed to
keep peace in Croatia and Bosnia.

indispensable player. Americans see the Europeans as too divided to play a major role. Europeans had gotten used to America looking after their security, so they never spent enough on defense and now spend less because they face few threats. Europe's big project, however, is not security but the **European Union**, which aims to have its own voice in the world.

Europe had been working toward unification and on two tracks, the security track (NATO) and the economic track (the European Union). During the long Cold War, the two tracks ran closely parallel, one reinforcing the other. With the end of the Cold War—which some date to the fall of the Berlin Wall in 1989—the two tracks diverged, as the two pillars of NATO, the United States and West Europe, increasingly sniped at each other. Without a main enemy, the divergent forces latent in the Western alliance pulled it apart. NATO had been held together by fear of Soviet expansion; when that vanished, the life went out of NATO. Now West Europe and the United States have an increasingly conflictual relationship, over trade, ex-Yugoslavia, Iraq, Iran, and many other questions.

A problem buried at the heart of NATO from its founding helped turn it into a paper alliance: its limited scope. The 1949 North Atlantic Treaty provided that an attack on a member country in Europe or North America will be treated as an attack against all. Places such as the Persian Gulf are "out of area," and genocidal war in ex-Yugoslavia was not an attack on a member. Americans kept expecting their NATO allies to follow the U.S. lead worldwide; Europeans kept saying, "That's not part of NATO, and we aren't following you." This first appeared in the Balkans in the early 1990s but got much worse with the Persian Gulf. West Europe said it would take the lead in stopping the horrors in Bosnia but then shrank back. Europeans were unwilling to use force to preserve Europe's security. Frustration grew on both sides of the Atlantic.

■ The Horrors of Ex-Yugoslavia

There were at least two horrors about ex-Yugoslavia. One was its war against civilians; the other was West Europe's inability to stop it. In 1991, the leading European powers told Washington they would handle this problem in their own backyard. With the blue helmets and white vehicles of the UN, most West European lands contributed at least a battalion of "peacekeepers" with very limited mandates: Oversee the latest cease-fire and get food and medicine to civilians. Their orders never included fighting. And that's why **UNPROFOR** proved to be mission impossible. There was no peace to keep; all sides were willing to fight for what they deemed justly theirs. Serbian forces simply arrested and handcuffed West European soldiers who were in the way.

The Bosnia fighting ended in November 1995 after the United States took an active interest. American diplomats arranged for arms to flow in, and "retired" U.S. officers trained Croatian and Bosnian forces. NATO, under U.S. leadership, then enforced a deal made in

Geography

THE RISE AND FALL OF YUGOSLAVIA

Yugoslavia was a rather artificial country that was created and broken by Europe's twentieth-century wars: It was born after World War I, conquered in World War II, and fell apart after the Cold War. The nationalities of ex-Yugoslavia did not hate each other for centuries; for most of history they got along. The main language, Serbo-Croatian, is little different from Belgrade (Serbia) to Zagreb (Croatia). Croats, however, are Catholic, Serbs Eastern Orthodox, and a plurality (but not a majority) of Bosnians are Muslim, having been converted by the Turks.

They earlier got along because sovereignty (see Chapter 1) was far away, either in Istanbul for Ottoman-controlled Serbia and Bosnia or in Vienna (and Budapest) for the Austro-Hungarian areas of Slovenia and Croatia. In the 1690s, many Serbs fled the Turks into Habsburg lands, accounting for the Serbian areas of Croatia, namely the Krajina, the old Military Frontier between the two great and hostile empires.

It was when sovereignty came up that Serb-Croat hostility flared. The Serbs, starting in the early nineteenth century, were the first to push back the Turks and to envision unifying all the South Slavic peoples under Serbian leadership. At the end of World War I, many Croats thought a joint state would be good, protecting them from Hungarian and Italian demands, but they soon resented Serbs bossing them around. A Croatian fascist movement, the Usatasha, formed after German conquest in 1941, took all of Bosnia, and murdered some 350,000 Serbs, a holocaust Serbs never forgot. The bitter hatred began during World War II.

The Communist-led *partizani* eluded many German divisions in the rough, mountainous terrain and emerged victorious in 1945. Under Marshal Joseph Tito, they quickly communized and federalized Yugoslavia and silenced all dissent. Stalin did not trust Tito and expelled Yugoslavia from the Communist camp in 1948. Tito did not fall from power but instead pioneered a new, more open type of socialism that featured "worker self-management" rather than Soviet-style central controls. Each major nationality of Yugoslavia had its own republic with great autonomy, although the Communist elite monopolized political power. The nationalities question was deemed settled on the basis of "brotherhood and unity."

The setup depended too much on one individual—President-for-Life Tito. There was still a certain social distance between nationalities but no outright hatred. Intermarriage occurred at an accelerating rate. Yugoslavia worked under Tito, who had the power, prestige, and cunning to squelch the nationalities question, but when he died in 1980, the system started coming apart. Opportunistic local politicians, such as Serbia's Slobodan Milosevic, played the nationalist card to build their personal power so that ten years after Tito's death Yugoslavia's main nationalities hated each other, most of the hatred artificially whipped up.

In 1991, Slovenia and Croatia pulled out of Yugoslavia, and fighting started. The Serbian areas of Croatia, with weapons and troops from Belgrade, declared their independence and instituted "ethnic cleansing" to push out Croats. Their methods included concentration camps, rape, and murder. Serbs took a quarter of Croatia, areas they claimed had a Serbian majority. In 1992, with Sarajevo's proclamation of independence, the same bloody process commenced in Bosnia until Serbs held some two-thirds of it. All together, over 200,000 people were killed, most of them civilians, and an additional 3 million were made refugees. In the worst massacre, in July 1995, Serbs shot some 7,000 Bosnian Muslim males into mass graves while Dutch troops stood by. The Netherlands and West Europe as a whole were humiliated.

IFOR   1995 Implementation
Force, mostly NATO.

KFOR   1999 Kosovo Force, mostly
NATO.

Dayton, Ohio, mediated by American diplomat Richard C. Holbrooke and Secretary of State Warren Christopher. The European members of NATO followed the U.S. lead and formed **IFOR**,
effective because it came after a cease-fire had been agreed to
and because IFOR had orders to shoot (see Chapter 22).

Next, trouble flared in Serbia's southern province of Koso-
vo, Serbia's medieval heartland but now inhabited mostly by ethnic Albanians. These *Kosovars*, Muslim and speaking an unrelated language, increasingly demanded autonomy and
then independence from Belgrade's rule. Underground parties and terrorism appeared,
brutally suppressed by Milosevic's police and soldiers, who drove tens of thousands of
Kosovars into neighboring Albania and Macedonia and prepared to massacre the rest.

This time the United States and West Europe, ashamed of having stood by while civilians were massacred in Bosnia, were ready to stop it. Under the command of U.S. Gen. Wesley Clark, seventy-eight days of aerial bombardment—no ground troops—persuaded
Milosevic to pull out of Kosovo. The bombs hit few good military targets, and Serbs killed
an estimated 10,000 Kosovars anyway. The Kosovo campaign should not be used as a
model for anything. The situation is inherently unstable, barely calmed by the patrols of
KFOR. (Our hunch: Eventually Kosovo will join Albania.)

From both Bosnia and Kosovo, Europe learned unhappily that only when America
leads do things get done. The United States has the airlift capacity, the satellite intelligence,
the communications network, the aircraft, the smart bombs, and the willingness to fight.
The message to Europe: Develop your own fighting technology and spirit or stay forever
dependent on the Americans. That is when the EU got serious about building its own rapid-
reaction force of 60,000. Ironically, the only times NATO was actually used contributed to
its splintering.

Concepts

ALLIANCES

An alliance is a treaty between two or more countries to come to each other's aid under specified
conditions, usually when one partner is attacked.
Forming alliances is an ancient technique, a natural tendency to band together in the face of threats.
When the threats subside, the alliance weakens and
falls apart. No alliance is permanent.

The reason for forming an alliance is called the
casus foederis (literally, "cause for federating,"
almost the opposite of *casus belli*, reason for
going to war). The *casus foederis* is almost always
a security threat. A purely ideological alliance—
"Let's get together because we think the same
way"—is a nonstarter, an idealistic wish that
doesn't get carried out. Many Americans believe
alliances are based on mutual liking or shared values. Not necessarily. An alliance is a rational calculation of national interests by the leaders in
power at a given time. Emphasized Britain's Lord
Palmerston in the nineteenth century: "Britain has
no permanent friends and no permanent enemies; she has permanent interests."

WHO JOINED NATO WHEN (TOTAL OF TWENTY-SIX MEMBERS)	
1949	Twelve original signers of the North Atlantic Treaty—the United States, Canada, Britain, France, Iceland, Portugal, Belgium, the Netherlands, Luxembourg, Italy, Denmark, and Norway
1952	Greece and Turkey
1954	West Germany (since 1990 all of Germany)
1982	Spain
1999	Poland, the Czech Republic, and Hungary
2004	Lithuania, Latvia, Estonia, Slovakia, Slovenia, Bulgaria, Romania

■ The Crumbling of NATO

For some, the eastward expansion of NATO breathed new life into it, but as it expanded it both hollowed out and irritated Russia. The new eastern members from the defunct Soviet bloc contribute little to NATO's strength but represent new strategic problems. Russia dislikes this expansion of NATO right up to its borders—implicitly, it's still an anti-Russian alliance—and influences Russia's foreign policy. Russia could turn hostile again.

NATO no longer faces a Soviet threat and refuses to get involved in the Middle East. Americans and Europeans just don't see the Middle East the same way. Washington sees a region on the brink of chaos that we must stabilize, to insure the flow of oil, to foster democratization, and to reach an Israel-Palestine compromise. Europeans see a complex region that outside intervention can only destabilize. Americans are generally pro-Israel, Europeans anti-Israel. No amount of diplomacy can bridge these different perceptions.

Ironically, the only time NATO invoked Article 5 ("attack on one . . . attack on all") was when a tentacle of the Middle East reached out and wounded America on 9/11. A German AWACS plane took a few turns around the Northeast, a little photo op that may be the only time Europe will ever come to the defense of America. Fewer and fewer U.S. troops are stationed in Europe; they simply aren't needed. But alliances are always crumbling; that is their nature. As long as states preserve their sovereignty, they also keep their options for independent courses of action.

NATO has always been shaky and dependent on the United States. The traditional European powers exhausted themselves in World War II; afterward, only the Soviet Union and the United States really mattered on the world scene. In 1945 the Soviet Union, too, was drained by the war but still had a large army and major occupation forces in East Europe. The United States, although it quickly demobilized its armed forces, was the only industrial and nuclear power in the world.

Europe was prostrate. The necessities of life were in short supply. In France and Italy, large, armed Communist parties threatened to take over. As the Soviets consolidated their hold on East Europe, fear rippled through West Europe that they would be next. In a major

NATO and EU Members

civil war, Greece tottered on the edge of Communist takeover. Moscow issued tough demands on Turkey, including control of the strategic Turkish Straits.

It was a turning point in U.S. foreign policy. Only ten years earlier, the United States had been isolationist toward Europe. By the spring of 1947, Washington had decided that we had to be deeply involved in Europe. As we considered in Chapter 2, Washington simultaneously produced the Truman Doctrine, the Marshall Plan, and Kennan's "X" article. These three major statements defined, respectively, the military, economic, and theoretical bases of the American position in the Cold War.

Two years later, in 1949, the **North Atlantic Treaty** for the first time committed the United States to the defense of foreign lands. NATO was more than a treaty. Its strength was its integrated command structure. Member countries would not decide on their own what to do in the event of attack. At its Paris headquarters, officers from all the member countries devised a joint, coordinated strategy. The top NATO commander—historically an American, although nothing in the treaty requires it—would be able to give orders to the forces of many countries.

North Atlantic Treaty   1949 treaty of alliance that formed NATO.

Common Market   Early and informal name for European Economic Community, now EU.

tariff   Tax on imports.

NATO worked best when the Europeans were genuinely scared, as in the early 1950s when it seemed the North Korean invasion of South Korea could signal Stalin's intention to do the same to West Europe. General Dwight D. Eisenhower was NATO supreme commander at this time, and, as skilled a diplomat as he was a soldier, he built the integration of NATO member forces. With Stalin's death in 1953, however, some of the fear that fed NATO subsided. His successors, starting with the flamboyant Khrushchev, launched several "peace offensives" to lull West Europeans into complacency, break up NATO, and reduce the military preparedness of its European members, who never spent much on defense. The crushing of Hungary in 1956 and the Berlin Wall in 1961 reminded Europeans that they still needed a U.S. presence, which Washington was glad to provide. America spent more on the defense of Europe than Europeans did, an inherently unbalanced relationship that had to end. With U.S. protection, Europeans turned their attention to the unification of their continent.

■ Europe Gropes for Unity

Staggering out of the rubble of World War II, most thinking West Europeans understood that they had to overcome their traditional national barriers in order both to avoid future conflicts and to achieve economic growth. The U.S. model was often mentioned: a continental federation with free movement of goods and people. Europe, chopped into many countries, each defending its anachronistic economic sovereignty, stunted the Continent's political and military capacity to look after itself. Washington understood this early; one of the provisions of the Marshall Plan was for joint European economic planning.

Economic integration, planned by France's Jean Monnet and Robert Schuman, was to be the engine of European unity. With the 1951 Paris Treaty, they forged the European Coal and Steel Community whereby all the member states—France, West Germany, Italy, Belgium, the Netherlands, and Luxembourg—agreed to pool their coal and steel resources by eliminating tariffs, quotas, and other restrictive practices. The ECSC worked and helped propel West Europe out of its postwar slump.

The next step was more ambitious. The same six countries in 1957 expanded the ECSC concept to include all economic sectors, including labor, hence the name **Common Market**. Members agreed to cut their many **tariffs** with each other by 10 percent a year until they reached zero and build up a common tariff toward the rest of the world. Workers from one member country could take jobs in another without special permits. With their economies interlocked like those of U.S. states, West Europe moved to "ever closer union."

confederation   Political union
looser than a federation.

The EU was a resounding economic success. Instead of hunkering behind their protectionist walls, European industries had to compete with each other, delivering better products at lower prices. Labor-surplus countries could send their workers to labor-short countries. Standards of living rose dramatically.

Economics led to integration rather than unification. That is, the economies of Europe's lands meshed, but politics and psychologies lagged behind. The EU has no constitution, only a treaty. In 2005 referendums the French and Dutch shot down the first EU constitution, which required approval by all members. Turning the EU into a federation is still a work in progress. Few Europeans call themselves citizens of Europe; most identify first as citizens of their country and only secondly as Europeans. But most Europeans feel the EU has benefited them, and the feeling of Europeanness is growing, spurred by common laws, currency, and policy differences with the United States.

Geography

GROWTH OF THE COMMON MARKET

The original six signers of the 1957 Treaty of Rome that created the Common Market, or, as it liked to be called, the European Economic Community (EEC), were France, West Germany, Italy, Belgium, the Netherlands, and Luxembourg. Interestingly, this "Europe of the Six" coincided closely with Charlemagne's original unified European kingdom founded in 800, the Holy Roman Empire.

Britain at first chose not to join, preferring its Commonwealth and U.S. connections. The Common Market worked so well, however, that by the early 1960s Britain decided to apply. This time, in 1963, President de Gaulle of France uttered his famous *Non!* to British entry, arguing that the British were not wholehearted Europeans (he was right). After de Gaulle left office (1969), negotiations resumed, and in 1973 the Six became the Nine with the addition of Britain, Denmark, and Ireland.

Norway was about to join at this time, but in a referendum most Norwegians decided they'd rather keep their sovereignty and oil and fishing rights to themselves.

Greece joined in 1981 and Spain and Portugal in 1986, making an even twelve in what since 1993 calls itself the European Union. At the start of 1995, Finland, Sweden, and Austria entered the EU. Norwegians for the second time rejected by referendum joining the EU. The East European lands were eager to join but first had to prove they were democracies with market economies. In 2004, after six years of complex negotiations, ten more, mostly ex-Communist countries in Central Europe, joined: Poland, Hungary, Czech Republic, Slovakia, Slovenia (remember, they are not the same), Lithuania, Latvia, Estonia, Malta, and Cyprus, making an EU of twenty-five members. Romania and Bulgaria are to join in 2007. The economic advantages of the EU persuade most European countries to join. Only Norway and Switzerland resist. Turkey has wanted in for years, but Brussels, fearing Turkey is too Middle Eastern and Muslim to be European, has gone very slowly in considering its application.

The EU is not yet a federation like the United States—it is a kind of **confederation**—but it is a single economy, one with a GDP of $11 trillion and a combined population of 455 million. The United States has a GDP of $12 trillion and 300 million people, and its economy and population grow faster than Europe's. The EU is more export-oriented and trade-protectionist than the United States.

Nasty old sovereignty blocks European unification. Sovereignty's chief—but not only—proponent was Charles de Gaulle of France, who was always a fierce French nationalist. He didn't much like NATO (for its American leadership) or the EEC (for trying to submerge French sovereignty). He called for a *Europe des patries*, a Europe of fatherlands, countries preserving their traditional powers and distinctiveness, with, of course, France in the lead. Paris demanded and got protection for France's overlarge agricultural sector. The EU's Common Agricultural Policy (CAP) eats half of the EU budget. The biggest chunk of CAP goes to France. An average European cow gets $2.50 a day in subsidies (a Japanese cow $7), giving new meaning to the phrase "cash cow."

De Gaulle also built his version of Europe when he ordered U.S. troops in France and NATO headquarters out of the country in 1966. He withdrew France from the integrated military structure that gives NATO so much of its strength. France is still a member of NATO but is not integrated into the command structure at its current headquarters near Brussels. One might say that France (and later Spain) are in NAT without the O.

Like de Gaulle, many Europeans want the EU's economic advantages without losing any of their countries' sovereign political rights. The 1991 Maastricht agreement, for example, aimed for deeper European integration, but some Europeans balked. The Danes narrowly voted it down in 1992, jolting Europe. In 2005, when the French and Dutch rejected the new EU constitution, many Europeans agreed with them. Their concerns are not trivial. The EU constitution had been a completely elite project with no popular input or consultation. A united Europe would mean each country giving up much of its sovereignty to distant bureaucrats in Brussels. Polish workers could take jobs in Belgium.

The biggest area of concern is the top-down, undemocratic EU structure. Europeans rightly complain of a "democratic deficit." The EU is run by remote bureaucrats and **technocrats**, who amass such a complex rulebook (the 80,000-plus pages of the *acquis*

> **technocrat**   Unelected governing official, usually a finance expert.

Geography

FOUR STAGES OF INTEGRATION

Integration comes in different levels or stages. The lowest is the "free trade area," where countries simply end their tariff barriers against each other. Example: NAFTA.

A step higher is the "customs union," where countries both lower their tariffs to each other and build a common tariff toward the outside world. Example: the *Zollverein* that helped Bismarck unify Germany.

Another step up is a "common market" that does all the above until barriers are zero, even to labor, and takes on some regulatory functions. Example: the original EEC.

The highest stage of integration is the economic union, essentially one big economy, with common currency and a quasi-federal structure. Example: the EU, which, if it keeps going, could turn into a federation, what some Europeans urge.

euro   Common EU currency; €1 was worth about $1.30 in 2006.

Eurodollars   U.S. dollars circulating in Europe.

EMU   European Monetary Union devised at Maastricht in 1991; set up new *euro* currency.

ECB   European Central Bank, the EU's Fed.

communitaire) that they bore Europeans into obedience. The most important body, the European Commission, both runs the EU's civil service and makes policy. Each member appoints one commissioner; no one elects them, and they became tarnished with fraud and mismanagement. The only elected body—and only half of Europeans bother to vote for it—is the 732-member European Parliament, with limited and uncertain powers.

Europe on Its Own?

During the Cold War, America, with its big military budget and nuclear weapons, defended West Europe. The Soviets kept many divisions ready to strike into West Germany. NATO forces, even with 300,000 Americans in Europe, were not enough. To deter a possible Soviet attack,

Economics

DOES THE EURO WORK?

The new **euro** currency, whose symbol is an "e" with two little lines across it (€), was adopted by twelve EU countries at the beginning of 1999. (Britain, Denmark, and Sweden stood outside the eurozone.) The euro had as many critics as supporters. Some hailed it as Europe's answer to the U.S. dollar. Others thought it would fail.

The euro was a major attempt to reach full European integration. Before the euro, European countries had to use either their own currencies or **Eurodollars** for trade with their neighbors. This meant heavy "transaction costs" of several percent whenever you had to change currencies. Second, Eurodollars meant depending on U.S. economic policy, which pushes the dollar up or down with Europe having no voice. And third, European politicians wanted to have a strong, respected currency of their own.

At Maastricht in the Netherlands in 1991, EU members set up the **EMU** to start the new euro in 1999, supervised by a new **ECB** in Frankfurt (equivalent to the U.S. Federal Reserve Board). At first the euro was used just for accounting and credit cards, but at the beginning of 2002 actual coins and bills replaced older currencies. After the initial

grumbling, most citizens of Euroland got used to the euro and even like it. American tourists especially like it, as it is worth about a dollar, and they do not have to change money so often.

Did the euro work? Initially valued at $1.17, it fell to 85 cents in 2001, but by 2003, as the dollar weakened in response to a massive U.S. budget deficit, the euro surpassed its starting worth and kept going. A "strong" currency is not necessarily good, as it makes it harder for you to export. The euro did not help Europe's economies recover from a long slump, caused in part by the ECB keeping interest rates too high in order to fight inflation. In contrast, the U.S. Fed massively cut our interest rates to fight recession. Some said the ECB was too cautious and too frightened of inflation. Meanwhile, several European countries, to fight chronic high unemployment, ran budget deficits over the EMU's limit of 3 percent of GDP. They got a scolding, but no one knew how to stop them. Now member countries cannot set their own interest rates, an important element of sovereignty that they have surrendered. Some worry that such conflicts could rip the EMU apart.

the United States in the 1960s kept some seven thousand relatively small tactical nuclear weapons—"tac nukes"—in West Europe, now reduced to zero.

Did it work? Sure, say its proponents; there was no Soviet invasion. In logic it's hard to prove why something *didn't* happen. More important was the psychological element to U.S. forces and nukes in Europe: to buck up our European allies as they recovered their political, economic, and military strength, which they did by the 1960s. As Europe got stronger, though, it started talking back to its U.S. big brother. De Gaulle (see the earlier discussion) withdrew France from NATO's integrated command and built France's own nuclear force. Europe should not rely on the Americans, preached de Gaulle. In 1961, the East German regime built the Berlin Wall, and the Americans made no move to pull it down. West Germans felt let down at the U.S. lack of firmness. Many Europeans began to think de Gaulle might be right.

In the 1970s the Soviets placed new missiles in East Europe, able to reach anywhere in West Europe. Moderate Europeans worried that the United States would not do enough to counteract the new Soviet threat, while radicals and pacifists were afraid the United States was too eager to challenge the Soviets, that U.S. impetuosity, especially under President Reagan, might lead to nuclear war. West European peace movements grew, complaining of "incineration without representation."

The Cold War ended before conflicts within NATO could pull it apart. But now many Europeans and Americans wonder if NATO can or should continue as before. U.S. troop strength in Europe is now a fraction of what it was and has no clear purpose. We may celebrate NATO's successes—keep the Soviets at bay, support European recovery and integration, and establish German democracy—but still ask what it is to do now. NATO members now participate—on a voluntary basis—in out-of-area peacekeeping in Bosnia, Kosovo, and Afghanistan. Some say such missions will give NATO a new reason for being.

Classic Thought

NOW MAKE EUROPEANS

One of Italy's unifiers in the late nineteenth century reflected, "Having made Italy, we must now make Italians." He meant that Italy, unified from the top down, lacked enthusiastic citizens who thought of themselves as Italians rather than as Venetians, Tuscans, or Sicilians. The same applies to Europe now. Europe exists as a set of bureaucratic institutions but not in the hearts of Europeans, who still think of themselves as French, German, or Italian. Said French Premier Lionel Jospin in 2001: "I want a Europe, but I remain attached to my own nation." Zbigniew Brzezinski, a political scientist and President Carter's national security advisor,

wisecracked in 2000 that "no 'European' is willing to die for 'Europe.'" (Actually, that is not completely true; dozens of European soldiers—with Spain in the lead—died for Europe in Bosnia.)

Constructing a European patriotism is much harder than setting up complex institutions few understand. Most Europeans go along with the EU but without passion: It's a good economic deal. Americans love the United States; Europeans do not love Europe. Building patriotism can take centuries and is helped by facing common threats and problems. We are likely to see a unified Europe long before we see "Europeans."

quota   Numerical limit on
imports.

subsidy   Government payment
to prop up an industry.

comparative advantage   Theory
that countries should make only
what they can produce efficiently
and trade for other products.

European armies are shrinking and not modernizing their
equipment. The EU's new rapid-reaction force faces the same
problem that has dogged European unity: Who is going to be in
charge of it? Twenty-five countries? Europe is reluctant to spend
on defense and lacks the high-tech items that make U.S. forces
effective. Washington did not favor the new EU force, fearing
it would splinter NATO, duplicate effort, and still leave Europe
weak. NATO works, said Washington; keep it unchanged. That
might not be possible.

Considering the resentment that has been building in Europe, Washington might let Europe find out what it can—and cannot—do for itself. It
would be better if they came to us seeking help rather than us hectoring them. We might
tell the Europeans, "Sure, go ahead and handle your own security." If they can, so much
the better. That will mean that the great postwar U.S. project of making Europe whole and
free has worked. And if they cannot, they will have to accept U.S. leadership again. It was,
after all, not the worst thing that's ever happened to Europe.

■ The Challenge of Trade Blocs

The United States and the EU quarrel bitterly over trade issues. Europe keeps out several U.S. products by means of tariffs, **quotas**, and **subsidies** designed to protect European farms and industries. They see protection of jobs as their number-one duty.

Classic Thought

COMPARATIVE ADVANTAGE

Any product should be produced where it is most advantageous, argued English economist David Ricardo nearly two centuries ago. If Spain grows the best oranges most cheaply—because of climate, soil, and work force—then it has a "**comparative advantage**" in growing oranges over England. Spain should concentrate on growing oranges. If England, on the other hand, makes the best cloth most cheaply, then that is its comparative advantage and it should concentrate on it. Then the two countries trade, Spanish oranges for English cloth, and this maximizes everyone's advantage because oranges and cloth are being produced where it is most efficient to do so.

Inefficiency comes when countries, out of an urge to be self-sufficient or protect local producers, try to produce things when they have no comparative advantage, like England growing oranges. How can you tell who has the comparative advantage? Just have free trade with no barriers or subsidies and soon you will see who can produce things best and cheapest. English orange growers will soon go out of business. Americans love this classic argument when it comes to explaining why Japanese should buy U.S. citrus and why Europeans should buy U.S. beef. We do not like it when it explains why Americans should buy Japanese cars.

Europe—like Japan—comes up with all manner of excuses to keep out U.S. products, like claiming hormone-fed beef or genetically modified grain is dangerous. We even got angry over bananas. The WTO (see Chapter 18) ruled against the EU, but the EU won't budge. In retaliation, Washington slaps high tariffs on certain European products. The dispute does not subside.

The EU protects its 15 million farmers (far too many) by providing half of their income in the form of subsidies. The United States helps its 3.4 million farmers (still too

Economics

THE RETIRED CONTINENT

Europe has built itself into an economic box, a series of interlocking problems that are hard to escape and sap the Continent of its vitality and ability to play a major world role. Most European countries have the following:

1. A large welfare state that provides nearly cradle-to-grave benefits, especially for the unemployed.

2. High taxes to pay for the welfare state, about 40 percent of GDP in contrast to 30 percent in the United States, Japan, and Australia.

3. Budget deficits to cover the shortfall between welfare expenditures and taxes. (As a percent of GDP, however, the United States now has even bigger budget deficits.)

4. Slow economic growth, slower than the United States and much slower than East Asia. (The new eastern EU members show good growth, thanks to their lower wages.) Europeans get long vacations (often a month) and short work weeks (often 35 hours), so that the average American works 350 hours longer a year.

5. High unemployment, sometimes over 10 percent, from slow economic growth, overly generous unemployment benefits, and "labor-force rigidities," such as anti-layoff laws and geographic immobility. Such unemployment would never be tolerated in the United States, where the labor force is less protected and more flexible.

6. An aging population that retires early (often before 60) and requires greater and greater pensions. With an extremely low birth rate—one that does not nearly replace Europeans who die—to provide the work force to pay for retirement benefits, governments go deeper into debt. By 2050, the average European is projected to be 52 years old, the average American 35.

7. Protected sectors, especially agriculture, that keep out foreign competition to try to hold down unemployment. This has made some sectors of the European economy inefficient.

8. A pacifist mentality. Europeans just don't want war and doubt that any war is justified. They may send forces for peacekeeping but under orders to avoid fighting. European opinion massively opposed the 2003 Iraq War.

These factors tend to make Europe preoccupied with its own domestic affairs and little interested in playing a leading role elsewhere, in the Balkans or Middle East. European concentration on how to pay for the welfare state also deepens frictions and disagreements with the Americans, who have a more open, flexible, and growing economy. Demographically and economically, Europe and America are increasingly different.

trade blocs   Geographic regions that trade mostly among themselves and keep out nonbloc goods.

many) by providing 30 percent of their income in the form of subsidies. Japan is far worse than Europe; it provides farmers with two-thirds of their income. (Australia and New Zealand subsidize farmers very little, resulting in the most efficient farms in the world.) But tell a Brussels Eurocrat that the EU has three times as many farmers as it needs, he shrugs and says, "But they get angry and vote when their livelihood is at stake. So the subsidies must continue." The result has been "mountains of butter and lakes of wine" in European surplus food warehouses, all useless and expensive.

Trade blocs can be terribly selfish. In looking after only the needs of their own producers, they keep out the products of others. The earlier selfishness of the individual nation-state just expands to become the collective selfishness of the trade bloc. France no longer keeps out non-French products; now the EU keeps out non-European products. Some fear a world of three major trading blocs—Europe, the Pacific, and North America—that erect trade walls against the rest of the world. Instead of a prosperity that expands until it covers the globe, closed-off trade blocs could lead to escalating rounds of retaliation that leave everyone poorer and angrier. Hitler, at the height of his conquests, dared the United States to invade his "Fortress Europe," implying a sealed-off empire. Could it indeed become such?

The brighter side is that trade blocs may be just temporary as the world progresses from one-country markets to a global market. Blocs may serve their purpose and fade. A trade bloc can be inward looking (bad) or outward looking (good). If the former, it will lock out foreign competition, damage its own citizens' prosperity, and retard growth worldwide. If the latter, it will be open to foreign competition, help lift up the poorer lands by means of trade, and give its citizens rising living standards. The great task of statesmanship in our day lies in keeping trade open. If America does not lead in this task, the world could slide back into protectionism.

Key Terms

Common Market (p. 251)

comparative advantage (p. 256)

confederation (p. 252)

ECB (p. 254)

EMU (p. 254)

euro (p. 254)

Eurodollars (p. 254)

European Union (EU) (p. 246)

IFOR (p. 248)

KFOR (p. 248)

North Atlantic Treaty (p. 251)

quota (p. 256)

soft power (p. 245)

subsidy (p. 256)

tariff (p. 251)

technocrat (p. 253)

trade bloc (p. 258)

UNPROFOR (p. 246)

Key Web Sites

European Union in the United States.
http://www.eurunion.org/home.htm

OSCE—Organisation on Security and Cooperation in Europe
http://www.fsk.ethz.ch/osce/

Europa (The European Union Web Site)
http://europa.eu.int/index.htm

Association for the Monetary Union of Europe
http://amue.lf.net/

Further Reference

Dinan, Desmond. *Ever Closer Union: An Introduction to European Integration,* 3rd ed. Boulder, CO: Lynne Rienner, 2005.

Garton Ash, Timothy. *Free World: Why a Crisis of the West Reveals the Opportunity of Our Time.* New York: Random House, 2004.

James, Harold. *Europe Reborn: A History, 1914–2000.* Upper Saddle River, NJ: Pearson Education, 2003.

Judt, Tony. *Postwar: A History of Europe since 1945.* New York: Penguin, 2005.

Kaplan, Lawrence S. *NATO Divided, NATO United: The Evolution of an Alliance.* Westport, CT: Praeger, 2004.

Lindberg, Tod, ed. *Beyond Paradise and Power: Europe, America and the Future of a Troubled Partnership.* New York: Routledge, 2004.

McCormick, John. *Understanding the European Union: A Concise Introduction,* 2nd ed. New York: Palgrave, 2002.

Moens, Alexander, Lenard J. Cohen, and Allen G. Sens, eds. *NATO and European Security: Alliance Politics from the End of the Cold War to the Age of Terrorism.* Westport, CT: Praeger, 2002.

Mowle, Thomas S. *Allies at Odds? The United States and the European Union.* New York: Palgrave, 2004.

Nugent, Neill. *European Union Enlargement.* New York: Palgrave, 2004.

Peterson, John, and Mark Pollack, eds. *Europe, America, Bush: Transatlantic Relations in the 21st Century.* New York: Routledge, 2003.

Tiersky, Ronald, ed. *Europe Today: National Politics, European Integration, and European Security,* 2nd ed. Lanham, MD: Rowman & Littlefield, 2004.

Zeff, Eleanor E., and Ellen B. Pirro, eds. *The European Union and the Member States,* 2nd ed. Boulder, CO: Lynne Rienner, 2006.

CHAPTER 17

ASIA

CHINA AS NUMBER ONE

QUESTIONS TO CONSIDER

1. Should we care if China becomes Asia's leading power?
2. How have the United States and East Asia historically misunderstood each other?
3. Is China now friendly or hostile? How quickly can this change?
4. Long term, is the Middle East or East Asia our biggest problem?
5. Is Taiwan a separate country from China? Should it be?
6. How did Japan handle Western penetration?
7. Was the U.S.-Japanese war inevitable? What steps led to it?
8. Is there some special formula for Japan's economic growth?
9. Why has East Asia been the center of economic growth?

In 2008 Beijing, bursting with pride, is set to host the summer Olympic games. China has been celebrating this international recognition since it won the Olympic nod in 2001. In 2003 China beamed at its earth-orbiting space launch. In these and other national-pride moves China's motive is to show the world that it is a great nation. China is quite open about its aim to become once again the leading power in Asia and the second power globally (after the United States). For centuries China was Asia's "Middle Kingdom," the cultural and political center to which its neighbors paid tribute and homage. Although brought low by "barbarians," Chinese never ceased thinking of themselves as the natural leading power of Asia.

It will still take many years, but China's goal is in view. After thirty years of record-setting growth, China has the world's second biggest economy (overall, not per capita, and corrected for purchasing-power parity). Japan, once the growth dragon of East Asia, has had either low or stagnant growth. Japanese firms now outsource much of their production to China. (Your new digital camera was likely made in China.)

China, the "factory of the world," now demands respect. China reckons that its "Century of Humiliation" began with its defeat in the 1839 Opium War—which Britain fought to sell opium in China, where it was illegal. The superior firepower of the European imperialists turned China into a semicolony. Then in the 1930s the Japanese imperialists began the conquest of China. Almost everything China does now, from rapid economic growth to acquiring nuclear weapons (see Chapter 14) to launching spacecraft to hosting the Olympics, is calculated to gain respect. Mao Zedong himself said it as he took power in 1949: "Our nation will never again be an insulted nation. We have stood up."

Should China's quest for power and prestige bother us? (What, by the way, does America strive for?) The answer to this question depends on what kind of China will emerge. If China is moving to democracy, great. But suppose China becomes rich but not free, a one-party Communist system with aggressive and expansionist designs on the region. Every few years, our picture of China alternates. One year we notice that China uses sweatshop labor, abuses human rights, crushes democracy, and threatens to invade Taiwan. The next year we notice that China is friendly and cooperative and has adopted pragmatic domestic and foreign policies. China's President Hu Jintao in 2005 called for a "harmonious world" where all live in peace. That has not always been the case with China. At one time or another, Communist China has had hostile relations with almost all of its fifteen immediate neighbors. It has fought with India, the Soviet Union, Vietnam, and with the United States in Korea.

Shanghai, center of China's rapid growth, has twice as many skyscrapers—most of them new—as New York. (Chang W. Lee/The New York Times)

The China problem has two parts. The first is the rapidly changing nature of the "real" China, which is difficult to discern in a country where politics is still secret. The second and perhaps bigger problem is America's tendency to embrace roller-coaster perceptions of China, one year too high, the next too low. How do we handle China? President Clinton argued that America gets "more influence in China with an outstretched hand than with a clenched fist." President Bush 43 denounced that view and portrayed China as our strategic competitor, but he soon returned to Clinton's policy and hosted more top Chinese leaders than those of any other nation.

East Asia

Modernization theory (see page 170) suggests that as China gets richer it will create a large, educated middle class, which will push for democracy. This is what happened in South Korea and Taiwan; as they became "middle-income countries" (those with per capita GDPs over $6,000), they moved from dictatorship to democracy. China will not necessarily follow this pattern. China is **totalitarian**; South Korea and Taiwan were **authoritarian**. No totalitarian system has reformed; instead, they have collapsed. Many authoritarian systems have reformed themselves into democracies. China is far bigger (population 1.3 billion) and more complex than those two little countries. China has an historical memory of past greatness and nurtures grievances against the foreign powers it believes

totalitarian Regime that attempts total control.

authoritarian Dictatorial regime but milder than *totalitarian*.

Open Door U.S. policy of China trade open to all and keeping China intact.

kept it down. Chief and permanent culprit in Beijing's eyes is Japan. Second and off-and-on culprit is the United States.

China's Communist leaders like the rapid growth of its partially market economy but refuse to go all the way to capitalism or relinquish political control. They permit no organizations or news media not controlled by the Communist party. Foreigners are watched, and few Chinese discuss controversial topics—such as democracy, religion, or Taiwan—with them. Dissidents—including writers, editors, medical doctors, and union organizers—get stiff prison terms. China even controls the Internet to keep out criticism and messages of freedom and democracy. This regime fears that any change could get out of hand—and it could.

America must take China's need for respect into account. It could become the most important problem of the twenty-first century. If handled well, it could move China in a free-market and democratic direction. If handled badly, it could move China in a nationalistic and aggressive direction. We should remember that America's involvement in East Asia has been a history of misperceptions, misunderstandings, and tragedies.

■ A History of Exaggerations

We should also remember that Asia did not ask to be "opened" by the West. It was perfectly content with its traditional civilizations when the first Portuguese sailors invited themselves into India, Indonesia, China, and Japan in the early sixteenth century, not long after Columbus journeyed to the Americas. Columbus and the Portuguese were looking for the same thing, a sea route to the spices of the East, then worth more than their weight in gold. Columbus did it by heading due west, the Portuguese by rounding Africa and crossing the Indian Ocean.

Early in the nineteenth century, extensive U.S. trade developed with China, soon followed by U.S. missionaries. But the United States never sought a "sphere of influence" and never participated in the imperialist carve-up of the China coast. Because of this, Chinese called Americans their "favorite people," and we were proud of that. At the beginning of the twentieth century, U.S. Secretary of State Hay issued the famous **Open Door** notes, telling all powers to keep trade with China open and to preserve China's territorial and administrative integrity.

We saw ourselves as China's big brother and in 1911 supported the new Chinese Republic and its Nationalist party. We especially favored Generalissimo Chiang Kai-shek, who was put on the cover of *Time* magazine ten times by publisher Henry Luce. (Luce was born

trade deficit Buying more from other countries than you sell to them.

bashing Accusing other countries of rigging their economies and trading practices to discriminate against the United States.

MITI Ministry of International Trade and Industry, guiding hand of Japan's economy; now called METI.

and raised in China of missionary parents.) As Japan warred against China in the 1930s, we tilted sharply toward China and eventually collided with Japan, which attacked Pearl Harbor because of U.S. support for China.

But after World War II, China went wrong. After years of fighting the Nationalists, the Chinese Communists under Mao Zedong won power in 1949 and in 1950 flung their army against us in Korea. McCarthyism looked for someone to blame (chiefly Democrats) for "who lost China?" China went from being our little brother to dangerous enemy; we fought in Vietnam to halt Chinese communist expansionism, or so we thought. Washington had nothing to do with Beijing until Nixon's 1972 visit. Then suddenly U.S.-China ties warmed as both sides used them as leverage against Moscow. Trade, exchanges, and embassies were established. We were buddies again.

By the 1990s, things turned sour again. In 1989 the regime bloodily crushed prodemocracy demonstrators in Beijing. China gave long prison terms to those who spoke out for democracy. The Chinese economy boomed, but China (like Japan) sold a lot more to America than it bought; U.S. **trade deficits** soared. Chinese manufacturers ignored U.S. patents and copyrights. Chinese Christians and Buddhist sects were harassed. Many Chinese, with regime approval, said they were tired of the Americans telling them what to do. Beijing and Moscow sometimes say they stand together against the "world hegemonic power," meaning us. In 2005 they staged their first joint military exercise, which looked like practice to invade Taiwan. But a strong China scares a weak Russia. Siberia is depopulating, and crowded China could use the land, some of which Russia took from China long ago by "unequal treaties." A China-Russia alliance does not seem likely.

Reflections

THE BASHING GAME

Late in the last century, Japan-**bashing** books, articles, and speeches washed over America, portraying a sinister conspiracy to take over the world by economic means. The powerful bureaucrats of the Ministry of International Trade and Industry (**MITI**) pushed Japan's industries to dominate key economic sectors. Japanese industries got protective tariffs, laws against foreign ownership, bank loans, and governmental planning. Japan's decade-long recession during the 1990s makes Japan-bashing look unfounded and ridiculous, and we worry more about the Japanese economy

failing to grow. Japan-bashing was a fraud, a gimmick to sell books.

Next, America turned to China-bashing. The new story is that Beijing is engaged in a sinister plot to dominate East Asia (and maybe further) by economic means, using cheap labor to suck in our high-tech industries and with them become a first-class power. China uses its growing economy to improve its army, a possible threat to us. Could we be engaging in another bout of exaggeration, one rooted in racism? Must we always have an East Asian nation to bash?

What does the roller coaster in U.S.-China relations mean? It suggests that we have almost continually misunderstood China, seeing it as a nation for us to either save or destroy, total friend or total enemy. We exaggerated China's friendship and then, after 1949, exaggerated its enmity. Starting with Nixon, we exaggerated it as a friend again. One exaggeration starting in the nineteenth century is the "China market," millions of customers for U.S. products. In truth, we never sold that much to China (it was too poor to buy much) and always did far more trade with Japan. The lure of a supposed China market still prompts U.S. business and agriculture to push for more trade. Now China sells far more to the United States than it buys, and this gives China incentive to not lose its biggest customer over, say, Taiwan.

No two countries can ever perfectly understand or agree with each other. Between nations there can be neither total friendship nor total enmity. China was not ours to either "save" or "lose." Americans must learn to avoid sentimentality, exaggeration, and hysteria in dealing with other countries.

◼ Which Way for China?

"Let China sleep," said Napoleon, "when she wakes, she will shake the world." Napoleon's prediction may now be coming true. China was actually easier to handle when it was a straight Communist dictatorship. It was revolutionary but isolated and poor, consumed by its latest self-destructive campaign (Great Leap Forward in the late 1950s, Great Proletarian Cultural Revolution in the late 1960s) unleashed by Chairman Mao. When it decided to come out of its shell under Deng Xiaoping in the late 1970s, it posed two questions, one economic and one political.

China's Special Economic Zones, mostly in the south and along the coast (in part, aiming to make Hong Kong easier to swallow) encouraged private enterprise and foreign investment. Taking advantage of China's low wages, Japanese, Taiwanese, and Hong Kong capital poured in and was soon producing textiles, clothing, footwear, and consumer electronics. China, starting in the 1980s, scored the fastest economic growth in history. Now China depends on the taxes paid by its market sector to prop up its state-owned industries, most of them decrepit and money-losing. China can't go back to communism. The problem here is how much of the world's production should shift to China. Should there be any limits? Other startup economies are hobbled, because few can compete with China. Mexico, for example, loses factory jobs to China. How many gigantic low-cost producers can the world take?

The political problem is that China is still governed by an old generation that was trained in revolutionary Marxism and "socialist" industry. They are reluctant to admit that the whole Maoist enterprise—including the death of perhaps 50 million of their own citizens—has been a mistake. Beijing's rulers thought they could liberalize China's economy but not its political system, which would stay under tight Communist central control. Can that work? Or do market economies create pressures for democracy, as they did in Taiwan?

As China's market economy grew, it undermined the legitimacy of communism. Desperate, Beijing sought to deflect its citizens' discontent into nationalism—an old trick—by

bluff Declaring a firm policy but not supporting it militarily.

rapprochement French for "approaching"; two countries drawing diplomatically closer to each other.

calling Japan unrepentant and the United States a bully and by staking out territorial claims far into the South and East China Seas. Possible major oil deposits around the Paracel, Spratly, and Senkaku Islands brought China into disputes with Vietnam, Indonesia, the Philippines, Malaysia, Brunei, and Japan. After getting nothing good out of these disputes, China ended them in favor of a "cooperative" solution. Beijing turns quarrels off and on as suits it.

Turning Point

WAR OVER TAIWAN?

Will China invade Taiwan? Beijing swears that if Taipei (Taiwan's capital) ever declares independence, China will invade and reunite with Taiwan by force. And Beijing adds that if Taipei hesitates too long to return to China, it may invade anyway. China's military buildup—including amphibious forces—makes this plausible. Some see a serious threat from Beijing; others see a **bluff**. China and Taiwan do a lot of business with each other, and neither wishes to hurt that.

When the Chinese Communists beat the Nationalists in 1949, Chiang Kai-shek's army retreated to the large island of Taiwan with the promise to return soon to liberate the mainland from the "bandit clique of Mao Zedong." Today, Beijing demands the reunification of Taiwan with the mainland. For both Nationalists and Communists, there is only one China, a dogma that is part of China's political culture.

For all intents and purposes, Taiwan really is a separate country. The Manchu dynasty annexed Taiwan in 1683 to stop piracy and a Dutch takeover. It was run by Japan from 1895 to 1945, and many older Taiwanese still speak Japanese. Their native dialect is quite distinct from Mandarin, and Taiwanese do not much like mainlanders. When the Nationalists took over after World War II, Taiwanese complaints about the new government led to rioting, which Chiang brutally suppressed. Until recently, no Taiwanese were allowed in Taipei's top ranks; those positions were reserved for mainland Nationalists. Many Taiwanese felt like a colony; some formed the opposition Democratic Progressive party.

Taiwan was a military dictatorship until 1987, with only one party, the Nationalists, but vigorous economic growth turned Taiwan into a vibrant democracy. Taiwan-born Lee Teng-hui, a Nationalist, won Taiwan's first free presidential election in 1996. In 2000, Chen Shui-bian of the Democratic Progressive party won the presidency. Both Lee and Chen said Taiwan is a sovereign state, a point that angered Beijing, which sees Taiwan as a renegade province.

When the United States, under President Nixon, began a **rapprochement** with mainland China, some Americans talked about a "two-Chinas" policy, that is, recognizing that they are two separate countries. Neither Taipei nor Beijing would hear of it, so the United States shifted its diplomatic recognition from the former to the latter. Informally, U.S.-Taiwan relations continue (see Chapter 19).

The question for the United States: Should we guarantee the independence of Taiwan? Would threats to cut off China's burgeoning U.S. trade ties be sufficient? Or would we really use military force? Current U.S. policy is to oppose the forcible unification of the two Chinas; if it's peaceful, we have no problem. Quietly, Washington urges Taipei to pipe down about sovereignty or independence and preserve Taiwan's strange status—a country that is legally not a country. As you review the tragedy of U.S.-Japan relations in the twentieth century—a history of misunderstanding and bluff—ask if the same could happen between us and China.

China is modernizing its large but poorly equipped armed forces, as if to say, "Nobody is going to push us around any more. We have been victims for too long. Now we take what we're entitled to." The Pentagon especially worries about this, fearing China could soon confront its neighbors with military strength. At what point, if any, should the United States take an interest? Should we, for example, be prepared to defend Taiwan against a forcible mainland takeover?

◼ Japan Encounters the West

The reasons for Japan's success are many. Geography and history helped. The island archipelago was close enough to China to assimilate much Chinese culture—such as ideographic writing, architecture, Buddhism—but sufficiently distant to resist invasion. Two invasion attempts by the Mongol emperor of China, Kublai Khan, in 1274 and 1281, had Japan petrified with fear until a "divine wind" (in Japanese, *kamikaze*) wrecked the invasion fleets. With few natural resources, Japan had to rely on human resources of thrift and cleverness.

Unlike China, Japan did not unify early into a bureaucratic empire but stayed a squabbling series of feudal ministates for centuries. Gradually and by conquest, these coalesced by 1600 into a feudal kingdom that covered the island chain. An emperor, virtually a prisoner of the court, served as a symbolic descendant of the sun goddess. Real power lay in the hands of a *shogun,* a military chief who ruled by armed force and by carefully balancing the powers of lesser lords. By the nineteenth century, Japan was a highly developed feudal system—with power dispersed among many groups, each with right of veto, and insufficient central authority.

Some thinkers argue that feudalism was so deeply ingrained in Japanese culture that Japan has never come out of it and remains feudal to this day. Tokyo lacks the central authority we take for granted in other modern countries. This is what makes Japanese government so difficult to deal with. Japan's leaders seem to promise one thing, but back home they knuckle under to domestic economic interests. It also means that Tokyo has great difficulty in reforming Japan's ailing financial system.

The arrival of the first Westerners—daring Portuguese navigators in 1542—confused the Japanese. Some traded with the Europeans, and hundreds of thousands embraced the Catholic faith brought to Japan by Jesuits. Others feared the dynamic outside influence would wreck Japan's delicate balance. In 1622 the newly established Tokugawa shogun decided the foreigners and their ways were destabilizing. He had the Westerners expelled and Japanese Catholics butchered. Then he firmly closed the door to outsiders; there was little trade or contact for over two centuries.

As the China trade grew, however, the West became increasingly curious and annoyed about Japan. How could this strange country resist us and our goods? The West wanted some way to recover shipwrecked sailors held in Japan. In 1853, the Americans made the opening move as Commodore Perry's black, fire-belching ships entered Tokyo Bay. The worried Japanese officials asked Perry to return next year for their answer. It was no longer possible to keep the foreigners out, so Japan in 1854 exchanged diplomatic recognition with the United States.

Meiji   Japan's period of rapid
modernization starting in 1868.

What took place next was amazing. Having accepted the opening, Japan could not continue as a pretty, picture-book traditional land. Officials saw that Japan had to modernize quickly or be taken over, as China was. In 1868, upon the accession of the new Emperor **Meiji**, a group of vigorous samurai pushed through a series of reforms called the Meiji Restoration, which modernized everything from government and industry through education and clothing. Under the slogan, "Rich nation, strong army!" Japan went from the crafts age to the industrial age in one generation. In 1895, Japan beat China, a decade later Russia.

■ The Road to Pearl Harbor and Hiroshima

Economics played a major role in the march to war. Japan depended—as it does today—on exports. Japanese goods, especially textiles, flooded the American market until they were limited by quotas. Japanese felt they were being denied a chance to compete. This played into the hands of militarists who argued that only imperial possessions could give Japan the economic growing room she needed. As the world economic depression deepened in the 1930s, everyone locked out foreign goods, hurting Japan even more. (See Chapter 18.)

Japan also resented U.S. laws in the early 1900s against Asian immigrants. In California, local laws discriminated against Japanese (and Chinese), and Tokyo felt insulted. Domestic matters have international repercussions.

Like newly unified Germany, Japan began to demand her "place in the sun." If the Europeans could grab colonies, why couldn't Japan? Japanese democrats tried to transplant Britain's constitutional monarchy—with a parliament and cabinet—but they were soon subverted by Japanese ways, a pattern also seen later. The Japanese armed forces were hotbeds of militant nationalism that demanded imperial expansion. They knew this would

Turning Point

THE FIRST PEARL HARBOR

Americans did not like tsarist Russia, which was infamous for its tyranny, Siberian penal colonies, and persecution of Jews. Americans rather admired Japan, which quickly copied everything Western and embraced dynamic, modern values. Accordingly, when the Japanese mounted their 1904 sneak attack on the Russian fleet at Port Arthur in China, President Theodore Roosevelt applauded them as the "plucky little Nips." (They didn't seem quite so cute when they repeated the stunt in 1941 against us.) Roosevelt personally mediated the Treaty of Portsmouth (New Hampshire) that ended the war. Japan's victory in the 1904–1905 Russo-Japanese War attracted other Asians (Chinese and Vietnamese) to copy Japan and resist European takeover. Japan's taste for imperial expansion was only whetted.

mean eventual collision with the United States and started quietly thinking about it after World War I. When U.S. Colonel Billy Mitchell demonstrated that aircraft could sink ships in 1926, the Japanese military delegation paid special attention.

The Japanese army in southern Manchuria—there since victory over the Russians—decided on its own to seize all of Manchuria in 1931. They staged a fake bombing and then "punished" the Chinese. Tokyo politicians who opposed this were assassinated. Japan set up the puppet state of **Manchukuo**, but U.S. Secretary of State Henry Stimson did not recognize it. Stimson's **nonrecognition** doctrine showed our indignation in a verbal rather than military way, and Tokyo didn't take it seriously. As Stimson recalled later, the Japanese bomb at the Mukden railroad tracks in 1931 led straight to Pearl Harbor in 1941 and Hiroshima in 1945. By the mid-1930s, the Japanese government was in the hands of the military and its allies. In 1937, Japan began the slow conquest of China and was still at it when Tokyo capitulated in 1945. The United States hotly denounced every Japanese move, but words unsupported by power are rarely taken seriously.

The U.S. military was remiss in not anticipating Pearl Harbor. Many signs pointed to it, but the intelligence was scattered and under no single authority. (One upshot: the

Manchukuo Japanese puppet state in Manchuria, 1931–1945.

nonrecognition Refusal to grant diplomatic recognition.

embargo Ban on shipping goods to certain countries.

attaché Military officer serving in an embassy, a legal spy.

Turning Point

THE U.S.–JAPAN WAR

Was war between the United States and Japan inevitable? It was as long as we were China's friend and protector. If we had been willing to look the other way as Japan pillaged China—using live Chinese, including babies, for bayonet practice—we could have avoided war with Japan. The entire Far East would be united under a single, hostile hand, which then would have linked up with Hitler to divide and dominate Eurasia.

Yes, we could have defined our interests narrowly, ending at Hawaii, but the world in general and Asia in particular would have been an uncomfortable place for us, to say nothing of those suffering under Imperial Japanese rule. The Japanese view of themselves paralleled the Nazi view of Germans as a superior, conquering race. Recognizing kindred spirits, Hitler put aside his Nordic image of race to declare Japanese "honorary Aryans."

If the United States had had strong forces in the Pacific and the readiness to use them, that might have persuaded the Japanese militarists to desist. But the United States was lightly armed and uninterested in going to war, and the Japanese militarists knew it. Instead of firm military steps, Washington used verbal protests and **embargoes** to try to make Japan stop conquering China. The Japanese thought we were bluffing and supposed they would call our bluff at Pearl Harbor.

The calculation omitted the crucial psychological factor—how Americans would react. The brilliant Admiral Yamamoto who planned Pearl Harbor knew he was awakening a sleeping giant and warned Tokyo. He had served several years in Washington as naval **attaché** and knew how Americans would react, but as a good soldier he obeyed orders. The U.S. reaction exceeded his fears. Americans instantly put aside isolationism and rose with vengeful hatred on December 7, 1941.

second-order consequence The later impact of a policy choice.

creation of the Central Intelligence Agency to collate all intelligence data.) Where had the Japanese fleet disappeared to? Why was a special telegram (whose code we had broken) scheduled from Tokyo to the Japanese embassy in Washington on December 7? And the complacent U.S. commanders in Hawaii had depth-charged one Japanese minisub and sighted their air squadrons on radar but didn't understand they were under attack until the bombs fell.

Pearl Harbor gave one major break to the Americans. By chance—or was it chance?—the carriers *Lexington* and *Enterprise* were on maneuvers at sea that day, and carriers were the ships that really mattered in the Pacific war. The battleships and cruisers that went down at Pearl were largely irrelevant. Pearl Harbor roused the Americans

Turning Point

WHAT SET UP NORTH KOREA?

The world's first Communist dynasty—the current dictator is the son of the founding dictator—North Korea got its start in the way World War II ended. Not knowing that the atomic bomb then nearing completion would actually work, Roosevelt at Yalta in early 1945 persuaded Stalin to enter the war against Japan three months after Germany surrendered. (Moscow and Tokyo had adhered faithfully to their 1941 neutrality pact.) When Truman learned that the bomb worked—he was at Potsdam conferring with Stalin after Germany's defeat—he tried to talk Stalin out of entering the war with Japan, but Stalin was happy to grab new territory.

Just as the U.S. bombs exploded at Hiroshima and Nagasaki in early August of 1945, Soviet forces smashed the Japanese in Manchuria. This brought Communist power into North Korea where Stalin set up a puppet Communist regime under Kim Il Sung. The expansion of Soviet influence in Northeast Asia, originally meant just to finish off Japan, led to the Korean War in 1950 and to an aggressive North Korea that kidnaps Japanese children (so its spies can perfect their Japanese), practices terrorism against South Korea, sells missiles to Middle East regimes, and develops nuclear bombs.

For a few years, North Korea, now under Dear Leader Kim Jong Il, looked like it might come out of its shell. As some 2 million North Koreans died of hunger in the 1990s (under the slogan, "Let's Eat Just Two Meals a Day!"), Pyongyang made contacts with Seoul, Tokyo, and Washington, asking for food and money but continued its nuclear program to show how tough it is. President Bush named North Korea one of the "axis of evil" in January 2002. Pyongyang took this literally and feared a U.S. invasion, which its nukes would deter. (Iran feared the same and also works toward nuclear weapons.) Washington immediately read this as a nuclear threat. North Korea, paranoid and ignorant of the outside world, is a far more dangerous nuclear threat than Iraq had ever been, one that might force Japan to develop its own nukes. Even Beijing worries about North Korea—not least because thousands of desperate North Koreans seek refuge in China each year—and has urged Pyongyang to join multilateral talks to defuse tensions.

Policy analysts use **second-order consequence** to designate an aftereffect, often unforeseen and undesirable, that flows from a policy's initial result. A third-order consequence is the same, only one step later. With Korea, the initial World War II decision brought an initial consequence of Soviet power in North Korea. A second-order consequence was the Korean War. A third-order consequence is the current dangerous nuclear impasse. The moral: Be careful with those initial decisions; they bring unexpected consequences.

without seriously harming them. Could Roosevelt have had an inkling of what Japan was up to and decided to let it happen? There is zero direct evidence, but we do know that FDR had promised Churchill to bring America into the war by the end of 1941. For the two Western leaders, Pearl was perfect: An enthusiastic America was now in the war, something that would have been impossible on December 6.

Could the war have ended sooner? A "war party" of extreme militarists in Tokyo would not consider calling it quits, and they prevailed. One of their arguments was that the "unconditional surrender" demanded by the Allies seemed to include getting rid of Emperor Hirohito, still regarded by some Japanese as a living god. Actually, that was never the Allies' plan, but there was no way to communicate this to Tokyo. Again, misunderstanding fed war.

Were the atomic bombs absolutely necessary? No, but we didn't know that at the time. As usual in war, Japan presented an image of willingness to fight forever. Japanese soldiers often refused to surrender. (The unofficial U.S. policy of executing some Japanese prisoners contributed to this.) A U.S. invasion of the main Japanese islands would have been bloody. But the war had become impossible for Japan. American submarines had cut Japanese shipping, and American air attacks had burned cities, industries, and crops. If the war had lasted another year, millions of Japanese would have starved to death. We didn't realize how close Tokyo was to surrender in the summer of 1945.

And the United States had, at great expense, just produced and tested the first atomic bombs. It seemed a pity not to use them. Some radical historians argue that Truman wanted to drop the bombs to show Stalin how tough we were and that we weren't going to put up with his demands. The evidence for this alleged "atomic diplomacy," however, is disputed. Truman ordered the bombings because he wanted to get the war over with. Was it immoral? Would death by starvation of millions of Japanese have been moral? Could we have dropped just the one Hiroshima bomb on August 6, 1945? Tokyo, still torn between war and peace parties, did not reply. The Nagasaki bomb came August 9, the emperor tilted against the war, and Japan asked for peace the next day. Ultimately, the Japanese can blame only their own militarists for the horror.

■ From Rubble to Riches

Japan's cities after the war were seas of gray rubble. A military occupation government under General Douglas MacArthur ran the country. Hirohito was demoted from living god to ordinary human but stayed figurehead emperor. A new constitution—still called the "MacArthur constitution" because it was drafted by Americans on his staff—set up a British-style system in 1946.

Economically, the defeat had certain beneficial aftereffects. The Japanese had nothing else to do with their energy but work. Everyone was poor; there was a rough equality. Gone was the dream of imperial expansion; they would have to make do with their little archipelago. Expectations were low; Japanese concentrated on survival and did not ask for much. At first Japanese products were cheap copies of American and European goods made of old tin cans. "Made in Japan" meant shoddy.

High-quality Japanese goods started appearing with the Korean War. Photojournalists tried Nikon and Canon lenses on their German cameras and found they were excellent.

Economics

Like medieval alchemists, American observers from the 1960s through the 1980s made a small industry trying to divine what the Japanese did that made them so productive. Many saw a combination of factors:

1. A political culture that stresses cooperation, as opposed to the fierce and sometimes destructive U.S. individualism. Employees work for the good of the firm, not just for themselves. Japanese unions rarely strike; that would hurt the company.

2. Modest pay for all members of the firm, from worker to president. Rather than suck money out of the company, Japanese want to make sure it prospers. Japanese executives of large firms make half of what their U.S. counterparts do.

3. A better-educated work force. Most Japanese graduate from high school, and their schools are demanding, especially in math. (Japanese high school graduates on average know more math than American college graduates.) Only three-quarters of Americans graduate from high school, some with only partial literacy and numeracy. International tests of math and science abilities show East Asia, led by Singapore, clustering at the top, far ahead of the United States.

4. Lifetime employment in key sectors of Japanese industry. Major manufacturers, covering about 30 percent of the work force, tried to guarantee their people lifetime jobs. This built terrific employee loyalty and meant companies could invest in training, knowing the worker won't leave. U.S. employees at all levels easily change firms either for better jobs or because they're "downsized" (fired).

5. Bank loans to fund expansion rather than sale of stock, as in most U.S. companies. Japanese banks take the long view; they want to make sure of their loans rather than wring maximum quick profits from risky loans, the pattern of many U.S. banks. U.S. shareholders also demand speedy returns on their money. Some Japanese loans, to be sure, were mistakes that left Japanese banks a lot poorer.

6. Long-term thinking within Japanese firms. Profits this year or the next are not so important; dominating the market in five or ten years is what counts. In a U.S. corporation, managers either make bigger profits for the shareholders every quarter or they're out. Without immediate profits to buoy its stock price, the firm will be "raided," taken over by hustlers who milk it for assets and then throw it away. Result: U.S. firms think short term.

7. Major investment in research and development. Because they're building for the long term, Japanese firms invest millions in new designs. This leads to tremendous technological innovation and the domination of more markets as U.S. designs fall behind.

8. Careful attention to efficiency, productivity, and quality. Japanese workers actually come in early, on their own time, to participate in "quality-control circles" to improve plant operations. Workers are encouraged to spot flaws on the assembly line. The U.S. attitude, of both managers and workers: "You didn't say 'good,' you said 'Tuesday.'"

9. Hands-on managers who roll up their sleeves and help on the shop floor. Japanese managers do not form a separate caste but mix freely with workers. Arrogant U.S. managers tend to hold themselves above and apart from workers. When Japanese managers take over a U.S. factory, it runs better.

10. A guiding hand from the Tokyo government. MITI (now METI) was sometimes described as the brains of Japanese government. MITI officials, the smartest in Tokyo, made suggestions and arranged loans for "sunrise" industries and politely told "sunset" industries to get into new lines or die. American industry hates governmental planning.

Soon the cameras—at first blatant copies but soon quite original—were excellent too, and Japan replaced Germany in the camera business. A GI took his U.S.-made Wollensak tape recorder to a dingy Tokyo shop for repair. The owner decided the machine was not so mysterious; he copied it and founded Sony. (There is no more Wollensak.)

In all this, desperation gave the Japanese a fine, competitive edge. They had to work harder and smarter, innovate more, and boost productivity. Both workers' wages and executives' salaries stayed low. Companies did not feel confined to a single product line; they continually branched out.

Japanese growth rates, for many years at or above 10 percent a year, awed the rest of the world. Japan is now the third largest industrial economy in the world, after the United States and China (Germany is fourth). And it has less than half the U.S. population. Japan's success gives several hopeful lessons: A poor nation can quickly climb from the Third World to the First. The poor country has a competitive edge over rich ones by dint of low wage rates. Natural resources are not the basis for growth; human resources are. Japan's stable population—actually it has begun to decline—shows that rapid population growth in the Third World slows as the country industrializes.

Take the "Secrets of Japan's Success" (see box on page 272) with many grains of salt. By 1990 Japan suffered recession, bad debts, and tumbling stock and property markets. Some of Japan's once-praised features made things worse: foolish loans, not enough attention to profit, inability to let failed banks and businesses go bankrupt, and (thanks to poor advice from MITI) overexpansion of major industries. Japan has eleven (11!) car makers, most losing money. Some Japanese giants, such as Sony, never sought or got government help. Many economists now think that Japan just got its economic "fundamentals" right:

Economics

ASIA'S GROWTH TIGERS

By the 1970s, four smaller Pacific Rim countries had rapidly growing economies—South Korea, Taiwan, Hong Kong, and Singapore—sometimes called the "Four Tigers" or "Four Little Dragons." As Japan's wages rose and its productivity gains slowed, the four lands used lower wages and strong work ethics to earn much of the world market in clothing, footwear, consumer electronics, tools, and shipbuilding. Their economic growth followed Japan's.

Two of the four, South Korea and Taiwan, turned into full-fledged democracies in the 1980s. Singapore stayed under the thumb of a forceful leader and a single party that tolerated little criticism. In time, it too may join the ranks of full democracies. Hong Kong—a British colony for a century and a half—started demanding democracy, but Britain gave it back to China in 1997. Beijing promised to respect Hong Kong's freedoms and capitalism but slowly choked them off as it restored Shanghai as China's great commercial hub, as it had been before World War II. Shanghai will soon be East Asia's financial center.

Other Asian lands tried to follow the Four Tigers, with mixed success. Malaysia, Thailand, and Indonesia showed rapid growth in the 1980s until currency collapses in 1997 slowed them down. The first two recovered, but in Indonesia massive corruption, ethnic unrest, and inept leadership threatened to pull it apart into a "zone of chaos" and major regional headache. Now India (population: 1 billion) has shed its anticapitalist founding biases and plunged into globalization with fast inroads into computer software.

APEC   Asia-Pacific Economic Cooperation; loose organization aimed at free trade among Pacific rim countries.

yen bloc   Areas of East Asia where Japan is the major investor.

low inflation, low interest rates, rising productivity, and high savings rates that provided ample capital for business expansion. The other factors did little except sell books and lectures in the United States on the "secrets" of Japan's success. And if the U.S. economy was so bad, why did it perform so well in the 1990s, precisely when the Japanese economy was in a prolonged slump?

◼ What Went Wrong?

In 1997, East Asia's financial systems stumbled, and the world feared a major crash. There were several lessons here. First, it showed how important East Asia had become to the world economy. Second, it showed that while these economies had enjoyed stupendous growth, they too could suffer downturns. Third, it showed that they had not done everything right and needed reforms. And fourth, it showed that the rest of the world was now smart enough to rush to the financial rescue to head off a ripple effect. China avoided trouble in 1997, but some fear its banking system also disguises weaknesses.

The common problem of many (but not all) of East Asia's economies: banking. Too much money, much of it foreign investment, had flooded in for the poorly developed banking systems of East Asia to handle. They loaned recklessly and sometimes crookedly, to friends or government officials: "crony capitalism." But rapid economic growth masked their mountains of bad debt. When the economies of the region slowed, the debts could not be paid, revealing that some banking and brokerage giants were actually broke. At the first hint of this, speculators dumped these currencies, drastically devaluing them and

Geography

AN EMERGING "YEN BLOC"?

Asia has nothing as formal as the European Union or even the North American Free Trade Association (NAFTA), but it does have the Asia-Pacific Economic Cooperation (**APEC**), an eighteen-nation forum of most countries that touch the Pacific (including the United States, Canada, Mexico, Chile, Australia, and New Zealand). In 1994 APEC informally agreed to move toward a free-trade area. By 2010 the richer APEC members are to end their tariffs on other members' goods.

If this process really covers both sides of the Pacific, all may be well. But if the Asian side forms its own trade bloc it will erect a trade barrier that splits the Pacific. Already, half of East Asia's trade is with other East Asian countries. Some analysts already see East Asia as a Japanese-dominated "**yen bloc**." Japan is the region's biggest investor and does more business with Asia than it does with the United States. China, however, has power ambitions of its own and would not willingly let Japan lead. Sino-Japanese friction and rivalry grow.

making the foreign loans even harder to repay. Asia's stock markets plunged. The prospect of default loomed and, with that, the possibility of worldwide recession. But the major financial countries plus the International Monetary Fund (IMF) assembled multibillion-dollar loan packages in record time, and this calmed the panic.

trade surplus Selling more to other countries than you buy from them.

As in the U.S. savings-and-loans scandal of the 1980s, the problem is a too-close relationship among politicians, banks, and businesses, each doing favors for the other. Bribes ("campaign expenses") flow to politicians, who recommend loans for their business friends, who get the loans from under-regulated banks that reap great profits and reward favorite politicians, all behind a veil of secrecy. The message: Free market, yes; unregulated market, no. By the start of the new millennium, the crisis was over, but many fear that East Asian banking reforms (including China's) are more apparent than real.

Viewed from the twenty-first century, the big story of the second half of the twentieth century was not the Cold War but the shift of the economic center of the world to East Asia. What could go wrong with this economic dynamo? The growth of trade protectionism would snip off economic growth throughout the region. Some countries already put up barriers to East Asian products. They do this in part because the Asian exporters are reluctant to import more than a little. Japan is not the only Asian country that limits U.S. products; China, South Korea, and Taiwan are also protectionist and insist on running **trade surpluses**. If trade doesn't roughly balance (over the long term, not necessarily in a given year), eventually it will decline. Currency exchange rates (see next chapter) cause friction. Washington charges Beijing with keeping its currency, the yuan, seriously undervalued in order to export more. China says it will revalue its yuan upward when it is good and ready. This makes the U.S. Congress protectionist against Chinese imports. Prudent steps by all the nations of the Pacific could prevent worse deterioration. And if not, consider the results of the economic protectionism that locked Japan out of trade between the two world wars. Could something similar happen again?

Key Terms

APEC (p. 274)

attaché (p. 269)

authoritarian (p. 263)

bashing (p. 264)

bluff (p. 266)

embargo (p. 269)

Manchukuo (p. 269)

Meiji (p. 268)

MITI (p. 264)

nonrecognition (p. 269)

Open Door (p. 263)

rapprochement (p. 266)

second-order consequence (p. 270)

totalitarian (p. 263)

trade deficit (p. 264)

trade surplus (p. 275)

yen bloc (p. 274)

Key Web Sites

China Information Office
http://www.china.org.cn

Center for Defense Information, Asia Forum
http://www.cdi.org/asia/fa/asp

Asahi Shimbun (Tokyo daily)
http://www.asahi.com/english/asahi/index.html

Daily Yomiuri On-Line (Tokyo daily)
http.//www.yomiuri.co.jp/index-e.htm

Taiwan Information Office
http://www.gio.gov.tw/

Chinese Foreign Ministry
http://www.fmprc.gov.cn

South Korean Embassy
http://www.korea.emb.washington.dc.us/KoreaGov.htm

Singapore Government
http://www.gov.sg/

Japan's Ministry of Foreign Affairs
http://www.mofa.go.jp/whats.html

Hong Kong Government
http://www.info.gov.hk/

Embassy of the People's Republic of China
http://www.china-embassy.org/

Further Reference

Alexander, Arthur J. *The Japanese Economy since the End of the Miracle: Trouble, Bubble, and Muddle*. Lanham, MD: Lexington Books, 2001.

Bush, Richard C. *Untying the Knot: Making Peace in the Taiwan Strait*. Washington, D.C.: Brookings, 2005.

Fishman, Ted C. *China, Inc.: How the Rise of the Next Superpower Challenges America and the World*. New York: Scribner, 2005.

Garrison, Jean A. *Making China Policy: From Nixon to G. W. Bush*. Boulder, CO: Lynne Rienner, 2005.

Gutmann, Ethan. *Losing the New China: A Story of American Commerce, Desire and Betrayal*. San Francisco, CA: Encounter, 2003.

Kornberg, Judith F., and John R. Faust. *China in World Politics,* 2nd ed. Boulder, CO: Lynne Rienner, 2005.

LaFeber, Walter. *The Clash: A History of U.S.-Japan Relations.* New York: Norton, 1997.

Lim, Robyn. *The Geopolitics of East Asia: Search for Equilibrium.* Philadelphia, PA: Taylor & Frances, 2003.

McGregor, James. *One Billion Customers: Lessons from the Front Lines of Doing Business in China.* New York: Free Press, 2005.

Terrill, Ross. *The New Chinese Empire: And What It Means for the United States.* New York: Basic Books, 2004.

Tyler, Patrick. *A Great Wall: Six Presidents and China.* New York, PublicAffairs, 1999.

Zhao, Suisheng, ed. *Chinese Foreign Policy: Pragmatism and Strategic Behavior.* Armonk, NY: M. E. Sharpe, 2004.

CHAPTER 18

THE UNITED STATES AND GLOBALIZATION

1. Is globalization still growing or has it peaked?
2. What international economic institutions did the United States sponsor to promote global prosperity?
3. What caused, deepened, and finally solved the Great Depression?
4. Which countries are the richest? Why is this tricky to calculate?
5. Which country has the biggest foreign debt?
6. How does NAFTA differ from the European Union?
7. If free trade is so good, why is it hard to expand?
8. Which is more likely, globalization or regionalization?

We should be asking three questions about globalization: (1) Is it still the main trend? (2) Is it desirable? (3) Is it stable? Our take: It never covered the entire globe and now may be fading. It is largely confined to a broad band stretching from West Europe across North America to the Pacific Rim, but even here plenty of barriers block truly open trade. Some globalization seeps down into newly industrializing countries, but the really poor countries are still out of it. Globalization is generally a good thing, but not all are able to take advantage of it. We now see that it is also unstable, vulnerable to banking and currency crises and trade protectionism. Globalization depends totally on world markets staying open, and many are now quietly limiting them. Only U.S. leadership can keep world trade open, but the United States is turning protectionist. Remember what happened the last time world trade constricted: the Great Depression.

■ What Is a Dollar Worth?

The dollar is the world's **reserve currency**, much as the British pound was in the nineteenth century. But few currencies are steady, and defining their **exchange rate** is hard. The basic choice is between **fixed** and **floating exchange rates**. China uses a fixed rate in relation to the dollar, one that keeps the **yuan** undervalued in relation to the dollar. This gives China a terrific advantage in gaining world markets but infuriates countries, such as the United States, whose industries are put out of business by Chinese goods. Accordingly, Washington urges China to "float" the yuan.

A floating exchange rate uses the market to determine the value of a dollar or yuan. When foreigners want more dollars, they bid the price up. When they want fewer—the case recently—they bid the price down. In theory, floating currencies find their own level based on who produces what and which currencies are the safest. In practice, currency markets—like all markets—overshoot both ways, like roller coasters. All **bubbles** burst. Speculators bet which currency is going up or down, and these billion-dollar bets themselves often make it happen.

reserve currency   World standard for money, used for most trade deals.

exchange rate   How much one currency buys of another.

fixed exchange rate   One currency buys a set number of other currencies.

floating exchange rate   One currency buys a varying number of other currencies, depending on the market for them.

yuan   (symbol: ¥) China's currency (in 2006, ¥8=$1).

bubble   Market that has gone too high.

Keynesian economics   The use of government spending to fight recessions.

Concepts

GREAT DEPRESSION

The Great Depression dominated the 1930s and led to World War II. It started with a U.S. recession in 1929 that got much worse with the collapse of the overvalued New York stock market that fall and the disastrous 1930 Hawley-Smoot tariff. Other countries immediately retaliated by raising their own tariffs, and world trade shriveled. A "liquidity crisis" appeared: not enough cash flowing to buy the world's goods. Factories and banks closed, and unemployment climbed to over one-quarter of the work force in the industrialized lands.

Most of the world's governments did the wrong things and made matters worse. They prescribed balanced budgets to get out of the Depression, but these further depressed the economy. The Depression did not cure itself. In the United States, Franklin D. Roosevelt's administration cautiously applied the new **Keynesian economics** to reflate

the economy. Instead of balancing the budget, the federal government went mildly into debt to provide jobs, loans, and price supports. Aside from the symbolic lift, however, little improved. In Germany, unemployment brought Hitler to power in 1933. He applied a massive Keynesian solution: gigantic public works projects and large government loans to get industry moving again. He also started World War II, and that cured the Great Depression for all countries.

Since then, there have been no depressions. Smaller economic downturns are called "recessions," defined as two or more consecutive quarters (i.e., at least half a year) of a declining GDP. Some economists believe that government controls and policies prevent major downturns. Others worry that factors leading to another world depression are in place.

The shock of the Depression and World War II made the major trading countries turn from floating to fixed exchange rates with the **Bretton Woods** agreement (see box below). The West German mark and Japanese yen, for example, went at rather low rates, respectively 4 and 310 to the dollar. Americans could buy Volkswagens and Sonys at good prices, and German and Japanese industry surged;they became export giants. By the 1960s, pricey U.S. products were losing out to West European and Japanese competition. U.S. corporations and tourists pumped dollars overseas. The United States became a debtor nation and stayed that way.

If we had been under a system of floating exchange rates, the dollar might have devalued itself. But the system of semifixed rates kept the dollar too high. The massive U.S. spending for the Vietnam War, for example, created not only domestic inflation but, when the dollars were sent abroad to pay for our purchases, inflation worldwide. We exported inflation. The Bretton Woods agreement got shakier and shakier. The dollar was clearly too high, and for our own and the world's good, something had to be done about it. President Nixon finally devalued the dollar in 1971 (see box below) and ushered in an era of floating exchange rates.

Over many years a dollar has bought fewer euros or yen. U.S. budget deficits of a quarter or a third of a trillion dollars persuaded many that the dollar was an unsound currency, so "speculators" sold them in favor of other currencies. Speculators are not necessarily greedy or evil gamblers (although they do tend to place multimillion dollar bets). They can be anyone with currency on hand: corporate executives, bankers, investors, even tourists. If they hear the dollar is "under pressure," that is, more are being sold than bought, they tend to bet the pressure will continue and they sell their dollars for other currency, such as euros, Swiss francs, or yen. They fear that if they hang on to their dollars they will lose value. Thus, even a rumor that a currency is under pressure may bring a wave of speculative selling of that currency that makes the rumor come true. In 1993, financier George Soros bet that the British pound would soon be devalued. He sold pounds for other currencies and overnight made $1 billion. (He has also bet wrong and lost billions.) No currency is completely stable, not even the dollar.

Economics

BRETTON WOODS AGREEMENT

Meeting at a New Hampshire resort in 1944, the Western allies agreed to fixed rates of exchange based on the dollar. An ounce of gold was to be worth $35, and other currencies were to be worth a set number of dollars. Bretton Woods was designed to coordinate policy among central banks, which would buy and sell dollars to fine-tune supply and demand. The system was not totally fixed, for if one currency got too far out of line, it could be adjusted downward (devalued) or upward (revalued). For about a generation, the Bretton Woods system worked pretty well and aided West Europe's and Japan's postwar recovery. But it was based on the fiction that gold was worth only $35 an ounce, and when that became totally unbelievable, the system cracked. Nixon ended the gold-backed dollar in 1971.

The Biggest Debtor

One area of concern about the U.S. dollar is the large and growing U.S. foreign-trade deficit, fueled in part by the tremendous
debt that America runs at all levels—international, federal, business, and personal. Americans spend money they don't have.

stagflation Slow economic
growth plus inflation.

Many top economists and business people and even the International Monetary Fund (see
box on page 282) warn that America's huge foreign debt could lead to a loss of confidence
in the dollar and a long and deep global recession.

Americans consume more than they produce and import about a third more than they
export, making the United States the world's biggest debtor nation (far ahead of Mexico or
Brazil), owing a trillion dollars. We are still among the world's biggest exporters, but we are
even bigger importers. We live beyond our means, paying for foreign products with overvalued dollars.

This works only as long as our trading partners continue to accept dollars, which they
did during the long Cold War. Billions of dollars flowed overseas, and many of them stayed
there, becoming the world's reserve currency. This was great for us. We pumped dollars
overseas and did not have to redeem many of them with our own goods; the foreigners were
content to hold the dollars forever. This was the origin of the "Eurodollar" (page 254).
After many years, though, as foreigners notice the size of the U.S. budget and trade deficits,
they worry about the value of the dollars they hold. Now, depending on economic conditions, foreigners devalue dollars by selling lots of them for euros, Swiss francs, or yen. The

Economics

ADDICTED TO OIL

Oil plays a mammoth and sometimes destabilizing
role in the U.S. and world economy. Through World
War II, the United States was the world's biggest
oil producer and exporter, but then the Persian Gulf
fields came on line, keeping world oil prices low. In
response, Americans built energy-inefficient cars,
homes, suburbs, and industries. Our main trading
partners try to avoid oil addiction by taxing oil heavily and encouraging energy efficiency. Europeans
pay some $6 a gallon for gas, use a third less fuel
per mile, and drive half as many miles as Americans. Overall, an American uses two and a half
times as much energy as a European or Japanese,
making us vulnerable to oil cutoffs or price hikes.

Americans received a fourth reminder of this in
2005, when gas prices doubled. The first warning
came with the 1973 Arab-Israeli war, after which

world oil prices jumped from about $2.50 to $11
a barrel; the second with the 1979 Iranian revolution, which in four years brought oil to $34 a bar-
rel. The result was a **stagflation** that kept U.S.
workers' incomes stuck at the 1973 level. Then oil
prices slumped to $11 a barrel in 1998, U.S. gaso-
line prices dropped to $1 a gallon, and Americans
purchased more large SUVs and pickups. Later,
though, OPEC got its act together and forced the
price back up to over $70 a barrel. China and India,
with growing energy appetites, suggest that oil will
never be $30 a barrel again. In 2006 Americans
paid over $3 a gallon at the pump. After several
warnings, Americans should learn about energy
vulnerability and efficiency. The next oil crisis could
severely damage the U.S. economy and a president's chances for reelection.

conventional wisdom   A set of
unexamined but widely believed
assumptions.

austerity   Belt-tightening; major
budget cutting.

euro, for example, debuted in 1999 at $1.17, fell to $0.85 in 2001, but by 2004 topped $1.25 as investors worried about U.S. budget deficits. If the dollar declines gradually and moderately it is not a bad thing, as it makes U.S. products cheaper on the world market.

But if the dollar becomes too dubious and its value drops suddenly, what could replace it as the world reserve currency, the standard money of international commerce? Europe disliked the unstable dollar and proposed its new euro currency as an alternative to the dollar; worldwide investors began shifting to euros. But some question the reliability of the euro, as many European governments exceed the EMU's limit of 3 percent budget deficit. Two-thirds of world foreign-exchange reserves are in dollars, one-fourth in euros, 4 percent in Japanese yen, and 3 percent in British pounds. This mix may shift away from the dollar if the United States cannot cure its persistent budgetary and foreign-trade deficits.

■ Globalization and Its Enemies

In the 1990s globalization became the **conventional wisdom**: Everyone said it, so it must be true. Corporate executives said: "Think global. There are no more one-country markets any more. Our products are now made in several countries and sold in many countries. And our competition is doing the same." They told their workers: "Restrain your wage demands or we'll move this operation overseas. Remember, you can be replaced by an Indian." (Many are.) Globalization thus held down wages and inflation, but employees, worried about their jobs going overseas, fear it. Consumers heard: "You get the best products at the lowest prices. Never mind where it's made, just enjoy it." The trouble with conventional wisdom, though, is that it's often wrong. There was nothing automatic or inevitable about globalization.

Economics

INTERNATIONAL MONETARY FUND

The IMF was established at Bretton Woods (see box on page 280) to keep exchange rates stable and help countries pay their international debts. IMF headquarters is in Washington, but most countries are members. Funds come from a pool of member countries' contributions. The industrialized First World contributes the lion's share, so it dominates IMF policy.

A sister of the IMF is the World Bank, which makes low-interest loans to developing countries.

Both help countries in need but only if they practice **austerity** and hold down inflation. Some poor countries say these demands are impossible and denounce the IMF and World Bank. Antiglobalists protest the IMF and World Bank and want to abolish them. They got a good target when Paul Wolfowitz—one of the Pentagon architects of the Iraq War—became president of the World Bank.

Economics

WHO IS RICHEST?

Who is richest depends on what you mean by "rich." If you mean overall economic clout, you look at a country's Gross Domestic Product (discussed in Chapter 11), the first column in the table below. This is not "per capita" (divided by population) and is in trillions of dollars. Here even countries commonly called poor—such as China and Brazil—now have considerable global economic clout. GDP can change considerably over the course of a few years. When world oil prices jumped up, Russia's GDP climbed rapidly.

GDP is now usually expressed in **Purchasing Power Parity** (PPP), which takes cost of living into account. The old way, GDP at exchange rates, misleads, as currencies can get seriously under- or overvalued in relation to each other. To correct for this, PPP collects prices on a standard market basket of goods and services in every country.

If by rich you mean how well people live, check the second column in the table below, per capita GDP at PPP. Now Chinese and Brazilians appear as much poorer, although not nearly as poor as the old exchange-rate comparisons made them out to be.

To get a rough idea of how much over- or undervalued a currency is in relation to the dollar, the British newsweekly The Economist publishes its "Big Mac Index," a quick PPP comparison of the cost of the identical hamburger worldwide. The Big Mac is actually a mini-market basket that includes ingredients, rent, energy, and labor. Although it's too urban and tourist-oriented to rely on, the Big Mac Index usually points the same way as more complicated calculations. Big Mac prices go up and down worldwide as currency rates change. With the euro and pound high in early 2006, a Big Mac in Germany and Britain was more expensive than the U.S. price of $3.15, indicating that the euro was overvalued. Cheap Big Macs, as in Russia and China, indicated their currencies were undervalued. Many countries like to keep their currencies cheap to boost exports and economic growth.

Country	2005 GDP (Trillion)	2005 Per Capita GDP	Early 2006 Big Mac in a Big City
United States	12.3	$40,800	$3.15
China	8.9	6,800	1.30
Japan	4.0	31,500	2.19
Germany	2.5	30,400	3.51[*]
Britain	1.8	30,300	3.32
Russia	1.6	11,100	1.60
Brazil	1.5	8,400	2.74
Mexico	1.1	10,000	2.66
Canada	1.0	34,000	3.01

[*]price in euro area

Sources: CIA World Factbook, The Economist.

purchasing power parity (PPP)
True worth of a currency; what it
can actually buy. (See page 283.)

Victorian Related to reign of
Britain's Queen Victoria,
1837–1901.

We need some perspective on globalization. First, it is not truly global. The World Bank found that roughly 3 billion people (half the world's population) live in twenty-four low-income "globalizer" countries (mostly in Asia) that increased their international trade and enjoyed an average of 5 percent a year growth in per capita GDP in the 1990s. How can you tell if a country is a globalizer? By an increase in trade as a percent of its GDP. But another 2 billion live in countries (mostly in Africa and Muslim lands) where trade as a percent of GDP has diminished—"nonglobalizers"—and they grew poorer by about 1 percent a year. Free trade works, but it needs certain policy and cultural prerequisites. Some countries take to it, others not.

Globalization is not a new concept. Basically, "globalization" is another word for saying "lots of trade among countries." The practice of globalization began with the Portuguese and the Spanish voyages of discovery to Asia and to the Americas, which produced a world trade boom during the sixteenth century. Then Great Britain led a "**Victorian** globalization" in the nineteenth century, but World War I and the Depression ended it. After World War II, a U.S.-led globalization zoomed exports as a percent of the world's GDP from 8 percent in 1950 to 28 percent in 2000. There are many reasons for the new globalization:

Globalization: Tokyo youth get their cholesterol at McDonald's, Japan's biggest restaurant chain. The second biggest is Kentucky Fried Chicken. (Michael G. Roskin)

1. American corporations invested heavily in West Europe after the war, setting the style for transnational (probably a better name than multinational) firms that were delighted to manufacture and sell anywhere.
2. Tariff barriers fell. Pushed by GATT (now the WTO), tariffs are at an all-time low. (There are still, to be sure, other barriers to free trade.)
3. Transportation became cheap. Thanks to containerization (loading goods at the factory in big metal boxes), it can be cheaper to ship across an ocean than across a country. High-end and perishable goods can be airfreighted at reasonable cost.

4. Communication became instantaneous and cheap. International phone calls, faxes, and the Internet make your contacts around the world seem like they're next door. (One by-product of this communication revolution: English is confirmed as the standard world language.)

5. Capital flowed across borders. International banking expanded, making transfers and loans quick and easy. This also created a world capital market in which funds seek investments that yield the highest returns.

6. Wages in the Global South were so much lower than First World labor costs that many firms set up shop in China, India, and other newly industrializing lands. Especially burdensome are West Europe's high "social overhead": taxes for medical insurance, pensions, unemployment, and welfare.

Some supporters of globalization, such as *New York Times* columnist Thomas Friedman, got ecstatic, hailing it as a revolution, a new historical epoch. They claimed it would uplift the developing countries, bring down dictatorships, and lead to peace. Said Friedman only half in jest: "No two countries with McDonald's have ever fought each other." (Actually, India, Pakistan, and Yugoslavia had McDonald's.) Borders become irrelevant, as information, capital, and goods move like an "electronic herd" to wherever there is a market. Governments and banks must offer open, incorrupt business environments; otherwise investors will stay away. And the whole process is self-enforcing; governments just get in the way. Like the Internet, no one is in charge.

Some thinkers were skeptical. Economist Paul Krugman noted that most goods are still consumed in the countries where they are produced; only a fraction are exported.

Economics

FROM GATT TO WTO

The founders of the IMF (see box on page 282) in 1947 wanted to set up an International Trade Organization (ITO) with enforcement powers, but many feared the ITO would infringe on national sovereignty (a point some Americans still fear). As a weaker substitute, the General Agreement on Tariffs and Trade (GATT) was a treaty among most nations to work for tariff reductions. Headquartered in Geneva, GATT members for decades slogged away at tariff and other trade barriers in a series of "rounds," each lasting many years and with over a hundred countries haggling. Over half a century, GATT cut tariffs by around 90 percent.

GATT turned into the World Trade Organization (WTO) in 1995. It now has 149 members (including China but not yet Russia) and more power than GATT. WTO has a court to adjudicate trade disputes. Soon there were angry charges of unfair practices, especially between the EU and United States and between the developing and rich countries. The 2003 WTO meeting in Cancún, Mexico, collapsed as Global South delegates walked out in protest over the high agricultural tariffs and huge subsidies—roughly $1 billion a day—that the EU, Japan, and the United States use to protect their farmers (and win their votes). These drive poor countries' products off the world market and keep them poor. We keep saying "free trade" but, especially in agriculture, do not practice it ourselves.

WTO   World Trade Organization, UN-related body, successor to GATT, promotes free trade.

protectionism   Policy of keeping out foreign goods.

Globalization in this view is mostly hype. In terms of percentage of GDP, Europe before World War I exported and imported more than now. In those days, some thought countries were too busy and happy to ever go to war again: Trade interdependence would ensure peace. In 1914, this globalization collapsed and did not revive until after World War II. Does globalization cause peace, or does peace cause globalization? Could war end the recent round of globalization?

And in Seattle in 1999, we learned that some hated and feared globalization and tried to block or reverse it. At the Seattle meeting of the World Trade Organization (**WTO**), as talks among members stalled over important differences, on the streets protesters denounced the whole enterprise. They saw globalization as an elite thing guided only by transnational corporations and government specialists. No one votes on it. Workers saw their jobs being exported to low-wage countries. Environmentalists saw global pollution. Leftists protested exploitive wages and working conditions in Global South sweatshops. Nationalists feared erosion of U.S. sovereignty. And self-styled "anarchists" just had fun trashing downtown Seattle.

The charge of exploitation of workers in the Global South doesn't hold up. They do not come from a rural idyll; they flee rural poverty and flock to the cities. What are "sweatshops" to us are great jobs to them, vastly better than picking through garbage dumps. Some Global Southerners pay bribes to get a factory job paying $2 a day. If the wages were too low and working conditions too bad, factories in the Global South (or anywhere, for that matter) would get no workers. Actually, multinationals (many U.S.-based) pay above-average wages and introduce new technologies. If workers were paid First World wages, their products could not sell on the world market. Their low wages give poor countries a chance to start climbing the ladder.

Likewise, First World environmental standards applied now in the Global South would close many industries. It takes a fairly rich country to afford pollution controls. Most of the Democratic hopefuls of 2004 proposed minimum wages and environmental standards to "help" the Global South. (More likely, it was trade protectionism to win votes from workers who feared the exportation of jobs.) Global South leaders say that is no help at all. They know their recent economic growth is based on trade, and any such restrictions hurt growth. "Helping" the Third World by demanding First World wage and environmental standards would pull the ladder away from those trying climb up it.

The real antiglobalist force, however, is not street protests but old-fashioned trade **protectionism**, much of it coming from Washington. As we discussed in Chapter 11, some U.S. jobs are lost. Traditionally, these have been low-paying, low-skilled factory jobs, but recently all manner of jobs, including high-tech professional ones, have also been sent overseas. American computer specialists who earn $100,000 a year are replaced by Indians at $20,000 a year. Some U.S. telephone support and service operations are now staffed by Indians trained in American accents. Indian radiologists read digitalized American X-rays. Although such trends are overstated (especially by Democrats in an election year), they feed American protectionist sentiments, and both parties quickly respond. Bill Clinton was the last free-trade president. Free trade always has rough going.

■ The Coming of NAFTA

West Europe and Japan contrived ways to keep out U.S. goods and services. The U.S. trade deficit got bigger, and Americans grew cranky at what they perceived as trade unfairness across both oceans. In part to combat this alleged trade discrimination, Washington began building its own trade bloc, the North American Free Trade Association. While never calling NAFTA a warning to or retaliation against the EU or the "yen bloc," the authors believe that is what Washington had in mind when it formed NAFTA (with Canada) in 1988 and expanded it to Mexico in 1992 (ratified after a hard Senate fight in late

Concepts

PROTECTIONISM

Scottish economist Adam Smith was among the first to argue, in 1776, that free trade makes everyone more prosperous: "If a foreign country can supply us with a commodity cheaper than we ourselves can make it, better buy it of them with some part of the produce of our own industry." Even *unilaterally* lowering your trade barriers is good for you. Few people understand it or believe it; historically most countries have kept out foreign goods on the theory that they hurt the domestic economy. They build protective barriers in the form of tariffs and quotas (see pages 251 and 256). You hear one excuse after another for protectionism. Developing countries say they must protect their "infant industries" from more efficient foreign competition to give them a chance to take hold. Developed countries say they must protect their mature industries from foreign goods made with cheap labor. Many argue that the country must not grow dependent on foreign supplies of strategic items.

Everybody wants to protect their farmers, and farm subsidies in rich countries—running at nearly $1 billion *a day!*—are the most egregious form of it. U.S. cotton growers, for example, get $4 billion a year from taxpayers for a crop worth less than that. We then dump our subsidized cotton on the world market at below production cost and devastate struggling Third World cotton growers. Similarly, the EU pays its growers €50 a ton for sugar beets (five times world prices) that nobody needs,

and this drives out Third World producers of cane sugar. Thanks to absurd subsidies, Europe is a major sugar exporter. Neither Europe, nor America, nor Japan has the guts to tell their farmers to go into another line of business. The result is increased Third World poverty and slow economic growth.

Most people instinctively seek trade protection. During the "jobless recovery" of the early 2000s, Americans complained about the "export of jobs" to low-wage countries. To stay competitive, companies have to manufacture where costs are low. Bush 43 talked free trade but became the biggest protectionist in decades with props for steel, agriculture, textiles, and clothing, all based on winning votes. Europe, China, and others brought suits against U.S. trade restrictions before the WTO and threatened retaliation. In late 2003 Bush lifted his tariff on steel, narrowly averting a trade war with Europe. Whatever you do to protect domestic producers angers foreign producers, and they retaliate.

Clinton was far more supportive of free trade, but in 2004 Democrats denounced the Republican administration for "deindustrializing America," always a good vote-getter. Promotion of free trade inherently comes from elites of corporate executives, economists, and some government officials. Left to the masses—or to politicians chasing votes—tariff and other barriers quickly rise, and everyone is the poorer for it.

1993). Washington, looking across both the Atlantic and the Pacific, said in effect, "All right, you lock us out of your area and we'll build our own bloc."

NAFTA and the EU are structurally very different. The EU is a much more highly developed and integrated bloc, one aiming at a single market and European federation. NAFTA has no such aim; it just wants to eliminate tariffs between members, nothing more. The EU has the free flow not only of goods and services but of labor and capital as well. It has a complex governing body, something NAFTA utterly lacks. The EU, since it began as the Common Market, sets up common external tariffs; NAFTA members set their own tariffs with nonmembers.

NAFTA has not had smooth sailing. Although both Canada and the United States benefited from cutting the tariffs between them—they were the world's biggest trading partners before NAFTA anyway—individual industries suffered as production went to the more efficient producers, which is precisely what is supposed to happen. American timbermen or Canadian retail clerks who have lost their jobs are in no mood to discuss the energizing effects of free trade. Polls indicate that many Canadians would be happy to abolish NAFTA, and it could happen.

American and Canadian workers fear competing with low-wage Mexican workers. Ross Perot campaigned against NAFTA ratification, claiming "a giant sucking sound" was the drain of U.S. jobs into Mexico. Actually, in the late 1990s U.S. unemployment dropped to a very low 4 percent. Lower-skilled U.S. jobs had been moving to Mexico for years anyway. People tend to get hysterical over trade liberalization. The effects of NAFTA on the gigantic U.S. economy were almost too trivial to measure. Its effects on Mexico were at first good and helped pull the Mexican economy out of a crisis. But much industrial growth projected for Mexico shifted to China, where wages are much lower. Over the first ten years of NAFTA, Mexico's per capita GDP growth averaged only 1 percent a year.

Mexico's slow growth made many wonder if NAFTA should expand to cover the entire hemisphere. If so, how fast? Discussions on a Free Trade Area of the Americas (FTAA) began in 1997, aimed at creating a thirty-four-nation hemispheric market. It would have fabulous growth potential. Unfortunately, the Bush presidency and U.S. Congress, frightened of worker and voter backlash, go slow or go backwards. Much of Latin America, plagued by slow growth and fearing U.S. domination, oppose a hemispheric trade bloc. Many claim the United States just wants to export freely to Latin America but still protect U.S. agricultural sectors. Brazil complains that the U.S. market for its orange juice—you probably drank some this morning—is unfairly limited to protect Florida growers. Would a president who narrowly won Florida and whose brother is governor of Florida do anything that hurts Florida orange growers? Not a chance. With the myriad of problems like this, efforts to build FTAA flopped at a 2003 meeting at Cancún, Mexico. One big problem with FTAA: It's unpronounceable.

Both NAFTA and WTO aim at lowering trade restrictions and expanding trade, but they are at odds over their geographical scope. A trade bloc, such as NAFTA or the EU, says in effect, "We're for free trade in our region, because that is all we can handle and feel comfortable with. We limit imports from other blocs because they are threats to our jobs." The WTO says in effect, "Make the whole world one big trade bloc; let all goods and services flow everywhere without hindrance." Washington promoted both NAFTA and the WTO, but in the long run they are contradictions.

The more successful WTO is, the less relevant NAFTA or any other trade blocs will be. If WTO really eliminates all trade barriers—something that will take many decades, at best—there will be no point to regional trade blocs that have eliminated barriers between members. If your tariffs and other barriers are already zero with everybody, they cannot be less than zero for your fellow members of NAFTA or the EU.

▮ Trade Wars?

A basic point of international trade is poorly understood. When two or more countries trade, they are in a win-win situation. They are not in a zero-sum game in which what one wins the other loses. Everybody gains; they all get more and better products at lower prices. If, for example, you tried to keep shirt-making in America for the sake of fellow Americans who make shirts, you would have $50 shirts instead of $15 shirts. If you import most of your shirts and export high-tech, high-value-added goods, such as jetliners and oil rigs, you have more well-paid workers at home and they can buy all the shirts they wish. To be sure, some jobs in the United States are lost; they are in the sectors that compete directly with the imports, such as shirt factories. Usually, though, after a while better jobs are gained.

Concepts

GLOBE.COM?

Is the Internet truly revolutionizing the world's flow of information and commerce? Is it binding us together into the "one world" philosophers have dreamed about? Beware of exaggeration. A century and a half ago the telegraph was supposed to make one world. Television was supposed to produce a "global village."

There have been many predictions that new and faster communications will bring peace. They are based on the view that wars and conflict occur because people do not understand other groups and nations. Often they understand each other all too well. Israelis and Palestinians want exactly the same thing: a small land called Palestine. Communications are often used to whip up nationalism and hatred. The independent Arab-language satellite TV station Al Jazeera attracted a huge audience with its broadcasts of tapes of Osama bin Laden and anti-U.S. coverage of the Iraq War.

Now some say that information technology (IT) will bring world peace. The Web and e-mail are growing rapidly and help economic growth. Indian farmers check Chicago soybean prices on the Web to see if they should sell or hold. IT also undermines one-party dictatorships, precisely why China filters the Internet for dangerous words like "freedom" and "democracy." But IT can also carry messages of hate and bomb-making; racists, neo-Nazis, and Islamic terrorists (the "virtual caliphate") are on-line. IT is responsible for much of the recent explosion of inequality. Some bright young people became (briefly) rich from IT, but many—including much of the Global South—are still on the wrong side of the "digital divide." Take IT with a grain of salt.

But, you say, let's suppose that some of the players are intent on minimizing consumption and maximizing exports. They export a lot—with government encouragement—but they import far less, thereby building a massive trade surplus. So much the worse for them. They have worked very hard and accumulated billions of dollars but have chosen to forgo the joy of spending those dollars. They live more poorly than they are entitled to live, and, at their expense, Americans live better. They put their hard-earned money into bad investments, and they suffer economic difficulties, just as Japan has.

But politicians and purveyors of "airport economics" (Paul Krugman's term for threateningly titled paperbacks sold at airport news-stands) persist in telling us that we are in an economic war with much of the rest of the world. It is not a war, however; it is an endless win-win exchange of goods and services. The more barriers that are placed in the way, the slower the gains for all sides. The trouble is that if people and nations as a whole begin to think that they are in an economic war, then they will turn increasingly protectionist. Remember, the road to World War II was paved with high tariffs.

Economic historians point out that global prosperity requires one major country to lead it—to keep trade open, enforce rules, and make its currency the world standard. Without a strong stabilizer nation, trade constricts and prosperity dims. In the nineteenth century, Britain and the pound sterling were indispensable, but a weakened Britain could no longer play stabilizer after World War I, and the world economy spiraled downward in the Depression. After World War II, the United States and its dollars led the world toward ever-freer trade and growing prosperity. But does the United States have the economic strength and political will to continue to lead, or will protectionists bring down the whole structure? The great tasks of statesmanship have shifted to the economic realm, to keeping the globe open to trade. If we don't lead, no one else will.

Key Terms

austerity (p. 282)

Bretton Woods (p. 280)

bubble (p. 279)

conventional wisdom (p. 282)

exchange rate (p. 279)

fixed exchange rate (p. 279)

floating exchange rate (p. 279)

Keynesian economics (p. 279)

protectionism (p. 286)

purchasing power parity (PPP) (p. 284)

reserve currency (p. 279)

stagflation (p. 281)

Victorian (p. 284)

WTO (p. 286)

yuan (p. 279)

Key Web Sites

International Monetary Fund
http://www.imf.org/

World Bank
http://www.worldbank.org/

International Trade Administration
http://www.ita.doc.gov/ita_home/itaabout.html

NAFTA Homepage
http://www.itaiep.doc.gov/nafta/nafta2.htm

World Trade Organization
http://www.wto.org/

Export-Import Bank
http://www.exim.gov/

G8 information Center
http://www.g7.utoronto.ca/

Further Reference

Bhagwati, Jagdish. *In Defense of Globalization*. New York: Oxford University Press, 2004.

Friedman, Thomas L. *The World Is Flat: A Brief History of the Twenty-First Century*. New York: Farrar, Straus and Giroux, 2005.

Grieco, Joseph M., and G. John Ikenberry. *State Power + World Markets: The International Political Economy*. New York: Norton, 2002.

Irwin, Douglas A. *Free Trade under Fire*. Princeton, NJ: Princeton University Press, 2002.

James, Harold. *The End of Globalization: Lessons from the Great Depression*. Cambridge, MA: Harvard University Press, 2001.

Legrain, Philippe. *Open World: The Truth about Globalization*. London: Abacus, 2002.

Mallaby, Sebastian. *The World's Banker: A Story of Failed State, Financial Crises and the Wealth and Poverty of Nations*. New York: Penguin, 2004.

Mandelbaum, Michael. *The Ideas that Conquered the World: Peace, Democracy, and the Free Markets in the Twenty-First Century*. New York: PublicAffairs, 2004.

Naím, Moisés. *Surprises of Globalization*. Washington, D.C.: Carnegie Endowment, 2003.

O'Brien, Robert, and Marc Williams. *Global Political Economy: Evolution and Dynamics*. New York: Palgrave, 2004.

Rapley, John. *Globalization and Inequality: Neoliberalism's Downward Spiral.* Boulder, CO: Lynne Rienner, 2004.

Soros, George. *The Bubble of American Supremacy.* New York: PublicAffairs, 2004.

Stiglitz, Joseph E. *Making Globalization Work.* New York: Norton, 2006.

Veseth, Michael. *Globaloney: Unraveling the Myths of Globalization.* Lanham, MD: Rowman & Littlefield, 2005.

Wolf, Martin. *Why Globalization Works.* New Haven, CT: Yale University Press, 2005.

PART V

THE POLITICS OF A NEW WORLD

Economic pressures are pushing toward some kind of new world, but economics alone cannot make a better world and can even create new conflicts. The world is trying, imperfectly, to civilize conflicts.

Chapter 19 describes the functions and methods of diplomacy and its changing role. Ambassadors are now largely symbolic as foreign policy is increasingly centralized, due to fast communications and travel. Diplomacy focuses on negotiations and compromise, for which there are some rules for success.

Chapter 20 argues that international law (IL) is generally preferred to war. The foundation of IL is consistency and reciprocity, and laws now exist to regulate state behavior in every area of international relations. The growing volume of exchanges, from economic to the Internet, mean more IL, most of which is based on treaties. With no world police, sanctions used to back laws rely on self-help. Although international courts are limited as long as sovereignty reigns, human rights are increasingly a subject of IL.

Chapter 21 describes the new activism of the United Nations. With the end of the Cold War, Security Council vetoes are now rare. Many countries now favor the UN, especially for "peace operations." The short, sad League of Nations and its collective security caution us not to expect a world government. Third-party diplomacy increasingly contains and settles conflicts. UN specialized agencies are indispensable in an integrating world.

Chapter 22 wonders if war has begun to fade. For war, states need motives, opportunity, the will, and an opponent, and these are shrinking. Democracies never fight other democracies. Major-power peace operations also inhibit wars. States tend to fight only if they think they can win, and this is becoming rarer. Preventive diplomacy, peace making, peacekeeping, peace enforcement, and peace building now internationalize wars and move them to resolution. There is, indeed, a new world of international relations.

CHAPTER 19

DIPLOMACY

QUESTIONS TO CONSIDER

1. How did U.S. diplomacy manipulate a Bosnian peace?
2. How did nationalism and democracy hamper traditional diplomacy?
3. Has diplomacy outlived its usefulness?
4. What offices are typically found in a U.S. embassy?
5. How has diplomacy been misused in our time?
6. What are the problems with political appointees as ambassadors?
7. What is the relationship between diplomats and soldiers?
8. Can diplomacy end wars? How?
9. How did Morgenthau think diplomacy could be revived?

In his State of the Union address in early 2002, President Bush charged that Iraq, Iran, and North Korea formed an "axis of evil" that we had to stop. In 2003 we invaded Iraq to make sure that it could not harm us. But for Iran and North Korea—which are actually far greater nuclear dangers—Washington used diplomacy. This raised the question: Why go to war when you can open diplomatic contacts, hold multilateral meetings, and devise ways to lower tensions? To be sure, diplomacy cannot solve every conflict. Each case is different. But with domestic and world opinion critical of the U.S. role in Iraq, the Bush administration had no immediate desire for new wars, and diplomacy was a convenient way to avoid them. Diplomacy can be useful.

Diplomacy is the putting of foreign policies into practice. A country's diplomats are its eyes, ears, mind, and mouth. They are present at almost every stage of a nation's foreign policy but are often undervalued in the modern world. The Bush 43 administration initially had little use for diplomacy, preferring blunt words and unilateral actions. **Diplomacy** is the way nations communicate with each other, feeling out their positions and defusing incidents before they get nasty.

For example, in April 2001 a U.S. Navy electronics surveillance aircraft collided with a Chinese jet fighter over the South China Sea and landed on the Chinese island of Hainan.

Beijing was furious—or pretended to be—claiming the U.S. spy plane had been in Chinese airspace and had rammed the Chinese jet. Beijing demanded that Washington apologize. The real issue: China's claims to vast areas of the East and South China Seas would be reinforced by a U.S. "apology." Washington's reply was firm but not angry. Said U.S. Secretary of State Colin Powell: "We have nothing to apologize for." The Chinese pilot was to blame, and the U.S. plane was over what most of the world (but not Beijing) calls international waters. China held the U.S. crew of twenty-four. U.S. Congressional anger grew.

> **diplomacy** Official political contact among governments. (See page 294.)
>
> **embassy** Chief diplomatic representation of one country to another.
>
> **bilateral** Two countries.
>
> **multilateral** Several countries.

Relations could have been damaged, but neither side wanted that. Beijing had too much at stake in its world economic ties, and Washington knew it. After quiet negotiations, an American letter said we were "very sorry" about the Chinese pilot and about entering China's airspace for the emergency landing. The subtleties of the Chinese translation allowed Beijing to claim it was a "form of apology," and they released the crew. When both sides want it, diplomacy can work. In six months China decided it needed good relations with America and forgot the whole thing. What did China want? Respect (see Chapter 17), and diplomacy delivered that, calming a potentially dangerous crisis.

■ The Rise and Decline of Diplomacy

A crude diplomacy can be found far back in human history, whenever kings had contact with each other. At first this involved personal visits, such as the Queen of Sheba's journey to Solomon, probably to arrange trade. Never mind how the deal was sealed. Later, monarchs sent ambassadors, usually court noblemen, for temporary visits to another king to present gifts and make requests. With the rise of sovereignty in the sixteenth century (discussed in Chapter 1) came permanent **embassies**, houses in the capital of foreign lands to report on and steer developments. Bribery was an acceptable method. Before the French Revolution unleashed nationalism, ambassadors were suave, of noble rank, and spoke French, the language of classic European diplomacy.

Concepts

DIPLOMACY

Diplomacy is political contact between national governments. It is usually carried out by ambassadors, foreign ministers (such as the U.S. secretary of state), or heads of government (such as the U.S. president), in which case it is called *summit* diplomacy. Diplomatic negotiations can be **bilateral** or **multilateral**.

Concepts

DIPLOMACY AND FOREIGN POLICY

Diplomacy is the feedback loop by which foreign policy is constantly adjusted. It works like this:

1. An act, usually by a government, starts the process; for example, government B announces it will raise tariffs on imported goods.
2. Government A's embassy in B's capital hears the news and cables A's foreign ministry. A may perceive the act as a threat or opportunity (or both). For example, B's move is a threat if A has an export market in B.
3. Defining the national interest generally takes place in the foreign office (e.g., Department of State) of government A. This is the crux of diplomacy. A's officials decide what they want of country B, in this case, continuation of the export market for A's goods.
4. They establish a goal of trying to get government B to shift its policy, to do

something or not do something. In this example, A wants B to not raise tariffs.

5. They plan a strategy to make B conclude that going along with A's goal is in B's national interest too. The diplomats of A are instructed to suggest promises, threats, punishments, or rewards to government B.
6. They conduct the actual diplomacy by sending A's ambassador to see B's top officials to emphasize that B's goods will enter country A only so long as B does not raise its tariffs on A's goods. This is a threat, but it is presented politely. As a sweetener, ambassador A offers minister B a ten-year trade treaty that benefits both sides.
7. Diplomats monitor and evaluate the policy. If government B takes the deal, A has conducted successful diplomacy. If not, the officials of A would have to go back to points 3, 4, or 5 and try again.

A Model of Foreign Policy

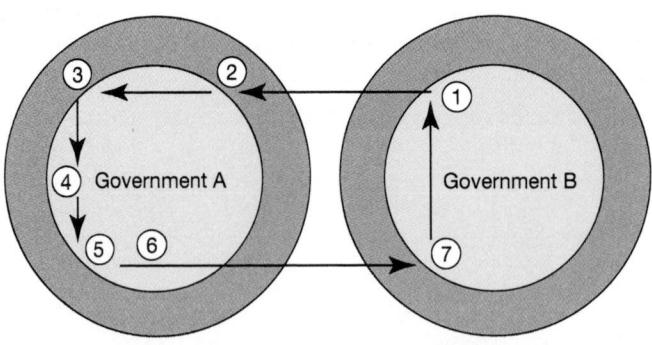

State A

1. Some act
2. Seen as a threat or opportunity because it affects the needs and capabilities of the state
3. National interest defined
4. Goal defined

State B

5. Strategy planned
6. Foreign policy action
7. To get B to reduce threats and enhance opportunities for A

From the end of the Thirty Years War in 1648 to the French Revolution in 1789, diplomacy worked moderately well. It didn't prevent wars, but it helped keep them limited because ruling elites shared a common culture and common interests, namely, preserving their power. All players accepted the principle of monarchy, and none tried to overthrow the other. Their quarrels were relatively minor ones, and their wars were not wars of total destruction. Armies were small and professional. Classic diplomacy, operating on the basis of "balance of power" (see Chapter 1), tried to preserve a stable, conservative system by adjusting borders and alliances. Public opinion did not count in this predemocratic age.

> **foreign ministry** Branch of national government dealing with IR; called State Department in U.S. and Foreign Office in Britain.
>
> **anachronism** Something that no longer fits the times.

Nationalism and democracy changed diplomacy. Gone were the shared values and culture. Conservative monarchs were replaced by nationalistic states. Enthusiasm, that most dangerous of virtues, appeared as nationalistic regimes expanded their borders and colonies. With increased education, mass media, and democracy, public opinion counted for more and more. In the twentieth century, politicians worried that public opinion could cost them reelection. With the electorate watching, diplomacy became much more difficult.

Particularly difficult for diplomacy to handle were the totalitarian dictatorships of Soviet Russia, Fascist Italy, and Nazi Germany, which used diplomacy as a cover to spread propaganda, subvert other countries, and grab pieces of Europe. Recently, states such as Iran and Libya use their embassies as bases to carry out terrorist bombings and assassinations. Clearly, diplomacy changed in the twentieth century.

Should we do without conventional diplomacy? It is tempting. Modern telecommunications let **foreign ministries** contact each other directly by e-mail, fax, and telephone without going through embassies. The Washington-Moscow hotline was established in 1963 precisely because normal diplomatic channels were much too slow for the missile age. To understand each nation's position on major questions, all one needs is a mission to the United Nations, the world's greatest listening post (more on this in Chapter 21). For face-to-face meetings, top officials can fly to any capital overnight. Heads of government can meet in "summits," as Presidents Reagan and Gorbachev did in Geneva in 1985. No embassy by itself carries out important negotiations any more. Some observers say conventional diplomacy has become an **anachronism**.

Classic Thought

"SURTOUT, MESSIEURS, POINT DE ZÉLE"

French statesman Talleyrand, who served both kings and Napoleon with equal aplomb, emphasized, "Above all, gentlemen, not the slightest zeal." Diplomacy must be conducted in calm with a cool head, not with enthusiasm. Zealots make poor diplomats; their commitment leads them to overlook complexity and commit blunders.

■ The Uses of an Anachronism

There are still reasons for traditional diplomacy, complete with embassies and titles. Diplomatic **recognition** is an important **symbol**; a country recognized diplomatically by many lands gains legitimacy and sovereignty. If no one recognizes a country, its very existence is dubious. Under apartheid, South Africa granted four of its black "homelands" nominal independence, but no other government recognized them. They were considered fake countries and are now again part of South Africa. Iran, which broke diplomatic ties with the United States in 1979, could not purchase U.S. weapons in its desperate war with Iraq. Iran's mistreatment of America was a blunder.

recognition   One country's opening of diplomatic relations with another.

symbol   Small thing or gesture that makes a political statement.

Countries can signal their relationship by what they call their diplomatic missions. The highest level is embassy, but other units do the same work without that rank. Israel began relations with West Germany with a "purchasing mission." Later, it became an embassy, indicating full-level diplomatic contact. When the United States opened relations with China in 1972, there was already a U.S. embassy in Taiwan. If we had opened an embassy in Beijing, we would have had to close the one in Taipei, something Nixon did not wish to do. We finessed the problem by opening "liaison offices" in each other's capital. They did everything embassies do. When, under President Carter, the time was ripe to turn them into embassies, we scaled down the U.S. embassy in Taipei to a "cultural institute" that does everything an embassy does. It is staffed by State Department personnel "on leave" who continue to collect their salaries and benefits. This phony setup got around the question of how to deal with Taiwan when Beijing claims to be the one and only China. Diplomacy must be flexible.

Diplomatic contact continues even when countries get mad at each other and "break relations." They rarely break them all the way, for contacts are still necessary. Instead, they turn their mission into part of the embassy of a third country. The United States broke relations with Castro's Cuba in 1961, but a few American diplomats staffed the "U.S. interests section of the Swiss embassy" in Havana. The Cubans, in turn, had a

Classic Thought

BALANCE-OF-POWER DIPLOMACY

Balance-of-power diplomacy is still around and is often quite useful, although few would say we have a balance-of-power system. Henry Kissinger, a scholar of nineteenth-century balance of power, noted carefully the differences between the eras but added that an "equilibrium of strength" was still necessary and desirable between the United States and the Soviet Union. President Nixon, who read a great deal about IR, said in 1971, "I think it will be a safer world and a better world if we have a strong, healthy United States, Europe, Soviet Union, China, Japan, each balancing the other, not playing one against the other, an even balance." Nixon's rapprochement with China is a classic example of balance-of-power diplomacy and helped set the stage for a world of several major powers.

"Cuban interests section" in the Czech embassy in Washington. Hostile countries can both break and maintain relations with each other.

persona non grata   Latin for "unwanted person"; order to expel a diplomat.

■ Diplomats

Not everyone who works in an embassy is a diplomat; indeed, only a minority have diplomatic status. Secretaries, drivers, communications people, and other staffers do not have diplomatic status, which is accorded by the host country foreign ministry in limited numbers to embassy officials only. Those accepted have their name, rank, and function printed in a "diplomatic list." They also get diplomatic license plates but still have to pay parking and traffic tickets.

Accredited diplomats enjoy "diplomatic immunity" from arrest, trial, or imprisonment. These immunities developed over the centuries so diplomats could do their job without harassment. They operate on the basis of reciprocity: You treat me well, and I will treat you well. The embassy is considered foreign territory and may not be entered or searched by host-country police. The Soviet bugging and penetration of the U.S. embassy in Moscow, of course, made mincemeat of this tradition. U.S. diplomats there assumed that all their conversations were electronically overheard. The diplomatic pouch and other official shipments are likewise not supposed to be tampered with. The worst a host country can do to those on the diplomatic list is declare them **persona non grata**, an "unwanted person," and order them out of the country within a few days.

In a revolutionary world, some of these niceties have been grossly violated. Iran broke every rule in the book by holding U.S. embassy personnel hostage for over a year. When a crowd of anti-Kaddafy Libyans protested at the Libyan embassy in London in 1984, an embassy employee opened up from a window with a submachine gun, killing a policewoman. The most Britain could do was break relations with Libya, forcing the closure of both embassies. In 1987 French officials learned that a translator at the Iranian embassy was actually supervising terrorism. The man was not covered by diplomatic immunity, but he stayed hidden in the Iranian embassy. French police surrounded the embassy, and the Iranians did the same with the French embassy in Tehran. Here we see the importance of "shared values" in making diplomacy work; when they erode, diplomatic rules collapse.

Classic Thought

CRIMES AND BLUNDERS

Commenting on Napoleon's 1812 invasion of Russia, French statesman Talleyrand said, "It was worse than a crime, it was a blunder." He drew a tongue-in-cheek distinction between a crime, which hurts someone else, and a blunder, which hurts you. Enthusiasts often commit blunders.

Ambassadors are treated with deference, a carry-over from the days when most were aristocrats. The new ambassador presents his or her "credentials" to the host country's head of state, not necessarily the head of government. Most countries (but not the United States) split the two functions. A U.S. ambassador appointed to the "Court of St. James" (Britain), for example, presents his or her credentials to Queen Elizabeth, the symbolic head of state, rather than to the prime minister. This is a holdover from the days when an ambassador was a personal representative from one sovereign to another. A new U.S. ambassador in Germany presents his or her credentials to the figurehead president, not the chancellor. Ambassadors are conventionally listed as "extraordinary and plenipotentiary" (full-powered), another carry-over from the days when slow communications meant an ambassador really had the full power to negotiate for his sovereign. Nowadays, foreign ministries back home guide negotiations.

Do ambassadors have any purpose, or are they just for public relations? Much of their activity, of course, is meeting, greeting, and socializing. These are not strictly social occasions, however, for good ambassadors learn a lot from conversations, much of which is reported back to their foreign office. Some ambassadors, however, do little of substance, and some embassies work perfectly well without them—maybe better. Part of the problem here is the way some countries, especially the United States, fill ambassadorships.

Approximately a third of U.S. ambassadors are political appointees, many with little background in foreign affairs. Often they are prestige-seekers who contribute big money to the president's election campaign. They rarely speak the local language or understand diplomacy. Some flamboyant types think they can solve difficult problems "the way we used to back home." The U.S. ambassador to the Vatican, a political appointee, hopped over to Libya to straighten things out with Kaddafy. The visit was strictly unauthorized. Shortly thereafter, we bombed Libya and the ambassador resigned. It's no job for amateurs.

Other political appointees have done well. Arthur F. Burns, former chairman of the Federal Reserve Board, was an excellent ambassador to Germany; he spoke both German and economics. Former Senator Mike Mansfield (D-Mont.) served as ambassador to Tokyo for years; he had been a professor of Asian studies and knew Japan well. But in the main, political appointees have down-graded the importance of the job. If a hotel owner or perfume-company heir buys an ambassadorship, we in effect tell the host country and our own embassy staff that the position is unimportant.

Turning Point

PING-PONG DIPLOMACY

In 1971, at an international table-tennis tournament in Tokyo, the Chinese delegation invited the American team to tour China. They did and had great fun. What was dubbed "ping-pong diplomacy" was actually Beijing's signal that they were interested in reestablishing relations. The White House got the signal. Kissinger visited Beijing secretly later that year, and Nixon arrived with great fanfare in early 1972. In diplomacy, symbols can be important signaling devices.

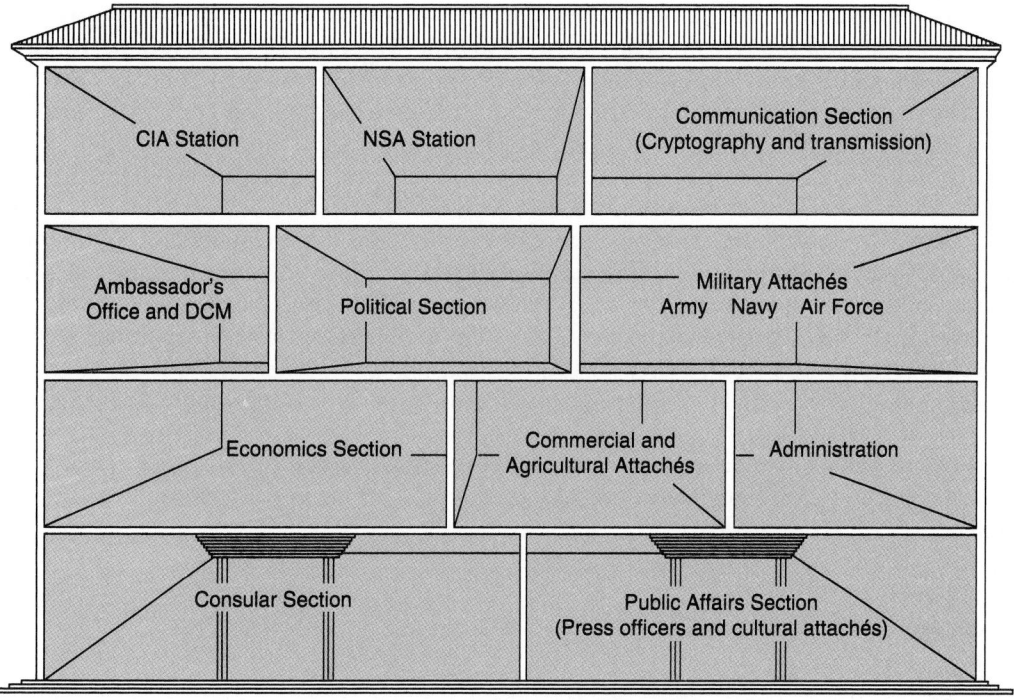

A Typical U.S. Embassy

▌ Inside an Embassy

A modern embassy is complex. It monitors its host country's economy, politics, public opinion, military capability, you name it. The embassy cutaway drawing represents a typical U.S. embassy, usually a multistory building. Security is tight. A Marine guard behind bulletproof glass carefully scrutinizes your passport. If possible, the building is situated well back from the street, away from car bombs. Large concrete "flower beds" on the sidewalk prevent cars from getting too close to the building.

The more sensitive offices are on the higher floors. On the ground floor is the consular section, which needs public access. American consuls, assisted by a staff of local employees (they're often cheaper and know the language), screen applicants and issue visas to come to the United States. A tourist visa is quick and easy to get, a student visa more complicated, and a prized immigration visa ("green card") usually requires a long, laborious process. Americans who need help—lost passports, emergency evacuations, lists of doctors and lawyers, registering a birth or marriage—also come to the consular section. Their staff do not generally lend you money but can e-mail home.

Also on the first floor would likely be the public affairs section (formerly U.S. Information Service), which explains U.S. foreign and domestic policies, arranges scholarly and cultural exchanges, sets up exhibits, and sometimes maintains an American library.

Semipublic offices might be on the second floor. The commercial and agricultural attachés provide information and contacts to help American firms sell their products abroad. The economics section might be here too, keeping tabs on the host country's growth, interest and inflation rates, and the general business climate. The administration section, which distributes paychecks, finds housing, and runs the motor pool, might also be on this floor. Documents on the first and second floors are mostly unclassified and most of the people working there are locals, not Americans.

About the third floor, things get more interesting and more classified. Here might be the ambassador's office and political section. There are few or no local employees. The ambassador or deputy chief of mission (DCM) represents the United States to the host government, conveying its wishes, requests, support, or disapproval. The political section, probably also on this floor, monitors parties, personalities, and policies. If its officers do a good job, there should be no surprises, such as unexpected coups, revolutions, electoral upsets, or wars.

The military attachés—army, naval, and air—may also be on this floor. Their work too is classified. They are considered "legal spies," gathering information on the host

Reflections

HOW TO JOIN THE FOREIGN SERVICE

The U.S. Foreign Service, the elite of the State Department, is the closest an American can get to a title of nobility. Foreign Service Officers (FSOs) are few and carefully recruited, trained, and promoted. Many aspire to join; few are chosen. Should you be interested, here's what you should do:

- Get a really thorough liberal-arts education, one heavy on economics, political science, history, and English. Command of a foreign language helps. Read good periodicals for background on everything from culture to currency markets.

- In your senior year, sign up to take the Foreign Service exam, given across the country. Your college career office has information and forms.

- The exam is difficult, selecting about the top 10 percent of the thousands who take it. All you have to know is everything, especially economics. Don't be too disappointed if you don't pass the first time; you can take it again.

- Go to graduate school to get the education you should have obtained as an undergraduate. The typical FSO has a master's degree; some have doctorates. The average age of a new junior Foreign Service Officer is twenty-nine.

- Gain relevant work experience in business, banking, journalism, or the military. Experience in developing countries shows you can live and work in the Global South, where many diplomatic postings are.

- If you pass the written exam, then comes the oral exam, which skims off a minority of those who passed the written exam. To test your smarts and leadership ability, the examiners, veteran FSOs, might ask you anything from U.S. geography to the best fiction you've read lately. They may put you in a group of fellow test-takers to see how you interact and lead.

- Didn't make it? Don't feel too badly; only a few hundred a year do. And think what a marvelous education and background you now have for private-sector international work, which often pays much better.

country's defenses, size and quality of army, types of weapons, and so on. They may also encourage the host country to purchase U.S. weapons, as this earns foreign currency, spreads out research and manufacturing costs, and ties the country to the United States.

> **consulate** Branch of an embassy with limited functions.
>
> **Foreign Service** Career corps of professional diplomats.

On the top floor are usually the most sensitive and secret offices. The CIA station, whose personnel pass as State Department people, keeps tabs on underground happenings and may try to influence them. Contact with opposition groups, funding of local friends, and surveillance of hostile embassies are all part of their duties. When it comes to certain matters, the CIA station chief may know more and be more important than the ambassador. Nearby might be an electronic eavesdropping office of the National Security Agency. The NSA, which is far more secret than the CIA, conducts signals intelligence ("sigint"), monitoring the radio traffic of other countries and cracking their codes. Probably next door is a conventional communications room that transmits the embassy's reports to Washington, often encrypted. These electronics offices are on the top floor, not only to be close to their antennas but also to give staffers time to destroy files and cryptographic machines should the embassy be attacked.

The embassy is in the capital, but other important cities may have **consulates**, branches of the embassy that perform some of the functions of an embassy, usually in serving visa applicants and Americans abroad. A big consulate is called a consulate general. Some consulates general (e.g., Frankfurt) are much bigger than a small embassy in an out-of-the-way country.

Only a minority of the people who work in a U.S. embassy are State Department **Foreign Service** Officers. The American secretaries and communications people are a separate category called Foreign Service Specialists. The attachés are from the military, commerce, agriculture, or other departments. Fewer than 30 percent of Americans at our posts abroad work for the State Department. And the local employees typically outnumber the Americans.

Turning Point

PURGE OF THE "OLD CHINA HANDS"

During World War II, several bright, Chinese-speaking (they had been missionary kids) U.S. diplomats in China predicted that the Chinese Communists would beat the Nationalists after the war. They were right, but when the Communists took over in 1949, Republicans demanded to know "Who lost China?" These U.S. Foreign Service Officers—dubbed the "old China hands" because they had long experience in China—were accused of being pro-Communist (they weren't) and fired. Although later exonerated, their purge was a warning to U.S. diplomats to report only good news. Accurate reporting can get you fired. In this way, political hysteria blinded U.S. policy in Asia for a generation and may have contributed to Vietnam. Politics can wreck good diplomacy.

■ Diplomacy and War

Many people see diplomats and warriors as opposites. In some ways they are. Military officers are precise, definite, enthusiastic, can-do guys. Diplomats are subtle, cautious, and used to dealing with ambiguities, more likely to tell you why something *shouldn't* be done. The common view is that diplomats work for peace while soldiers practice war, and that the two don't have much in common.

This is not accurate. The two, diplomats and warriors, are, or should be, part of the same foreign policy. One does not make sense without the other. Diplomats from a militarily weak country may have trouble making their point. Those from a militarily strong country are listened to carefully, for if worst comes to worst, they can deliver on their warnings. U.S. diplomats in the 1930s, representing a lightly armed country with no military forces in China, could admonish the Japanese to cease their conquest of China, but the Japanese did not take them seriously. By the same token, military might operating without diplomatic guidance is a blind, raging force that destroys to no good purpose. In the 1930s, Japanese militarists seized control of their government and began the conquest of China, which led them into a devastating war with the United States. The Pacific War might have been avoided if American diplomats had had military backup and Japanese generals had had diplomatic guidance.

Diplomacy can prevent or end wars if the countries engaged in them are willing to compromise. If they are too angry to speak to each other, "third-party diplomacy" can help. Here, a neutral third country extends its "good offices" so the disputants can meet on neutral ground. This may go a little further if the third country practices "mediation," the carrying back and forth of proposals and counterproposals, sometimes with the third country adding suggestions of its own.

One of the high points of U.S. diplomacy was the 1979 Camp David accords between Egypt and Israel, the first peace treaty between Israel and an Arab country. President Carter mediated personally between President Sadat of Egypt and Prime Minister Begin of Israel, smoothing feelings, suggesting compromises, and not letting his guests leave until they agreed. Notice here how the negotiating was done by heads of government, not by diplomats. A psychological incentive for Sadat and Begin to agree was the fact that the year before they had shared a Nobel Peace Prize. Both were proud of the award, and to

Classic Thought

WAR BY OTHER MEANS

Some people think Carl von Clausewitz, an early nineteenth-century Prussian military thinker, cynically favored war. They take his famous statement that "war is the continuation of diplomacy by other means" as the sort of policy Hitler pursued. Actually, Clausewitz urged that wars be limited to policy goals—set by a civilian government—rather than escalate to an extreme, which is what they might do if left entirely to generals. He is saying don't go to war for its own sake, but only for clearly delineated goals that cannot be reached otherwise. Do not divorce war from diplomacy.

have left Camp David without a treaty would have tarnished their reputations as men of peace. Unfortunately, Israelis and Palestinians in 2000 were too far apart for President Clinton's summit diplomacy to work.

President Theodore Roosevelt was successful in the Russo-Japanese War of 1904–1905. The Japanese trounced the Russians on land and sea but were running short of men and yen. They asked Roosevelt to mediate, and he called Japanese and Russian delegates to Portsmouth, New Hampshire, where he twisted arms to get the Treaty of Portsmouth and end the war. For this, Teddy Roosevelt, the most bellicose of all U.S. presidents, won the 1906 Nobel Peace Prize. Roosevelt, too, recognized the importance of military backup in diplomacy. Said he in 1905: "I never take a step in foreign policy unless I am assured that I shall be able eventually to carry out my will by force."

The crux of diplomacy is willingness to compromise. Diplomacy worked best when monarchs played limited games. In a nationalistic world, compromise is hard. Countries may severely distrust one another and fear that giving up anything will be seen as weakness. Public opinion may undermine settlements of serious conflicts. Norwegian diplomats mediated the 1993 Oslo agreement between Israel and the Palestinian Authority, but hotheads on both sides, by acts of violence, brought the peace process to a standstill. An Israeli fanatic assassinated Prime Minister Rabin for being too willing to compromise. Prime Minister Barak's cabinet collapsed in 2000 for the same reasons. Palestinian suicide bombings killed any peace process. Kings didn't have to worry about public opinion.

Could there be a revival of diplomacy in our day? It is possible, and there are a few good signs. The end of the Cold War made some previous antagonists more cooperative. Gone are the ideologies and arms races. Even the most rabidly nationalistic regimes gradually come to their senses after years of the stupendous costs that come with modern warfare. Egypt's Sadat didn't love Israel, but by the late 1970s Egypt was so financially strapped and war-weary that Sadat found it possible to make his historic 1977 visit to Jerusalem, the capital of his archenemy. This dramatic example of "personal diplomacy" paved the way for the 1979 Camp David accords. In 2004, the leaders of India and Pakistan met personally to restart a peace process after years of tension between the two nuclear powers.

Many wondered that with the right kind of diplomacy Saddam Hussein of Iraq, diplomatically isolated and rebuked by all the major powers, might have permitted thorough international inspection. Germany unified in 1990 with a series of diplomatic agreements that assured its neighbors that Germany would not be a threat. Canada and Spain used diplomacy to calm disputes over fishing rights.

Classic Thought

MUSIC WITHOUT INSTRUMENTS

The expression "Diplomacy without an army is like music without instruments" is attributed to Frederick the Great of Prussia, who ruled from 1740 to 1786. Frederick was both an excellent military commander and a clever diplomat (and fine musician) who helped build Prussia into one of Europe's major powers. He fully understood the military component of diplomacy.

Effective diplomacy, however, depends on the context. In a hostile situation, where the parties seriously fear and mistrust each other, as between Washington and Baghdad in 2002 and 2003, diplomacy can accomplish little. Diplomats can meet and sometimes draft agreements, but they seldom calm hostilities. The Cold War was a long era of extreme mistrust during which only small points could be settled (e.g., the 1963 "hotline" agreement). As the Cold War faded, diplomacy accomplished more serious tasks, such as the 1987 INF treaty that banned intermediate-range missiles. With the end of Cold War hostilities, many questions between the United States and Russia were settled with businesslike diplomacy, as there was no longer much to fear or mistrust.

Classic Thought

MORGENTHAU'S NINE RULES

Hans Morgenthau (see page 27) had a profound impact on the study of international relations in the United States. This refugee scholar from Nazi Germany expounded a "realist" theory that stripped away wishful thinking. He warned against both German and Soviet expansionism but cautioned Americans against indiscriminate use of force. He deplored, for example, the Vietnam War. Morgenthau did not think diplomacy was dead. It could be revived, and he offered nine rules for successful diplomacy.

1. "Diplomacy must be divested of the crusading spirit." Ideological or religious doctrines aimed at remaking the world can only lead to war.

2. "The objectives of foreign policy must be defined in terms of the national interest and must be supported with adequate power." Define your interests narrowly, stressing that which really matters, and make sure you have enough military power for that purpose.

3. "Diplomacy must look at the political scene from the point of view of other nations." Other countries have national interests, too, and so long as they are limited and rational they are legitimate.

4. "Nations must be willing to compromise on all issues that are not vital to them." If you've observed the first three rules, you will be able to see what is vital and what is not. If your adversary does the same, you can find a middle ground.

5. "Give up the shadow of worthless rights for the substance of real advantage." Don't worry about scoring legal or propaganda points; look to see what you're really getting in terms of national interest.

6. "Never put yourself in a position from which you cannot retreat without losing face or cannot advance without grave risks." Before you enter into negotiations, always ask how they can go wrong and how you can get out gracefully. Don't make unrealistic demands; you may have to back down on them.

7. "Never allow a weak ally to make decisions for you." Countries' national interests are seldom identical, and if you let a smaller ally define yours, you lose your freedom of action.

8. "The armed forces are the instrument of foreign policy, not its master." The military mind is blunt and destructive; the diplomatic mind is "complicated and subtle." With the military in charge, there can be no compromise.

9. "The government is the leader of public opinion, not its slave." Leaders of democracies must, of course, pay attention to public opinion, but they must also inform and educate it.

Source: Hans J. Morgenthau and Kenneth W. Thompson, *Politics among Nations: The Struggle for Power and Peace*, 6th ed. New York: Oxford University Press, 1985.

The post–Cold War context prompted a revival of diplomacy in other areas. Third-party diplomats from the UN, EU, and the United States helped bring together warring sides in Namibia and in the former Yugoslavia. Arabs and Israelis occasionally made some progress. China set up negotiations to try to get North Korea to drop its nuclear-weapons program. Even Washington liked Beijing's diplomacy here. Much of the world agreed: "Give diplomacy a chance."

Key Terms

anachronism (p. 297)

bilateral (p. 295)

consulate (p. 303)

diplomacy (p. 295)

embassy (p. 295)

foreign ministry (p. 297)

Foreign Service (p. 303)

multilateral (p. 295)

persona non grata (p. 299)

recognition (p. 298)

symbol (p. 298)

Key Web Sites

Department of State
http://www.state.gov/

CIA
http://www.odci.gov/

Strategic Intelligence
http://www.loyola.edu/dept/politics/intel.html

The Electronic Embassy
http://www.embassy.org/

American Foreign Service Association
http://www.afsa.org/

Further Reference

Art, Robert J., and Patrick M. Cronin. eds. *The United States and Coercive Diplomacy.* Herndon, VA: USIP Press, 2003.

Barston, R. P. *Modern Diplomacy,* 2nd ed. New York: Longman, 1997.

Berridge, Geoffrey R. *A Dictionary of Diplomacy.* New York: Palgrave, 2001.

Cohen, Raymond. *Theatre of Power: The Art of Diplomatic Signalling.* White Plains, NY: Longman, 1987.

Craig, Gordon A., Alexander L. George, and Paul G. Lauren. *Force and Statecraft: Diplomatic Problems of Our Time,* 4th ed. New York: Oxford University Press, 2006.

Dizard, Wilson, Jr. *Inventing Public Diplomacy: The Story of the U.S. Information Agency.* Boulder, CO: Lynne Rienner, 2004.

Dorman, Shawn, ed. *Inside a U.S. Embassy: How the Foreign Service Works for America,* rev. ed. Washington, D.C.: American Foreign Service Association, 2005.

Dunn, David H., ed. *Diplomacy at the Highest Level: The Evolution of International Summitry.* New York: St. Martin's Press, 1996.

Holbrooke, Richard. *To End a War.* New York: Random House, 1998.

Kissinger, Henry. *Diplomacy.* New York: Simon & Schuster, 1994.

Marshall, Peter. *Positive Diplomacy.* New York: St. Martin's, 1997.

Newnham, Randall E. *Deutsch Mark Diplomacy: Positive Economic Sanctions in German-Russian Relations.* University Park, PA: Penn State University Press, 2002.

Small, Melvin. *Democracy & Diplomacy: The Impact of Domestic Politics on U.S. Foreign Policy, 1789–1994.* Baltimore, MD: Johns Hopkins University Press, 1996.

CHAPTER 20

INTERNATIONAL LAW

QUESTIONS TO CONSIDER

1. How is international law (IL) like domestic law?
2. How do consistency and reciprocity over time build IL?
3. If IL lacks the enforcement mechanism of domestic law, why is it generally obeyed?
4. What is "self help" in international law?
5. What are the several sources of IL? Which is the most important?
6. How can war be legal under IL? And if war is legal, how can "war crimes" be illegal?
7. How far out from its shores does a state extend?
8. What does diplomatic "recognition" mean?
9. How can piracy law be relevant in our day?
10. What precedent did Nuremberg set?

For many years, Greece and Turkey glared uneasily at each other. Under the Aegean Sea between them could be oil. Who owns it? Both countries claim the areas are within their territorial waters. Billions are at stake. Wars have been started for less, and the two countries have a long history of bitter hostility toward each other. Instead of reaching for their guns, however, the two countries reach for their lawyers. War is a last resort that neither country wants nor can afford. They hire international lawyers, court law professors, measure their continental shelves, and haggle endlessly. It is better than fighting. By turning an economic and political dispute into a legal and technical dispute, they take some of the tension out of it.

International law (IL) may or may not eventually settle who has undersea drilling rights. More important is the fact that the two states wish to avoid war and find IL a convenient mechanism to do so. Some people who dismiss IL as weak and ineffectual—because it lacks the authority and sanctions of domestic law—fail to grasp its basic purpose.

International law regulates exchanges between states in predictable ways, if existing law is followed or new law is created. Bluntly put, IL allows countries to page through law books instead of marching their troops. If both countries use IL they avoid war, and what is wrong with that?

If you think about it a minute, isn't that what domestic law does? Instead of obtaining satisfaction through dueling, disputants obtain it in court. The same anger present in duels is present in lawsuits. But the emotions have been calmed and civilized to eliminate recourse to violence. Much domestic law exists to prevent violence, and this is the case with international law, too. IL, like domestic law, is a calmer-downer. In the post–Cold War era, IL has increased in volume, constraining more state behavior, and injecting more lawyers into the foreign policy process.

■ Consistency and Reciprocity

One of the major—and valid—complaints about IL is that it is used to justify whatever the powerful wish. The major powers are especially prone to cynically cloaking their actions with IL. They are inclined to apply IL to others but not to themselves (see box on page 311). International lawyers, like all lawyers, are for hire.

But even the cynical use of IL is helpful. Once you have asserted, even for self-serving purposes, a point of IL, you find yourself under pressure to observe it consistently. If you denounce a rival for "illegally" aiding rebels who are trying to overthrow a friendly government, then you are "hoist with your own petard" when you are caught aiding rebels who are trying to overthrow a government. You must either cease complaining about aiding rebels in general or stop aiding your favorite rebels. The U.S. government was in an embarrassing position when several Floridians were charged with breaking U.S. neutrality laws by helping the Nicaraguan *contras,* for that is precisely what the CIA and White House had been doing. Governments try to avoid looking hypocritical.

This exerts some restraint on decision makers. During the 1962 missile crisis, President Kennedy rejected a surprise air attack on Cuba because it sounded too much like Pearl Harbor, and he didn't wish to be remembered as a "Tojo."

Classic Thought

FREDERICK THE GREAT AND IL

It was said of Prussia's Frederick the Great: "First he conquered Silesia, and then he ordered his international lawyers to justify it." The expression epitomizes the cynical use of IL. Unfortunately, the same process goes on in most foreign offices today: First do it, then justify it.

The human mind generally likes **consistency**. One of the surest ways to make people mad is to point out their inconsistencies. If they have claimed one thing in IL, they have some trouble claiming the opposite. What's sauce for the goose is sauce for the gander. Over the centuries, these pressures for consistency build up what is called "customary international law," law that has grown up because most countries preach it and don't

> **consistency**   Observation of rules with no exceptions for oneself.
>
> **reciprocity**   Threat to do to others what they have done to you.

want to be caught violating it. Contributing to this is the principle of **reciprocity**: What you do to me, I do to you. Nations, like people, cannot expect to get a whole lot better than they have given. Their obnoxious behavior will soon be returned by offended countries.

Reciprocity tends to be self-enforcing and contagious. Traditionally, cars with diplomatic license plates had been exempt from parking tickets—an extension of diplomatic immunity. Diplomats in Washington often abused the privilege by parking anywhere they liked, even in the middle of the street. In the 1960s, with permission from the State Department, D.C. police began ticketing diplomatic offenders, and the tickets had to be paid. Soon every country in the world dropped diplomatic immunity for misparked cars. (Actually, many other capitals were just itching to do what Washington did first.) Almost instantly, law governing diplomats had been modified by the simple principle of reciprocity.

The easiest area in which to apply reciprocity is diplomacy, one of the original topics of IL. Countries that break reciprocity suffer penalties. Obviously, Iran broke every rule in the book when it held U.S. hostages in Tehran for over a year. No one retaliated directly

Turning Point

LEGALISTIC EUROPE

One basic point driving Europe and the United States apart (see Chapter 16) is that since World War II, Europeans have become highly legalistic while Americans have rejected legalism in favor of military power. Europeans, after centuries of bloody wars, have come to appreciate governing their relations through treaties, IL, and the United Nations. They look at the many treaties leading to peace in Europe and to the step-by-step building of the EU and say, "See, treaties work." They believe that the expansion of IL through current and new treaties can do the same for much of the world, a view that presumes the rest of the world is eager for peaceful and orderly relations.

America has been going the other way and tends to see the world as violent and disorderly,

unripe for treaties and IL. Ironically, from the late nineteenth century through the middle of the twentieth century, American scholars and statesmen concentrated on treaties and IL and denounced "power politics." Woodrow Wilson took us into World War I because German submarines were violating IL. Naively, Washington tried to outlaw war with the 1928 Kellogg-Briand Pact. (It didn't work.) After World War II, "realist" thinkers such as Hans Morgenthau and George Kennan persuaded Americans to abandon the "legalist-moralist" approach in favor of the rational application of U.S. power. Some in the Bush 43 administration disparaged IL and treaties and argued they were not binding on us. Europe and America split wide apart on this issue.

treaty   Contract between nations.

ratify   To formally accept treaty as binding.

against Iran, but most of the world ostracized Iran and severely limited diplomatic contacts. Tehran could scoff at this, but it hurt Iran in its war against Iraq. There was a price to be paid for breaking IL. International law is observed, studies show, to about the same degree as domestic law. In fact, law is about as essential in providing order and predictability to international relations as it is for domestic relations.

■ Origins of International Law

The great mechanism for developing IL is the **treaty**, an analog to the contract in domestic law. Treaty-making grew with the rise of the modern "strong state" in the sixteenth century (see page 16). States and IL were born twins, for IL serves to protect and preserve states. IL also grew with the volume and importance of international exchanges. The opening of the New World spawned colonies, commerce, shipping, piracy, and wars, the worst of which was the Thirty Years War (1618–1648). Indeed, one of the first thinkers on IL, Grotius, wrote during and in horror at that massive war.

Concepts

HOW TO MAKE A TREATY

Some treaties are bilateral, some multilateral. A treaty can also be called an accord, convention, pact, protocol, agreement, compact, or arrangement. Here's how they make and break them.

1. Negotiation: Any designated representative of a state can negotiate a treaty. Usually this is an official diplomat, but it can be a president, prime minister, or foreign minister. Negotiators generally come with proposals prepared by their governments and don't have much leeway to make changes or compromises, which have to be approved back home. Diplomats are not free agents.

2. Signing: Once the parties have agreed to the text, a top figure signs it. If it's an important treaty, presidents may sign it with fanfare. Even unratified, IL stipulates that the parties cannot act contrary to the treaty until ratification has failed.

3. Ratification: Every state has constitutional procedures for its formal consent to treaties. In the United States, two-thirds of the Senate (the House is not involved) must consent to a treaty to allow the president to **ratify** it formally. Technically, the Senate does not ratify, which is done only by the executive. Understandings and reservations may be attached; if important they have to be renegotiated with the other parties. Failure to ratify releases that state of obligations. Finally, the treaty is registered with the UN Secretariat.

4. Termination. Some treaties are of unlimited duration, some fixed. Some set a time for renewal. Treaties end when one or more parties violate it, when a new treaty supersedes the old one, by war between the parties, and by the disappearance of a state. The Bush 43 administration, desiring to build a national strategic defense, told Moscow that it regarded their 1972 Anti-Missile Treaty as obsolete. Moscow noted that this would end it on both sides, so in effect the 1972 treaty died.

The Spaniard Francisco de Victoria (1480–1546), influenced by medieval Catholic thought, wrote that "natural law" from reason and necessity required orderly relations between states. IL transcended the will and consent of kings because states had to recognize the logic and interests of an international community. Another Spaniard, Francisco Suarez (1548–1617), took a more modern view and held that states had to first consent to IL.

sanction Punishment for violation of IL.

territorial limit Extent of sovereignty from states' shores.

Bridging both views was the true father of international law, Hugh de Groot (1583–1645), known as Grotius. (Latin names were fashionable in the seventeenth century.) His 1625 work, *On the Law of War and Peace,* written (in Latin) in reaction to the barbarity of the Thirty Years' War, made the case for moderation in warfare and for open, peaceful intercourse between nations. Sovereignty, he said, was limited by divine law, natural law, and the law of nations. The latter arises from both reason and the practice of international relations. Treaties must be obeyed, he said, because it was in the nature of all law that legal commands one has consented to must be obeyed.

The growth of nationalism and democracy made governments emphasize state interests that could be sold to peoples and parliaments. IL arose in Europe, the birthplace of the modern state, but spread worldwide. Not everyone liked IL. Revolutionary regimes, such as Lenin's in Russia, rejected the state concept and IL. Workers had no country, Lenin argued, and existing "bourgeois" agreements were to be scrapped. It took years before the Soviet Union and then China rediscovered the utility of IL. Nazi Germany never accepted IL and paid for it. More recently, Global South states denounced IL as made by colonialists for their own interests, but these lands too have gradually appreciated the value of IL. Eventually, even Iran may get the message.

■ Commands

Like domestic law, international law has both commands and **sanctions**. The command obliges states to behave in particular ways. Maritime law, for example, commands extensive freedom of the seas beyond the twelve-mile **territorial limit** but not within it. Diplomatic immunity commands that there be no arrest or trial of accredited diplomats even if

Concepts

SUCCESSOR STATES

Is Russia the continuation of the Soviet Union and Serbia of Yugoslavia? Most states follow the "continuity rule" and recognize the rights and duties of what are called successor states. Treaties the old government signed carry over to the new. Russia got the Soviet Union's permanent seat on the Security Council but also agreed to existing treaties, such as those on arms control. Serbia stopped calling itself Yugoslavia in 2003 but strove to make sure its treaties, signed under the name Yugoslavia, on the use of the Danube and its borders with Hungary and Albania are not questioned.

executive agreement   A commitment of less importance than a treaty.

they commit a serious crime. In 1986, a South Korean diplomat in New Zealand who habitually drove drunk ran over a pedestrian. All the New Zealand government could do was declare the diplomat *persona non grata* (an unwanted person) and expel him.

Since there is no supergovernment to tell states what to do, commands must be those that states impose upon themselves, an important characteristic of IL. States must consent to the commands they will follow. Without consent, there is no IL. Clearly, this is different from domestic law, where citizens may not consent to a law but are under its command anyway. Domestic law occurs within sovereign entities, IL among them.

IL is a direct expression of *raison d'état*, the "reason of the state" or the "interests of the state." Some believe that IL serves and protects the "global community," but it is secondary to treaties, which are negotiated among states and command only those who ratify them. Treaties are negotiated by diplomats to get commitments from other states to behave a certain way. They are contracts between states that serve state interests.

Weaker than treaties but still binding are **executive agreements**, widely used by U.S. presidents because Senate approval of treaties is slow and often turns into a political football. The United States now signs few treaties—the Bush administration does not like them—but many executive agreements. Critics do not like executive agreements, viewing them as end runs around Senate scrutiny. The early 1950s isolationist Bricker Amendment tried to block use of executive agreements, and the 1972 liberal Case Act required that they be reported to Congress.

Custom creates commands if a particular right or obligation is practiced and not challenged by other states. For example, the United States treats the Chesapeake Bay as its territory, and no one has challenged the U.S. claim. Libya, on the other hand, claims the Gulf of Sidra, but no one accepts that claim because it's too wide. U.S. warships periodically enter it to express lack of consent.

The International Court of Justice, better known as the World Court and located in the Hague, Netherlands, started with the League of Nations and is now a branch of the UN. Its fifteen judges are nominated by national groupings of states and elected by the UN. Usually experienced jurists, they serve nine-year terms. (United Nations)

Commands based on custom take time to develop and can be ambiguous because they are usually unwritten. The same is true of IL based on reason, morality, and justice. Few states explicitly consent to them. Treaties are a firmer foundation for IL.

■ Sanctions

Why do states obey international law? Because they benefit from it. Arms control agreements lessen the risk of war, stop arms races, and reduce defense costs. Trade agreements establish markets and the flow of goods. Extradition treaties remove sanctuaries for criminals. To violate treaties and IL would remove these benefits. When you break a contract, you don't get the benefit of the contract.

But why do states obey IL when it costs them something and they don't want to obey? No world police force exists to keep states law-abiding, but there are sanctions that make states obey even though they do not want to.

Courts, even at the national level, backed by national police powers, can enforce IL as if it were domestic law. In *Missouri v. Holland* (1920), the state of Missouri did not want to carry out provisions of a treaty with Britain (for Canada) that protected migratory birds. The U.S. Supreme Court ruled the treaty was valid as U.S. law. Now using national courts to sue foreign wrongdoers is a growing trend. A 1993 Belgian law opened its

Concepts

INTERNATIONAL SANCTIONS

The UN Charter states that "armed force shall not be used, save in the common interest." In 1950 the Security Council charged North Korea with "breach of the peace" and called on it to withdraw from South Korea. Then the UN urged members to assist the South militarily. In 1990, the Security Council authorized war to expel Iraqi forces from Kuwait. Both were examples of international sanctions, which include the following:

1. Reprisals include confiscation of property, boycotts, and punitive raids, normally illegal under IL. They become legal when an injured party responds to violations of law. The UN Charter doesn't like any use of force, but it also acknowledges the right of self-defense. Reprisals are far more limited than war. In 1986, the United States bombed military installations in Libya, claiming it was a reprisal to Libyan-sponsored terrorist bombing.

2. A retorsion is a milder sanction, a reply against a state that does something objectionable. Iran's support of terrorism and its nuclear program led the United States to cut off all trade with Iran in 1995.

3. War is an acceptable sanction in IL. "Contending by force," Grotius's definition of war, can be used legally against those who start aggressive wars. Defining "aggression," however, is hard; no definition is accepted by all. Often the side that fires first (preempts) is the defender; the aggressor is often the side that mobilizes first.

exclusive economic zone Fishing and mineral rights 200 miles from shore belong to that country.

courts to lawsuits over human rights that had nothing to do with Belgium. The cases seemed designed to embarrass leaders rather than actually collect damages. A little-used 1789 U.S. law was dusted off and used to sue the former leaders of Serbia, China, and Britain as well as terrorists and German companies that used slave labor during World War II. The United States has a consistency problem here. We let U.S. courts try foreigners but reject the jurisdiction of foreign courts to try American wrongdoers, as in the new International Criminal Court. Either way we resolve the inconsistency expands the realm of IL.

Treaties on human rights have opened governments to suits in domestic and international courts. In 1996, a Spanish prosecutor charged the former military presidents of Argentina and Chile with killing Spanish citizens. When Chilean General Augusto Pinochet visited Britain for medical treatment in 1998, Spain demanded his extradition, and Britain had to (house) arrest him. Britain skirted the difficult legal issue by letting Pinochet return to Chile for (fake) health reasons, but the episode showed that ex-dictators are not immune to human-rights charges. The European Court of Human Rights faulted Britain for

Economics

LAW OF THE SEA

One of the first subjects of IL and one of Grotius's main points is still a hot topic: law of the sea, which continually evolves. Who owns the sea? For most of history it was considered *res nullius* (nobody's thing), so anybody could take its fish. (Big current problem: overfishing.) More recently, some countries, especially poor and landlocked ones, want the sea considered *res omnes* (everybody's thing), so the UN can redistribute profits to them from undersea oil and minerals.

How far from shore a country's territory extends has been debated for centuries. By the eighteenth century, three miles from shore was defined as a country's territorial limit (sometimes called the "cannonball rule," although old cannons could not shoot nearly that far). Anything beyond three miles was considered international waters. Not every country liked that. The Soviet Union didn't like foreign spy ships getting that close to its shores and proclaimed twelve miles as its limit. Other maritime powers adopted the same view, and now twelve miles is standard. Ecuador and Peru didn't like others fishing

so close and proclaimed a 200-mile limit. They even arrested U.S. tuna boats. Countries now agree to a 200-mile **exclusive economic zone** (EEZ) beyond territorial limit for their own fishing and mineral rights. The EEZ is still open sea for ship movement; it is not sovereign territory.

Global warming is making territorial limits newly relevant. Melting Arctic ice opens up the legendary Northwest Passage to shipping north of Canada. Canada has claimed Arctic regions since 1895 but in 1969 added a law proclaiming a 100-mile Canadian "management zone" over Arctic waters. Any ship, such as a U.S. tanker, must ask Canada's permission to transit the zone.

After many years of negotiation, a UN Convention on the Law of the Sea (UNCLOS) covering territorial limits, EEZs, military uses, piracy, environmental pollution, and many other points was concluded in 1982. The United States, fearing infringement on its economic rights, voted against it but informally abides by its rules. The United States is leery of being bound by treaties.

Turning Point

FROM NUREMBERG TO SADDAM

The trial of Saddam Hussein continued the expansion of IL that started at Nuremberg in 1945. Where and how to try Saddam—an international tribunal or an Iraqi court? Was he primarily a war criminal or a domestic murderer? He was tried by an Iraqi court, a decision that could serve as a **precedent** for similar cases in the future. Before World War II, he would likely not have been considered a criminal, merely the head of a defeated state.

Before World War II there had been little law on **human rights**; Hitler and the Holocaust changed that. The Nuremberg War Crimes Trials in 1945–1946 established a major precedent by trying the top twenty-one Nazis and sentencing eleven of them to death. Nuremberg, staffed by U.S., British, French, and Soviet judges, was controversial at the time. There had been no category called **war crimes** before, but Nazi Germany had committed "crimes against humanity" on civilians and prisoners,

Some criticized Nuremberg as "victors' justice" or legalistic revenge that invented dubious laws after the fact and applied them to soldiers who had just been carrying out orders. The legal reasoning against these arguments has been cited ever since. U.S. prosecutor Telford Taylor argued "there are some universal standards of human behavior that transcend the duty of obedience to national laws." Nuremberg set the precedent for the Tokyo war crimes trials after Japan's defeat, the 1961 Eichmann trial (see page 320), and the ongoing Bosnian and Rwandan war crimes tribunals. In 2001 the Hague tribunal sentenced a Serb general to forty-six years for genocide for the 1995 massacre of 7,000 unarmed Muslims in Srebrenica (see page 247).

Nuremberg actually continued the Western tradition of trying to limit war and its horrors. Medieval Catholic churchmen expounded **jus ad bellum** and **jus in bello** (see page 49). The tradition, expanded with the **Geneva Convention**—actually a compilation of four conventions held between 1864 and 1949 to which over 150 countries (including the United States) now adhere—

codifies principles on noncombatants, prisoners, wounded, occupation, and permissible weapons. One Geneva-type question on Al Qaeda suspects we held at Guantánamo was whether they should be treated as POWs. (We said terrorists do not qualify as POWs.) Torture at Abu Ghraib prison clearly flunked the Geneva Conventions and massively embarrassed the United States.

Human rights were included in the UN Charter, and the new UN drew up the Universal Declaration of Human Rights in 1948. Although not a treaty, the Declaration set the stage for more specific covenants, such as one on **civil rights** (United States ratified in 1992); racial discrimination (United States ratified in 1994); economic, social, and cultural rights; women and children; torture; and most recently (2002) the International Criminal Court. The U.S. delay or failure to ratify these later covenants came from the notion that U.S. sovereignty and Constitution are supreme, to be controlled by no outside power. The new International Criminal Court started without U.S. participation. President Bush and Congress feared it would bring frivolous charges against American officials and soldiers.

Human-rights law protects private individuals, not states. In Haiti in 1994, egregious violations of human rights brought intervention. UN-established tribunals are trying political leaders and soldiers who violated human rights in the former Yugoslavia and Rwanda. While state preservation remains the guiding principle of IL, the old norm that states can do whatever they wish to their citizens has vanished.

The U.S. invasion of Iraq in 2003 contributed to the new norm that dictators cannot use "sovereignty" to murder with impunity. The Bush administration had earlier proclaimed indifference to IL but soon set a major IL precedent, namely, that dictators are responsible for crimes against their people. (The Nuremberg and Tokyo trials were for crimes against civilians in other countries.) Some of the biggest expansion of IL occurred under the Bush 43 administration.

precedent   Legal reasoning based on previous examples. (See page 317.)

human rights   Freedom from government mistreatment such as torture, jail, or death without due process. (See page 317.)

war crimes   Mistreating prisoners or civilians. (See page 317.)

jus ad bellum   Traditional rules on right to go to war. (See page 317.)

jus in bello   Traditional rules on behavior in war. (See page 317.)

Geneva Convention   Modern rules on behavior in war. (See page 317.)

civil rights   Ability to participate in politics and society, such as voting, free speech, and equality. (See page 317.)

its harsh treatment of suspected IRA terrorists. Britain in 2000 adopted the European Convention on Human Rights as domestic law, thereby giving itself the equivalent of a U.S. Bill of Rights for the first time.

The UN Security Council can establish special tribunals to try war criminals and human rights violators. Two such tribunals, both with Judge Richard Goldstone of South Africa as chief prosecutor, began functioning in 1995—one in the Hague to try offenders in the wars in the former Yugoslavia and one in Tanzania to judge Hutu and Tutsi perpetrators of genocide in Rwanda. Although faced with questions of how to catch the accused and what laws to employ, they did get some convictions and warned future war criminals that they could be brought to justice.

States can take cases against other states to the World Court, but the accused state has to consent in advance. A country cannot be dragged into the World Court. Many states make their participation conditional. The United States is especially cautious. The 1946 Connally Amendment rejects the Court's jurisdiction on "matters which are essentially within the domestic jurisdiction of the United States of America as determined by the United States of America."

■ Self-Help

Injured states can also use a sanction known as "self-help." Weaker states rarely try this against stronger states. The United States indirectly attacked Cuba in 1961, but Cuba did not retaliate by attacking the United States. Some states use extralegal sanctions, such as terrorism and supporting the opposition in the other country.

States that break international agreements have difficulty making new agreements and are isolated diplomatically. For example, Uganda's abuse of foreigners under Idi Amin in the 1970s, Libya's sponsorship of international terrorism in the 1980s, and Iraq's aggression in the Persian Gulf in the 1990s left these regimes shunned in negotiations and reduced their foreign relations.

Worldwide news coverage can damage an offending state. Soviet intervention in Afghanistan and the 2003 U.S. invasion of Iraq hurt both on the world scene. No country likes to be called an aggressor; that can lead to realignments, loss of allies, and intervention. The Idi Amin regime in Uganda was finally toppled when Tanzania aligned with Ugandan rebels and intervened militarily in 1979.

U.S. action against Panama in 1989 is a dramatic example of extralegal self-help. With not one vote of support in the Organization of American States, the United States invaded Panama, overthrew its corrupt government, and carted off its leader, Manuel Antonio Noriega, for trial in Miami on drug charges.

Self-help often leads to violation of IL. Strong states with important national interests at stake tend to ignore legal commands. It was common during the Cold War. The United States tried to subvert Nicaragua's revolutionary government to preserve its sphere of influence. The Soviet Union invaded Afghanistan to keep a buffer client state. In each case the injured party either could not or would not employ sanctions to stop the breaking of international law. Lawbreaking states are willing to suffer some long-term costs when violating IL for what their leaders perceive as short-term necessities.

de facto "In fact"; simplest form of recognition, often informal, without embassies.

de jure "In law"; higher form of recognition, formal and with embassies.

■ Recognition

Recognition acknowledges the existence of another state and its government. It is important in the lives of countries. If most states, especially the major powers, recognize a country, it buttresses its sovereignty and makes it accepted. In the 1970s, South Africa pretended four little black homelands were independent states, but no other country recognized them, and they legally returned to South Africa when Nelson Mandela became president. Recognition does not necessarily mean diplomats are exchanged. Some poor countries recognize other states but do not maintain embassies there. (They meet at the UN.) Recognition can be **de facto** (in fact) by provisionally dealing with that state's representatives or, at a higher level, **de jure** (by law) upon an official pronouncement to that effect.

When the Chinese Communists, for example, took over the mainland in 1949, the United States continued to recognize the Nationalist government, which had fled to the island province of Taiwan. The Korean War, in which Communist China fought the United States, made recognition politically impossible. When the Sino-Soviet rift changed U.S. perceptions of China, President Nixon made his dramatic 1972 trip to Beijing, a form of de facto recognition. In 1979, Beijing and Washington de jure recognized each other. This required Washington to de-recognize Taiwan, as Beijing insists it is the one and only China. U.S. Secretary of State Albright's visit to North Korea in 2000 gave that country de facto but not yet de jure recognition.

Recognition helps make states participants in IL because it gives them certain rights; for example, the right of continued existence, which means the right of self-defense. Article 51 of the UN Charter confirms this right. The duties of states come from respecting the rights of other states. States have a duty to obey treaties. They have a duty not to intervene in another state, although this is widely ignored. Some argue they have the right to protect their citizens in other lands and to render humanitarian service where natural or political disasters "shock the conscience of humankind." In 2003, even the United States sent civilian and military personal to Iran to help after a terrible earthquake.

The UN Security Council said the international community had a duty to intervene in Haiti in 1994, where a military regime was abusing civil and political rights. Haitians fled in unsafe boats, and hundreds drowned. More interventions are now UN-sanctioned than ever before, and most involve human rights abuses (see Chapter 22).

◼ IL and Individuals

Individuals have some rights under various conventions on human rights. Citizens have a right to claim protection by their state. Sometimes they do not get it, and some become refugees. The 1951 Geneva Convention on the Status of Refugees, has given refugees some not very clear rights. Criminals can be extradited to the state where the crime was committed, but some states reject extradition and grant foreign political offenders asylum.

Criminals committing crimes within the jurisdiction of a foreign state are usually subject to prosecution by that state, as Americans caught using drugs abroad have discovered. So have hijackers, pirates, slave traders, and terrorists.

◼ Territory

Under IL, conquest and annexation of territory are frowned upon. Disputes over territory can lead quickly to violent conflict. The best way to prevent this is to establish and observe boundaries under IL. First, a border must be agreed upon in a boundary treaty and carefully marked on maps and on the ground, as with concrete pylons and posted signs. Unfortunately, few borders in the world have been so clearly established.

IL tries to move disputes to settlement, often using historic or geographic indicators. There are many boundary questions that IL has tried to solve: the India-Pakistan fight over

Reflections

EICHMANN AND PIRACY

As a young journalist I landed a job with the Associated Press at the Eichmann trial in Jerusalem in 1961. This got me into the meticulously secured building for a firsthand view of the "trial of the century." Adolph Eichmann had been a mid-level Nazi official in charge of rounding up Europe's Jews and shipping them to death camps. He had been living in Argentina under an assumed name when Israeli agents kidnapped him and brought him to Israel for trial.

There was a lot of discussion in the courtroom about the IL aspects of the Eichmann case. How could Israel (1) kidnap someone from another country; (2) try him for crimes committed in distant countries before Israel even existed; and (3) call him a criminal when he was just following orders?

These arguments took weeks and were highly complex, but the main argument of Attorney General Gideon Hausner was piracy. IL had long held that pirates can be tried by whomever catches them; their crimes are not specific to a nation or place. Hausner argued that piracy law set a precedent for other types of international lawlessness. As for Eichmann just following orders, Hausner demonstrated that (1) the orders themselves were illegal, and (2) Eichmann exceeded them in his personal eagerness to kill Jews. Eichmann was found guilty, among other points, of "crimes against humanity" and was hanged the following year.

—M. G. R.

Kashmir, Venezuela with Guyana, Peru with Ecuador, Argentina with Chile over Tierra del Fuego, Morocco with Algeria over the Spanish Sahara, and Iran with Iraq over the Shatt al-Arab waterway. In this last case, customary IL puts the boundaries between two **riparian** states at the deepest point of the river. In all such cases, IL can work only if the disputants want to settle. Then IL becomes a convenient and sometimes face-saving way to do so.

riparian   Country bordering a river.

In a parallel with the law of the sea, states control the air above their territory to the edge of the earth's atmosphere, generally taken to mean as high as a plane can fly. Custom and a UN resolution say that orbiting satellites are outside the state's jurisdiction, like international waters.

■ War

The Kellogg-Briand Pact of 1928 actually outlawed war. Some use this as an example of the irrelevance of IL. Article 51 of the UN Charter allows war for self-defense. In 1625 Grotius wrote that it is lawful "to kill him who is preparing to kill." The difficulty in defining who is the aggressor and who the defender has left international law largely impotent in eliminating the use of armed force. Where IL has been more successful is in limiting the use of armed force. Customary IL prohibits the excessive use of force to defeat an enemy.

Multilateral conventions, going back to the 1864 Geneva Convention, prohibit certain practices and weapons and establish various procedures for the conduct of war. Poison gas, exploding bullets, and shotguns have been prohibited. Neutrals, civilians, and prisoners of war are supposed to have rights and obligations. Victors occupying conquered land have been constrained in their treatment of the defeated. Trials for war crimes are becoming more frequent. Nevertheless, it is safe to say that every side in every war has violated the rules of war.

Turning Point

HOLE IN THE OZONE

IL plays a major role in the world's growing awareness of man-made environmental damage. Ultraviolet (UV) radiation from the sun causes skin cancer and other damage. A fragile layer of ozone shields the earth from much UV. Scientists discovered that chlorofluorocarbons (CFCs), chemicals in aerosol sprays and refrigerants, attack and deplete the ozone layer. In 1987 a hole in the ozone layer was discovered over Antarctica. A series of negotiations produced a protocol signed and ratified by many states to reduce the production and use of CFCs. Your air conditioner and hair spray are now different because of that. Discussions are underway to reduce the gases that contribute to global warming.

Attacking harmless civilians is a war crime under the Geneva Convention of 1949, seconded by the U.S. Uniform Code of Military Justice. In 1968, U.S. soldiers slaughtered over three hundred Vietnamese civilians in My Lai, South Vietnam. The U.S. military had never instructed its soldiers about war crimes. Now representatives of the Judge Advocate General (JAG) advise all operations and draw up rules of engagement (ROEs), especially important in tricky peace operations.

■ The Future of IL

The legitimacy of IL is on the rise in spite of the obvious violations we now see in regional wars, terrorism, and human-rights violations. Even the Bush 43 administration was compelled to say it respected IL. The present, unsettled world leaves regional conflicts uncontrolled and with the potential to spread, to disrupt trade, and to result in massacres of people. These threats create common national interests for a more stable, orderly world. IL can help.

Half of the world's states are at least approximately democratic and favor rule of law in guiding international relations. Communication and transportation has vastly accelerated exchanges between states, exchanges that have to be regulated. The cyberworld was unhappy in 2000 when the Filipino "love bug" hacker, who caused millions in damage, walked free because the Philippines had no law against it. It has now.

One indicator of the growth of IL is the number of U.S. law schools that teach it. In 1900, only six had such programs. Now, ten times that number exist. One way to produce more law—as Americans well know—is to produce more lawyers. If a new, more peaceful IR system consolidates around the world, there will be a major growth of IL.

Key Terms

civil rights (p. 318)

consistency (p. 311)

de facto (p. 319)

de jure (p. 319)

exclusive economic zone (p. 316)

executive agreement (p. 314)

Geneva Convention (p. 318)

human rights (p. 318)

jus ad bellum (p. 318)

jus in bello (p. 318)

precedent (p. 318)

ratify (p. 312)

reciprocity (p. 311)

riparian (p. 321)

sanction (p. 313)

territorial limit (p. 313)

treaty (p. 312)

war crimes (p. 318)

Key Web Sites

Multilateral Treaty Texts
http://www.tufts.edu/fletcher/multilaterals.html

United Nations Treaty DataBase
http://www.un.org/Depts/Treaty/

Foreign and International Law
http://lawlib.wuacc.edu/forint/forintmain.html

International Court of Justice
http://www.icj-cij.org/

International Law from the United Nations
http://www.un.org/law/

International Law (The WWW Virtual Library Site)
http://www.pitt.edu/~ian/resource/law.htm

Transitional Justice Forum
http://tj-forum.org/

Further Reference

Bass, Gary J. *Stay the Hand of Vengeance: The Politics of War Crimes Tribunals.* Princeton, NJ: Princeton University Press, 2000.

Bederman, David J. *International Law Frameworks.* New York: Foundation Press, 2001.

Byers, Michael. *War Law: Understanding International Law and Armed Conflict.* New York: Grove, 2006.

Donnelly, Jack. *International Human Rights,* 3rd ed. Boulder, CO: Westview, 2006.

Glahn, Gerhard von, and James L. Taulbee. *Law among Nations: An Introduction to Public International Law,* 8th ed. Boston, MA: Longman, 2006.

Goldsmith, Jack, and Eric Posner. *The Limits of International Law.* New York: Oxford University Press, 2006.

Malanczuk, Peter. *Akehurst's Modern Introduction to International Law,* 8th ed. New York: Routledge, 2004.

Maogoto, Jackson Nyamuya. *War Crimes and Realpolitik: International Justice from World War I to the 21st Century.* Boulder, CO: Lynne Rienner, 2004.

Murphy, John F. *The United States and the Rule of Law in International Affairs.* New York: Cambridge University Press, 2004.

Rabkin, Jeremy A. *Law without Nations? Why Constitutional Government Requires Sovereign States.* Princeton, NJ: Princeton University Press, 2005.

Rawls, John. *The Law of Peoples.* Cambridge, MA: Harvard University Press, 2000.

Rochester, J. Martin. *Between Peril and Promise: The Politics of International Law.* Washington, D.C.: CQ Press, 2006.

Scott, Shirley V. *International Law in World Politics: An Introduction.* Boulder, CO: Lynne Rienner, 2004.

Stover, Eric. *The Witnesses: War Crimes and the Promise of Justice in the Hague.* Philadelphia, PA: University of Pennsylvania Press, 2005.

Trimble, Phillip R. *International Law: United States Foreign Relations Law.* New York: Foundation Press, 2002.

Tuck, Richard. *The Rights of War and Peace: Political Thought and the International Order from Grotius to Kant.* New York: Oxford University Press, 2000.

Williams, Paul R., and Michael P. Scharf. *Peace with Justice? War Crimes and Accountability in the Former Yugoslavia.* Lanham, MD: Rowman & Littlefield, 2002.

CHAPTER 21

THE UNITED NATIONS

QUESTIONS TO CONSIDER

1. Why was the UN designed to have little power?
2. What was Emery Reves's theory of world government?
3. Who authored the League of Nations? Why did it fail?
4. What was Roosevelt's concept of the "four policemen"?
5. Who are the permanent members of the Security Council? Should they be permanent?
6. Who were the UN secretaries general?
7. What are the various types of third-party diplomacy?
8. How was functionalism supposed to work?
9. Why and over what is the United States at odds with the UN?

The standard approach to the United Nations is to expect too much from it and then denounce it for not delivering. Many look to the UN to solve horrendous problems of war, bloody dictators, genocide, and nuclear proliferation. But the UN has next to no enforcement mechanism—no police, no courts, and no armed forces. It can sometimes borrow—at high salaries—the armed forces of willing countries for peacekeeping missions (see Chapter 22) that the major powers have agreed to in advance. On its own, the UN can do nothing. If anything gets enforced, it's because the major powers, if they are in agreement, want it enforced. In many ways the UN really is just a big debating society whose conclusions, if they are ever reached, are not always obeyed.

But often the very people who denounce the UN for its weakness are precisely the ones who would not stand for it infringing on their nation's sovereignty. How many Americans would obey a UN vote requiring the United States to pull out of Iraq or cut its emission of greenhouse gases? "No way!" they would say, "We don't knuckle under to any other power." In a world of sovereign states, "world government" is a misnomer. The UN cannot govern much of anything and was not designed to. It was made deliberately powerless because its founders did not want anyone else telling them what to do. Voluntary compliance based on reason and national interest is the best it can hope to achieve. The UN was born weak and is likely to stay that way.

The United Nations is not worthless. Most countries try to persuade it and work through it. It's a good place to talk, and the talking can sometimes prevent fighting. Few countries totally reject the UN because they do not want to be regarded as international bullies. Even U.S. Republican administrations, which often disdain the UN, do not seriously consider withdrawing from it, for such a move would isolate and weaken the United States. The number of UN operations to settle or contain regional and civil wars has more than doubled since 1987. The major powers want the UN to stabilize world politics. Could the world now be ready, in the words of the Preamble to the UN Charter, for an international organization "to save succeeding generations from the scourge of war"?

◼ Theory of World Government

The idea of an international body that would prevent war has been around for a long time. The Romans proudly spoke of *Pax Romana,* the "Roman peace" that came with being part of the empire, which was, of course, not voluntary. Rome simply crushed those who did not obey and was constantly at war.

The medieval Roman Catholic Church planted the idea of a unified world—which in those centuries meant Europe—in which kings would acknowledge the supremacy of the pope. The church would provide guidance and try to dampen conflict among monarchs. The Middle Ages closed, however, with monarchs deciding they didn't need to obey the pope; instead they instituted their own absolute rule, strengthened their kingdoms, and turned them into nation-states. The Protestant Reformation shattered the tenuous unity of the Middle Ages.

Classic Thought

LE RÊVE DE REVES

Just as the United Nations was born amid great hopes in 1945, American writer Emery Reves published *The Anatomy of Peace,* a reasoned defense of a supranational entity that would take away each nation's sovereign right to make war. Reves's reasoning:

Wars between groups of men forming social units always take place when these units—tribes, dynasties, churches, cities, nations—exercise unrestricted sovereign power.

Wars between these social units cease the moment sovereign power is transferred from them to a larger or higher unit.

It was an optimistic line of thought, one that suited the times. The historical progression is from smaller to larger units. Logically, the next step is to enroll the nations into a single, large unit: the United Nations. Reves may have been too early with his vision, but was he totally dreaming?

As the Thirty Years War raged early in the seventeenth century, the Frenchman Emeric Crucé proposed a world organization that would promote trade and settle disputes by a majority decision of a council of ambassadors. William Penn, founder of Pennsylvania, proposed a world parliament that would settle conflicts by a three-fourths vote and enforce its decisions by armed force. The great German philosopher Immanuel Kant proposed a "League for Perpetual Peace."

Versailles 1919 treaty that ended World War I.

In the wake of the Napoleonic wars, Austrian Prince Metternich set up a Concert of Europe in which all the major European monarchs would consult and suppress nationalism and liberalism. This was an international organization based on the balance-of-power theory (see Chapter 1) with a reactionary twist; it fell apart as the forces of modernity made impossible the old order of conservative monarchies. Its final collapse was World War I.

■ The Short, Sad League of Nations

For some observers—especially Americans—World War I or the Great War, as it was then called, proved the wickedness and perversity of the "balance-of-power" system used by European statesmen to justify the cynical moves that led to the giant conflagration. U.S. President Woodrow Wilson, one of America's first political scientists, slowly and reluctantly brought the United States into the war in 1917 on an idealistic basis, a "war fought to end all wars." Wilson went to the **Versailles** peace conference insisting that it set up a League of Nations to prevent future wars. Britain and France accepted the League idea but slanted it to keep themselves in the top spots globally and to retain their vast empires. The Covenant of the League of Nations was part of the Versailles treaty.

But Wilson couldn't get the Senate to approve the treaty. Slightly over one-third of the senators found something to object to, and it takes two-thirds to ratify. Some of their objections seemed valid. Could the League Covenant force the United States to go to war, bypassing a congressional

Woodrow Wilson is commemorated in this statue of the signs of the zodiac that adorns the lawn of the League of Nations building in Geneva, Switzerland. It is now the European headquarters of the UN and home to many negotiations. (Michael G. Roskin)

collective security Agreement by all countries to automatically punish aggressor states.

declaration of war? Would the United States have to keep Britain and France permanently on the victors' throne? Important for Irish-Americans: Did the League mean that Britain could keep Ireland forever? Important for German-Americans: Did League membership mean the United States would assist France in keeping Germany down? In addition, some Republican senators just plain hated Wilson, who was a cold, rigid personality. The treaty failed, and Wilson left office a bitter man. Fed up with Wilson's idealistic rhetoric, America slouched into isolationism.

One of the arguments during and after World War II was whether U.S. participation in the League might have headed off World War II. Most Democrats, certainly Roosevelt and Truman, believed that America's absence from the League had been a terrible mistake—primitive Republican isolationism—that had led to its failure and to war. But passive U.S. membership would have changed nothing, and during the 1920s and 1930s an isolationist America supported only rhetorical peace gestures. An active America willing to contribute military force for "collective security" might have made a huge difference. But that was simply not America in those years.

The League got off to a reasonable start in 1920 with forty-two member states (later it grew to sixty). All members had one vote in the Assembly, which met about one month a year. (The UN equivalent is the General Assembly.) The Council, consisting of from eight to fifteen members, met more frequently to conciliate disputes. (The UN equivalent is the Security Council.) A permanent Secretariat under a secretary general (just like the UN) ran day-to-day affairs. A magnificent headquarters, the Palais des Nations (Palace of the Nations), was constructed in Geneva, Switzerland.

The crux of the League was **collective security** under Article 16 of the Covenant. Members agreed to leave other states alone. In a dispute, the two sides were to refrain

Concepts

COLLECTIVE SECURITY

Elements of collective security can be found in ancient Greece and the Middle Ages, but it did not come into its own until the League of Nations. The idea, magnificent on paper, offered a middle way between the instability of the balance-of-power system, which had just failed to prevent World War I, and a total world government, which would enforce the peace by a near-monopoly on military power, which was too much to ask for in a world where all nations jealously guard their sovereignty.

The middle way was as follows: All nations would agree to collectively punish any nation that practiced aggression. Like balance of power, collective security was willing to meet aggression by forming an alliance against it. The difference was that collective security was a permanent, standing alliance against any aggressor. Each nation would give up some of its sovereignty regarding when to go to war; instead, the League's Council would decide. Any country contemplating aggression would thus know that it would face the combined strength of all other nations. Ergo, there would be no aggression; however, it didn't work that way.

from war for at least three months while the League looked for a solution. If one party turned out to be the aggressor, all League members were required to break economic and political ties with it. If that didn't curb the aggressor, the Council could recommend military actions against it. Surely no would-be aggressor could withstand the combined boycott and military threat of the rest of the world.

The failure of collective security spelled the end of the League. The idea had at least two weaknesses: (1) the difficulty of agreeing on what aggression is, and (2) getting member states to go along with Council requests to apply sanctions.

Aggression is often hard to define. What looks like aggression to some is merely vigorous defense to others. Israelis in the 1967 war, Americans in Iraq, Soviets in Afghanistan, and Iraqis in Kuwait were all convinced they were acting defensively. Even Hitler claimed he was acting to defend Germany against a fiendish threat, and many Germans believed him. In the modern world, everyone is defensive. There are no more "war ministries"; now they are all "defense ministries." The last conqueror to admit that he was practicing aggression was probably Genghis Khan.

Real aggressors often disguise their misdeeds. The beginning of the end for the League came with the Japanese conquest of Manchuria in 1931. The Japanese military set off a small bomb on some railroad tracks and said the Chinese did it. Who could prove otherwise? By the time the League's Council could send a commission of inquiry, the conquest was complete. The commission noted that the conquest was not ordered by the civilian government and found it difficult to condemn Tokyo. Soon Japan withdrew from the League anyway.

Most of the world didn't care about Manchuria, and a few admired Japan. Britain and France, the leading democracies of the League, were not about to send troops to the other side of the world for an area neither of them cared about. There was no point in antagonizing Japan by a boycott, because Britain and France had extensive colonies in Southeast Asia that were vulnerable to Japanese attack. (These colonies were, of course, quickly taken over by Japan early in World War II.) In terms of the national interests of the democracies, Manchuria wasn't worth making a fuss about.

Turning Point

WAS KOREA COLLECTIVE SECURITY?

When North Korea invaded South Korea in 1950, President Truman saw an analogy to the aggression of the 1930s and asked the United Nations for a collective military response. U.S. forces fought under the UN flag, and the U.S. commander was called the supreme commander of UN forces, but it was not collective security. Most U.S. allies contributed only token forces. If the Soviet Union and China had been on our side, that would have been collective security. They, of course, supported North Korea. The 1991 and 2003 Iraq war don't qualify either. The coalition forces were ad hoc responses and not prearranged.

veto   Blocking a measure by just one vote against.

And a few dictators intended to do the same as Japan. Mussolini conquered Ethiopia in 1935, and Emperor Haile Selassie addressed the League's Assembly to warn them with tears in his eyes that Ethiopia may seem far away to them, but soon they too would be victims of aggression. He was right, of course, but Britain, which could have easily ended the Ethiopian campaign by denying Italy use of the Suez Canal, didn't want to risk pushing Mussolini into the arms of Hitler. (He willingly embraced Hitler anyway.)

Hitler noted the League's weak response to the Japanese and Italians. He withdrew Germany from the League and picked up one piece of Europe after another, claiming he was just consolidating the German people into one country. Until 1939, nobody tried to stop him. Then Hitler invaded Poland, and it was too late to stop the aggressors with collective security; it took a war. With the outbreak of World War II, the League was effectively dead, although it kept a skeleton staff to hand over its buildings and mandates to the United Nations after the war. (The Palais des Nations in Geneva is now the European headquarters of the United Nations and the site of many important conferences.)

Some say it is unfair to condemn collective security because it was never really tried. Had it not been for the timidity and cowardice of Britain and France (and the isolationism of America), some argue, collective security might have worked. But nations do what they do for good reasons. The democracies couldn't understand at the time the aggressive, world-conquering nature of the dictatorships. They could not foretell the future and feared that sanctions imposed under collective security would only make things worse. And they were in no mood to go to war for distant lands. The trouble with collective security was that it asked nations to be what they aren't: farsighted, altruistic, and willing to let others make decisions for them.

The Rise of the UN

Franklin D. Roosevelt had been assistant secretary of the Navy under Wilson and still had some of Wilson's idealism. If America participated in World War II, it must be with an eye toward setting up a United Nations to prevent future wars. FDR saw this as a chance to rectify the tragic failure of the League. In wartime meetings, FDR obtained Churchill's lukewarm support for a postwar UN and Stalin's indifferent consent. The American president was so enthusiastic about the idea, and America was supplying so much war aid, that they felt they must humor the man. Truman continued FDR's hopes for the United Nations when it swung into operation in 1945. This time America was the United Nations' most enthusiastic backer.

As noted, in structure the UN is very much like the old League of Nations: a General Assembly (GA) that meets every fall in which all nations have one vote; a fifteen-nation (enlarged from ten) Security Council that can meet any time to preserve peace; and a Secretariat to run the organization. A secretary general is elected by the GA for renewable five-year terms. The GA has only the power to recommend action. In contrast, the Security Council can order compliance with its resolutions. Each of the five permanent members of the Security Council has the right to **veto** any resolution. That is, if the

United States, Russia, China, Britain, or France dislike some measure, their lone vote—even fourteen-to-one—shoots the resolution down. The ten nonpermanent members, who are elected by the GA for two-year terms, have an ordinary vote without veto. Nothing, in other words, can go against the wishes of even one of the Big Five.

You can see problems here. Are these five really the most important or powerful countries in the world? The United States is, but Britain and France have long since been overtaken economically by Germany and Japan, who have both requested permanent seats on the Security Council. China—since 1971 mainland Communist China rather than Nationalist Taiwan—is the most populous country and enjoying rapid economic growth. Russia is big but no longer an impressive force. Some countries are campaigning to add six new permanent seats to the Security Council. Brazil and India, claiming to speak for the Third World, and Egypt, Nigeria, and South Africa, claiming to speak for Africa, each want permanent seats. The Big Five do not like adding permanent members—it would dilute their power—but might consider it if the newcomers have no right of veto. Who is to decide which nations can keep the peace? What we have with the Big Five is FDR's wartime notions of who should guide the world. What may have been a reasonable choice then no longer corresponds to power realities decades later. And there is no mechanism for adding permanent Security Council members.

A more basic problem is why any major country should have a veto over the will of the majority. Stalin at Yalta in 1945 insisted on the veto provision, and Churchill and Roosevelt went along. Stalin felt (correctly) that the Soviet Union would be so outnumbered by non-Communist countries that it would suffer permanent condemnation. The UN framers put in the unit veto as a mechanism to enable a major power to stay in the UN and not withdraw over something it didn't like—the way Germany, Japan, and Italy had withdrawn from the League in the 1930s. They understood that the veto could render

Turning Point

THE FOUR POLICEMEN

President Roosevelt saw the possibility of world stability after World War II because the four most powerful nations of the world would cooperate in running the UN. The United States, Soviet Union, Britain, and China would be the globe's "four policemen," each preventing disorder in its area of influence and keeping the peace as the "Big Four" permanent members of the new UN Security Council. (When de Gaulle squawked, France was made the fifth permanent member.)

FDR projected the temporary and illusory unity of World War II onto the postwar future. First, China was big but weak; it had barely resisted the Japanese during the war. With the Communist victory in 1949, China turned into an enemy. Second, FDR, a personally charming man, thought he could charm Stalin into cooperative behavior after the war. FDR was mistakenly projecting his domestic political skills onto the world stage, a common error of American presidents. Britain had been drained by the war and soon lost its colonies. And this was another problem: the rapid growth in number of nations in the world and members in the United Nations, many of them with anticolonial chips on their shoulders. Even if the "Big Four" held together, much of the world would not have obeyed them.

President Bush speaks to the General Assembly at the United Nations in New York in 2002. (Ruth Fremson/The New York Times)

the Security Council toothless, but better to keep the big powers talking, they reasoned. At first, only the Soviet Union used the veto, but later the Western powers, including the United States, also found it convenient.

In fairness, the veto system has kept the UN alive a lot longer than the League. Without it, one or several of the Big Five powers would long since have withdrawn from the UN. The veto in the Security Council has been likened to a fuse in a house wiring system. If the system overheats, better to have a fuse blow (a veto) than the house burn down. The price for holding the system together in this way, though, is its powerlessness to solve many disputes. The U.S.-led Kosovo campaign had no UN authorization because Russia and China would have vetoed it. The Security Council did not specifically authorize the 2003 U.S. invasion of Iraq, although we said earlier resolutions amounted to the same thing.

■ The UN: Early Idealism

When it started, many people believed in the UN, especially Americans. Washington looked first to the UN to contribute to peaceful solutions to conflicts. In some measure, the UN did, but often not in a permanent way. The superpowers rarely agreed to final settlements; they were happy just to end expensive combat in deadlocked Cold War contests. Still, here and there, the UN has helped.

Palestine was one of the UN's first problems (see Chapter 8). The British, who had a mandate to govern Palestine from the old League of Nations, were fed up with Arab-Jewish fighting and announced in 1947 that they would pull out the following spring. They threw the issue to the UN, which devised a partition plan, dividing Palestine into a checkerboard of Jewish and Arab territories. It was probably unworkable, but the General Assembly voted thirty-three to thirteen in favor of partition. The Jews accepted it; the Arabs rejected it.

The 1947 UN partition plan illustrates the difficulty of an outside body trying to settle a local fight. True, a majority of the UN supported the plan, but none of the countries in the immediate region did. Should the vote of a Central American republic (under U.S. pressure) count as much as the vote of a country that would be immediately affected? To the Arabs, the UN vote lacked legitimacy, and they invaded the newly proclaimed state of Israel in the spring of 1948. The UN system didn't work here.

mediation Suggesting compromises to disputants.

After the Arab attack failed, though, they grudgingly consented to UN **mediation**. Here the UN was useful, although the result was an unstable armistice rather than a peace treaty. A UN Truce Supervision Organization (UNTSO), staffed by unarmed professional soldiers from neutral countries, helped to keep the peace by reporting violations. The way the truce was reached by Ralph Bunche gives Americans cause for pride (see box below).

The Korean War, although it was not collective security, gave at least a temporary boost to the authority of the UN. Truman, still a believer in the UN, immediately referred the 1950 North Korean invasion to the Security Council. A resolution urged all UN members to "furnish assistance" to repel North Korean aggression, and it passed. Why didn't the Soviets veto it?

The explanation is half comical. The Soviet delegation had been demanding that Communist China, which had just won a civil war, take the UN seat occupied by Nationalist China, which had recently retreated to Taiwan. The Security Council, dominated by Western powers, wouldn't comply, so the Soviets showed their displeasure by stalking out. In their absence, the Security Council passed the resolution condemning

Turning Point

RALPH BUNCHE: UN HERO

From black civil-rights advocate in the 1930s to world statesman in the 1940s, Ralph Bunche illustrates the American involvement with the founding of the United Nations and how third-party diplomacy can work. Bunche earned a Ph.D. in political science at Harvard, taught at Howard in Washington, then went into the State Department and served on the U.S. delegation to draft the UN Charter in 1946. Bunche wanted decolonization as one of the UN's main goals, but his own delegation showed no interest, so Bunche quietly took his draft to the Australian delegation, which got it included in the Charter. Bunche knew how to manipulate procedures, a cardinal diplomatic skill.

Bunche then joined the UN Secretariat as director of trusteeship affairs (i.e., decolonization) and was assigned the delicate task of mediating an end to the first Arab–Israeli war of 1948–1949. With no guidance from superiors and improvising as he went, Bunche finally got the Arabs to agree to "proximity talks" with the Israelis. The Arabs refused to meet the Israelis face to face, so Bunche gathered them into a hotel on the Greek island of Rhodes—on separate floors. Endlessly climbing from one floor to another, Bunche carried negotiating points back and forth, deftly adding his own suggestions. In the armistice, all sides agreed to stop fighting along lines that became Israel's borders until 1967. Ralph Bunche won the Nobel Peace Prize in 1950 but was proudest of developing the concept of "peacekeeping" (see Chapter 22).

North Korea and asking for help in resisting aggression. No member has missed a Security Council session since. As the French say, *Les absents ont toujours tort* ("Those absent are always wrong").

■ Disillusion with the UN

Would the right leadership have given the UN strength to solve world problems? This intriguing question can never be settled. The first two secretaries general (see box below) were respected and with that came respect for the UN in general. The next two were weak, indecisive figures, and the UN's reputation as a whole declined.

But was it completely their fault? The UN changed a lot in the 1960s, becoming bigger and more complex. First, membership more than tripled. From fifty-one founding members—mostly from Europe and Latin America—UN membership ballooned with decolonization in the 1950s and 1960s. In just two years, 1960 and 1961, most of Africa went from being British, French, or Belgian colonies to independent states, all of which immediately joined the UN. With the addition of former Soviet and Yugoslav republics, there are now 192 UN members, most of them Global South and poor, some of them ministates.

Turning Point

GREAT AND NOT-SO-GREAT SECRETARIES GENERAL

The UN's first two secretaries general, Trygve Lie of Norway (1946–1953) and Dag Hammarskjöld of Sweden (1953–1961), were strong personalities who deeply believed in the UN's peace missions. Both stood up for peace even when criticized from East and West, and neither was afraid of committing the UN to difficult situations. Hammarskjöld actually died in the line of duty, in a plane crash while supervising UN forces trying to bring peace to the strife-torn Congo.

Their two immediate successors were lesser men, afraid to use the UN as anything more than a debating society. U Thant of Burma (1961–1971) had such a pro-Third World orientation that he could see no wrong in demands from developing countries. He speedily acquiesced to Nasser's demand to remove UN forces from the Sinai, a step that led to the 1967 Mideast War. Kurt Waldheim of Austria (1972–1981) was a courtly ex-Nazi who hid his past in order to posture as a world leader while doing little.

Stronger leadership returned with Javier Pérez de Cuéllar of Peru (1982–1991). He skillfully projected the UN into conflicts in which the superpowers lost interest as the Cold War faded. UN negotiators mediated a cease-fire in the Iran-Iraq War, the independence of Namibia, the end to the Angolan, Cambodian, and Salvadorean civil wars, and the status of Western Sahara (see Third-Party Diplomacy box on page 335). Boutros Boutros-Ghali of Egypt (1992–1996) inherited a UN at the height of its activity and took a strong leadership role. He sometimes ran afoul of the major powers on the Security Council, including the United States, which vetoed him for a second term for not cutting costs. Kofi Annan of Ghana, the UN undersecretary general for peacekeeping, won U.S. approval and took over in 1997. Annan, with the Rwanda massacres in mind, wanted a more activist UN, but he, too, ran afoul of U.S. isolationism. South Korea's foreign minister, Ban Ki-moon, was slated to take over at the end of 2006.

Poor countries often have a radical perspective on the world economy and demand vast sums for development (see Chapter 11). Organized as the Group of 77 in the GA, they also condemn any situation that looks like colonialism and routinely vote against Israel, Russia, and America.

During the Cold War, North-South conflicts merged with East-West conflicts to paralyze the UN. Majorities, especially including the five permanent members of the Security Council, were hard to come by. Sometimes, however, majorities appeared when particular conflicts threatened just about every member's interest. A breakdown in authority in the former Belgian Congo between 1960 and 1963, the 1967 and 1973 Middle East wars, and the ethnic struggles in Cyprus in 1964 and 1974 brought cooperation under the aegis of the UN.

Both the United States and Soviet Union used the UN as a foreign policy tool in their battles. They introduced resolutions to embarrass each other and larded their speeches with propaganda. (UN delegates are instructed by their foreign ministries on what to say and how to vote.) During the Cold War, they never allowed the UN to control any conflict in which they had an interest. The Vietnamese and Afghan wars were kept out of the UN, which was unable to fulfill its Charter's peacekeeping purposes.

third party   Someone not party to a dispute.

good offices   Giving disputants a meeting place.

arbitration   Disputants' agreement to obey third-party decision.

Concepts

THIRD-PARTY DIPLOMACY

One way to settle disputes is to have a neutral **third party** come between the two hostile parties. Third-party diplomacy is often the only way to bring warring nations to the conference table. Their hostility prevents a bilateral (two-party) meeting. The UN is the perfect instrument for third-party diplomacy, offering a face-saving way out of conflict. The Iran-Iraq War, the Soviet occupation of Afghanistan, and the decolonization of Namibia were negotiated under UN auspices. If for no other reason, the third-party function of the United Nations makes the organization worthwhile.

There are three ways a third party may facilitate the resolution of conflict:

Good Offices   Here, the third party gets the conflicting parties together, providing a meeting place, support services, and security. Secretary General Javier Pérez de Cuéllar brought France and New Zealand together under his **good offices** to settle the sinking of a Greenpeace protest vessel, for example.

Mediation and Conciliation   In more difficult situations, the third party may make proposals and give advice. Presidents Carter and Clinton tried to mediate Arab-Israeli conflicts at Camp David. Conciliation goes one step further; the third party, such as U.S. envoy Richard Holbrooke at Dayton in 1995, offers solutions to the disputants.

Arbitration   **Arbitration** has the disputants select arbitrators, who actually make a decision after hearing the evidence. The parties are supposed to accept the decision, but there is no way to force them, and arbitration is rare.

■ The Uses of the UN

The UN is a fabulous listening post. Diplomats, journalists, and scholars can learn more about what's happening in the world in a few weeks at the UN than anywhere else. Border disputes, regional weather calamities, desperate refugees—often stories that don't appear in the news media—are the standard fare of UN committees. The UN thus serves as an early-warning system for tomorrow's problems and controversies.

The UN is also a diplomatic bargain for small, poor countries that can afford only two or three embassies around the world. At the UN headquarters in Manhattan, for the price of one mission to the UN, they can have diplomatic contact with all nations. Manhattan itself is not a bad location for the UN. There are already so many strange people in New York City that foreign diplomats don't attract much attention. Even enemies can get together discreetly. Israel could talk to Jordan, Iran to the United States.

The world faces a growing class of issues that require international solutions, the so-called "world-order issues," which can include everything from uses of the seabed to climate changes. Although not yet uniformly appreciated, they are probably the great issues of twenty-first-century politics.

Reflections

PAYING ATTENTION TO THE DEEP SEABED

As a journalist for the Associated Press, I covered some of the activities of the 1968 General Assembly. (The GA meets every fall.) Some of the meetings were dull, and many were unintelligible to a newcomer. One meeting I had to cover seemed pointless until years later. I had actually witnessed an important strategic discussion and didn't know it.

The committee was on the uses of the seabed, chiefly on who owned its mineral rights. One of the points was on "peaceful uses of the seabed." I thought that was pretty silly, for how could anyone use the seabed for war? Even sillier, I thought, was the quibble between the U.S. and Soviet delegates. The American wanted to prohibit using the deep seabed for "any weapon"; the Soviet wanted to prohibit "any military uses" of the deep seabed. I strained to make a news story out of what seemed to be a dispute about nothing.

Years later, I found out what they had really been talking about. At that very time, in secrecy,

the United States was implanting undersea listening devices on the seabed to monitor the coming and going of Soviet nuclear submarines. Soviet subs were then rather noisy and easy to pick up as they passed the North Cape, Skagerrak, Turkish Straits, and Pérouse Strait. This gave us a terrific advantage.

The Soviets knew what we were doing and hated it. So they tried to use obscure wording in a UN seabed convention to prohibit such devices—"any military uses." The United States knew full well what this meant, so they wanted only a prohibition on weapons (and a listening device is not a weapon). The veiled language used by both sides concealed a major step in the arms race that they wished to keep quiet. If I had known this, I could have had a page-one story. The UN is a great listening post, but you need considerable background to follow its debates.

—M. G. R.

What, for example, are we going to do about the "green-house effect" that may be heating the planet and affecting weather and farming? Carbon dioxide from burning fuel traps more of the sun's heat, melting the polar icecaps and raising the level of the oceans. One or even a few countries can do nothing. To cut back the use of fossil fuels requires global planning and compliance with international standards. Americans may not like limits on their cars and smokestacks, but neither do they like hurricanes and floods. The world is getting crowded and polluted, and this may force greater international cooperation.

functionalism   Gaining countries' cooperation in specialized matters so it spills over into general cooperation.

■ The Functionalist Dream

World-order issues may reawaken the **functionalist** dream, a view that waxed and waned along with enthusiasm for the UN. The crux of functionalism is the presumed spillover effect that grows out of cooperation on immediate problems. If Arabs and Israelis, for example, can work together on smallpox eradication, they may temper their hostilities and even learn to live together.

Besides, many of the specialized agencies linked to the UN do fine work, tasks that would have to be undertaken even if there were no UN. Under the supervision of the World Health Organization, for example, the world wiped out smallpox. Some of the agencies, such as the Universal Postal Union, long antedate the UN. The UPU makes sure mail flows between countries and keeps tabs on which countries owe postage due. The many agencies also let more countries have an organization in their capital. Geneva, Switzerland, of course, has many agencies, holdovers from the League of Nations.

Some of these agencies became political footballs, especially when Global South members in cooperation with the Soviet bloc took them over and used them as platforms to excoriate Israel, South Africa, or the United States. For this reason, the United States and Britain withdrew from UNESCO. (The United States also withdrew for a year from the International Labor Organization, accusing it of subservience to Communist aims.) UNESCO

Concepts

FUNCTIONALISM

Political tension prevents the direct building of world authority, but if we can get nations working together on relatively small, "functional" issues—disease, weather, famine, air traffic—gradually they will learn to cooperate, and this will form the basis of an international community, argues functionalist theory. Cooperation in a narrow area will "spill over" into the broader arena. Americans, who like technological fixes, are often drawn to the functionalist theory.

MAJOR SPECIALIZED UN AGENCIES		
Agency	**Location**	**Chief Function**
International Court of Justice (ICJ)	The Hague, Netherlands	Adjudicate claims between nations
International Seabed Authority (ISA)	Kingston, Jamaica	Enforce conventions on seabed
International Labor Organization (ILO)	Geneva	Improve labor conditions
Food and Agriculture Organization (FAO)	Rome	Fight famine
UN Educational, Scientific and Cultural Organization (UNESCO)	Paris	Promote exchange of ideas
UN Environment Program (UNEP)	Nairobi, Kenya	Protect environment
UN Children's Fund (UNICEF)	New York	Help world's poorest children
UN Conference on Trade and Development (UNCTAD)	Geneva	Promote economic growth of poor countries
UN High Commissioner for Refugees (UNHCR)	Geneva	Protects refugees
World Health Organization (WHO)	Geneva	Fight plagues
International Monetary Fund (IMF)*	Washington	Stabilize currencies
World Bank*	Washington	Make loans to poor countries
International Civil Aviation Organization (ICAO)	Montreal	Promote air travel
International Telecommunication Union (ITU)	Geneva	Promote telecom flow
Universal Postal Union (UPU)	Bern	Promote mail flow
International Telecommunication Union (ITU)	Geneva	Allocate radio frequencies
World Meteorological Organization (WMO)	Geneva	Share weather information
International Maritime Organization (IMO)	London	Promote world shipping
World Intellectual Property Organization (WIPO)	Geneva	Protect patents
International Atomic Energy Agency (IAEA)	Vienna	Oversee peaceful nuclear development

*For more on these agencies, see Chapter 18. The WTO, although headquartered in Geneva, is not part of the UN.

developed a bad reputation as its Senegalese director hired friends at lush salaries to enjoy Paris and politicize the organization. He held office thirteen years, immune to criticism because most developing lands supported him.

Necessary as some may be, the international agencies have not fulfilled the functionalists' hopes. There is little or no spillover effect because the specialists who staff the agencies have little influence on national policymakers, who respond primarily to national pressures and interests. The agencies, many overstaffed and inefficient, are highly autonomous and almost impossible to reform. **NGOs** are vastly more efficient (see Chapter 22). The UN agencies talk about it; the NGOs do it.

NGO   Nongovernmental organization, international charities and voluntary groups.

■ The UN: Humankind's Last, Best Hope?

Too much was expected of the UN too early. Any international organization (IO) is only as effective as its members make it. If national interests converge, cooperation becomes more likely. The present international system may be leading to a convergence of interests not seen since the heyday of the early nineteenth century's Concert of Europe. No country, not even Russia or China, wants North Korea to have nuclear weapons. The UN can be the instrument for converting common interests into common policies.

Turning Point

THE UNITED STATES AND THE UN

The U.S. Congress, especially Republicans from traditionally isolationist states, does not love the UN and deliberately ran up $1.3 billion in UN arrears to get the spendthrift UN to economize. UN officials are very well paid, and some of them are not needed. Congress rejected UN demands as too high and paid less than $1 billion in 1999. (Ted Turner personally contributed an even $1 billion to the UN.) Congress also got the U.S. share of the UN budget trimmed from 25 percent to 22 percent. When the UN was founded, argued Congress, the United States was the only rich country in the world, but now there are many rich countries, and they should pay their fair shares.

The Bush 43 White House shared Congress's dislike of the UN. The State Department under Secretary Powell tried to exercise U.S. world leadership within the UN, but he was isolated in the Bush administration. The former chairman of the Senate Foreign Relations Committee, Jesse Helms (R-NC), wanted the UN greatly trimmed and in 2000 personally warned the Security Council that

the United States would withdraw from the UN if it tried "to impose its presumed authority on the American people without their consent." It was the identical argument—don't touch our sovereignty—used by the Republican senators who voted against joining the League of Nations in 1919.

The United States has gone from inventing and supporting the UN to ignoring and distancing itself from the UN. In turn, the United States lost influence in the UN. Leading up to the 2003 Iraq War, many countries urged the United States to operate within the UN framework in dealing with Iraq, but the White House was in no mood for such restraint. U.S.–UN relations dipped lower with the 2005 appointment of John Bolton as U.S. ambassador. Bolton, a Republican unilateralist, made no secret of his disdain for the UN. He demanded major reforms—and many are needed—and threatened to block the UN's budget if he didn't get them.

The UN and the secretary general depend upon the votes of the members of the Security Council and General Assembly to act in every area. Secretaries general can rarely act on their own. Members' support is essential for peacekeeping operations because they supply the troops, financing, and logistics. Only Australia's push for UN intervention in East Timor (led by Australia) in 1999, made it happen. The effectiveness of the UN reflects members' interest. Australia is close to Timor.

UN resolutions can denounce human-rights violations, such as Iraq's in Kuwait or Milosevic's in Kosovo. There is a growing consensus among members on human rights. The 1948 Universal Declaration of Human Rights is developing some respect because governments are embarrassed to conduct business with bloody-hand regimes. Barbarity is becoming unfashionable.

International conferences under UN auspices abound, some 7,500 a year in Geneva alone. Defining issues, especially those labeled "world order," is a prelude to multilateral treaties for global problems. From the fast spread of AIDS to vitamin A deficiency, scores of international conferences capture TV coverage and focus world attention, forcing national governments to respond.

The UN's role in peacekeeping and peacemaking is more accepted than ever. There were failures in the former Yugoslavia and in Somalia but successes in the Iran-Iraq War, the Salvadoran, Angolan, and Mozambican civil wars, and in Haiti's political and economic reconstruction. The U.S. share of UN peacekeeping expenses annually is around $1 billion, a reasonable sum if it keeps regional conflicts from growing out of control.

The UN does need reform. Its related agencies are sprawling, overstaffed, overlapping, and unaccountable. (There are three UN food agencies, all in Rome.) The dues formula hasn't been updated in decades, and some countries pay too much in relation to their GDPs, others too little. (Biggest overpayer: Japan, which demands a reduction. Biggest underpayer: China, which does not complain.) Security Council membership does not reflect power and wealth realities; Germany and Japan should become permanent members. If General Assembly resolutions are to be respected, the GA will have to go to some form of weighted voting to get around the problem of a microstate counting as much as a big country. The UN, however, is highly resistant to change because many countries can block reform. If the UN does not reform and slim down to its core competencies—dispute resolution—it could fade before it fully blossoms.

Key Terms

arbitration (p. 335)

collective security (p. 328)

functionalism (p. 337)

good offices (p. 335)

mediation (p. 333)

NGO (p. 339)

third party (p. 335)

Versailles (p. 327)

veto (p. 330)

Key Web Sites

United Nations Home Page
http://www.un.org

Charter of the United Nations
http://www.un.org/aboutun/charter

United Nations Foundation news service
http://www.unwire.org

Further Reference

Chasek, Pamela S. *Earth Negotiations: Analyzing Thirty Years of Environmental Diplomacy.* Tokyo: United Nations University Press, 2001.

Diehl, Paul F., ed. *The Politics of Global Governance: International Organizations in an Interdependent World,* 3rd ed. Boulder, CO: Lynne Rienner, 2005.

Fasulo, Linda. *An Insider's Guide to the UN.* New Haven, CT: Yale University Press, 2003.

Jordan, Robert S. *International Organizations: A Comparative Approach to the Management of Cooperation,* 4th ed. Westport, CT: Praeger, 2001.

Kennedy, Paul. *The Parliament of Man: The Past, Present, and Future of the United Nations.* New York: Random House, 2006.

Krasno, Jean E. *The United Nations: Confronting the Challenges of a Global Society.* Boulder, CO: Lynne Rienner, 2004.

Malone, David M., ed. *The UN Security Council: From the Cold War to the 21st Century.* Boulder, CO: Lynne Rienner, 2004.

Mingst, Karen A., and Margaret P. Karns. *The United Nations in the Twenty-First Century,* 3rd ed. Boulder, CO: Westview, 2006.

Muldoon, James P., JoAnn Fagot Aveil, Richard Reitano, and Earl Sullivan. *Multilateral Diplomacy and the United Nations Today,* 2nd ed. Boulder, CO: Westview, 2005.

Schabas, William A. *Genocide in International Law: The Crime of Crimes.* New York: Cambridge University Press, 2000.

Schlesinger, Stephen. *Act of Creation: The Founding of the United Nations.* Boulder, CO: Westview, 2004.

Weiss, Thomas, David Forsythe, Roger Coate, and Kelly-Kate Pease. *The United Nations and Changing World Politics,* 5th ed. Boulder, CO: Westview, 2006.

White, Nigel D. *The United Nations System: Toward International Justice.* Boulder, CO: Lynne Rienner, 2002.

Chapter 22

Giving Peace a Chance

Questions to Consider

1. Post–Cold War, has war been a growing or declining thing? Why?
2. Of the wars now ongoing, which are about territory?
3. Has ideology waned as a factor leading to wars?
4. Looking at this week's news, what is the likeliest cause of a major war?
5. Do democracies not go to war against other democracies?
6. Why is peace enforcement extremely difficult and risky?
7. Can peacekeeping work without a previously agreed-to cease-fire?
8. Is peacekeeping a growth industry? Should we do more of it?

Looking at the globe as a whole, the 2003 Iraq War stands out as an **anomaly**, for there are now fewer wars than there used to be. To be sure, problem areas—Israel-Arab, India-Pakistan, North Korea—can erupt in war, but the world is less tense than it was during the Cold War. For many, war doesn't have the appeal, the glamour, or the efficacy it once had. Most countries focus on domestic affairs and pay little attention to foreign policy. Prior to 9/11 it was a non-issue in U.S. presidential campaigns. What is the future of war? We get some clues by looking the traditional uses of **war**.

War as an Instrument of Policy

The Prussian military theorist Clausewitz (see box on page 190) said war was the "continuation of politics by other means"; war makes no sense without a political objective. A given war is likely to show one of five basic objectives.

1. **Wars to seize or take back territory.** States long expanded wherever they could. New lands made them richer and more powerful. And if they didn't take it, someone else

would. Look at U.S. expansion in the nineteenth century. Territory is still a hot issue for Israelis, Palestinians, Chinese, Indians, and Pakistanis.

2. **Wars to redeem people.** Nationalism unleashed the idea that people of the same nation should live in one state. Old borders, migrations, and states have left peoples in other states—Kurds in Turkey, Palestinians in Israel, Serbs in Croatia—and these have led to some of the longest and most intense wars because they are about the very definition of the nation and its sovereignty. They become especially violent when they mix in religion or ideology.

3. **Wars to spread religion or ideology.** Wars that grew out of religion—the Muslim conquests, Crusades, and Thirty Years War—have been historical turning points. In the twentieth century, ideology ran amok with communism and fascism. The Cold War was in part ideological. Samuel Huntington now sees a clash of civilizations based largely on religion, especially Islam, as the main source of conflict (see page 189).

4. **Revolutionary war.** The great revolutions in France, Russia, China, and Iran changed the whole pattern of IR, making it more ideological and conflictual. Revolutionary regimes feel compelled to spread their revolution, and this produced the Napoleonic wars, Communist expansion, and several Middle East wars. Islamic fundamentalism fosters revolutionary wars.

5. **Civil wars and wars of separation.** One region trying to separate from a state it dislikes underlay the American Revolutionary War and Civil War. Civil and separatist wars still burn in Northern Ireland, Spain's Basque country, Kashmir, Sri Lanka, and Sudan. Such wars are intense and long.

anomaly   An exception to an overall pattern. (See page 342.)

war   Contending by force. (See page 342.)

The Future of War

The world situation suggests a decline in war. Those now locked in war dislike it, especially the civilians who now do most of the dying. (Governments in the twentieth century killed far more civilians in wars and repressions than they did enemy soldiers.) Americans thrilled to the quick victory over Iraq in 2003 but soon turned against the casualties and costs of occupation. Bush recognized that Americans were in no mood for another war and used diplomacy with Iran and North Korea rather than military threats. Big war could be nearly obsolete, and regional and civil wars are increasingly opposed and isolated by the world. "Peace operations," some under the aegis of the UN, have become a major task of armies. War as an instrument of policy may be declining.

There are fewer motives for war. Territorial violence flared in the former Soviet Union and former Yugoslavia. China occasionally threatens Taiwan with war if it declares independence. Beijing is not kidding on this point, but it also understands that a forcible takeover of Taiwan would disrupt its amazing economic growth. Washington urged Taipei not to push the question of independence, for that would start a war. Even hermit North Korea, faced with starvation, has made signs of coming out of its shell. India and Pakistan, after threatening each other with nuclear weapons over Kashmir concluded it wasn't worth mutual destruction and resumed their peace dialogue. The list of disputed borders is shrinking, and few of these disputes cause wars. In Europe, borders have been confirmed in the 1975 Helsinki Final Act. The flow of people, goods, and ideas through borders is making borders less relevant for the security of states—part of the globalization argument (see page 285).

Except for Islam—especially its militant strain—ideologies have generally declined after the Cold War. Truth with a capital T has less credibility in the global information age. Internet users in China double every year, a fact that frightened the regime into trying to control the Internet. Can you in fact control it? What will be the impact of having much of the world on-line? The present authors routinely e-mail other continents. Francis Fukuyama predicted the "end of history": the end of global ideological conflict because the ideas of liberal democracy and market economics are growing worldwide. Ideology no longer burns as brightly.

Revolutions and civil wars will still occur, but the international community has increasingly intervened to calm them. These peace operations have contained, stalemated, and frustrated local wars, sometimes leading to settlement. Power is now harder to

Concepts

WAR AND POWER

Countries can have motives for war, but they do not automatically lead to war. Other causes are necessary. There must be an opportunity to go to war, and that usually means having superior power. The side that initiates war, as Geoffrey Blainey emphasizes in his classic *The Causes of War*, must believe that it will win. No one starts wars they think they will lose. Many IR thinkers argue that failure to deter an aggressor is a prologue to every war. Then an aggressor starts thinking he can win because he faces either a weak or weak-willed opponent. That would be the story of Britain and France not standing up to Hitler until it was almost too late.

The will to fight comes from an aggressive leader mobilizing his government, armed forces, and people (Clausewitz's "remarkable trinity"). This gives the aggressor superior power and the will to use it. Such leaders also try to legitimize the conflict, invoking justice and the national interest. The enemy must be demonized as lacking in basic human qualities. Death is too good for them. (How groups of people stereotype other groups is a growing area of study in international relations.) Finally, the leader lies, saying that, although he is a man of peace, war is the only way to obtain the desired goal. Diplomacy has not and will not work—at least so the leader says.

It is often forgotten that war takes two sides willing to fight. The side attacked must also perceive the opportunity to prevail and have the will to fight back. There have been few cases where a state threatened with attack or attacked simply gave up. Czechoslovakia, abandoned by Britain and France, let Hitler take it over in 1939. Thailand, surrounded by overwhelming Japanese power, became Japan's only "voluntary" ally in World War II. Unarmed Denmark immediately surrendered after the German threat to bomb Copenhagen. Most states that are attacked, however, fight back because honor and hope fuel the idea that somehow, perhaps with help, the aggressor will be defeated. For a year (1940-41), Britain fought alone against mighty Germany. Things looked grim. British Foreign Secretary Lord Halifax suggested seeking a deal with Hitler to end the war leaving Germany in control of the Continent. Churchill fired him. Willpower counts for a lot.

calculate, making it harder to predict who will win a war. Clausewitz wrote: "First, be very strong." An aggressor who does not feel very strong is unlikely to go to war. Few national leaderships now argue that victory is certain.

Power is now dangerous and harder to calculate. Hitler could calculate that a certain number of *Panzer* (tank) divisions would beat the Poles or French. Numbers meant something. Now the ability to deliver fifty or one hundred nuclear warheads deters an aggressor, even one with a thousand nukes. Calculating superiority and winning decisive victories are becoming harder. The 2003 U.S.-led military victory in Iraq looked quick and decisive but appeared less so over the years of bombings and ambushes. Many recent wars have stalemated and ended in negotiations, the case with the Arab-Israel wars, the Iran-Iraq War, the 1991 Gulf War, and wars in Cambodia, Angola, Mozambique, and the former Yugoslavia. Who wants to fight a war to a draw?

Other factors stalemate wars. Today's integrated world means conflicts pull in many powers. The Iran-Iraq War stalemated because over a dozen countries, including the United States, supplied arms and intelligence to both sides. Neither side could win. In the 1990s, the Serbs in Croatia and Bosnia thought they would win, but the United States quietly supplied trainers and arms, and Muslim countries sent arms to the Bosnian Muslims. Serbia changed its mind and settled. Thanks to outsiders, the powerless sometimes gain power.

Concepts

THE DEMOCRATIC PEACE

Democracies confronting other democracies do not, and seemingly cannot, develop the will to attack other democracies. Yale's Bruce Russett studied all wars since 1816 and demonstrated in his *Grasping the Democratic Peace* that a democratic culture doesn't like to mobilize against another like itself. Democracies prefer to negotiate and compromise. It is hard to demonize another democracy.

Do not count on democratic elections to solve all problems. The 2006 election of the fundamentalist Hamas to Palestinian leadership puts the theory of the democratic peace to a severe test. Democratic Israel and democratic Palestine sincerely hate each other. The 2005 Iraqi elections further shattered the country between Shias and Sunnis as Iraq lurched toward civil war. The 2005 Egyptian elections gave a major victory to the shadowy Muslim Brotherhood, the original Islamist movement. Perhaps we could insert a Huntington exception to the Russett rule: Democracy brings peace, except in Muslim lands.

Democracies fight almost as much as dictatorships, but they only fight dictatorships (and mostly win). Democracies tend to have developed market economies and advanced military forces. If they can convince their people to support the war, then the popular will to win will be strong. But leaders know that a wrong, unsuccessful war will cost them reelection. Since LBJ saw Vietnam end his political career, U.S. presidents have been cautious over how U.S. voters will react to war. A long war could cost them votes, as in 2006. Democracies also make and keep allies much better than dictatorships do, a key factor in the defeat of the Axis in World War II and of Iraq in 1991.

doctrine   Planned military response to given situations.

preventive diplomacy   Third-party efforts to dampen disputes before they turn violent.

peace enforcement   Use of force by third parties to impose *cease-fires*.

peace building   Third-party efforts to turn *cease-fires* into lasting settlements.

peacekeeping   Maintaining peace after peace has been agreed upon.

peacemaking   Encouraging hostile parties to agree to peace.

With these uncertainties, leaders worry about a "quagmire," about becoming "bogged down" in an unending situation. Enthusiasm for war is on a shorter leash. In sum, the motives, power, and will to make war are in decline.

A major factor inhibiting war is that democracies do not go to war against other democracies. This "democratic peace" means that with roughly half the world's states at least approximately democratic, the number of possible wars is shrinking. It takes two sides—at least one of them a dictatorship—to make war nowadays.

Nevertheless, wars still happen. They tend to be low-tech, on the world's fringes or in remote areas, and frequently indecisive. The major powers oppose these little wars and use the UN to reduce their negative effects. Refugees burden neighboring states. Brutality and ethnic cleansing affront humanitarian norms. Wars damage markets and sources of vital raw materials. Prolonged conflicts can escalate. UN peace operations now discourage future wars by threatening to take them out of the control of the belligerents, and they seek to settle existing wars (or gum them up to make them unproductive and therefore ready for resolution).

Peace Operations

New vocabulary and **doctrines** are being created for peace operations in the post–Cold War era. Strategies of **preventive diplomacy**, peacemaking, peacekeeping, **peace enforcement**, and **peace building** are being developed and refined. Conflicts go

Concepts

PEACEKEEPING AND PEACEMAKING

Peacekeeping is not mentioned in the UN Charter. Secretary General Dag Hammarskjöld invented the concept after the 1956 Middle East war. Citing Chapter VI of the Charter—entitled "Pacific Settlement of Disputes"—as sufficient authority, he proposed putting UN troops between combatants to preserve the cease-fire, and the Security Council went along. With more than thirty peacekeeping operations authorized, past and present, the definition of the activity has expanded to include providing security, monitoring elections, resettling refugees, disarming belligerents, and giving humanitarian assistance. Peacekeeping also buys time for peacemaking.

Peacemaking, which is what the UN was designed to do under Chapter VI, involves resolving disputes. In Cambodia, for example, peacekeeping and peacemaking were combined, and a new regime was instituted under UN supervision. (See later text for more on "peace operations.")

through stages, so third-party efforts to prevent, halt, and resolve conflicts must fit the particular stage of conflict. It makes no sense, for example, to use a preventive strategy if a war is raging. Failure to employ the proper strategies by the UN, the United States, NATO, and others has led to failure and discredited peace operations among some critics, but these doctrines are still new and rough.

cease-fire Mutually agreed-upon pause in a war; the first step to peace but much less than a treaty.

Preventive Diplomacy

Preventive diplomacy tries to get the two sides to negotiate to resolve their differences. The third party must be alert to the danger signs of possible war: threatening goals, military mobilization, and the whipping up of hatred. Preventive diplomacy depends on the major powers recognizing dangers and developing a strategy to deter the aggressor and provide incentives for a diplomatic solution.

For example, Jimmy Carter, with official U.S. support, brokered a deal with North Korea in 1994. The North Korean nuclear program and its overall isolation seemed to threaten war. The United States pledged two power-generating nuclear reactors (that don't yield weapons-grade plutonium) plus oil, and suggested diplomatic and economic relations. Clinton also traveled to South Korea and recommitted the United States to South Korea's defense. The combination of deterrent threat plus incentives started a process to settle a smoldering quarrel. North Korean dishonesty and Bush's "axis of evil" approach to North Korea set back the effort, but both sides soon saw the utility of renewed negotiations.

The six-nation Contact Group for Yugoslavia (the United States, Britain, France, Italy, Germany, and Russia) also used deterrence and diplomatic initiatives to try to head off a massacre of ethnic Albanians in Kosovo by Serbs in 1999. When negotiations failed, a U.S.-led bombing campaign helped persuade Belgrade to back down (see Chapter 16).

Recent wars are examples of neglected or failed preventive diplomacy. The leaders of Croatia failed to anticipate the dangers of separating from Serb-dominated Yugoslavia and made no agreement on the status of local Serbs. War followed. Similarly, the United States misread Iraq's grievances against Kuwait in 1990 and its war preparations. Saddam Hussein thought he had a green light to attack Kuwait (see Chapter 9). The danger of warrior clans in Somalia was ignored in the early 1990s.

Peacemaking

Peacemaking tries to get both sides to sign a **cease-fire** and stick to it. Peacemaking cannot use deterrence because the fight is on. Instead, third parties and diplomats provide mediation and contain and stalemate the conflict. The mediator explores the interests of both sides, develops ways to reconcile them, and sets up meetings. Containing the conflict helps to stalemate it by blocking outside help that could favor one side. Containment imposes arms and economic embargoes, gets neighboring states to stay out, and delivers humanitarian assistance. Peacemakers must not favor one side. Patience is the principal virtue of this third-party mediation.

In Mozambique, a local archbishop and an Italian Catholic NGO helped settle the horrifying war between the Marxist FRELIMO and the rebel RENAMO. Both sides lost their foreign patrons—respectively, the Soviet Union and South Africa. Mozambique's neighbors agreed not to take sides but to support a diplomatic settlement. In the friendly atmosphere of a villa overlooking Rome, the mediators arranged for a cease-fire, organized a peacekeeping operation under the UN, brokered a new multiparty constitution, and then monitored elections. In 1994, FRELIMO won fair elections, and peace was stabilized.

Peacemaking helps make conflicts "ripe" for resolution. The peacemaker is invaluable in establishing the negotiating process and the formula that satisfies the warring parties. UN-sponsored or UN-administered peacemaking efforts in the Iran-Iraq War and in the revolutionary wars in Cambodia, Namibia, Angola, and El Salvador eventually came to successful conclusions. Peacemakers fail when they are not perceived as neutral. Efforts to contain the conflict may fail. Sometimes the warring parties say they want a cease-fire but just use it to win support or buy time.

Concepts

THE PACIFIST FALLACY

Pacifists deem any use of arms immoral. American Protestant theologian Reinhold Niebuhr wrestled with this problem on the eve of World War II, when many American Christians took the pacifist view that we should keep out of war. Niebuhr concluded that pacifism is a type of heresy because it requires Christians to do nothing in the face of evil; you just stand there and let the murders continue.

Pacifism is still around. Some people were morally outraged over U.S. actions in the Gulf, Bosnia, and Kosovo. This is a "politics of conviction," a rigid and simplistic rejection of force no matter what the situation. The opposite: a "politics of responsibility" that asks, "If I don't act, what will happen? Would my military intervention make things better or worse?" If you proclaim your country will never intervene militarily, you notify the world's dictators that they can murder with impunity.

Yes, of course we should pursue peace, but notice how many of the peace efforts described here need a military component. Without it, good intentions lack credibility. Remember, you're dealing with some very mean characters. Underequipped and unprepared peacekeeping forces stumbled into civil wars and looked pathetic. Effective peacekeeping forces must be ready for war-fighting. Much U.S. military activity now is peace operations. The politically correct may recoil in horror, but one of the best ways to serve peace nowadays is as a soldier.

All these negative factors were present when the United States tried peacemaking in Lebanon after the 1982 Israeli invasion. Lebanon was in a civil war with Syrian-backed Muslim and Druze forces contesting the Christian government (see page 128). It was a multisided war, too complex for the new U.S. secretary of state, George Shultz, to broker a deal. The massacre of Palestinian civilians by Christian militias brought hurried U.S. diplomacy, because Washington had pledged to protect the Palestinians. Shultz tried to get the Israeli and Syrian forces to leave and the Lebanese warring parties to sign a cease-fire. Unfortunately, Shultz ignored the interests of the Muslim and Druze forces, which in effect made the United States pro-Christian. The Christian government tried to use U.S. backing to win. Syrian and Israeli forces remained in Lebanon to back their Lebanese clients. Outside peacemakers, including the United States, had a hazy mandate and soon came under fire and left.

Similarly, UN peacemakers in Somalia in 1992 did not get a genuine cease-fire, which is the only way peacekeeping operations can work. The militia loyal to Muhammad Farah Aideed believed the UN was plotting his demise, and his rival, Ali Mahdi, tried

force configuration How an army is trained, equipped, and deployed.

light forces An army with few tanks and artillery, mobile but not so strong.

heavy forces An army with lots of tanks and artillery, powerful but slow.

Concepts

MILITARY FORCE FOR WHAT?

Everyone agrees that U.S. armed forces should be trained and ready, but ready for what? The way we perceive the world scene determines how we **configure** our forces. If we face a powerful foe, as during the Cold War, we must go heavy, ready to repel a massive attack in all-out war. Say many U.S. Army officers: Never send **light forces** against **heavy forces**. On the other hand, with civil wars and massacres, we need light, agile forces. In such situations, heavy forces may be overkill and take too long to get there. Don't use sledgehammers when you need fly swatters. U.S. action in Afghanistan in late 2001 required light U.S. forces, but Iraq in 2003 required U.S. heavy forces.

Training is also quite different and not easily switched. If you're expecting a war, you train to destroy the enemy. Such troops, however, make poor peacekeepers, as they tend to treat everyone as the enemy. Tragedies occur when war-fighting troops are used for essentially police duties. We made this mistake in Iraq in 2003. MPs and civil-affairs specialists—mostly in reserve U.S. units—should have arrived one day after our combat troops. Instead, too few of them arrived weeks later, after looting and lawlessness had turned Iraq into chaos. By 2004, the Army was retraining thousands of combat soldiers to serve as badly needed MPs and civil affairs specialists.

Republicans tend to favor a heavy war-fighting configuration that avoids peace operations. Democrats tend to favor a lighter, peacekeeping configuration and are more willing to use it in peace operations. One solution: have two distinct missions with units trained and equipped differently.

ROEs Rules of engagement, stating when peacekeepers may shoot back.

to get UN support for his militia. Both militias signed bogus cease-fires to allow in humanitarian food aid, which they stole at gunpoint. The moral: no cease-fire, no peacekeeping. Instead, disaster.

■ Peacekeeping

Peacekeepers try to get the parties who have signed a cease-fire to maintain it so a final settlement can be worked out. Peacekeeping needs a firm cease-fire in place that all parties consent to. They must also allow peacekeeping forces to take up positions between the parties. The peacekeepers shoot only in self-defense and take no sides as they monitor the cease-fire, resolve violations, and promote humanitarian relief, government reformation and elections, and economic recovery. This is hard and stressful, and mistakes are made. Since 1948, over 1,600 peacekeepers have been killed.

Turning Point

UNPROFOR LOUSY, IFOR EXCELLENT

The UN Protective Force, originally designed to supervise the Serb-Croat ceasefire of 1992, quickly found its mission expanded to Bosnia, where, without benefit of any cease-fire agreement, it was to get food and medicine to civilians and prevent civilian casualties. The wrong mission in the wrong place with the wrong rules quickly became not only a failure but also a laughingstock—and not due to the abilities of the French, British, Spanish and other soldiers assigned to UNPROFOR.

The problem was weak and vague **ROEs**, the rules that tell soldiers when and how they may shoot back. They were assigned strictly as peacekeepers—when there was no peace to keep—and allowed to shoot only if clearly attacked. They were under specific orders not to participate in any fighting—even to defend UN-designated "safe areas." As a result, Bosnian Serb forces laughed at them, ignored them, and sometimes arrested and handcuffed them before proceeding

to massacre Muslim civilians, as in Srebrenica in 1995, where the Dutch UNPROFOR unit, good soldiers all, just stood by. UNPROFOR's ROEs were inherently weak because the UN can be no stronger than its quarreling members, and they never wanted UNPROFOR to fight a war. The Serbs knew this and took full advantage of it.

IFOR (Implementation Force) took over in 1996 and was totally different. First, it wasn't UN; it was NATO, at that time still an effective alliance, with an integrated command structure and lots of practice working together. This time the United States was there, contributing about a third of IFOR's 60,000 personnel. IFOR came only *after* the Dayton accord produced a cease-fire, the only way peacekeeping can possibly work. And IFOR arrived with heavy weapons, ready to fight a war, and with "robust ROEs" to shoot whenever necessary. Serb forces did not laugh at IFOR. With IFOR in place, the cease-fire held. Peacekeeping is not for peace marchers; it's for war fighters.

Peacekeepers have helped situations between Egypt and Israel, Jordan and Israel, and among El Salvador, Mozambique, Angola, and Cambodia. They have stabilized unresolved conflicts in Kashmir between Pakistan-backed Muslims and the Indian authorities, in Western Sahara between the

mission creep Tendency of modest peacekeeping goals to expand into bigger ones.

Polisario independence movement and the Moroccan government, in ex-Yugoslavia, and in Cyprus between the Turkish and Greek communities. Now some 40,000 soldiers from eighteen countries in the International Security Assistance Force (ISAF) attempt to bring order and security to Afghanistan after the U.S.-led ouster of the Taliban government. Unfortunately, ISAF is reluctant to venture out of Kabul into the dangerous countryside.

Cyprus shows both the worth and problems of peacekeeping. Civil war broke out in this former British colony in 1963 between the Greek Cypriots who wanted *enosis* (union with Greece) and the Turkish Cypriots who wanted *taksim* (partition). Britain, Greece, and Turkey mediated a truce, and UN peacekeepers (UNFICYP) arrived in 1964. In 1974, a Greek military junta, still dreaming of *enosis*, overthrew the Cyprus government and provoked a Turkish invasion that occupied 40 percent of the island. With fighting stalemated, a reinforced UNFICYP interposed itself between the communities, negotiated local cease-fires, and policed population transfers. UNFICYP froze the civil war and is still there, calming an unresolved conflict. Peacekeeping can take decades; it is not for the impatient. In 2004 the prosperous Greek portion of Cyprus joined the EU, a lesson that stability and economic growth are much better than civil war.

Peacekeepers in Lebanon—where there was no peace to keep—failed in 1982–1984 when the French and U.S. contingents took the Christian side. Shia militias truck-bombed the French and U.S. Marine barracks. Containment disappeared as Iran and Syria increased their support to the militias fighting the Christian-dominated government.

In Somalia, UN peacekeepers tried to restore order and put Somalia back together, leading to the new expression "**mission creep**." Aideed saw the move as aiding his rival and plotted the ouster of UN peacekeepers and U.S. forces (who were not under UN command). Knowing that Americans hate protracted conflict, Aideed in 1993 first killed twenty-four Pakistani UN soldiers, which provoked the Americans to put a price on his head. U.S. Rangers attempted to snatch Aideed but stumbled into street fighting that killed eighteen of them ("Black Hawk Down"). President Clinton ordered U.S. forces out; UN forces left in 1995. Tens of thousands of lives were saved by the UN's protection of relief supplies, but the expanded mandate was mission impossible. When that happens, it is the duty of peacekeepers to say so.

Peace Enforcement

Peace enforcement tries to induce an aggressor to accept and maintain a cease-fire. It may be a last hope when peacemaking and peacekeeping fail. War is raging, and the aggressor is on the move. A strong third party may decide that it will not accept the likely outcome if the war runs its course. If this third party is willing to use force to prevent an aggressor from winning, it may practice peace enforcement. Such operations are often bolstered by UN Security Council approval for forceful measures. Peace enforcement, although it has different and limited goals, starts to resemble war; it is not a neutral operation. In Kosovo in 1999, we saw how peace enforcement blends into war.

Peace enforcement identifies and isolates the aggressor. It introduces combat forces to block the aggressor's military capability. It also offers the aggressor a beneficial cease-fire. While doing this, it tries not to back the victim of aggression to the point that it tries to win. Once the aggressor accepts a fair cease-fire, the combat stops without victory for any side.

Peace enforcement's limited goals compared to war confuse people. The Korean War started as a war—each side sought victory and the unification of all of Korea under its control. But then UN forces under U.S. command stopped seeking victory and accepted the goal of imposing a cease-fire on North Korea, and the operation became peace enforcement. Many Americans were frustrated and rallied to Gen. Douglas MacArthur, whom Truman fired, and his famous words, "In war, there is no substitute for victory."

Reflections

FROM RWANDA TO SIERRA LEONE TO LIBERIA

As we saw in Chapter 7, Hutu-Tutsi civil war in Rwanda killed some 800,000 and then spilled over into the Congo, where perhaps another 1.7 million died while the outside world largely stood by. President Clinton, visiting Africa later, expressed regret at our inaction. Shame perhaps explains why we were willing to do a little more in Sierra Leone.

Sierra Leone, a former British colony on the western bulge of Africa, had been in civil war since 1991, when the Revolutionary United Front (RUF) rebelled. RUF seemed mostly interested in grabbing local diamonds (traded for guns) and chopping off the arms of civilians, including children. In 1999, government and rebels signed cease-fires and peace deals, and 6,000 UN peacekeepers arrived, but RUF quickly returned to fighting. In early 2000, the UN expanded its forces to 11,000, but they were unprepared and unequipped, and RUF grabbed 500 of them as hostages. To repeat, peacekeepers must be ready to fight.

U.S. policy mirrors the contradictions of the American people and Congress: Do something, but don't get too involved. The lame U.S. response to Sierra Leone: Send several hundred U.S. Special Forces to Nigeria to train West African battalions for peace enforcement. If intervention at arm's length doesn't work, if the African peacekeepers are ineffective, should we take a direct role? The costs of not acting include more child amputees.

The United States eventually took a little interest in Liberia after a fourteen-year civil war among greedy and murderous bands. Over 100,000 Liberians died. Here we had a historical connection: Liberia was set up in 1822 with U.S. dollars and freed U.S. slaves, who formed an elite modeled on their Southern white masters. As starvation and massacre spread, many Liberians begged for U.S. intervention. The Bush administration ignored the pleas but under pressure in 2003 encouraged Nigerian peacekeepers to go and even sent a handful of U.S. Marines. Some Americans were ashamed that we had not done more sooner to help our offspring.

In 1960 the UN Security Council voted for a peace-enforcement operation to prevent mineral-rich Katanga from leaving the Congo (see page 113). With Congo's government and army in shambles, many UN members saw in Katanga's separation a continuation of colonialism (it was). After the UN Operations in the Congo (ONUC) got mercenary forces out of Katanga and bloodied the Katangese army, Katanga agreed to return to the Congo. Peace operations that work can then turn into peace-building operations.

■ Peace Building

Peace building tries to preserve and deepen a settlement. It is a last step that comes only after the other steps. It may include confidence-building measures, foreign aid, and international organizations to help the parties manage their problems. Peace building creates incentives to maintain peace and makes clear the penalties for resuming conflict.

Monitoring borders and human rights are important confidence-building measures. U.S. monitors in the Sinai assure Israel and Egypt that neither will attack. SFOR and KFOR (see Chapter 16) monitor zones in ex-Yugoslavia. Human-rights monitors in El Salvador provided the former rebels the security to integrate themselves into the political system.

Some outside parties remove land mines, cheap maiming devices of which there are millions. They train the police, military, and civil service to become professionals who obey

Reflections

NON-GOVERNMENTAL ORGANIZATIONS

"Non-Governmental Organization" was coined when the UN was founded, and now some 25,000 NGOs operate around the globe, especially in Global South famines, disasters, and wars. Going where governments cannot, NGOs include the International Committee of the Red Cross, Save the Children, Médecins sans Frontières (Doctors without Borders), World Vision, CARE, and Oxfam. Most religious denominations have an NGO (dubbed RINGO). Real doers, NGOs raise some $6 billion a year and provide more aid than all governments and UN agencies put together and do it far more efficiently. Their downsides: too many of them, wildly decentralized, not always well thought-out, and with overlapping projects that are sometimes public relations for the NGO and culturally at odds with local traditions.

Everyone connected with peace operations has high praise for NGOs. Most focus on food and medical care, but some clear land mines, care for orphans, and foster peace agreements. You might consider a stint with an NGO. By serving humanity, you can learn a language, develop skills, and have an adventure. (Warning: You can also get killed. NGOs are not for the fainthearted.) Such background helps you get into graduate school, government service, journalism, and international business.

the law and serve their citizens. Such UN assistance went to the Congo, Mozambique, the Palestinian Authority, Haiti, and Cambodia. Economic help goes for electricity, roads, harbors, railroads, potable water, sanitation, health care, and education. Delivery of food and medicine is usually in the hands of NGOs. Foreign investment can integrate a former conflict area into the world economy, as does membership in WTO, IMF, and World Bank.

If one side then resumes hostilities it loses assistance while the other, peaceful side keeps it. When Angolan rebel leader Jonas Savimbi refused to accept his loss in a fair, UN-monitored 1992 election and renewed his war, he lost and his adversaries gained. The United States had been Savimbi's main supporter, but then the Clinton administration cut off all aid to him and assisted the Angolan government in putting down Savimbi's offensive. Isolated and unsupported, Savimbi gave up the war in 1995.

■ Beyond War?

Are we gradually putting wars behind us? There are glimmers of hope. Some of the international systems discussed in Chapter 1, by becoming more integrated, constrain state behavior. Isolation severely penalizes aggressors. But the world still does not run by itself. Governments make it work by facilitating and civilizing global exchanges of goods, people, and information and by penalizing aggressors.

Unfortunately, domestic pressures in all major powers now push governments to turn inward. Now that the Cold War is over, concern for taxes, domestic reform, and the loss of sovereignty make citizens forget the importance of the condition of the world for their own safety and prosperity. The governments of major powers that bow to these isolationist pressures do their people no good. Major powers' commitment to diplomacy and peace operations help future generations avoid war. We have, in the words of Harvard's Stanley Hoffmann, "duties beyond borders."

Key Terms

anomaly (p. 343)

cease-fire (p. 347)

doctrine (p. 346)

force configuration (p. 349)

heavy forces (p. 349)

light forces (p. 349)

mission creep (p. 351)

peace building (p. 346)

peace enforcement (p. 346)

peacekeeping (p. 346)

peacemaking (p. 346)

preventive diplomacy (p. 346)

ROEs (p. 350)

war (p. 343)

Key Web Sites

UN Peace-Keeping Operations
http://www.un.org/Depts/dpko/

United Nations Security Council
http://www.un.org/Overview/Organs/sc.html

SFOR (NATO Peacekeepers in Bosnia)
http://www.nato.int/latest/home.htm#ifor

Clausewitz's Principles of War
http://www.mnsinc.com/cbassfrd/CWZHOME/PrincWar/Princwr1.htm

Further Reference

Barnett, Michael. *Eyewitness to a Genocide: The United Nations and Rwanda.* Ithaca, NY: Cornell University Press, 2002.

Crocker, Chester A., Fen Osler Hampson, and Pamela Aall, eds. *Leashing the Dogs of War: Conflict Management in a Divided World.* Herndon, VA: U.S. Institute of Peace, 2006.

Durch, William J., ed. *Twenty-First-Century Peace Operations.* Herndon, VA: U.S. Institute of Peace, 2006.

Fleitz, Frederick H., Jr. *Peacekeeping Fiascoes of the 1990s: Causes, Solutions, and U.S. Interests.* Westport, CT: Praeger, 2002.

Goodhand, Jonathan, *Aiding Peace? The Role of NGOs in Armed Conflict.* Boulder, CO: Lynne Rienner, 2006.

Hamburg, David A. *No More Killing Fields: Preventing Deadly Conflict.* Lanham, MD: Rowman & Littlefield, 2003.

Marten, Kimberly Zisk. *Enforcing the Peace: Learning from the Imperial Past.* New York: Columbia University Press, 2006.

Perito, Robert M. *Where Is the Lone Ranger When We Need Him? America's Search for a Post-Conflict Stability Force.* Herndon, VA: U.S. Institute of Peace, 2004.

Power, Samantha. *"A Problem from Hell": America and the Age of Genocide.* New York: HarperCollins, 2003.

Russet, Bruce, and John R. Oneal. *Triangulating Peace: Democracy, Interdependence, and International Organizations.* New York: W. W. Norton, 2001.

Sokalski, Henryk J. *An Ounce of Prevention: Macedonia and the UN Experience in Preventive Diplomacy.* Herndon, VA: USIP Press, 2003.

Sriram, Chandra Lekha, and Karin Wermester, eds. *From Promise to Practice: Strengthening UN Capacities for the Prevention of Violent Conflict.* Boulder, CO: Lynne Rienner, 2003.

Zartman, I. William. *Cowardly Lions: Missed Opportunities to Prevent Deadly Conflict and State Collapse.* Boulder, CO: Lynne Rienner, 2005.

INDEX